ZAGAT SURVEY

Back in 1979, we never imagined that an idea born during a wine-fueled dinner with friends would take us on an adventure that's lasted three decades – and counting.

The idea – that the collective opinions of avid consumers can be more accurate than the judgments of an individual critic – led to a hobby involving friends rating NYC restaurants. And that hobby grew into Zagat Survey, which today has over 350,000 participants worldwide weighing in on everything from airlines, bars, dining and golf to hotels, movies, shopping, tourist attractions and more.

By giving consumers a voice, we – and our surveyors – had unwittingly joined a revolution whose concepts (user-generated content, social networking) were largely unknown 30 years ago. However, those concepts caught fire with the rise of the Internet and have since transformed not only restaurant criticism but also virtually every aspect of the media, and we feel lucky to have been at the start of it all.

And that wasn't the only revolution we happily stumbled into. Our first survey was published as a revolution began to reshape the culinary landscape. Thanks to a host of converging trends – the declining supremacy of old-school formal restaurants; the growing sophistication of diners; the availability of ever-more diverse cuisines and techniques; the improved range and quality of ingredients; the rise of chefs as rock stars – dining out has never been better or more exciting, and we've been privileged to witness its progress through the eyes of our surveyors. And it's still going strong.

As we celebrate Zagat's 30th year, we'd like to thank everyone who has participated in our surveys. We've enjoyed hearing and sharing your frank opinions and look forward to doing so for many years to come. As we always say, our guides and online content are really "yours."

We'd also like to express our gratitude by supporting **Action Against Hunger,** an organization that works to meet the needs of the hungry in over 40 countries. To find out more, visit www.zagat.com/action.

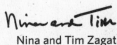

Nina and Tim Zagat

ZAGAT®

CELEBRATING 30 YEARS

Boston
Restaurants
2009/10

Including Cape Cod,
Martha's Vineyard, Nantucket
and The Berkshires

LOCAL EDITORS
Eric Grossman, Lynn Hazlewood and Naomi Kooker
LOCAL COORDINATOR
Maryanne Muller
STAFF EDITOR
Bill Corsello

Published and distributed by
Zagat Survey, LLC
4 Columbus Circle
New York, NY 10019
T: 212.977.6000
E: boston@zagat.com
www.zagat.com

ACKNOWLEDGMENTS

We thank Jack Dew, Dave Krugman, Kit Krugman, Gerrish Lopez, Chelsey Minnis, Ellen Roberts, Matthew Tharp, Brit Withey and The Culinary Guild of New England, as well as the following members of our staff: Christina Livadiotis (assistant editor), Brian Albert, Sean Beachell, Maryanne Bertollo, Jane Chang, Sandy Cheng, Reni Chin, Larry Cohn, Alison Flick, Jeff Freier, Curt Gathje, Andrew Gelardi, Justin Hartung, Roy Jacob, Garth Johnston, Ashunta Joseph, Cynthia Kilian, Natalie Lebert, Mike Liao, Dave Makulec, Andre Pilette, Kimberly Rosado, Becky Ruthenburg, Jacqueline Wasilczyk, Sharon Yates, Anna Zappia and Kyle Zolner.

The reviews in this guide are based on public opinion surveys. The ratings reflect the average scores given by the survey participants who voted on each establishment. The text is based on quotes from, or paraphrasings of, the surveyors' comments. Phone numbers, addresses and other factual data were correct to the best of our knowledge when published in this guide.

Our guides are printed using environmentally preferable inks containing 20%, by weight, renewable resources on papers sourced from well-managed forests. Deluxe editions are covered with Skivertex Recover® Double containing a minimum of 30% post-consumer waste fiber.

SUSTAINABLE FORESTRY INITIATIVE	Certified Chain of Custody Promoting Sustainable Forest Management www.sfiprogram.org

PWC-SFICOC-260

ENVIROINK™

The inks used to print the body of this publication contain a minimum of 20%, by weight, renewable resources.

Maps © 2009 GeoNova Publishing, Inc.

Contents

Ratings & Symbols

Zagat Top Spot	Name	Symbols	Cuisine	Zagat Ratings			
				FOOD	DECOR	SERVICE	COST

Area, Address & Contact

Z Tim & Nina's ◑ *Eclectic* — ▽ 27 | 4 | 13 | $15

North End | 1000 Thatcher St. (Margin St.) | 617-555-1234 | www.zagat.com

Review, surveyor comments in quotes

In the "red sauce–centric North End" comes this "weird, wonderful and welcome" bastion of "Eclectic fodder with gourmet twists" – think "scrumptious truffled grits", "Beluga-infused polenta" and "sea urchin muffins"; the fare has foodies "dreaming all day long", but the "ramshackle" digs in a converted ATM vestibule and "slow service" have aesthetes "fearing nightmares."

Ratings

Food, Decor and **Service** are rated on the Zagat 0 to 30 scale.

0	–	9	poor to fair
10	–	15	fair to good
16	–	19	good to very good
20	–	25	very good to excellent
26	–	30	extraordinary to perfection
	▽		low response	less reliable

Cost

Our surveyors' estimated price of a dinner with one drink and tip. Lunch is usually 25 to 30% less. At prix fixe–only places we show the charge for the lowest-priced menu plus 30%. For unrated **newcomers** or **write-ins**, the price range is shown as follows:

I	$25 and below	E	$41 to $65
M	$26 to $40	VE	$66 or more

Symbols

Z	highest ratings, popularity and importance
◑	serves after 11 PM
Ⓢ	closed on Sunday
Ⓜ	closed on Monday
⊄	no credit cards accepted

Maps

Index maps show restaurants with the highest Food ratings in those areas.

About This Survey

Here are the results of our **2009/10 Boston Restaurants Survey,** covering 1,214 eateries in Boston and its surroundings, as well as in Cape Cod, Martha's Vineyard, Nantucket and The Berkshires. Like all our guides, this one is based on the collective opinions of avid consumers – 6,767 all told.

WHO PARTICIPATED: Input from these enthusiasts forms the basis for the ratings and reviews in this guide (their comments are shown in quotation marks within the reviews). These surveyors are a diverse group: 51% are women, 49% men; 14% are in their 20s; 24%, 30s; 20%, 40s; 22%, 50s; and 20%, 60s or above. Collectively they bring roughly 900,000 annual meals' worth of experience to this Survey. We sincerely thank these participants – this book is really "theirs."

HELPFUL LISTS: Our top lists and indexes can help you find exactly the right place for any occasion. See Most Popular (page 7), Key Newcomers (page 9), Top Ratings (pages 10–16), Best Buys (page 17) and the 33 handy indexes starting on page 208.

OUR EDITORS: Special thanks go to our local editors, Eric Grossman, a Boston-based food and travel writer; Lynn Hazlewood, former editor-in-chief of *Hudson Valley* magazine; and Naomi Kooker, a food and wine writer for *Wine Spectator* and others; and to our coordinator, Maryanne Muller, a personal chef and cooking instructor.

ABOUT ZAGAT: This marks our 30th year reporting on the shared experiences of consumers like you. Today we have over 350,000 surveyors and now cover airlines, bars, dining, entertaining, fast food, golf, hotels, movies, music, resorts, shopping, spas, theater and tourist attractions in over 100 countries.

INTERACTIVE: Up-to-the-minute news about restaurant openings plus menus, photos and more are free on **ZAGAT.com** and the award-winning **ZAGAT.mobi** (for web-enabled mobile devices). They also enable reserving at thousands of places with just one click.

VOTE AND COMMENT: We invite you to join any of our surveys at **ZAGAT.com.** There you can rate and review establishments year-round. In exchange for doing so, you'll receive a free copy of the resulting guide when published.

AVAILABILITY: Zagat guides are available in all major bookstores as well as on **ZAGAT.com.** You can also access our content when on the go via **ZAGAT.mobi** and **ZAGAT TO GO** (for smartphones).

FEEDBACK: To improve this guide, we invite your comments about any aspect of our performance. Did we miss anything? Just contact us at **boston@zagat.com.**

New York, NY
April 8, 2009

Nina and Tim

Nina and Tim Zagat

What's New

$ All signs point toward the Boston dining scene holding up well despite the economic crisis. A spate of newcomers has premiered – most of them moderately or inexpensively priced – and Bostonians are filling their seats in droves. Indeed, 75% of surveyors say they are eating out as much as or more than they were two years ago. But that doesn't mean they're being foolhardy with their funds. Roughly two-thirds say they are paying more attention to prices, patronizing less expensive places and skipping appetizers, desserts and/or alcohol.

HIGHS & LOWS: With the average price of a meal in Boston having risen to $33.64 – a 4.6% annualized increase from our last survey and a higher rate of inflation than in other major cities such as Chicago (2.1%), Los Angeles (3.3%) and New York (3.3%) – it comes as no surprise that 63% of respondents say they are spending more to dine out than they were two years ago. Still, Beantown's average per-meal cost remains below the national mean of $34.15, thanks in part to its wealth of bargains. Adding to the list of the city's Best Buys (see page 17) are cheap arrivals like **Franky N the Boys, Lavender Asian Cuisine, Rudi's Resto-Café & Bar, Thaitation** and **Wheeler's Café & Ice Cream Bar.**

THE NAME GAME: Forty-three percent of surveyors say they would be more likely to patronize the restaurant of a famous chef, and several newcomers are increasing those options. Among these premieres, the real deals are lower priced options from high-profile chefs, including Barbara Lynch's **Drink** and **Sportello,** Jimmy Burke's **Orta,** Ana Sortun's **Sofra Bakery & Café** and Chris Douglass' **Tavolo.** Also of note are **Hungry Mother** (from Barry Maiden, ex **Lumière**), **Scampo** (Lydia Shire) and **Sensing** (the first Stateside endeavor from French toque Guy Martin). Of course, sometimes the known name belongs more to the venue rather than the chef, as in the case of Asian–New American arrival **Asana** in the Back Bay's ritzy new Mandarin Oriental.

NEIGHBORHOOD WATCH: While the South End has cooled off a bit, with only a single high-profile entry (Spanish tapas specialist **Estragon**), there's been lots of action in the Downtown Crossing/Financial District areas. Tellingly, most of the freshmen – **Bina Osteria, Bond, The Littlest Bar, Marliave** and **Max & Dylans Kitchen & Bar** – offer many sensibly priced options, a boon to the vicinity's belt-tightening professionals.

FACTS & FIGURES: Poor service (cited by 72%) again tops the list of dining-out irritants, with noise and prices tied as distant seconds (8% each) . . . The Internet keeps gaining ground as a reservations tool: 38% typically book online, up from just 5% in 2006 . . . Concerns about mercury have prompted 21% to avoid certain types of fish . . . Recession notwithstanding, 64% will pay more for sustainably produced goods, and 60% will pay more for organic.

Boston, MA
April 8, 2009

Eric Grossman

Menus, photos, voting and more – free at ZAGAT.com

Most Popular

Plotted on the map at the back of this book.

BOSTON

1 Legal Sea Foods | *Seafood*	**21** East Coast | *BBQ/Seafood*
2 Blue Ginger | *Asian Fusion*	**22** Lumière | *French*
3 L'Espalier | *French*	**23** Sel de la Terre | *French*
4 No. 9 Park | *French/Italian*	**24** Ruth's Chris | *Steak*
5 Hamersley's Bistro | *French*	**25** FuGaKyu | *Japanese*
6 Abe & Louie's | *Steak*	**26** Rialto | *Italian*
7 Oleana | *Mediterranean*	**27** Petit Robert Bistro | *French*
8 Aujourd'hui | *French*	**28** Union Oyster* | *Seafood*
9 Capital Grille | *Steak*	**29** Sorellina | *Italian*
10 B&G Oysters | *Seafood*	**30** Olives | *Mediterranean*
11 Mistral | *French/Mediterranean*	**31** Davio's | *Italian/Steak*
12 Oishii | *Japanese*	**32** Radius | *French*
13 Grill 23 & Bar | *Steak*	**33** Helmand | *Afghan*
14 EVOO | *Eclectic*	**34** Il Capriccio | *Italian*
15 Cheesecake Factory | *American*	**35** Giacomo's | *Italian*
16 Craigie on Main | *French*	**36** Morton's | *Steak*
17 Clio/Uni | *French*	**37** UpStairs on the Sq. | *Amer.*
18 Anna's Taqueria | *Tex-Mex*	**38** Aquitaine | *French*
19 Elephant Walk | *Cambodian*	**39** Eastern Standard | *Amer./Euro.*
20 La Campania | *Italian*	**40** Icarus | *American*

CAPE COD, MARTHA'S VINEYARD & NANTUCKET

C=Cape Cod; M=Martha's Vineyard; N=Nantucket

1 Abba/C | *Mediterranean/Thai*	**11** Cape Sea Grille/C | *American*
2 Brewster Fish/C* | *Seafood*	**12** 28 Atlantic/C | *Amer.*
3 21 Federal/N | *American*	**13** Arnold's Lobster/C | *Seafood*
4 Chillingsworth/C | *French*	**14** Topper's/N | *American*
5 American Seasons/N | *Amer.*	**15** Wicked Oyster/C* | *Amer./Sea.*
6 Chatham Bars Inn/C | *American*	**16** Chatham Squire/C | *Pub Food*
7 Mews/C | *American*	**17** Nauset Beach Club/C | *Italian*
8 Lobster Pot/C | *Eclectic/Seafood*	**18** Straight Wharf/N | *Seafood*
9 Ocean House/C | *American*	**19** Red Pheasant | *Amer./French*
10 Impudent Oyster/C | *Seafood*	**20** Black Dog Tav./M | *American*

---

* Indicates a tie with restaurant above

KEY NEWCOMERS

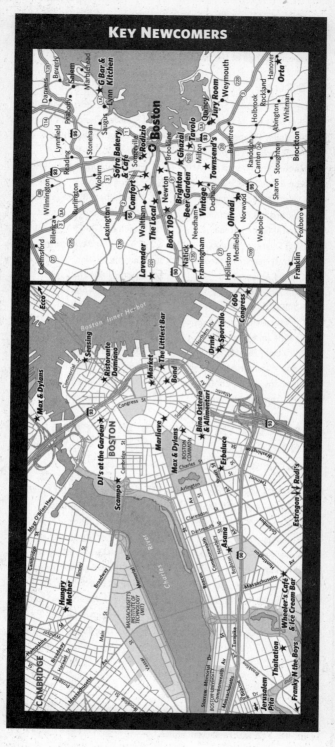

Menus, photos, voting and more – free at ZAGAT.com

Key Newcomers

Our editors' take on the year's top arrivals. See page 261 for a full list.

Asana | *Asian*

Bina Osteria | *Italian*

Bokx 109 | *Steak*

Bond | *Eclectic*

Brighton Beer Garden | *Pub Food*

Comfort | *American*

DJ's at the Garden | *American*

Drink | *American*

Ecco | *American*

Erbaluce | *Italian*

Estragon | *Spanish*

Franky N the Boys | *Burgers*

G Bar & Kitchen | *American*

Ghazal | *Indian*

Hungry Mother | *American*

Jerusalem Pita | *Israeli*

Jury Room | *American*

Lavender | *Asian*

Littlest Bar | *Pub Food*

Local, The | *American*

Market | *American*

Marliave | *Continental/Italian*

Max & Dylans | *American*

Olivadi | *Italian*

Orta | *Italian*

Ristorante Damiano | *Italian*

Rodizio | *Brazilian*

Rudi's | *American*

Scampo | *Italian*

Sensing | *French*

606 Congress | *American*

Sofra Bakery | *Middle Eastern*

Sportello | *Italian*

Tavolo | *Italian*

Thaitation | *Thai*

Townsend's | *American*

Vintage | *Amer./Steak*

Wheeler's Café | *Vegan*

In the year to come, some familiar favorites will present fresh endeavors: the Back Bay's Stephanie's on Newbury will beget **Stephi's on Tremont** in the South End; chef Dante de Magistris, of East Cambridge's dante, will branch out to Belmont with **Il Casale**; and Barbara Lynch will continue her quest for Fort Point Channel domination with a fine-dining concept to augment the more casual Drink and Sportello. The Back Bay's former Excelsior will be retooled into an upscale-casual French-Mediterranean bistro, while Excelsior's chef, Eric Brennan, is expected to head the kitchen at American brasserie **Post 390,** slated to open at luxury condo complex The Clarendon, also in the Back Bay. In Harvard Square's former Greenhouse Café space, the folks behind Audubon Circle, Cambridge, 1. and Miracle of Science will present **Tory Row,** serving American and European cafe fare from sunup to sundown and beyond. Also set to debut are a pair of high-profile hotels with eateries that are undefined at press time but sure to be buzz-worthy: the **W Boston** in the Back Bay and **The Ames,** a chic Morgans Hotel property situated near Faneuil Hall and Government Center. Finally, on Martha's Vineyard, veteran restaurateurs Mary and Jackson Kenworth (ex Slice of Life and Sweet Life Café) are constructing **State Road** in West Tisbury, featuring all-day New American fare with a sustainable bent.

Top Food Ratings

Excludes places with low votes, unless indicated by a ▽. See also Cape Cod, Martha's Vineyard and Nantucket Top Spots on pages 169, 192 and 199, respectively.

BOSTON, CAMBRIDGE, NEARBY SUBURBS

__28__ L'Espalier | *French*
Aujourd'hui | *French*
Oleana | *Mediterranean*
o ya | *Japanese*
La Campania | *Italian*
No. 9 Park | *French/Italian*

__27__ Ten Tables | *Amer./Euro.*
Bistro 5 | *Italian*
Clio/Uni | *French*
Neptune Oyster | *Seafood*
Troquet | *American/French*
Oishii | *Japanese*
Hamersley's Bistro | *French*
EVOO | *Eclectic*
Meritage | *American*
Taranta | *Italian/Peruvian*

Catch | *American/Seafood*
Sorellina | *Italian*
Hungry Mother | *American*
Lumière | *French*
Il Capriccio | *Italian*
Delfino | *Italian*
Prezza | *Italian*
Craigie on Main | *French*
Mistral | *French/Med.*

__26__ Carmen | *Italian*
Trattoria di Monica/
  Vinoteca | *Italian*
Trattoria Toscana | *Italian*
Galleria Umberto | *Italian*
Toro | *Spanish*

OUTLYING SUBURBS

__29__ Duckworth's | *American*

__27__ Oishii | *Japanese*
Coriander Bistro | *French*
Sichuan Gourmet | *Chinese*

__26__ Ithaki | *Mediterranean*

Square Café | *American*
Blue Ginger | *Asian Fusion*
Maxwell's 148 | *Asian Fusion/Italian*
Clam Box | *Seafood*
Caffe Bella | *Mediterranean*

BY CUISINE

AMERICAN (NEW)
__29__ Duckworth's
__27__ Ten Tables
Troquet
Meritage
Catch

AMERICAN (TRAD.)
__25__ Oak Room
__24__ Mr. Bartley's
Oceana
NewBridge Cafe
Summer Winter

BARBECUE
__25__ East Coast Grill
Blue Ribbon BBQ
Uncle Pete's Ribs
__24__ NewBridge Cafe
__22__ Redbones BBQ

BURGERS
__24__ Mr. Bartley's
__23__ UBurger
__21__ Audubon Circle
__19__ Miracle of Science
b. good

CAMBODIAN/VIETNAMESE
__23__ Elephant Walk
Pho Pasteur
__21__ Le's
Wonder Spice
Lam's

CHINESE
__27__ Sichuan Gourmet
__25__ Peach Farm
__24__ Qingdao Garden
Bernard's
East Ocean City

ECLECTIC

27	EVOO
25	Blue Room
	Centre St. Café
23	Scutra
	Metropolis Cafe

FRENCH

28	No. 9 Park
27	Mistral
26	Salts
25	Butcher Shop
24	Sandrine's

FRENCH (BISTRO)

27	Troquet
	Hamersley's Bistro
	Coriander Bistro
	Craigie on Main
26	Pigalle

FRENCH (NEW)

28	L'Espalier
	Aujourd'hui
27	Clio/Uni
	Lumière
26	Radius

INDIAN

25	Punjab
24	Kebab Factory
	India Quality
	Rangoli
	Himalayan Bistro

ITALIAN

27	Sorellina
	Taranta
	Delfino
	Prezza
26	Carmen

ITALIAN (NORTHERN)

27	Bistro 5
	Il Capriccio
26	Trattoria Toscana
	Bridgeman's
25	Tosca

JAPANESE

28	o ya
27	Oishii
26	Oga
25	FuGaKyu
	Sakurabana

MEDITERRANEAN

28	Oleana
27	Mistral
26	Ithaki Med.
	Caffe Bella
	Chiara

MEXICAN

25	Tacos Lupita
	El Sarape
24	Olecito/Olé
	Tu Y Yo
	Cantina la Mexicana

MIDDLE EASTERN

26	Sofra Bakery & Café
	Helmand
25	Café Mangal
24	Byblos
	Sultan's Kitchen

NEW ENGLAND

24	Gibbet Hill Grill
	Green Street
23	Henrietta's Table
	Woodman's
22	Parker's

PAN-ASIAN

23	Myers + Chang
21	Pho République
20	Billy Tse
	Grasshopper
	Ma Soba

PIZZA

26	Galleria Umberto
25	Santarpio's Pizza
	Za
24	Emma's Pizza
	Pizzeria Regina

PUB FOOD

22	Matt Murphy's
21	Audubon Circle
	Publick House
20	Sunset Cantina
19	Mission B&G

SEAFOOD (AMERICAN)

27	Neptune Oyster
	Catch
26	Clam Box
	B&G Oysters
25	East Coast Grill

SEAFOOD (ETHNIC)

- 25 Giacomo's
  Peach Farm
- 24 Tamarind Bay
  Daily Catch
  East Ocean City*

SPANISH

- 26 Toro
- 25 Dalí
- 23 Taberna de Haro
  Solea
  Tasca

STEAKHOUSES

- 26 Capital Grille
  Abe & Louie's
- 25 Morton's
  Grill 23 & Bar
  Davio's

THAI

- 25 Brown Sugar/Similans
- 24 Dok Bua
  House of Siam
  Khao Sarn Cuisine
- 23 Thai Basil

BY SPECIAL FEATURE

BRUNCH

- 28 Aujourd'hui
- 27 Meritage
- 25 Centre St. Café
- 23 Henrietta's Table
  Metropolis Cafe

CHILD-FRIENDLY

- 26 Clam Box
  flour bakery
- 25 Blue Ribbon BBQ
- 21 Jasper White's
- 20 Full Moon

CHOWDER

- 27 Neptune Oyster
- 26 B&G Oysters
- 22 Legal Sea Foods
- 21 Turner Fisheries
- 20 Union Oyster House

DESSERT

- 26 flour bakery
- 24 Bristol
  Hi-Rise
- 23 Finale
- 22 Picco

HOTEL DINING

- 28 Aujourd'hui
  (Four Seasons Hotel)
- 27 Clio/Uni
  (Eliot Hotel)
  Meritage
  (Boston Harbor Hotel)
- 26 Rialto
  (Charles Hotel)
- 25 Oak Room
  (Fairmont Copley Plaza)

LANDMARKS

- 24 Locke-Ober
- 23 Charlie's Sandwich
- 20 Union Oyster House
- 17 Jacob Wirth
  Durgin-Park

LATE DINING

- 26 Franklin Café
- 25 FuGaKyu
- 24 Peach Farm
- 22 Eastern Standard
- 21 Chau Chow

NEWCOMERS (RATED)

- 27 Hungry Mother
- 26 Sofra Bakery
- 23 Bokx 109▽
- 22 Scampo
  Rodizio▽

PEOPLE-WATCHING

- 25 Butcher Shop
- 22 Scampo
  Parish Cafe
- 20 Stephanie's
  Sonsie

POWER LUNCH

- 26 Radius
  Abe & Louie's
- 25 Harvest
- 24 Bristol
- 23 Smith & Wollensky

WINNING WINE LISTS

- 28 L'Espalier
  Aujourd'hui
  La Campania
  No. 9 Park
- 27 Troquet

BY LOCATION

BACK BAY

28 L'Espalier
Aujourd'hui
27 Clio/Uni
Sorellina
26 Capital Grille

BEACON HILL

28 No. 9 Park
25 Grotto
24 Pierrot Bistrot
Rist. Toscano
Mooo . . .

BROOKLINE/ CHESTNUT HILL

27 Oishii
26 Capital Grille
25 FuGaKyu
Orinoco: A Latin Kitchen
24 Pomodoro

CENTRAL/ INMAN SQS./ EAST CAMBRIDGE

28 Oleana
27 Craigie on Main
26 Baraka Cafe
Salts
Helmand

CHARLESTOWN

25 Olives
24 Tangierino
23 Figs
Navy Yard Bistro
16 Warren Tavern

CHINATOWN

25 Peach Farm
24 East Ocean City
23 Kaze
Taiwan Cafe
New Jumbo Seafood

DOWNTOWN CROSS./ FINANCIAL DICTRICT

26 Radius
25 Sakurabana
24 Ruth's Chris
Sultan's Kitchen
Locke-Ober

FENWAY/KENMORE SQ.

26 Trattoria Toscana
24 India Quality
Petit Robert Bistro
23 Great Bay
Elephant Walk

HARVARD SQ.

27 Ten Tables Cambridge
26 Rialto
25 Garden at The Cellar
Harvest
24 Darwin's Ltd.

JAMAICA PLAN

27 Ten Tables
25 Centre St. Café
24 Zon's
El Oriental de Cuba
23 JP Seafood

NEEDHAM/NEWTON/ WELLESLEY

27 Lumière
26 Blue Ginger
25 Blue Ribbon BBQ
Sweet Basil
Fava

NORTH END

27 Neptune Oyster
Taranta
Prezza
26 Carmen
Trattoria di Monica/Vinoteca

PARK SQ.

25 Via Matta
Davio's
24 Fleming's Prime
23 Finale
22 Da Vinci

SEAPORT/ WATERFRONT

27 Meritage
26 flour bakery
25 Morton's
Persephone
24 Oceana

SOMERVILLE

27 EVOO
25 Dalí
Tacos Lupita
24 Kebab Factory
Tu Y Yo

SOUTH END

27 Oishii Boston
Hamersley's Bistro
Mistral
26 Toro
flour bakery

THEATER DISTRICT

27 Troquet
26 Pigalle
24 Avila
Teatro
23 Montien

WALTHAM/ WATERTOWN

28 La Campania
27 Il Capriccio
24 New Ginza
Tuscan Grill
23 Solea

CAPE COD

27 Inaho
Front Street

Pisces
Red Pheasant
Bramble Inn

MARTHA'S VINEYARD

27 Détente
Larsen's Fish Mkt.
26 Bite
L'Étoile
25 Atria

NANTUCKET

28 Company/Cauldron
27 Topper's
26 Le Languedoc
Black-Eyed Susan's
25 Straight Wharf

THE BERKSHIRES

28 Old Inn/Green
27 Wheatleigh
Blantyre
25 Gramercy Bistro
Elizabeth's

Top Decor Ratings

28	Aujourd'hui		Bravo
	Sorellina	24	No. 9 Park
27	Meritage		Bistro 5
	Banq		Parker's
	Oak Room		Dalí
26	Top of the Hub		Beehive
	Gibbet Hill Grill		Scarlet Oak Tavern
	Bristol		Oceanaire
	Tangierino		Maxwell's 148
	Mistral		Hungry i
	J's at Nashoba		Longfellow's Inn
	Square Café*		Rocca
	Cuchi Cuchi		Scampo
	Clio/Uni		L'Andana
25	La Campania		Mooo . . .
	Clink		Davio's
	Radius		Chiara
	28 Degrees		Barker Tavern
	Locke-Ober		UpStairs on the Square
	Rialto		Avila

OUTDOORS

B&G Oysters	J's at Nashoba
Barking Crab	Oleana
Casa Romero	Red Rock Bistro
Hamersley's Bistro	Stella
Harvest	Stellina
Henrietta's Table	Stephanie's

ROMANCE

Carmen	L'Espalier
Casa Romero	Mamma Maria
Dalí	Oleana
Hungry i	Pigalle
Il Capriccio	Tangierino
Lala Rokh	Taranta

ROOMS

Beehive	La Campania
Bridgeman's	Mistral
Clink	Oak Room
Clio/Uni	Radius
Cuchi Cuchi	Sorellina
Dalí	Tangierino

VIEWS

Anthony's	Meritage
Back Eddy	Oceana
Barking Crab	Red Rock Bistro
Bristol	Tavern on Water
dante	Top of the Hub
J's at Nashoba	Upstairs on the Square

Top Service Ratings

28	Aujourd'hui		Hamersley's Bistro

28 | Aujourd'hui
L'Espalier

27 | Trattoria Toscana
Maxwell's 148
No. 9 Park

26 | Bistro 5
Bristol
Meritage
Sorellina
Oak Room
EVOO
o ya
Lumière
Clio/Uni
Coriander Bistro
Duckworth's*
Salts
La Campania

25 | Marco Romana
Mistral

Hamersley's Bistro
T.W. Food
Craigie on Main
Gibbet Hill Grill
Capital Grille
Troquet
Blue Ginger
Hungry Mother
Il Capriccio
Abe & Louie's
Grapevine
Oleana
Mooo . . .
Radius
Rialto
Persephone
Ten Tables

24 | flora
Pigalle
Fava

Best Buys

BOSTON

In order of Bang for the Buck rating.

1. 1369 Coffee Hse.
2. Anna's Taqueria
3. Baja Betty's
4. Boloco
5. b. good
6. Galleria Umberto
7. UBurger
8. Sofra Bakery & Café
9. Boca Grande
10. Tacos Lupita
11. Athan's Café
12. Darwin's Ltd.
13. flour bakery
14. Oxford Spa
15. Paris Creperie
16. UFood Grill
17. Charlie's Sandwich
18. Cantina la Mexicana
19. Bottega Fiorentina
20. Punjabi Dhaba
21. Picante Mexican
22. Il Panino Express
23. Mr. Crepe
24. Hi-Rise Bread Co.
25. All Star Sandwich
26. Rami's
27. Sound Bites
28. Deluxe Town
29. Blue Ribbon BBQ
30. Shawarma King
31. Pie Bakery & Café
32. El Oriental de Cuba
33. Dok Bua
34. Mr. Bartley's
35. Cafe Jaffa
36. South End Buttery
37. Veggie Planet
38. Upper Crust
39. Basta Pasta
40. Rosebud Diner

OTHER GOOD VALUES

Addis Red Sea
Border Cafe
Boston/Salem Beer
Brown Sugar Café
Bukowski Tavern
Café Polonia
Cambridge Common
Carlo's Cucina
Centre St. Café
Delux Café
Demos
Fajitas & 'Ritas
Giacomo's
Halfway Café
Hot Tomatoes
India Quality/Punjab
Johnny's Lunch.
Kebab Factory
Koreana
Le's
Mike's City Diner
Miracle of Science
Muqueca
NewBridge Café
Other Side Café
Paramount
Pho Lemongrass
Pizzeria Regina
Redbones BBQ
Santarpio's Pizza
Silvertone B&G
South St. Diner
Steve's Greek
Sultan's Kitchen
Sunset Grill/Cantina
Sweet Basil
Taqueria Mexico
Vinny's at Night
Za
Zaftigs

PRIX FIXE MENUS

Call for availability. All-you-can-eat options are for lunch and/or brunch.

PRIX FIXE LUNCH

28 L'Espalier ($24)
26 Radius ($29)
25 Little Q Hot Pot ($9)
24 Kayuga II ($9)
   Punjab Palace ($7)
   Sandrine's ($20)
   Sel de la Terre ($21)
   UpStairs on the Square ($20)
23 Elephant ($17)
22 Lotus Blossom ($11)

PRIX FIXE DINNER

27 Catch ($36)
   EVOO ($35)
   Lumière ($35)
26 Rendezvous($38)
25 Grotto ($36)

   Little Q Hot Pot ($14)
24 Chez Henri ($39)
   La Morra ($35)
   Pierrot Bistrot ($34)
   Sandrine's ($40)

ALL YOU CAN EAT

26 J's at Nashoba ($23)
25 Blue Room ($23)
24 Bristol ($39)
   Himalayan Bistro ($8)
   Kebab Factory ($8)
   Mela ($10)
   Tamarind Bay ($9)
23 Kashmir ($10)
   Henrietta's Table ($45)
   Bukhara ($9)

BEST BUYS: CAPE COD

In order of Bang for the Buck Rating.

1. Betsy's Diner
2. Sir Cricket's
3. Captain Frosty's
4. Dunbar Tea Room
5. Liam's at Nauset Bch.
6. Cobie's Clam Shack
7. Stir Crazy
8. Catch of the Day
9. Captain Kidd
10. Clancy's

BEST BUYS: MARTHA'S VINEYARD

1. Art Cliff Diner
2. Sharky's Cantina
3. Net Result
4. Bite
5. Larsen's Fish Mkt.
6. Offshore Ale
7. Newes From America
8. Zapotec
9. Black Dog Tavern
10. Jimmy Seas Pan Pasta

BEST BUYS: NANTUCKET

1. Fog Island Café
2. Black-Eyed Susan's
3. Brotherhood of Thieves
4. Even Keel Cafe
5. Sushi by Yoshi
6. Queequeg's
7. Arno's
8. SeaGrille
9. Sconset Café
10. Le Languedoc

BEST BUYS: BERKSHIRES

1. Baba Louie's
2. Café Latino
3. Barrington Brewery
4. Siam Square
5. Aroma B&G
6. Thai Garden
7. Bombay
8. Elizabeth's
9. Route 7 Grill
10. Truc Orient

BOSTON/
CAPE COD & THE ISLANDS
RESTAURANT
DIRECTORY

Boston

Abbondanza Ristorante Italiano ⬧ *Italian* ▽ 23 | 16 | 21 | $31

Everett | 195 Main St. (bet. Appleton St. & Forest Ave.) | 617-387-8422

"In the wilds of Everett", this "quintessential" "old-school" Italian doles out "large portions" of "simple, delicious" and "consistently fresh seafood and pasta" that admirers aver "hold their own" against any "red-sauce royalty"; relatively "low prices" match the "quaint but not kitschy" atmosphere, which feels "welcoming" thanks to a "friendly staff."

Ƶ Abe & Louie's *Steak* 26 | 22 | 25 | $61

Back Bay | 793 Boylston St. (Fairfield St.) | 617-536-6300 | www.abeandlouies.com

"You'll swear you died and went to fat-cat heaven" at this "manly" Back Bay steakhouse where the "melt-on-your-tongue" beef served with "all the bells and whistles" is "worth every penny", especially if you "go on someone else's expense account"; while the "'in' crowd" downs "fantastic wines" at the bar, others enjoy the "elegant" (if "noisy") dining room where "top-notch", "seasoned" staffers help make any meal feel "celebratory."

Addis Red Sea *Ethiopian* 22 | 19 | 18 | $26

South End | 544 Tremont St. (Clarendon St.) | 617-426-8727
Porter Square | 1755 Massachusetts Ave. (Linnean St.) | Cambridge | 617-441-8727
www.addisredsea.com

"Leave your fork at home" when heading to one of these Porter Square and South End "bargain" Ethiopians where "spongy" injera bread is used to sop up "delectable morsels" of "authentic" fare cooked with "amazing spices" and "served family-style"; the "traditional settings" come complete with "evocative decor", seats that can be "uncomfortable" (because you're practically "sitting on your haunches") and "friendly" though "somewhat slow service."

Aegean *Greek* 21 | 19 | 20 | $28

Watertown | 640 Arsenal St. (Coolidge Ave.) | 617-923-7771
Framingham | 257 Cochituate Rd. (bet. Caldor Rd. & Greenview St.) | 508-879-8424
www.aegeanrestaurants.com

The "homestyle", "well-seasoned" Greek fare "made with love" at this duo is offered in "generous portions" and at "wallet-friendly" prices to boot, just like the "affordable" Hellenic wines; the newer Framingham location, boasting a "great bar", is "more chichi", the one in Watertown is "spacious" yet "homey" and both employ "friendly" staffs.

Alchemist Lounge *American* 17 | 17 | 18 | $27

Jamaica Plain | 435 S. Huntington Ave. (Centre St.) | 617-477-5741 | www.alchemistlounge.com

"Funky" digs plus "swanky drinks" plus "live music at times" is this Jamaica Plain bar/eatery's formula for an "unpretentious" "neigh-

borhood hangout"; but there are minuses in the equation: the New American "comfort food" with a "twist" is "inconsistent", just like service can be "iffy" (still, the "hipster" staffers are "generally happy to be there"); P.S. "sitting outside" for "brunch is nice."

Al Dente *Italian*
22 | 17 | 22 | $34

North End | 109 Salem St. (Cooper St.) | 617-523-0990 | www.aldenteboston.com

A "bountiful selection" of "always-pleasing", "homestyle red-sauce Italian" dished out in "huge portions" "at reasonable prices" makes this North Ender "a good value"; plus, the "nice peeps" who work here "treat you as family", making up for the "tight quarters."

All Star Sandwich Bar *Sandwiches*
23 | 15 | 18 | $16

Inman Square | 1245 Cambridge St. (Prospect St.) | Cambridge | 617-868-3065 | www.allstarsandwichbar.com

"Awesome" "concoctions", often filled with "unexpected ingredients" that "challenge the imagination", make this Inman Square storefront a "sandwich-lover's paradise"; the "friendly" staff can get "understandably overwhelmed" at peak times, but it's "worth the wait" in "simple", somewhat "squished" surroundings for such "ample" (albeit "overpriced") eats; P.S. "no wraps allowed", so carbo-phobes should skedaddle.

Alta Strada *Italian*
21 | 18 | 20 | $39

Wellesley | 92 Central St. (Weston Rd.) | 781-237-6100 | www.altastradarestaurant.com

Chef Michael Schlow brings a "hip vibe" and "stylish" Italian fare focusing on "imaginative" small plates to Wellesley via this eatery, but numbers-crunchers can't decide whether it's "overpriced" or "affordable for what you get"; however, everyone's in concert when it comes to the "bustling", "modern"-"minimalist" setting: it's "noisy beyond belief" ("glad there's takeout available" at the "gourmet market in the basement").

Amarin of Thailand *Thai*
22 | 19 | 20 | $27

Newton | 287 Centre St. (Jefferson St.) | 617-527-5255
Wellesley | 27 Grove St. (bet. Central & Spring Sts.) | 781-239-1350
www.amarinofthailand.com

There may be "no surprises" at these Newton and Wellesley Thais, but there's "never a dud" on the "wide"-ranging menu thanks in part to "high-quality" ingredients and "reasonable prices"; "pleasant", "casual atmospheres" that "invite conversation" and "efficient", "kid-friendly" service mean they're "much more than just take-out joints."

Amelia's Kitchen *Italian*
22 | 16 | 18 | $27

Somerville | Teele Sq. | 1137 Broadway (Curtis St.) | 617-776-2800 | www.ameliaskitchen.com

"If you live in Somerville", it's "worth the trip to Teele Square" for this "understated", "family-owned" storefront – or so say regulars who find "value" in the selection of "reliable" pizzas, pastas and other Italian staples; on the other hand, some dollar-watchers deem it "pricey for the portions" and perhaps too "ordinary."

| | FOOD | DECOR | SERVICE | COST |

Amelia's Trattoria 🗗 *Italian* — 22 | 17 | 19 | $32

Kendall Square | 111 Harvard St. (Portland St.) | Cambridge | 617-868-7600 | www.ameliastrattoria.com

"MIT techies" and Kendall Square locals hit this "quaint" "hole-in-the-wall" for "killer pastas", "unique pizzas" and other Italian "goodies" ranging from "light to hearty"; the "cozy" space with "tiny aisles" gets "packed" at key times and service varies between "efficient" and "bored", but "decent prices" make it "fantastic", especially for lunch.

Amrheins *American* — 18 | 17 | 18 | $28

South Boston | 80 W. Broadway (A St.) | 617-268-6189 | www.amrheinsboston.com

"Commune with old South Boston" at this "casual" "standby" serving "hearty, flavorful", "reasonably priced" American grub amid "dark" yet "pleasant" environs; there's "outdoor dining in the summer", but "sports enthusiasts" prefer hunkering down around the "large", "beautiful" hand-carved bar and its "big TVs."

Anchovies ● *Italian* — 20 | 14 | 18 | $24

South End | 433 Columbus Ave. (bet. Braddock Park & Holyoke St.) | 617-266-5088

"Always busy" with "straights, gays" and South Enders "old and new", this "salty hideout" attracts with a "noisy bar" pouring "strong", "cheap drinks" and "affordable" fare from Italy brought to table until late into the night; highlights of the "flea-market" decor include "moose heads, road signs and voodoo masks", while service proves to be a bright spot when it's "friendly" (as opposed to "cranky").

Angelo's 🗗 *Italian* — ∇ 26 | 17 | 22 | $44

Stoneham | 237 Main St. (bet. Elm & William Sts.) | 781-279-9035 | www.angeloristorante.com

Even if there were more dining options in Stoneham, this "tiny" "storefront" would still be a "treasure", as its "authentic" Italian fare is "cooked to order", "fantastic" and complemented by a "good wine selection"; prices on the "tablecloth side" are "commensurate with the quality of the food", those in the "pizzeria area" are more "reasonable", while the decor in both "leaves lots to be desired" (post-Survey renovations may help with that).

⚡ Anna's Taqueria *Tex-Mex* — 22 | 10 | 18 | $9

Beacon Hill | 242 Cambridge St. (Garden St.) | 617-227-8822
Cambridgeport | MIT Stratton Student Ctr. | 84 Massachusetts Ave. (Vassar St.) | Cambridge | 617-324-2662 ●🝮
Porter Square | Porter Exchange Mall | 822 Somerville Ave. (Mass. Ave.) | Cambridge | 617-661-8500 🝮
Brookline | 1412 Beacon St. (Summit Ave.) | 617-739-7300 🝮
Brookline | 446 Harvard St. (bet. Coolidge & Thorndike Sts.) | 617-277-7111 🝮
Somerville | 236 Elm St. (bet. Bower Ave. & Chester St.) | 617-666-3900 ●🝮
www.annastaqueria.com

"Starving students" and other "deal"-seekers flock to these "no-frills" Tex-Mex taquerias where "lightning-fast" "burrito cowboys"

whip up "gut-busting" "bundles of joy" along with "fresh, hot and filling" tacos and quesadillas at "easy-to-digest" prices; though doubters deem them "not worthy of the hype", everyone else admits to being "totally addicted."

Anthony's Pier 4 *Seafood* | 18 | 18 | 18 | $49 |
Seaport District | 140 Northern Ave. (Pier 4) | 617-482-6262 | www.pier4.com

Supporters say this Seaport District "stalwart" is a "reliable" "step back in time" for "quintessential" "New England seafood" ferried by "career waiters" in "white coats"; true, being a stop for "hordes" of tourists on "drive-by-eating excursions" may have caused it to have "lost its luster" somewhat, but it's still "worth the wait and the bucks", "at least once", for the "dynamite popovers" and "spectacular views of the harbor."

Antico Forno *Italian* | 23 | 17 | 19 | $32 |
North End | 93 Salem St. (bet. Cross & Parmenter Sts.) | 617-723-6733 | www.anticofornoboston.com

"One of the better deals in the North End", this "Southern Italian stalwart" "amazes" with "hearty", "ultrafresh" "red-sauce basics", plus pizzas and pastas "finished in a brick oven", then served by "unfussy" staffers; while the "simply decorated" "space is tight", "noisy" and "crowded" with "a lot of families", "all is forgotten after that first bite of bubbling cheese."

Antonio's Cucina Italiana ⓈI *Italian* | 22 | 13 | 21 | $27 |
Beacon Hill | 286 Cambridge St. (bet. Anderson & Grove Sts.) | 617-367-3310 | www.antoniosofbeaconhill.com

"Bringing North End" "real-deal" Italian to Beacon Hill without the "dressed-up prices", this "mundane storefront" "surprises" with "more-than-generous portions" of "homestyle" eats that "never fail to deliver"; the "tight quarters" are "always packed" (hence "noisy"), but the "friendly" "staff makes it work" by being "prompt" too.

Apollo Grill & Sushi ●Ⓜ *Japanese/Korean* ▽ | 17 | 13 | 15 | $33 |
Chinatown | 84-86 Harrison Ave. (Kneeland St.) | 617-423-3888

Though "not on the radar" when the sun shines, this open-till-4 AM Chinatownie becomes a "hidden gem" "after a long night of partying" "when you need sushi" or Korean barbecue ("average" though they may be); the "decor could use a little touch-up", but that matters not to clubbers for whom "affordability" and "availability" trump ambiance.

Appetito *Italian* | 19 | 17 | 19 | $36 |
Newton | 761 Beacon St. (Langley Rd.) | 617-244-9881

When "not aiming for fancy", Newton Center locals head to this "reliable neighborhood restaurant" for "ample portions" of "solid" Italian that some suspect is "more sophisticated" than the norm and others lament is "a bit heavy at times"; "smallish" digs with "tables too close together" and "erratic service" don't prevent it from being "always busy" – and "loud."

	FOOD	DECOR	SERVICE	COST

☑ Aquitaine *French* · 23 · 22 · 22 · $46

South End | 569 Tremont St. (Clarendon St.) | 617-424-8577 |
www.aquitaineboston.com

"A little trip to France" is as easy as booking this South End bistro
where steak frites are "the must" at dinner, mussels ("use bread to
soak up every drop of sauce") reign at lunch and "out-of-this-world
waffles" rule at brunch – and though everything's slightly "pricey",
it's "fair" for the "high quality"; the elevated noise level "remains both
exciting and annoying", but the "stylish" setting and "polite, prompt"
service make it "impressive" "for business and romance" alike.

Aquitaine Bis *French* · 23 · 21 · 21 · $45

Chestnut Hill | Chestnut Hill Shopping Ctr. | 11 Boylston St. (Hammond St.) |
617-734-8400 | www.aquitainebis.com

At this "smaller version" of the South End original, the "biggest
issue" is the "intrusive noise" – but that only adds to the "chic",
"you're-in-France" vibe (indeed, "you totally forget" you're in a
Chestnut Hill strip mall); likewise, the "traditional bistro" fare is
"way above what you would expect" in the 'burbs, and though
it's "not cheap", it's "worth it", especially factoring in "plenty
of free parking."

Ariadne ☒ *American* · 21 · 22 · 20 · $47

Newton | 344 Walnut St. (Washington Park) | 617-332-4653 |
www.ariadnerestaurant.com

For "romance" and "sophistication", Newtonians know this New
American offers "old-school luxe" by way of "plush", "comfortable
booths", "tall ceilings, big curtains" and "soothing colors and fab-
rics"; the "Mediterranean-influenced" menu is itself "wonderful", as
are the "well-chosen wines", and while they're "pricey", more "casual bites" are available at the "gorgeous bar" (where one is more
likely to find less "glacial service").

Artichokes Ristorante Trattoria ☒ *Italian* · 21 · 17 · 21 · $34

Malden | 2 Florence St. (Pleasant St.) | 781-397-8338

The "mouthwatering aroma of garlic" and the promise of "huge portions" of "delicious" "homemade Italian" that yield "leftovers for a
week" lead to "long waits" at this "small", "loud and crowded"
Malden venue; however, the lines to get in may get shorter when it
moves to bigger digs at 317 Main Street in Wakefield post-Survey,
at which time the scores may be outdated.

Artú *Italian* · 21 · 16 · 20 · $32

Beacon Hill | 89 Charles St. (Pinckney St.) | 617-227-9023
North End | 6 Prince St. (Hanover St.) | 617-742-4336
www.artuboston.com

"Simple", "moderately priced" "Italian standards of consistent quality" make this pair a "go-to" for "to-go" lunches and dinners; they're
dine-in destinations too: if you hope to "impress a date", hit the
"quaint", "spare" Beacon Hill "basement" where "exposed brick
abounds", or if you're with "friends and family", the "long and narrow" North End locale has "more space" and a "wonderful bar."

	FOOD	DECOR	SERVICE	COST

NEW Asana *American/Asian*
| - | - | - | E |

Back Bay | Mandarin Oriental | 776 Boylston St. (Fairfield St.) |
617-535-8888 | www.mandarinoriental.com/boston

Open for breakfast, lunch and dinner, the signature restaurant of the
Back Bay's Mandarin Oriental hotel puts the spotlight on pricey New
American and Asian fare; during the day, light floods in from floor-
to-ceiling windows overlooking Boylston Street, while at night, dark
bamboo floors, aquatic blues and earth tones and a glassed-in wine
room create a sexy vibe.

Ashmont Grill *American*
| 22 | 19 | 22 | $31 |

Dorchester | 555 Talbot Ave. (Ashmont St.) | 617-825-4300 |
www.ashmontgrill.com

At this "urban oasis" in Dorchester, the "high-quality" American
"comfort food" leans toward the "gourmet", but the "modest
prices", "lively", "casual" vibe and "diverse mix" of clientele ensure
that it "remains a neighborhood joint"; the "dot-themed" interior
boasts a "great bar" where "fun, attentive" 'tenders mix "amazing
cocktails", which can also be enjoyed on the "beautiful", "private-
and-cozy-feeling" patio.

Asmara *Eritrean/Ethiopian*
| ∇ 21 | 16 | 20 | $24 |

Central Square | 739 Massachusetts Ave. (bet. Pleasant &
Prospect Sts.) | Cambridge | 617-864-7447 |
www.asmararestaurantboston.com

For "delicious" fare that seems "unusual and familiar at the same
time", adventurers head to this Central Square spot for "authentic",
"spicy" Eritrean-Ethiopian cuisine that you "eat with your
hands" (bring a new friend – it's "a real ice breaker"); despite
the spare surroundings, it's "worth a visit" for such "warm service"
and "affordable" prices.

Assaggio ● *Italian*
| 24 | 21 | 22 | $36 |

North End | 29 Prince St. (Hanover St.) | 617-227-7380 |
www.assaggioboston.com

"Why spend a fortune" in the North End when "huge plates" of
"reasonably priced" "old-country" Italian and "inventive specials" can be found here? – or so wonder this "dependable" eatery's backers who also appreciate that the "friendly" servers "stay
out of your hair" when appropriate so you can enjoy the "warm, inviting", statue-filled ground level or the "romantic", "vine-covered"
cellar in peace.

Atasca *Portuguese*
| 23 | 22 | 22 | $32 |

Kendall Square | 50 Hampshire St. (Webster Ave.) | Cambridge |
617-621-6991 | www.atasca.com

"Earthy", "flavorful" Portuguese dishes starring "jumping-fresh"
seafood are whipped up for "reasonable prices" at this "bustling"
Kendall Square site whose "vibrant atmosphere" and "friendly, efficient service" are "great for groups of friends" or "families"; it can
be "romantic" too, especially on the summertime patio where "it's
all about drinking *vinho verde.*"

	FOOD	DECOR	SERVICE	COST

Athan's European Bakery & Café *Mediterranean/Bakery*

| | 23 | 19 | 18 | $14 |

Brighton | 407 Washington St. (bet. Leicester & Parsons Sts.) | 617-783-0313

Brookline | 1621 Beacon St. (Washington St.) | 617-734-7028

www.athansbakery.com

This "sun-filled" "sanctuary" in Brighton may serve "delicious" Mediterranean meals, but the "decadent", "visually stunning" desserts ("buttery", "flaky pastries", "yummy gelato" and an "enormous selection of baklava") are the "main" events here and at the bakery-only Brookline original; some tally it's "a little overpriced" for what it is, but then again, if you're going to "blow your diet and then some", wouldn't you rather go "gourmet"?

Atlantica Ⓜ *Seafood*

| | ▽ 15 | 24 | 17 | $40 |

Cohasset | 44 Border St. (Summer St.) | 781-383-0900 | www.cohassetharborresort.com

"Lovely", even "magical" "views of Cohasset Harbor" are "alone worth the visit" (and what "you're paying for") at this "cavernous" seafooder; "unfortunately, that's all" that wows, as the "food is just ok" – in fact, you may prefer to just "sit at the bar and enjoy a glass of wine" or a cocktail; N.B. from October to May, it's open Wednesday–Saturday for dinner only.

Atlantic Fish Co. *Seafood*

| | 23 | 21 | 22 | $45 |

Back Bay | 761 Boylston St. (bet. Exeter & Fairfield Sts.) | 617-267-4000 | www.atlanticfishco.com

"Many tourists" and "after-workers" hit this Back Bay fish house for "dependable", "high-quality" seafood "simply but tastily prepared"; it's "no bargain", but the "professional" – "if youthful" – staff, "warm atmosphere" and "great people-watching" from the outdoor-dining area make it "worth what you pay."

Audubon Circle *Pub Food*

| | 21 | 19 | 18 | $23 |

Kenmore Square | 838 Beacon St. (Arundel St.) | 617-421-1910 | www.auduboncircle.us

"Somewhere between grad-school shindig and real life" lies this "funky"/"classy" Kenmore Square venue with a "limited but choice menu" of American pub grub ("heavenly burgers", "always popular potstickers") whose "inexpensive" tabs belie their "high-end" preparations; "go here before a Red Sox game for little-to-no waits", "after work" for the "extensive drinks list and many kinds of beer" or "in the summer" for the "awesome patio."

Ⓩ Aujourd'hui Ⓜ *French*

| | 28 | 28 | 28 | $85 |

Back Bay | Four Seasons Hotel | 200 Boylston St. (Charles St.) | 617-351-2037 | www.fourseasons.com/boston

Voted Boston's No. 1 for both Decor and Service, this "elegant", "luxurious" room "overlooking the Public Gardens" in the Back Bay's Four Seasons retains the "ne plus ultra" of staffs to deliver "divine" New French cuisine that "dazzles both the eye and the palate"; yes, it's "a bit stuffy", but "that's kind of the point", and true, you

may be "shocked by the bill", but it's "worth every penny" for such a "sublime experience."

Aura *American* | 22 | 19 | 21 | $50 |

Seaport District | Seaport Hotel | 1 Seaport Ln. (bet. Congress St. & Northern Ave.) | 617-385-4300 | www.aurarestaurant.com

"Hidden in the convention jungle" that is the Seaport District, this "respectable" all-day establishment makes its mark with "refined", sometimes "whimsical" (and pricey) New American preparations as well as a "terrific bar"; the "intimate" setting, however, proves to be "unmemorable" – after all, it's "still a hotel lobby."

Avenue One *American* | ▽ 18 | 17 | 18 | $40 |

Downtown Crossing | Hyatt Regency Boston | 1 Ave. de Lafayette (bet. Chauncy & Washington Sts.) | 617-422-5579 | www.avenueoneboston.com

Though the mid- to upper-priced New American fare at this all-day venue in Downtown Crossing's Hyatt Regency straddles the line between "outstanding" and "weak", it's still not a bad choice for pre-theater; however, for every ticket-holder who appreciates the "bright, open" feel of the spacious room, there's another who can't escape the feeling they're "eating in a hotel lobby", causing them to "quickly eat and leave."

Avila *Mediterranean* | 24 | 24 | 23 | $51 |

Theater District | 1 Charles St. S. (Boylston St.) | 617-267-4810 | www.avilarestaurant.com

The "colorful, high-style surroundings" and "upbeat atmosphere" of this "hip" "oasis" in the Theater District complement an "imaginative", "pricey" Mediterranean menu enhanced by specials that "are in fact special" and an "expansive wine list" ("the sommelier hits the mark every time"); what's more, the "professional", "attentive" servers "get you in and out if you let them know" you've got a show.

Azure *American* | 22 | 23 | 21 | $54 |

Back Bay | Lenox Hotel | 61 Exeter St. (Boylston St.) | 617-933-4800 | www.azureboston.com

A "pretty palette of blues" fashions a "calm, cool" and "classy" backdrop for the "safely exotic" (read: "creative but not outlandish") seafood-centric New American menu at this venture in the Back Bay's Lenox Hotel; it continues to "fly under the radar" in spite of its "trendy vibe" and "right-on service", but aficionados assure "you won't regret eating here" – even though it's "expensive."

Bacco *Italian* | 21 | 19 | 20 | $38 |

North End | 107 Salem St. (Cooper St.) | 617-624-0454 | www.bacconorthend.com

"Watch the world go by" from an upstairs window or join the "chatty" crowd below at this North Ender offering "dependable" Italian fare whose value splits surveyors ("a little pricey" vs. "reasonable for the quality and quantity"); the "bustling" atmosphere is bolstered by "quite a large bar" where locals perch to "watch the game" with drinks poured by "friendly" 'tenders.

	FOOD	DECOR	SERVICE	COST

Back Eddy, The Ⓜ *Seafood* — 22 | 21 | 20 | $40

Westport | 1 Bridge Rd. (Rte. 88) | 508-636-6500 | www.thebackeddy.com

Dining on "fresh", "not-fancy" seafood alfresco or "having cocktails on the dock" at this Westport "pearl" is "what living in New England in summertime is all about" ("you pay for the view", but "watching the sunset over the water" alone is worth it); the service, while "friendly", can be "uneven", and though the somewhat "stark interior" can get "loud", what's a "party" without "buzz"?; N.B. closed January–March.

Baja Betty's Burritos ⬗ *Mexican* — 20 | 13 | 20 | $11

Brookline | 3 Harvard Sq. (Davis Ave.) | 617-277-8900 | www.bajabettys.com

"Always fun" for "cheap, fast" eats, this Brookliner rolls out "Californian-style Mexican" fare like "big, sloppy and delicious" burritos stuffed with "fresh", relatively "healthy ingredients" by a "friendly staff"; it's just a small "storefront", but it's so "relaxed", not to mention such an "excellent value", you won't mind bringing the kids.

Baker's Best Cafe *American* — 22 | 13 | 16 | $19

Newton | 27 Lincoln St. (Walnut St.) | 617-332-4588 | www.bakersbestcatering.com

"Soccer moms" and other "well-heeled suburbanites" crowd into this "much-loved" Newton New American bakery/cafe to "see and be seen" while "waiting in line forever" for "sensational" breakfasts, lunches, brunches and desserts ("on the pricey side for what" it is, but "worthwhile" nonetheless); those who can't cotton to the "chaotic" "cafeteria-style seating" opt for "wonderful takeout."

Bambara *American* — 20 | 22 | 19 | $40

East Cambridge | Hotel Marlowe | 25 Edwin H. Land Blvd. (Rte. 28) | Cambridge | 617-868-4444 | www.bambara-cambridge.com

"Modern" decor is "the most striking feature" of this "funky restaurant in a funky hotel" in Cambridge, but the "inventive" New American fare, "spiked with interesting colors and flavors", holds its own; it's especially "useful for business dining" (prix fixe lunches are "great deals", dinner tabs run toward the "high end"), while "after work", "exotic" cocktails "with unique spirits" render it a "great place to meet friends."

Bamboo *Thai* — 23 | 18 | 20 | $23

Brighton | 1616 Commonwealth Ave. (Washington St.) | 617-734-8192 | www.bamboothairestaurant.com

"Everything is fresh and dee-lish" at this Brighton Thai known for "cheap", "healthy dishes" and "lots of specials"; while surveyors split on whether the "small" space is "warm and cozy" or "long in the tooth", the majority finds the service "prompt" and "attentive", with bonus points bestowed on staffers who "recognize familiar faces."

ⓩ B&G Oysters *Seafood* — 26 | 20 | 22 | $46

South End | 550 Tremont St. (Waltham St.) | 617-423-0550 | www.bandgoysters.com

"Hipsters and yuppies slurp" up a "fabulous variety of freshly shucked oysters" and "deeply satisfying" (though "awfully pricey")

"New England–style" seafood washed down with "smart wines" at this "Barbara Lynch hit" "tucked under a brownstone" in the South End; the "tight quarters" are "always crowded", but the "knowledgeable" service and "lively atmosphere" make it feel like you're "crammed into someplace special"; P.S. try for the "gorgeous garden out back" in warm weather.

Bangkok Bistro *Thai*   22 | 13 | 18 | $21
Brighton | 1952 Beacon St. (Chestnut Hill Ave.) | 617-739-7270
At this Brighton Thai, the "nondescript" dining room is "a little dark" and the service is only "somewhat attentive", but "the taste of the food outweighs any concerns", as do the "hefty portions" and "reasonable prices"; "great lunch specials" and "quick takeaway" are two more reasons it's "not a bad choice" when in "hectic" Cleveland Circle.

Bangkok Blue *Thai*   21 | 13 | 16 | $23
Back Bay | 651 Boylston St. (bet. Dartmouth & Exeter Sts.) | 617-266-1010 | www.bkkblueboston.com
Desk jockeys call this Back Bay Thai an "awesome lunch spot", but it's "just right when you need a good, quick dinner too"; it may appear to be a "dubious" "hole-in-the-wall", but the "flavorful" fare ("delicious noodles", "curries with just the right spice") and "value" prices "more than make up for" that – still, you might be more comfortable on the "patio in the summer."

Bangkok City *Thai*   ▽ 20 | 20 | 20 | $29
Back Bay | 167 Massachusetts Ave. (Belvidere St.) | 617-266-8884 | www.bkkcityboston.com
"A nice meal before the symphony" can be had at this Thai "next to Berklee" in the Back Bay, where the "extensive menu" displays the "usual" suspects, "some different choices" and "reasonable costs"; a "pleasant atmosphere" and "pretty" decor (featuring Asian artifacts and an atrium) further make it "a good bet."

☑ Banq ● *Eclectic*   21 | 27 | 21 | $49
South End | 1375 Washington St. (Union Park) | 617-451-0077 | www.banqrestaurant.com
In this former South End Penny Savings Bank, the "hip and happening" convene amid "hypnotic", "spectacular wooden wave-form decor" for an Eclectic "adventure of flavors": Far-East inspired cocktails are the métier of the "loud", "lively bar", while "trendy" Asian-French-Indian fusion dishes fill the dining *carte*; fans find the fare "remarkable", while critics carp that "some dishes would benefit from simplification", further opining if the kitchen would eschew "shiny pretense", it might more duly "warrant" the "pricey" checks.

Baraka Cafe Ⓜ⌖ *African*   26 | 18 | 17 | $25
Central Square | 80½ Pearl St. (bet. Auburn & William Sts.) | Cambridge | 617-868-3951 | www.barakacafe.com
"Exquisite" North African cuisine is "prepared with love" at this "quaint", "homey", "family-run" "gem" in Central Square; it "doesn't take reservations" or credit cards and you'll have to "make do with-

nol" and with "borderline negligent service", but just
rly, "bring the greenbacks" (you won't need many), order
the "to-die-for rose-petal lemonade" and take the "time to enjoy"
the "exotic" experience.

Barker Tavern ⓜ *American*   23 | 24 | 24 | $48

Scituate | 21 Barker Rd. (bet. Brookline & Wellesley Rds.) | 781-545-6533 |
www.thebarker.com

The "charming Colonial atmosphere" that permeates this "rambling", "lovely old house" overlooking Scituate Harbor fosters "romantic, cozy" meals consisting of "well-prepared and -presented" American dishes ("the swordfish is a must"); "gracious service" abounds, both in the "pricey" main room and the adjoining pub, which "serves a lighter menu" and "generous cocktails."

Barking Crab *Seafood*   16 | 16 | 14 | $28

Seaport District | 88 Sleeper St. (Northern Ave.) | 617-426-2722 |
www.barkingcrab.com

"Rowdy young professionals" and "out-of-towners" "defy you not to have fun" at this "salt-of-the-earth" Seaport District "clam shack", an open-air tent known for "long waits", "shared" picnic tables, "ok" seafood and "frosty brews"; while it may have "all the ambiance of a listing ship" and service is sometimes "invisible", "as long as expectations are not high", you too will have a "rocking" time.

BarLola ❶ *Spanish*   18 | 21 | 18 | $34

Back Bay | 160 Commonwealth Ave. (Dartmouth St.) | 617-266-1122 |
www.barlola.com

With an "amazing" "sunken outdoor patio" ("beautifully appointed with flowering plants"), a "low-lit bar area that's cozy during the colder months" and a location "off-the-beaten" Back Bay path, this Spanish small-plates purveyor "seems like a secret" "romantic" "respite"; the "sangria is a must", and while many find the tapas "terrific", some connoisseurs deem them "too expensive" for being "lackluster."

Bar 10 ❶ *Mediterranean*   17 | 21 | 19 | $36

Back Bay | Westin Copley Pl. | 10 Huntington Ave. (Dartmouth St.) |
617-424-7446 | www.westin.com

"Those who know" this "sophisticated" lounge "hidden" within the Westin Copley Place realize "it's all about being seen" "cuddling" "in high back booths" amid "dim lights" and a "gorgeous bouquet of brown" tones with "innovative", "expensive" martinis in hand; to facilitate the transition from "after work" to "late night", there's also a "limited menu" of "light" Mediterranean "munchies."

Basta Pasta ⌿ *Italian*   24 | 8 | 17 | $16

Central Square | 319 Western Ave. (Putnam Ave.) | Cambridge |
617-576-6672 | www.bastapastacambridge.com

It's "not much to look at", but this "no-atmosphere" "sub shop"–style Central Square "hole-in-the-wall" serves a "vast menu" of "delectable" Italian fare (featuring "homemade pastas") "cooked with impeccable skill" and offered for "amazingly low prices"; service is

"decent at best" and "seating is limited", so many regulars "opt for takeout" and "savor every flavor" in the comfort of their own homes.

Beacon Hill Bistro *French*
22 | 21 | 20 | $42

Beacon Hill | Beacon Hill Hotel | 25 Charles St. (bet. Beacon & Chestnut Sts.) | 617-723-1133 | www.beaconhillbistro.com

With a "quaint", "long and narrow dining room", this "elegant yet unpretentious" French bistro in the Beacon Hill Hotel is a "charming", "date-night haunt", despite the fact that "service can vary"; though the selections and portions feel "limited" to some (and "a bit pricey" to others), they're "solid" and "satisfying", not to mention "delicious", to most.

Beacon Street Tavern *American*
20 | 20 | 20 | $31

Brookline | 1032 Beacon St. (bet. Carlton & St. Marys Sts.) | 617-713-2700

The "same" "friendly vibe" as its Washington Square Tavern sibling permeates this Brookline offshoot serving "fairly easy on the wallet" American pub fare alongside "great beers", "amazing drinks" and an "extensive wine list" that's "better than you could hope for" at such a "bustling pub"; "on a nice day", "ask for a seat on the patio."

Beehive ● *American*
18 | 24 | 18 | $36

South End | Boston Center for the Arts (BCA) | 541 Tremont St. (Clarendon St.) | 617-423-0069 | www.beehiveboston.com

When they're the recipients of "friendly, professional" service, South End "over-30s" buzz about this "artistic" restaurant/club's "sassy bordello vibe", "outstanding" live music, "amazing drinks" and "reasonably priced" New American menu that "changes regularly"; however, when the staff's "slow" and "too cool for you", they're "disappointed" they "waited" on the "ridiculous line" to get in.

Bella's *Italian*
▽ 19 | 16 | 22 | $39

Rockland | 933 Hingham St. (Commerce Rd.) | 781-871-5789 | www.bellasrestaurant.com

Rocklanders "always get" what they "expect" at this "comfy" Italian: a "great" staff vending "fantastic" "make-your-own" grilled pizzas and a "wide variety" of "traditional" "red-sauce" dishes at "not-over-the-top" prices; because it "can be a mob scene" – especially in the "fun lounge" – it "lacks" as a "first-date choice", but for vino and Keno with a "big local crowd", it's on the ball.

Bernard's *Chinese*
24 | 15 | 21 | $35

Chestnut Hill | The Mall at Chestnut Hill | 199 Boylston St. (Hammond Pond Pkwy.) | 617-969-3388

"Lots of imagination" is evident in the "fresh, flavorful", "upscale Chinese" cuisine served at this "delightful surprise" with a "solicitous" staff that "fawns" over everyone ("regulars get the royal treatment"); the "wine list is mountains above average" too, making it easier to "get over" that the "not-pretty" digs – with a "strange location" in The Mall at Chestnut Hill – get "crowded and noisy" with "grandparents, youngsters and large shopping bags."

	FOOD	DECOR	SERVICE	COST

Bertucci's *Italian*

| 17 | 14 | 16 | $22 |

Back Bay | 39-45 Stanhope St. (bet. Berkeley & Clarendon Sts.) | 617-247-6161

Faneuil Hall | Faneuil Hall Mktpl. | 22 Merchants Row (State St.) | 617-227-7889

Kenmore Square | 533 Commonwealth Ave. (Brookline Ave.) | 617-236-1030

Central Square | 799 Main St. (bet. Cherry & Windsor Sts.) | Cambridge | 617-661-8356

Harvard Square | 21 Brattle St. (Mt. Auburn St.) | Cambridge | 617-864-4748

Braintree | 412 Franklin St. (West St.) | 781-849-3066

Brookline | 4 Brookline Pl. (Washington St.) | 617-731-2300

Chestnut Hill | Atrium Mall | 300 Boylston St. (Florence St.) | 617-965-0022

Medford | 4054 Mystic Valley Pkwy. (Commercial St.) | 781-396-9933

Newton | 275 Centre St. (Pearl St.) | 617-244-4900

www.bertuccis.com

Additional locations throughout the Boston area

"For a fancy night out", this "ubiquitous chain" is "not the place" – however, it "hits the spot" for "solid brick-oven pizza" "on the fly", "especially for families" in need of "reasonable prices" but "not top-notch service"; Italian aficionados deem the other entrees merely "ok", but even they won't turn down the "highly addictive", "piping-hot rolls" "served pre-meal."

Betty's Wok & Noodle Diner *Nuevo Latino/Pan-Asian*

| 19 | 16 | 18 | $25 |

MFA | 250 Huntington Ave. (Mass. Ave.) | 617-424-1950 | www.bettyswokandnoodle.com

With a locale "convenient" to the MFA, this Nuevo Latino–Pan-Asian "'50s-style" diner with a "perky" staff and "loud oldies" provides a "funky" prelude to "the theater or the symphony"; "control"-freaks appreciate that you get to "customize your meal" by "choosing the meat, sauce" and vegetables to mix with your "oodles of noodles", even though it can seem "a little overpriced" for "doing the chef's work."

b. good *Health Food*

| 19 | 13 | 19 | $11 |

Back Bay | 131 Dartmouth St. (bet. Columbus Ave. & Stuart St.) | 617-424-5252

Back Bay | 272 Newbury St. (bet. Fairfield & Gloucester Sts.) | 617-236-0440

Harvard Square | 24 Dunster St. (bet. Mass. Ave. & Mt. Auburn St.) | Cambridge | 617-354-6500

Brookline | 455 Harvard St. (bet. Columbia St. & Thorndike St.) | 617-232-4800

www.bgood.com

"Be good to your waistband and your wallet" at this "unpretentious", "healthy alternative" to other fast-food joints doling out "a variety of low-calorie, low-fat" fare like "fresh burgers and sandwiches", "air-baked fries" and "surprisingly good milkshakes" that "cost a little more" than the standard, but are still pretty "cheap"; those who've sampled the sporadic menu "miss", however, say it buoys "the cliché that healthy food doesn't taste good."

	FOOD	DECOR	SERVICE	COST

Bhindi Bazaar Indian Cafe *Indian*   22 | 13 | 18 | $21

Back Bay | 95 Massachusetts Ave. (bet. Commonwealth Ave. & Newbury St.) | 617-450-0660 | www.bhindibazaar.com

Subcontinental connoisseurs say this Back Bay Indian's "bountiful portions" of "out-of-the-ordinary" cuisine from "different corners of the country" fall "above the mark", thanks in part to "helpful recommendations" from the "friendly staff"; even those who "have yet to experience the 'wow' factor" ("yawn"-inducing environs don't help) admit it's "consistent", not to mention "cheap."

bia bistro 🅜 *French/Italian*   ▽ 24 | 17 | 20 | $41

Cohasset | 35 S. Main St. (Elm St.) | 781-383-0464 | www.biabistro.com

Chef Brian Houlihan is "keen on pleasing" at this "cozy, rustic" Cohasset "gem", and he succeeds with "more than adequate" portions of "well-prepared" Italian–Southern French dishes complemented by a "varied wine list" and "thoughtful service"; it continues to "fly under the radar", but locals "would like to keep it that way", even though it can bia bit "pricey" (it's "worth it").

Billy Tse *Pan-Asian*   20 | 14 | 20 | $27

Revere | 441 Revere St. (Pierce St.) | 781-286-2882 | www.billytse-revere.com ●

North End | 240 Commercial St. (Atlantic Ave.) | 617-227-9990 | www.billytserestaurant.com

If you're in the North End and "not in the mood" for pasta, this Pan-Asian "diamond in the Italian rough" (with a Revere sibling) offers "yummy" if "Americanized" Chinese, Thai and sushi at "decent prices"; the "kitschy decor" "could be improved", but the more "fun drinks" you have from the "hopping bar", the less you'll care; P.S. it's "dependable for takeout" too.

Biltmore Bar & Grille, The *American*   18 | 15 | 18 | $30

Newton | 1205 Chestnut St. (Oak St.) | 617-527-2550 | www.thebiltmoregrill.com

"With an eye toward the upscale", this nonetheless "casual" watering hole/grill brings "slightly fancy" American fare to the "outer reaches of Newton" – and though it's "nothing extraordinary", it's for the most part "reliable and reasonable"; with pressed-tin ceilings and a mahogany bar, the decor leans toward the "retro", which gives patrons something to look at if it's "too loud" to converse and it "takes forever to get served."

NEW Bina Osteria & Alimentari *Italian*   - | - | - | M

Downtown Crossing | 571-581 Washington St. (Avery St.) | 617-956-0888 | www.binaboston.com

A frosted glass wall separates the dual concepts at this midpriced Italian in Downtown Crossing from the team behind Bin 26 and Lala Rokh; one side is a full-service restaurant with mother-of-pearl–specked terrazzo floors, a bar and a communal table, and the other is an upscale gourmet food-and-wine shop (the alimentari), which serves breakfast fare, panini and homemade gelato for takeout.

	FOOD	DECOR	SERVICE	COST

Bin 26 Enoteca *Italian* — 21 | 22 | 21 | $42

Beacon Hill | 26 Charles St. (Beacon St.) | 617-723-5939 | www.bin26.com

"Tucked away" on Beacon Hill, this "lively" "wine lover's delight" whose decor "uses corks and bottles" in "creative" ways (don't forget to "look up" in the "cool bathrooms") is known for a "dizzying array" of vino complemented by "sophisticated" Italian nibbles; the "small servings" are "steeply priced" for random pairings, so be sure to consult the "informative" (if slightly "arrogant") staff first.

Birch Street Bistro *American* — 19 | 20 | 19 | $34

Roslindale | 14 Birch St. (bet. Belgrade Ave. & Corinth St.) | 617-323-2184 | www.birchstbistro.com

An "anchor in the Roslindale eating scene", this "friendly neighborhood bistro" proffers "reasonably priced" American fare ("some inventive dishes, some comfort food"), and though it occasionally "varies" in execution, "most everything comes out fine"; the "warm", "pleasant" space – all "dark" tones and exposed brick – benefits from a "cool bar", a patio and "nice music on Thursdays."

Bison County BBQ ● *BBQ* — 18 | 12 | 16 | $24

Waltham | 275 Moody St. (Crescent St.) | 781-642-9720 | www.bisoncounty.com

"Dependable", "reasonably priced" ribs, brisket, pulled pork and other "smoked stuff", plus "unique and tasty bison burgers", fuel "fun times" at this Waltham joint with a "decent selection of draft beers" and an appropriately "no-fuss atmosphere"; BBQ buffs, however, warn "don't get buffaloed" into thinking the eats are authentic.

Z Bistro 5 Ⓩ Ⓜ *Italian* — 27 | 24 | 26 | $50

West Medford | 5 Playstead Rd. (High St.) | 781-395-7464 | www.bistro5.com

An "unprepossessing exterior" hides this Medford "jewel" where chef-owner Vittorio Ettore takes "great pride" in his "consistently wonderful" "gourmet" Northern Italian dishes bolstered by "local" ingredients with "explosive" flavors (he also "frequents" the "elegant" dining room to "chat" with his guests); adding to the "amazing" – and yes, "pricey" – experience are "fabulous" staffers who "offer great pairing" ideas from the "well-chosen wine list."

Bistro 712 Ⓩ Ⓜ *French* — ▽ 24 | 20 | 22 | $42

Norwood | Norwood Ctr. | 712 Washington St. (Day St.) | 781-769-7712 | www.bistro712.com

The "sure hand" in this Norwood kitchen produces "sophisticated", frequently "changing" French cuisine, which in turn is ferried by "great" staffers to the "intimate" converted-storefront dining room decked out in burgundy walls and cream accents; indeed, not least of all because it's "unique" for the 'burbs (and not even that expensive), it remains "a keeper."

Black Cow Tap & Grill *Pub Food* — 19 | 20 | 18 | $38

South Hamilton | 16 Bay Rd. (bet. Linden St. & Railroad Ave.) | 978-468-1166

(continued)

Black Cow Tap & Grill
Newburyport | 54R Merrimac St. (Green St.) | 978-499-8811
www.blackcowrestaurants.com

"Warm and welcoming atmospheres" draw "convivial" crowds to these "hopping" pubs serving "solid" American bar grub at "appropriate prices"; the "lively bar scenes" can make for "noisy" meals, but they could be quieter if you "opt for the deck" "overlooking the harbor" in Newburyport or "get a booth" in South Hamilton.

Black Sheep Restaurant *American* ∇ 21 | 20 | 15 | $27
Kendall Square | Kendall Hotel | 350 Main St. (Anne St.) | Cambridge | 617-577-1300 | www.kendallhotel.com

"Charming" and downright "adorable", this red Kendall Hotel restaurant filled with firefighter memorabilia proffers a "varied and appealing" menu of "most satisfactory" American classics from breakfast to dinner; "service is erratic", but the prices please every time.

Blarney Stone, The *Pub Food* 16 | 14 | 15 | $23
Dorchester | 1505 Dorchester Ave. (Park St.) | 617-436-8223 | www.blarneystoneboston.com

"Reinvented" from an "old-time pub" to a "somewhat hip after-work spot", this Dorchester "hangout" serves "basic" American grub to an "eclectic crowd" – and if the clientele brands the fare "nondescript", well, "you get what you pay for"; the lunch menu is merely "adequate" too, but "the patio is a bonus."

blu ⊠ *American* 21 | 21 | 20 | $46
Theater District | Millennium Complex | 4 Avery St. (bet. Tremont & Washington Sts.) | 617-375-8550 | www.blurestaurant.com

In "a nondescript gym" lies this "chic", "unusual" space with "great views" of the Theater District, where folks both "dressed up for the night and tumbling in after a workout" come for the "smallish", "pricey" menu of "healthy-tasting" American fare with "occasional flashes of inspiration"; some servers are "warm", others are "cold", but word is the bartenders – who mix "interesting drinks" – are "fun."

Blue Fin *Japanese* 22 | 16 | 19 | $33
Porter Square | Porter Exchange Bldg. | 1815 Massachusetts Ave. (Roseland St.) | Cambridge | 617-497-8022
Middleton | 260 S. Main St. (Lonergan Rd.) | 978-750-1411

"Crowds of all kinds" rush these "simple" Middleton and Porter Square "Japanese food houses" for "fantastic quality" sushi and "authentic" "cooked items" that most feel are "reasonably priced" (lunch offers some real "deals"); even when others are "waiting" for your table, you won't "feel rushed" by the "courteous servers" – you may, however, grow tired of the "below-par decor."

⊠ Blue Ginger *Asian Fusion* 26 | 23 | 25 | $58
Wellesley | 583 Washington St. (Church St.) | 781-283-5790 | www.ming.com

"As good as the hype" suggests, this "Wellesley wonder" stars Ming Tsai's "palate-popping" "East-meets-West" Asian-fusion "miracles" –

FOOD | DECOR | SERVICE | COST

and the best part is that the "gifted" "star chef" is "actually there" ("what a novelty!"), further rendering it "well worth" the "expensive" tabs; the "calming blue" decor is "even more inviting" thanks to a recent upgrade, and the addition of a "phenomenal new bar area" makes it "now possible to drop in for a light meal without having made a reservation a month in advance."

Blue on Highland   *American*   17 | 20 | 19 | $34

Needham | 882 Highland Ave. (West St.) | 781-444-7001 | www.blueonhighland.com

This "somewhat trendy" Needham New American features "quiet booths" in the "mod" dining room and an "upbeat atmosphere" at the bar; the "fun drinks list" is suitable for "girls' night out" or "watching the Sox", and while some find the fare "respectable", for others, the "uneven" menu "does not measure up", no matter how "relatively low priced" it is.

Blue Ribbon BBQ   *BBQ*   25 | 12 | 19 | $17

Arlington | 908 Massachusetts Ave. (Highland Ave.) | 781-648-7427
Newton | 1375 Washington St. (Elm St.) | 617-332-2583
www.blueribbonbbq.com

"A rare find north of the Mason-Dixon Line", the "heaping platters" of "lip-smacking", "fork-tender", "slow-cooked" BBQ at this "rowdy" pair in Arlington and Newton are "hands-down" "wow-wow-wow", as are the "fantastic sauces" and "out-of-this-world sides" dished out by "friendly" staffers; the "dinerlike settings" are "elbow-to-elbow", so "program the number into your speed dial" to get takeout "lickety-split quick" (and "for not a lot of money").

Blue Room, The   *Eclectic*   25 | 21 | 22 | $42

Kendall Square | One Kendall Square Complex | 1 Kendall Sq. (Hampshire St.) | Cambridge | 617-494-9034 | www.theblueroom.net

"Feel in-the-know for having found" this "almost hidden" Kendall Square purveyor of "truly Eclectic" fare featuring "complex", "inventive", "delicious oddities" "based on what's fresh"; "warm and pleasant decor and staff" facilitate the "come as you are" vibe, and if it's a smidge "pricey", the "fabulous" Sunday brunch buffet "won't break the bank" (while converting even "the most die-hard breakfast-skipper").

Bluestone Bistro ◑ *Pizza*   ▽ 17 | 11 | 17 | $18

Brighton | 1799 Commonwealth Ave. (Chiswick Rd.) | 617-254-8309 | www.bluestonebistro.com

"It's your typical college pizza and sub shop", "nothing more" admit "students" who deal with this Brighton joint's "so-so" chow because its requires from them so few ducats; those who only "get takeout" in the winter sometimes try the patio in summer "since there are very few in the area."

Blue22 Bar & Grille   *American/Pan-Asian*   ▽ 19 | 13 | 20 | $24

Quincy | 1237 Hancock St. (Saville Ave.) | 617-774-1200 | www.blue22-barandgrille.com

Sports fans "watch games" on "big-screen TVs", "trendy" "singles" "have a blast" at karaoke and trivia nights and everyone downs

| | FOOD | DECOR | SERVICE | COST |

"well-priced drinks" sopped up with a "fun mix" of "American bar food" and "Asian snacks" at this "interesting place in Downtown Quincy"; those perturbed that their "conversation was strained" due to all the activity scoff it's "still trying to settle on its identity", but "variety"-seekers dig the "unique" approach.

Boca Grande *Tex-Mex* 19 | 10 | 14 | $10

Kenmore Square | 642 Beacon St. (Commonwealth Ave.) | 617-437-9700
East Cambridge | 149 First St. (Bent St.) | Cambridge | 617-354-5550 🛃
Porter Square | 1728 Massachusetts Ave. (Linnaean St.) | Cambridge | 617-354-7400
Brookline | 1294 Beacon St. (bet. Harvard & Pleasant Sts.) | 617-739-3900
www.bocagrande.citysearch.com
"When you need a fix" of Tex-Mex, this quartet "won't knock your socks off", but will provide "well-prepared" "basics" from "over-stuffed burritos and quesadillas" to "real-deal" tamales and tacos; there's "no decor", "limited seating" and "typical counter service" ("some days on, some days lacking"), but it's "fast and cheap", which is just one reason why "there's always a line."

🆕 Bokx 109 American Prime *Steak* ▽ 23 | 27 | 21 | $60

Newton Lower Falls | Hotel Indigo | 399 Grove St. (Rte. 128) | 617-454-3399 | www.bokx109.com
"You'd never guess" to find such a "dynamic hot spot" in Newton Lower Falls, but that's exactly where the "glam" Hotel Indigo has constructed this modern/retro, brown-and-red steakhouse serving "large portions of grilled meats" alongside "creative" entrees and "innovative sides"; there are reports of "spotty" service ("kinks" that will surely be "ironed out"), but most deem it a "treat on every level" – "ridiculously expensive" tabs notwithstanding.

Boloco *Eclectic* 18 | 11 | 16 | $9

Brighton | 1940 Beacon St. (Chestnut Hill Ave.) | 617-739-0340
Back Bay | 137 Massachusetts Ave. (Boylston St.) | 617-369-9087
Back Bay | 247 Newbury St. (bet. Fairfield & Gloucester Sts.) | 617-262-2200
Fenway | 283 Longwood Ave. (Blackfan Circle) | 617-232-2166
Fenway | Marino Ctr. | 359-369 Huntington Ave. (bet. Forsyth St. & Opera Pl.) | 617-536-6814
Financial District | 125 Pearl St. (High St.) | 617-422-0162 🛃
Financial District | 133 Federal St. (Matthews St.) | 617-357-9727 🛃
Financial District | 50 Congress St. (bet. Exchange Pl. & Hawes St.) | 617-357-9013 🛃
Harvard Square | 71 Mt. Auburn St. (Holyoke St.) | Cambridge | 617-354-5838
Medford | Tufts University | 340 Boston Ave. (bet. Bellevue & Winthrop Sts.) | 339-674-9740
www.boloco.com
Additional locations throughout the Boston area
"Smart" bo-locals "who like to eat light" patronize this counter-serve chain for "customizable", "grab-and-go" "Mexican-esque" Eclectic wraps and "addictive smoothies" made from "fresh", "healthy" ingredients; "inconsistency" in both preparation and ser-

	FOOD	DECOR	SERVICE	COST

vice from store to store makes for "good and bad days", but it "won't hurt your wallet."

Bombay Club *Indian* — 20 | 17 | 18 | $28

Faneuil Hall | Faneuil Hall Mktpl. | 1 Faneuil Hall Mktpl. (bet. N. Market & S. Market Sts.) | 617-723-6001 ⊠
Harvard Square | 57 JFK St. (bet. Eliot & Winthrop Sts.) | Cambridge | 617-661-8100
www.bombayclub.com

"Giant picture windows" with "views of Harvard Square" make up for "undistinguished" decor at this eatery where "standard but well-prepared Indian" fare is served by "friendly" (if occasionally "flaky") staffers – and though a few feel "it's a little pricey" for the type, it's "a good value" nonetheless, especially the "bottomless lunch special"; fans also "enjoy eating" at the "pleasant" Faneuil Hall outpost.

Bon Caldo *Italian* — 22 | 20 | 20 | $38

Norwood | 1381 Providence Tpke. (Sumner St.) | 781-255-5800 | www.boncaldo.com

"Convenient" for Norwood Italian-cravers looking to save themselves "a trip to the North End", this midpriced "red-sauce" site plies "authentic", "well-prepared" "standards" supplemented by "enough extras" so one "won't get bored"; it's all conveyed by "friendly" servers, who also proffer a "nice selection of wines", both in the "comfortable" main room and in the "beautiful bar area."

NEW Bond *Eclectic* — - | - | - | M

Financial District | Langham Boston | 250 Franklin St. (Oliver St.) | 617-451-1900 | www.langhamhotels.com

Gourmands looking for an upscale escape in the Financial District find it at this Eclectic inside the luxurious Langham hotel, where a bygone era is evoked by original crystal chandeliers hanging from vaulted ceilings and a beautiful rosewood bar; casual lunch fare, small plates at dinner and a mezzanine lounge bring this classy act into the 21st century.

Bonfire ⊠ *Steak* — 21 | 22 | 20 | $49

Park Square | Park Plaza Hotel | 50 Park Plaza (bet. Arlington & Charles Sts.) | 617-262-3473 | www.bonfiresteakhouse.com

Is it a "Spanish villa", a "medieval hunting lodge" or a "Monty Python" movie set? – one thing's for sure, the "deep-red hues" and "oversized" furniture at this Todd English steakhouse in Park Square craft a suitably "shadowy" setting for the menu's "spicy, smoky twists"; the portions are "huge" and the wines are "fabulous", but penny-pinchers say it costs "way too much money" either way and instead opt for the "unbeatable" happy-hour "taco deal" at the bar.

Bon Savor *French/South American* — ∇ 20 | 19 | 19 | $26

Jamaica Plain | 605 Centre St. (Pond St.) | 617-971-0000 | www.bonsavor.com

The "welcoming owners" and "capable staff" of this "little" Jamaica Plain bistro provide "delectable", "reasonably priced" French–South American breakfasts and lunches in "attractive", "sunny" environs,

which at dinnertime take on a "romantic", "candlelit" gl... menu was reconcieved post-Survey, outdating the Food score); "wonderful brunches" make it "usually crowded on weekend mornings", while the recent procurement of a liquor license should keep it filled at other times as well.

Border Cafe *Cajun/Tex-Mex* | 19 | 17 | 18 | $21 |

Harvard Square | 32 Church St. (Palmer St.) | Cambridge | 617-864-6100 ◗

Saugus | 817 Broadway/Rte. 1 (bet. Lynn Fells Pkwy. & Main St.) | 781-233-5308

Burlington | 128 Middlesex Tpke. (3rd Ave.) | 781-505-2500 ◗ www.bordercafe.com

"Never-ending baskets of chips", "strong", "icy margaritas" and "quick", "reliable" Tex-Mex–Cajun "without the frills" leave "hordes of students" "satisfied" "for cheap" at these "happy zoos" in Burlington and Harvard Square; on the other hand, "every night is family night" at the Saugus iteration – just "be prepared" for the same "grueling seating process" and "tacky decor" as the others.

Boston Beer Works ◗ *Pub Food* | 18 | 16 | 17 | $23 |

Fenway | 61 Brookline Ave. (Lansdowne St.) | 617-536-2337

West End | 112 Canal St. (Causeway St.) | 617-896-2337

Salem Beer Works *Pub Food*

Salem | 278 Derby St. (bet. Congress & Lafayette Sts.) | 978-745-2337 www.beerworks.net

Inexpensive American pub grub (mostly "predictable", occasionally "surprising", always "filling") takes care of soaking up the "big selection" of beers made in-house ("try a sampler" of the seasonal ales) at this pack of microbreweries; "with all the TVs", they're "always filled to capacity" with "lively" "Sox fans", and if that can lead to "inattentive" staffers, at least they "make great recommendations" when you catch them.

Boston Sail Loft *Seafood* | 15 | 14 | 16 | $25 |

Waterfront | 80 Atlantic Ave. (Commerical Wharf) | 617-227-7280

Forever to be "described as a shack", this "nautical"-themed "old standby" on the Waterfront may serve "decent enough" seafood, but the kitchen is no match for the bar: "friendly 'tenders" pouring "reasonably priced" beers and cocktails make it "popular in the evenings" among "recent grads" and "young professionals" who try to "get a seat by the window and watch the boats go by" when not partaking in the "singles scene."

Bottega Fiorentina *Italian* | 24 | 14 | 18 | $16 |

NEW **Back Bay** | 264 Newbury St. (bet. Fairfield & Gloucester Sts.) | 617-266-0707 | www.botteganewbury.com

Brookline | 313B Harvard St. (Babcock St.) | 617-232-2661 | www.bottegabrookline.com

"True neighborhood gems", these Italian delis augment "hearty sandwiches" with "unforgettable" pastas and "amazing sauces", all at "bargain basement prices"; "seating is limited" at the "unassuming", counter-serve Brookline original ("takeout is your best op-

tion"), while the new Back Bay location has true "sit-down service" and a patio overlooking always-hopping Newbury Street.

Bouchée *French*   21 | 22 | 21 | $42

Back Bay | 159 Newbury St. (bet. Dartmouth & Exeter Sts.) | 617-450-4343 | www.boucheebrasserie.com

Francophiles applaud the "authentic brasserie" fare served at this "lively" Back Bay spot, just as grape groupies toast the "extensive wine menu" – and though "you pay for it", it's "worth" the cost; further making it "feel like a Parisian cafe" is a "stylish" interior ("dark woods, nice lighting"), while the "lovely" patio with its "prime people-watching", not to mention "skilled, friendly" service, is pure Newbury Street.

Brasserie Jo *French*   20 | 20 | 20 | $42

Back Bay | Colonnade Hotel | 120 Huntington Ave. (W. Newton St.) | 617-425-3240 | www.brasseriejoboston.com

With its "casually elegant", "art deco-ish" setting, "uniformed staff" and "classic French cuisine" – "well-executed", from the "succulent mussels" to the "heavenly profiteroles" – this Back Bay brasserie "takes you straight to Paris"; true, you'll find "no surprises" (except perhaps that "it's not cheap"), but it manages "reliability" while "filling the dining void in the Symphony Hall vicinity."

Bravo *Eclectic*   21 | 25 | 21 | $47

MFA | Museum of Fine Arts | 465 Huntington Ave. (bet. Forsyth Way & Museum Rd.) | 617-369-3474 | www.mfa.org

"The perfect ending to a visit to a great art museum", this MFA "class act" offers Eclectic lunches that "often echo" special exhibits, all "beautifully presented" by an "attentive staff"; "overlooking the courtyard", the "sophisticated", "modern" dining room is usually filled with "museum members taking advantage of their discount" (it's "pricey" otherwise); N.B. dinner served Wednesday–Friday only.

Brenden Crocker's Wild Horse Cafe *American*   ▽ 25 | 22 | 23 | $37

Beverly | 392 Cabot St. (Colon St.) | 978-922-6868 | www.wildhorsecafe.com

Beverly locals always "have a good time" "relaxing" on the "comfy chairs and sofas" while digging into "fun, interesting", midpriced New American dishes – recommended by "knowledgeable" staffers who ferry them from the open kitchen – at this cozy, folksy venue with a bar that's an "atmospheric" spot for "excellent drinks."

Bricco ◑ *Italian*   25 | 21 | 21 | $51

North End | 241 Hanover St. (bet. Cross & Richmond Sts.) | 617-248-6800 | www.bricco.com

"Outrageous views" of the North End, "especially in summer" when the windows are open, and often "rowdy" revelers "packed in like sardines" cause almost as big of a "commotion" as the "amazing", "artistically presented" "modern Italian" fare whipped up at this "tiny place"; "wonderful wines" and generally "attentive" service are

two more reasons why fans "go back and go back again", despite the fact that it's "an expensive evening."

Bridgeman's *Italian*
26 | 23 | 23 | $44

Hull | 145 Nantasket Ave. (bet. Berkley Rd. & Park Ave.) | 781-925-6336 | www.bridgemansrestaurant.com

Head to Hull to "dine by the sea" at this "sophisticated yet unpretentious" "gem" where the service is "attentive" and the reasonably priced Northern Italian cuisine features "out-of-site seafood" and "awesome specials"; though it's so "noisy" you should "bring your earplugs", a "stroll along the ocean" makes for a soothing ending to a "delicious" experience.

NEW Brighton Beer Garden ● *Pub Food*
- | - | - | M

Brighton | 386 Market St. (Washington St.) | 617-562-6000 | www.brightonbeergarden.com

The Brighton space that long housed SoHo has been transformed into this clubhouse-style jock bar; indeed, it's a sports fan's Shangri-la, with 40 HDTVs and a large menu that goes beyond pub grub while staying easy on the wallet.

Z Bristol, The *American*
24 | 26 | 26 | $53

Back Bay | Four Seasons Hotel | 200 Boylston St. (Charles St.) | 617-351-2053 | www.fourseasons.com/boston

"Money can buy happiness!" exclaim guests of the Back Bay's Four Seasons, who've shelled out for "informal dining at its regal best" in its "beautifully appointed", "sedate" lounge; whether for a "dignified afternoon tea", champagne and "dessert after a show" or a New American bite before (such as the "phenomenal burger"), "you can't go wrong" with a "romantic" table "overlooking the Public Gardens"; P.S. "don't miss" the "over-the-top" dessert buffet on Friday and Saturday evenings.

Brookline Family Restaurant *Turkish*
21 | 9 | 19 | $19

Brookline | 305 Washington St. (Harvard Sq.) | 617-277-4466 | www.brooklinefamilyrestaurant.com

"You'd never guess" from its "generic name" or "hole-in-the-wall" decor, but this Brookline storefront is a "haven of Turkish delights", with "enormous" portions of "exotic cuisine" that exhibits "all the right flavors" and "cheap" tabs; the "quirky" setup goes from "cafeteria-style" lunches to "table service for dinner", while the "helpful staff" helps to create a "real family atmosphere"; P.S. the American breakfasts are "popular" too.

Brownstone ● *American*
15 | 17 | 16 | $25

Back Bay | 111 Dartmouth St. (Columbus Ave.) | 617-867-4142 | www.irishconnection.com

A true "locals' place", this wood-and-leather tavern on the Back Bay–South End border offers New American pub fare that may be merely "mediocre" (and served by "spotty" staffers) but it's "cheap"; it's also a "relaxing" setting to "just have a drink" while "catching the Sox or Pats" on the "large TVs" – except when it gets "loud" with "spillover from the bar next door."

	FOOD	DECOR	SERVICE	COST

Brown Sugar Cafe *Thai* — 25 | 17 | 21 | $24

Boston University | 1033 Commonwealth Ave. (bet. Alcorn & Babcock Sts.) | 617-787-4242

Similans, The *Thai*

East Cambridge | 145 First St. (bet. Bent & Rogers Sts.) | Cambridge | 617-491-6999
www.brownsugarcafe.com

"Downright delicious" Thai "classics and originals" that "pack a punch" come from a "huge menu", for "affordable prices" and via "cheerful", "super-fast" staffers at these BU and East Cambridge siblings; those irked by "tight", "forgettable" quarters appreciate that "delivery is quick and efficient."

Bukhara *Indian* — 23 | 19 | 18 | $25

Jamaica Plain | 701 Centre St. (Burroughs St.) | 617-522-2195 | www.bukharabistro.com

Jamaica Plainers in search of "amazing" Indian cuisine at "reasonable prices" know to hit up this "quaint", "pleasant-enough" spot for both "standard" and "unusual" dishes, especially during the "wonderful lunch buffet"; though they never know whether they'll be saddled with "rushed" or "indifferent" service, the faithful claim it'd be "naan-sense" to pass it by.

Bukowski Tavern ◑⇄ *Pub Food* — 17 | 15 | 17 | $17

Back Bay | 50 Dalton St. (Boylston St.) | 617-437-9999
Inman Square | 1281 Cambridge St. (Prospect St.) | Cambridge | 617-497-7077

With a "surly staff", "rowdy" regulars ("not college kids") and the music "volume [turned up] to 11", these Back Bay and Inman Square taverns literally scream "dive"; "basic pub fare" fills folks up "for a fair dime", but it's really "all about" the "noteworthy" beers on a list with so much "depth", you'd do well to consult the "well-versed" bartenders – or spin the "wheel of indecision" at the Dalton Street branch.

Bullfinch's *Eclectic* — 21 | 21 | 23 | $38

Sudbury | 730 Boston Post Rd./Rte. 20 (bet. Lafayette Dr. & Stone Rd.) | 978-443-4094 | www.bullfinchs.com

"Small and large groups receive equal attention" from a "wonderful" staff at this "charming, quirky" "suburban family place" in a Sudbury strip mall, offering moderately priced Eclectic eats prepared with "imaginative" "flair"; the "warm atmosphere" ensures "a good time is had by all", especially on the "fun patio" and at the "fantastic" Sunday jazz brunch.

Burren, The *Pub Food* — 14 | 16 | 14 | $20

Somerville | 247 Elm St. (Chester St.) | 617-776-6896 | www.burren.com

"Jovial at all times", this bit of "Dublin" in Somerville's Davis Square is all "about draft beer" and "great entertainment, with live music every night of the week"; it's "no culinary beacon", "but if you're just looking for some" "cheap", "quick" Irish pub "munchies" served by "brogue"-sporting staffers in "standard" tavern environs, it's "fine."

	FOOD	DECOR	SERVICE	COST

Burtons Grill *American*

21 | 20 | 21 | $39

Fenway | 1363 Boylston St. (Kilmarnock St.) | 617-236-2236
North Andover | Eaglewood Shops | 145 Turnpike St. (Peters St.) |
978-688-5600
Hingham | The Derby Street Shoppes | 94 Derby St. (Hingham Plaza) |
781-749-1007
www.burtonsgrill.com

"Swarming" with the "ballgame crowd", this Fenway outpost of the
suburban New American franchise lures with a "diverse menu" of
"classy" meats and such "without [high] prices" or an overly "manly
atmosphere"; though many staffers also seem like "students",
they're "friendly", "eager" and help keep the joint "jumping";
N.B. the Hingham and North Andover branches were not surveyed.

Butcher Shop, The *French/Italian*

25 | 22 | 23 | $45

South End | 552 Tremont St. (Waltham St.) | 617-423-4800 |
www.thebutchershopboston.com

At Barbara Lynch's French-Italian vino bar/butcher shop, South
Enders jockey for "spots at the butcher block" or small tables
for "high-quality", "carefully prepared" meats and cheeses served
by "passionate", "knowledgeable" servers; the chance to get
their "socks rocked" by an "ever-changing" selection of "interesting" wines gets them to "come back frequently", even though
there's often a "wait" and the eats are "priced like entrees and
sized like canapés."

Byblos ⊠Ⓜ *Lebanese*

24 | 16 | 20 | $30

Norwood | 678 Washington St. (Vernon St.) | 781-278-0000 |
www.byblosrestaurant.com

"Plentiful" portions of "superb", "authentic Lebanese" cuisine is
served for "reasonable prices" at this Norwood Middle Eastern with
an "easy atmosphere" and "fun" weekend entertainment; the decor
may be a tad "tacky" and the "friendly" service "can be a little slow",
but fans say those should be no cause for concern: "go for the food,
go for the belly dancing, just go!"

Cactus Club *Tex-Mex*

16 | 16 | 16 | $25

Back Bay | 939 Boylston St. (Hereford St.) | 617-236-0200 |
www.bestmargaritas.com

"After-workers", lively "singles" and "college students" descend
upon this "rather predictable" Back Bay Tex-Mex "party place",
making its bar, "gimmicky" dining room and sidewalk patio "packed"
and "very loud"; while they're there and "wrecked on delicious frozen margaritas", they say the "fair-priced" "pseudo-Mexican food"
"tastes good" – but the morning after, it's often a different story.

Café Algiers *Mideastern*

18 | 20 | 14 | $19

Harvard Square | 40 Brattle St. (Church St.) | Cambridge | 617-492-1557

Students and "beatniks" get lost in "long", "deep discussions" over
"strong Arabic coffee" and "well-prepared, well-priced" Middle
Eastern "basics" at this "venerable", "bohemian" "Harvard Square
hangout" with "North African"–inspired decor; in warm weather, the

"beautiful but tiny roof deck" is "great", but be warned: "the higher you sit, the slower the service" from the sometimes "snarky" staffers.

Café at Taj Boston *Eclectic*   20 | 22 | 21 | $51

Back Bay | Taj Boston | 15 Arlington St. (Newbury St.) | 617-536-5700 | www.tajhotels.com/boston

All sorts of French, Indian, Italian and New England dishes can be found on the Eclectic menus proffered all day by a "warm staff" at this "elegant, peaceful" Back Bay hotel cafe boasting "great views" of Newbury Street through a wall of windows; numbers-crunchers calculate it's "way too expensive for what you get", but history buffs pronounce it "a Boston tradition that's well worth experiencing"; P.S. the lounge hosts a "wonderful" afternoon tea.

Cafe Barada 🖾 *Mideastern*   ▽ 23 | 12 | 23 | $19

Porter Square | 2269 Massachusetts Ave. (Dover St.) | Cambridge | 617-354-2112 | www.cafebarada.net

"Delicious", cheap Middle Eastern eats are "hard to find" – that's why Cambridgians are "so happy" to have this "small" bastion of "authentic Lebanese" "home cooking" right in Porter Square; the sparseness of the "too-brightly-lit" environs are of no concern when the "sweet", "adorable owner" is around.

Café Belô *Brazilian*   ▽ 20 | 11 | 17 | $13

Somerville | 120 Washington St. (Franklin St.) | 617-623-3696 ◐
Milford | 112 Main St. (bet. Jefferson & Spring Sts.) | 508-478-7818
www.cafebelo.com

"Fill your plate and pay by weight" at these Milford and Somerville Brazilians where "genuine" "homestyle" meats and other "delicious delights" are set out "buffet-style"; the "cafeteria"-like settings are "not glamorous", to put it mildly, but where else can you "stuff yourself" for such "an incredibly low price"?

Café Brazil *Brazilian*   23 | 14 | 22 | $24

Allston | 421 Cambridge St. (Harvard Ave.) | 617-789-5980 | www.cafebrazilrestaurant.com

"Real Brazilian food cooked by real Brazilians" is the stock in trade of this Allston spot where it's "hard to spend a lot of money" on the mounds of "impeccable meats" (there's plenty for "vegetarians" to fill up on too); "warm service" and frequent "live entertainment" "add to the charm", even when the somewhat "tacky decor" (there's a "mural of Copacabana Beach") does not.

Cafe Escadrille ◐🖾 *Continental*   19 | 18 | 19 | $47

Burlington | 26 Cambridge St. (Wayside Rd.) | 781-273-1916 | www.cafeescadrille.com

"Consistent for 35-plus years", this Burlington "standby" provides "traditional" Continental fare in two settings: the "fancy", "special-occasion worthy" Gourmet Room and the casual, more forward-thinking Greenhouse Cafe; while the latter serves as a "pleasant" "escape", the former gets the brunt of the criticism, with naysayers focusing on "overpriced" tabs for "outdated" dishes; P.S. the bar is a known "pickup place" for an "older crowd."

	FOOD	DECOR	SERVICE	COST

Café Fleuri *American/Continental*
22 | 23 | 23 | $48

Financial District | Langham Hotel | 250 Franklin St. (bet. Oliver & Pearl Sts.) | 617-451-1900 | boston.langhamhotels.com

"The place to be seen" in the Financial District for a "power break-fast", this "bright" and "lovely" Continental–New American "oasis" beneath a six-story glass atrium in the Langham Hotel is also a "great corporate lunch spot"; cocoa connoisseurs come for the "sin-fully delicious chocolate buffet" on Saturdays (September–June), while music lovers rave about the "awe-inspiring Sunday jazz brunch" (if not the "over-the-top prices").

Cafe Jaffa *Mideastern*
22 | 13 | 17 | $16

Back Bay | 48 Gloucester St. (bet. Boylston & Newbury Sts.) | 617-536-0230

"Astoundingly affordable" considering its location "just steps from tony Newbury Street" in the Back Bay, this "Middle Eastern pit stop" offers "authentic, tasty" kebabs, falafel and the like in "ample" por-tions; despite "courteous", "cheerful" service, the "far-from-fancy", "low-lit" environs get many to opt for takeout.

Café Mangal ☒ *Mediterranean*
25 | 19 | 22 | $37

Wellesley | 555 Washington St. (Grove St.) | 781-235-5322 | www.cafemangal.com

Wellesleyans anoint this "family-run" restaurant "neighborhood-gem" status for its "exotic menu" of "amazing" Med-Turkish fare served in a "shotgun-style" dining room that's "busy and boisterous for lunch" (when American options round out the menu) and "cozy and warm at night"; "attentive" servers are "happy to tell you about the dishes", while "BYO makes the expensive entrees [seem] more reasonable."

Cafe of India *Indian*
22 | 17 | 18 | $26

Harvard Square | 52A Brattle St. (Hilliard St.) | Cambridge | 617-661-0683 | www.cafeofindia.com

Harvard Square suppers say you can "bring the family or bring a date" to this Indian for the "value" lunch buffet and "reliable" din-ners; a location "near the A.R.T." makes it "convenient for pre-theater", and if the "cozy" interior could use a redecorating "rescue", it's "nice in summer" when the "front windows are open."

Cafe Podima *Sandwiches*
▽ 19 | 4 | 9 | $12

Beacon Hill | 168 Cambridge St. (Hancock St.) | 617-227-4959

Beacon Hill residents and workers appreciate this "convenient", inex-pensive "stop-in" for its "yummy sandwiches", "excellent smoothies" and "awesome frozen yogurt" "with about 100 toppings"; those dis-pleased over the "seen-better-days" setting (with only a handful of seats) and "slow", "cranky" service call for "free delivery."

Café Polonia *Polish*
24 | 16 | 21 | $24

South Boston | 611 Dorchester Ave. (Southampton St.) | 617-269-0110 | www.cafepolonia.com

Nearly "hidden" in South Boston, this eatery dishes out "large por-tions" of "low-cost", "home-cooked" Polish "goodness" to kielbasa-, pierogi- and potato pancake–craving natives and expats ("lots of

accents!"); "warm, knowledgeable" servers patrol the "tiny", "cottage"-like space, taking the time to "thoroughly explain" the menu when asked.

Café St. Petersburg Ⓜ *Russian*　　19 | 17 | 18 | $40

Newton | 57 Union St. (Langley Rd.) | 617-277-7100 | www.cafestpetersburg.com

"A touch of Russia in Newton" is found at this "cozy", colorful spot serving "wonderful" blini, "mouthwatering borscht" and other "authentic" fare, best paired with "ice-cold" "infused vodkas"; complaints include "Cold War–era service" (especially to outsiders) and somewhat "high" tabs – however, caviar is offered at "a decent price", while a live piano player is a weekend bonus.

Cafe Sushi *Japanese*　　▽ 17 | 11 | 18 | $26

Harvard Square | 1105 Massachusetts Ave. (Putnam Ave.) | Cambridge | 617-492-0434

"Students on a budget" appreciate that they "never have to wait" for the "great deals" on "basic" sushi – especially on Sunday nights when it's just "$1 per piece" – available at this low-key storefront outside of Harvard Square; but that's not enough to draw opponents of "unremarkable" quality and "small portions."

Cafeteria *Mediterranean*　　17 | 16 | 16 | $31

Back Bay | 279A Newbury St. (bet. Fairfield & Gloucester Sts.) | 617-536-2233 | www.cafeteriaboston.com

Situated on a high-profile corner of Newbury Street, this Back Bay canteen receives its "stylish" clientele on a large sidewalk patio ("good people-watching") and in a "trendy", minimalist dining room – which "modern"-decor detractors deem "a bit uncomfortable"; the "prices are reasonable", but many would welcome "more oomph" both in the "predictable", "passable" Mediterranean victuals and "inattentive service."

Ⓩ Caffe Bella Ⓧ *Mediterranean*　　26 | 19 | 23 | $46

Randolph | 19 Warren St. (Main St.) | 781-961-7729

For possibly "the best meal you'll ever have in a strip mall", program your GPS for this "unassuming" Randolph restaurant where "wonderful" servers proffer "huge portions of hearty", "exceptional" Med fare and an "awesome wine list"; it's "a little expensive" for the 'burbs, "deafeningly loud" and the "no-reservations policy" often yields "extraordinary waits", but in spite of all that, "if you haven't been, you're missing out."

Caffe Paradiso ❶ *Coffeehouse*　　17 | 16 | 15 | $19

North End | 255 Hanover St. (bet. Cross & Richmond Sts.) | 617-742-1768

"Tourists" take "light-lunch" breaks at this "dependable", "busy" Italian coffeehouse with a "classic" old-world atmosphere in the North End, while locals like to "unwind after a long day" with "reasonably priced wines" and "*futbol*" "playing on multiple screens"; its midnight closing time also renders it "great for dessert, espresso and people-watching" "after dinner."

	FOOD	DECOR	SERVICE	COST

Caffe Tosca *Italian*

| 24 | 21 | 23 | $37 |

Hingham | 15 North St. (Cottage St.) | 781-740-9400 |
www.eatwellinc.com

Known for a "fantastic" assortment of wood-fired Italian meats, pastas and pizzas, not to mention a "nice patio", this "casual" "offshoot of Hingham's Tosca restaurant" offers "real bargains" "compared to its big sister across the street"; partisans also sing the praises of the "reasonably priced wine list", which helps fuel the "lively bar scene."

Caliterra Bar & Grille *Californian/Italian*

| ▽ 16 | 18 | 17 | $41 |

Financial District | Hilton Boston Financial Dist. | 89 Broad St. (Franklin St.) | 617-556-0006 | www.caliterrarestaurant.com

"Before setting out" for the day, guests of the Hilton Boston Financial District enjoy "leisurely" breakfasts at this "contemporary" Californian-Italian eatery known as a "lively business-lunch rendezvous" among area workers; a "broad menu" is also offered at dinner – which some suspect is "overpriced" given the somewhat "unoriginal" fare.

Cambridge, 1. ◐ *Pizza*

| 22 | 18 | 19 | $21 |

Fenway | 1381 Boylston St. (bet. Kilmarnock St. & Park Dr.) | 617-437-1111
Harvard Square | 27 Church St. (Palmer St.) | Cambridge | 617-576-1111
cambridge1.us

"Fancy" "wood-grilled pizzas" that are "light in texture, big on flavor" and loaded with "unusual", "funky" "topping combinations" are the draws at these "hip", "reasonably priced" parlors (there's also a "limited range of appealing salads"); the "roomier" Fenway operation is a destination to "grab a beer and a bite before a game", while the "sharp-looking" Harvard Square original can get "insanely crowded" – thankfully, "service is prompt once seated."

Cambridge Common ◐ *Pub Food*

| 17 | 14 | 17 | $18 |

Harvard Square | 1667 Massachusetts Ave. (bet. Sacramento & Shepherd Sts.) | Cambridge | 617-547-1228 |
www.cambridgecommonrestaurant.com

One of the "best values in all of Cambridge", this "homey" Harvard Square pub serves "cheap" plates of comfort grub ("tasty burgers", fried pickles) alongside "local brews" to everyone "from famous professors" to "undergrads"; but many of them get frustrated by "slow-as-molasses" service and "noise" – both from fellow patrons and downstairs' Lizard Lounge – that makes "tables and heads vibrate."

Canestaro *Italian*

| ▽ 19 | 14 | 16 | $24 |

Fenway | 16 Peterborough St. (Park Dr.) | 617-266-8997 |
www.canestaro.com

Cheered for its "dependability", this Fenway Italian provides "good values" on "filling" sandwiches, "nice pasta dishes" and "delicious" pizzas; "friendly service", both in the simple, "cozy" dining room and "quaint" sidewalk area, makes it a "great bet" for "a relaxing meal without the huge crowds" "before a Red Sox game."

	FOOD	DECOR	SERVICE	COST

Cantina Italiana *Italian*

22	16	20	$36

North End | 346 Hanover St. (Fleet St.) | 617-723-4577 |
www.cantinaitaliana.com

With a "reasonably priced" menu "full of red-sauce favorites" offered in "really big portions" amid "old-school comforts" (read: "old decor"), this "cozy joint" "charms" patrons who can "accept it" on its own "throwback" terms; while "attentive" staffers and "lively" company abound, "you can usually get a table without reservations on weekends" – a large plus in the North End.

Cantina la Mexicana *Mexican*
(fka Taqueria la Mexicana)

24	14	20	$15

Somerville | 247 Washington St. (Union Sq.) | 617-776-5232 |
www.lataqueria.us

"Once tiny", this "festive" Somerville taqueria has expanded with a "new, adjoining", "proper sit-down" cantina that boasts the "added benefit of a full bar" with a "Mexican beer menu"; "friendly" staffers who "treat you like family" haven't changed, nor has the "authentic", "fresh and tasty" fare and its "bargain-basement prices."

Z Capital Grille, The *Steak*

26	24	25	$65

Back Bay | 359 Newbury St. (bet. Hereford St. & Mass. Ave.) |
617-262-8900
Chestnut Hill | 250 Boylston St. (bet. Hammond Pond Pkwy. & Langley Rd.) |
617-928-1400
Burlington | 10 Wayside Rd. (Cambridge St.) | 781-505-4130
www.thecapitalgrille.com

Even those who "don't like chains" agree these "clubby" beef emporiums do "fantastic" jobs when it comes to delivering "fabulous steaks", "spectacular sides" and "terrific wines"; it's "so unbelievably crowded and noisy" though, some "can't hear" the "attentive", "knowledgeable" servers describe the offerings – which are so "expensive", "it's best if your boss is paying."

Captain's Table & Take Away *Seafood*

–	–	–	I

Wellesley | 279 Linden St. (Kingsbury St.) | 781-235-3737 |
www.captainmardens.com

You can't get closer to the sea in the suburbs than at this casual diner-style Wellesley hot spot owned and operated by adjacent Captain Marden's Seafoods, one of Boston's top fishmongers; boosters roll up their sleeves to crack lobster or dig into inexpensive daily specials that seem like an even better deal when factoring in the BYO policy.

Carlo's Cucina Italiana *Italian*

25	12	22	$26

Allston | 131 Brighton Ave. (bet. Harvard Ave. & Linden St.) |
617-254-9759 | www.carloscucinaitaliana.com

"The secret's out" lament acolytes who have to suffer increasingly "long waits" (not to mention a "lack of parking") to get into this Allston "hole-in-the-wall" Italian's "snug", "noisy" digs; but it's "worth it" for such "generous portions" of "easy-on-the-pocket", "consistently excellent" fare, which is "delivered hot to table" by "friendly" servers.

	FOOD	DECOR	SERVICE	COST

☑ Carmen 🅜 *Italian* — 26 | 19 | 23 | $46

North End | 33 North Sq. (Prince St.) | 617-742-6421 |
www.carmenboston.com

"Small space, huge flavors" are how fans describe this North End
"closet" and its "creative", "expensive but magnificent" Italian
dishes, which are served amid "romantic" lighting and decor;
"gracious" servers ferry selections from the "wide-ranging wine
list" to eager diners, many of whom first had to "wait outside", "even
with reservations"; P.S. "no coffee or dessert", but there's plenty
of cannoli nearby.

Casablanca *Mediterranean* — 22 | 21 | 20 | $36

Harvard Square | Harvard Sq. | 40 Brattle St. (Church. St.) | Cambridge |
617-876-0999 | www.casablanca-restaurant.com

A "rare holdover from old-school Harvard Square", this
Mediterranean "fixture" "tucked underground" plies an "interesting
crowd" with "always delicious" "small and large plates" from a "reasonably priced", "small but varied menu"; festooned with
Casablanca movie frescoes", the "terrific atmosphere" features a
"fun bar" (a "noisy, crowded" "place to spot celebrities") as well as
a "cool dining room."

Casa Portugal *Portuguese* — 21 | 14 | 19 | $28

Inman Square | 1200 Cambridge St. (bet. Prospect & Tremont Sts.) |
Cambridge | 617-491-8880 | www.restaurantcasaportugal.com

Inman Square's "many Portuguese residents" can't get enough of
the "authentic", "reliable" dishes, featuring lots of "delicious seafood preparations", that are "efficiently served" at this "longtime
neighborhood" "standby"; though the digs may be looking a "bit
dowdy these days", it matters not when taking into account tabs
that "won't break the bank."

Casa Romero *Mexican* — 23 | 22 | 22 | $36

Back Bay | 30 Gloucester St. (bet. Commonwealth Ave. & Newbury St.) |
617-536-4341 | www.casaromero.com

"Truly a hidden gem", this "intimate" "cave" "tucked away" in a Back
Bay alley vends "authentic", "refined" Mexican fare; indeed, the
"upscale" menu "disappoints only those looking for a burrito" (probably the same folks who find it "a little pricey" for the genre), while
the "tasty margaritas" knock everyone "for a loop"; P.S. "wonderful
service" helps to make it a "great date spot", especially on the
"romantic back patio."

Cassis 🅢 🅜 *French* — ▽ 26 | 17 | 23 | $47

Andover | 16 Post Office Ave. (Main St.) | 978-474-8788 |
www.cassis-bistro.com

While Boston foodies opine it "deserves a better fate than to be hidden in the Northwest 'burbs", Andover locals hope this "teensy-
weensy hole-in-the-wall" serving slightly pricey, "wonderful"
modern interpretations of French bistro classics stays right where it
is; though it can get "a bit noisy", "romantic" candlelight soothes, as
does the "relaxed, friendly" staff.

	FOOD	DECOR	SERVICE	COST

☑ Catch 🅼 American/Seafood — 27 | 20 | 23 | $49

Winchester | 34 Church St. (bet. School St. & Waterfield Rd.) | 781-729-1040 | www.catchrestaurant.com

"Sublime", "astoundingly creative" and "attractively presented" New American seafood of "exceptional" "freshness" is the hook at this "cozy", "homey" Winchester spot whose daily changing menu is proffered by a "friendly, knowledgeable staff"; "the one real drawback" is the "minuscule portions", which quantity-controllers deem "pricey for what you get."

Central Kitchen American — 24 | 21 | 21 | $37

Central Square | 567 Massachusetts Ave. (Pearl St.) | Cambridge | 617-491-5599

"Cambridge date night" often begins at this "hip", "warm and homey" Central Square spot where "amazing wines" pair with a "well-edited", "frequently rotating menu" of "delectable" New American fare that some calculate as "reasonably priced" and others deem "expensive"; "solo diners" also feel welcome, especially at the bar, which is usually "lively" and "crowded" (good thing, since "it's too dark to read").

Centre Street Café Eclectic — 25 | 16 | 22 | $23

Jamaica Plain | 669A Centre St. (bet. Burroughs & Myrtle Sts.) | 617-524-9217 | www.centrestcafe.com

"What a way to start the day" cheer the "folks who wait outside" in "long lines" "in all sorts of weather" for this Eclectic "Jamaica Plain jewel's" "amazing", "value"-priced weekend brunch; inside, "friendly, caring" staffers make themselves heard over "loud" crowds to tout the venue's "commitment" to "local and organic ingredients" before ferrying "massive portions" of "inventive", "wholesome" fare, which is also served daily for lunch and dinner.

Chacarero Chilean — - | - | - | I

NEW **Downtown Crossing** | 101 Arch St. (bet. Franklin & Summer Sts.) | 617-542-0392

Downtown Crossing | 26 Province St. (bet. Bosworth & School Sts.) | 617-367-1167
www.chacarero.com

Downtown Crossing worker bees are abuzz about this duo's "excellent Chilean sandwiches", piled high on homemade bread with fresh ingredients and a secret recipe hot sauce (if you dare); "prices that can't be beat" have them arriving "early to avoid lines" at the takeout-only Arch Street storefront and the Province Street location, which offers limited seating, while both are only open through lunch and on weekdays; P.S. "yummy" breakfast items are also available.

Changsho Chinese — 20 | 19 | 19 | $28

Porter Square | 1712 Massachusetts Ave. (bet. Linnaean & Martin Sts.) | Cambridge | 617-547-6565 | www.lotuscuisine.com

You'll "never have to wait" to get into this "reliable" Cambridge "cavern" (set between Harvard and Porter squares) sporting a plethora

of tables, a "classy" design and "somewhat suburban Chinese food" that may be "more expensive than most" of its ilk, but is "generally worth it" (the lunch buffet is a "good deal"); it's a "great place for Sunday dim sum", not least of all because it boasts "free parking."

Charley's *American*   18 | 17 | 18 | $29
Back Bay | 284 Newbury St. (Gloucester St.) | 617-266-3000
Chestnut Hill | The Mall at Chestnut Hill | 199 Boylston St. (Hammond Pond Pkwy.) | 617-964-1200
www.charleys-restaurant.com
"Take the kids, grandparents, first dates, illicit lovers", anyone to these "casual" "saloons" for a "wide variety" of "affordable" American "comfort fare" (weekend brunches, which come with a "complimentary cocktail", are especially "great"); the Back Bay branch's patio is a "people-watching" paradise, while the Chestnut Hill locale is a "homey and relaxed" "mall favorite", despite service being a "crap-shoot" here.

Charlie's Kitchen ● *Diner*   17 | 13 | 15 | $16
Harvard Square | 10 Eliot St. (Winthrop St.) | Cambridge | 617-492-9646
One of the "last holdouts from the yuppie-fication of Harvard Square", this "old college hangout" still plies its "cheap, cheap, cheap" diner fare, including the "famous double cheeseburger", in a "boisterous" atmosphere ("punk kids singing Kenny Rogers karaoke" anyone?); if the service is "iffy" and the victuals "forgettable", the "cool" "new beer garden is perfect."

Charlie's Sandwich Shoppe ⊠⊅ *Diner*   23 | 13 | 20 | $15
South End | 429 Columbus Ave. (bet. Dartmouth & W. Newton Sts.) | 617-536-7669
Travel "back to a time when egg yolks were acceptable" by joining the "long line" to get into this inexpensive, idiosyncratic South End breakfast-and-lunch "landmark" whipping up "awesome" "greasy diner food" (the "turkey hash is the standout") for "local pols and celebs" who "share tables" with the hoi polloi; there's "no alcohol, no bathroom, no attitude", and if you're one of the "scores of people who turn up" on a Sunday, prepare for "disappointment", because it's closed.

Chart House *Seafood*   21 | 22 | 20 | $47
Waterfront | 60 Long Wharf (Atlantic Ave.) | 617-227-1576 | www.chart-house.com
"Expensive" tariffs for "delicious fish" are blunted by a "classic Boston seaside" atmosphere (it "doesn't feel like the chain that it is") at this "scenic", "upscale" Waterfront outpost; though the patrons skew "touristy" and the staff gets "inconsistent" marks, most report "enjoyable" experiences.

Chau Chow City ● *Chinese*   21 | 10 | 15 | $22
Chinatown | 83 Essex St. (bet. Chauncy & Oxford Sts.) | 617-338-8158
"If you're looking for a beautiful restaurant with personal service, go somewhere else", but if you're just seeking an "extensive" array of "amazing" daily dim sum from "authentic push carts" at "bargain"

prices, choose this "huge" Chinatown staple (it's "dingy" and "un-friendly", but "who cares?"); "big groups" descend for dinner, while "post-club-goers" keep it "always crowded" until 3 or 4 AM nightly.

Cheers *Pub Food*　　　　　　　14 | 18 | 16 | $27

Beacon Hill | 84 Beacon St. (bet. Arlington & Charles Sts.) | 617-227-9605 ◗

Faneuil Hall | Faneuil Hall Mktpl. | Quincy Mkt. (bet. Commercial & Congress Sts.) | 617-227-0150
www.cheersboston.com

"Die-hard *Cheers* fans" "don't care" if the Beacon Hill "bar that in-spired the TV show" and its Faneuil Hall facsimile are "total tourist traps" that "look nothing like the sitcom" – they "take a picture", "grab a T-shirt" and leave happy; however, non-"sentimental" types who "get dragged here when relatives visit" are "totally disap-pointed" by "character-themed" pub grub that "tastes like a prop" and staffers who "don't want to know your name, just your wallet."

Z Cheesecake Factory *American*　　18 | 17 | 17 | $28

Back Bay | Prudential Ctr. | 115 Huntington Ave. (Belvedere St.) | 617-399-7777 ◗

Braintree | 250 Granite St. (Forbes Rd.) | 781-849-1001

Burlington | Burlington Mall | 75 Middlesex Tpke. (I-95) | 781-273-0060

East Cambridge | Cambridgeside Galleria | 100 Cambridgeside Pl. (bet. 1st St. & Land Blvd.) | Cambridge | 617-252-3810

Chestnut Hill | Atrium Mall | 300 Boylston St. (Florence St.) | 617-964-3001

Peabody | North Shore Mall | 210 Andover St. (Cross St.) | 978-538-7599

Natick | Natick Collection | 1245 Worcester St. (Speen St.) | 508-653-0011
www.thecheesecakefactory.com

The menu's "mammoth" – and "so are the crowds" – at this "family-pleasing" chain where the "endless" American options arrive in equally "colossal" portions (ironically, "they give you so much there's no room" for their "heavenly" namesake desserts); despite "ordinary" settings, "spotty" staffing and "lots of commotion", these "well-oiled machines" are so "busy, busy, busy" that they're best accessed "off-hours" to avoid a "long wait."

Chef Chang's House *Chinese*　　　20 | 14 | 19 | $25

Brookline | 1004 Beacon St. (St. Mary's St.) | 617-277-4226 | www.chefchangshouse.com

"Chang's still got it" assure advocates of this nearly 30-year-old Brookline Chinese praised for its "perfectly prepared Peking duck" and other "delicious", "reasonably priced" classics; those with an eye on design feel the "tired" interior "needs a major redo", but "re-liable" service ensures they get in and out "quick."

Chef Chow's House *Chinese*　　　20 | 16 | 21 | $22

Brookline | 230 Harvard St. (Webster St.) | 617-739-2469 | www.chefchowshouse.com

Coolidge Corner's "neighborhood standby" for "fresh" and "great tasting", if "typical", Chinese fare employs a "prompt", "friendly staff" that brings "smiles" to Brookliners' faces; the decor boasts

"nothing special except a fish tank", but that feature makes it "kid-friendly", just like the "inexpensive" tabs.

Chef Lee's II *Southern*

| – | – | – | I |

Dorchester | 554 Columbia Rd. (Dudley St.) | 617-436-6634

Aficionados of "amazing soul food" pronounce this Dorchester Southerner's vittles – fried catfish, fried chicken, baked mac 'n' cheese and so on – "otherworldly"; "the decor's no-frills", but the "friendly staff" that mans the buffetlike steam tables helps to make it a "can't-miss" experience that many believe is "far better than anything else you can get north of the Mason-Dixon."

Chez Henri *Cuban/French*

| 24 | 20 | 22 | $45 |

Harvard Square | 1 Shepard St. (Mass. Ave.) | Cambridge | 617-354-8980 | www.chezhenri.com

"Charmingly French and amusingly Cuban", the "interesting twists" imbued in this Harvard Square spot's fare are as much a "joy" as its "cozy" dining room is "romantic" ("share plates" for a "great" "foodie date"); the "convivial" bar offers a "completely different", "less expensive menu" on which the "to-die-for Cuban sandwich" and "awesome drinks" are stars, while "engaging service" can be found throughout.

Chiara Ⓜ *Mediterranean*

| 26 | 24 | 24 | $50 |

Westwood | 569 High St. (Barlow Ln.) | 781-461-8118 | www.chiarabistro.com

Westwood's fine diners are "thrilled" with this "classy" establishment's "sophisticated", "well-executed" Mediterranean menu, which is served alongside "wonderful wines" by an "attentive staff" in "lovely", "tastefully furnished" digs (never mind the "unassuming strip-mall" locale); indeed, they assure it's "as good as Boston's best" – and just "as expensive."

Chilli Duck *Thai*

| 21 | 13 | 18 | $21 |

Back Bay | 829 Boylston St. (I-90) | 617-236-5208

Both "authentic" dishes "made with care" and "yummy" "American-friendly versions" reward "all levels of Thai enthusiasts" at this "easy-to-miss", "cozy basement secret" in the Back Bay; indeed, there's "far better food" than the "odd" "tiki-room" decor "would suggest", but it's as "light on the wallet" as one could hope.

China Pearl *Chinese*

| 21 | 11 | 14 | $20 |

Chinatown | 9 Tyler St. (Beach St.) | 617-426-4338
Quincy | 237 Quincy Ave. (bet. Circuit & Faxon Park Rds.) | 617-773-9838
Woburn | Woburn Mall | 288 Mishawum Rd. (Ryan Rd.) | 781-932-0031
www.chinapearlrestaurant.com

For a dim-sum "adventure", devotees "go early" to this "aging" Chinatown "factory", and they still must endure "long", "claustrophobia-inducing" lines that go "down the stairs and out to the street" – but it's "worth it" for such "super-inexpensive", "delectable treats", which "keep coming one after another" via "little carts"; for best lunch and dinner results, those in-the-know suggest "ordering off the menu"; P.S. the Quincy and Woburn iterations offer similar "real-deal" experiences.

	FOOD	DECOR	SERVICE	COST

China Sky *Chinese/Japanese* | 19 | 19 | 18 | $29

Wellesley | 11 Forest St. (Rte. 16) | 781-431-2388 |
www.chinaskyrestaurant.com

"Well-to-do" Wellesleyans "pay a bit of a premium" for the "white-tablecloth Chinese cuisine" and "respectable sushi" served at this "elegant", "restful" venture; it also provides "fast service", which ensures "easy takeout" service too.

Christopher's ● *Eclectic* | 17 | 15 | 18 | $21

Porter Square | 1920 Massachusetts Ave. (Porter Rd.) | Cambridge |
617-876-9180 | www.christopherscambridge.com

"First and foremost a bar", this "Porter Square icon" supplements "loads" of beer on tap and "Bloody Marys the size of your head" with a "nifty variety" of Eclectic comfort stuff, including "lots of options for vegetarians"; servers can either "smile" or act "bored", but the "great prices" help to leave the "multiculti, multigenerational" regulars "feeling that the world is a good place."

Church ● *American* | 20 | 21 | 19 | $30

Fenway | 69 Kilmarnock St. (bet. Peterborough & Queensberry Sts.) |
617-236-7600 | www.churchofboston.com

"Oh my Goth", Fenway folks totally dig this "dark", "cool" haunt, and "not just for the irony" of sipping "creative" signature cocktails inspired by the "seven deadly sins" in a "hook-up joint" with a hallowed name – the New American fare is quite "tasty", and "priced reasonably" to boot; the "restaurant side" sports stained-glass windows and velvet drapery, "the club side is kind of hardcore" and there's a "lovely outdoor area when the weather's nice."

Ciao Bella *Italian* | 19 | 18 | 18 | $37

Back Bay | 240A Newbury St. (Fairfield St.) | 617-536-2626 |
www.ciaobella.com

"Sitting outside watching all the characters walk by" makes for a "picturesque" respite at this Back Bay Italian offering "traditional" fare that, though "not memorable", is "decent" enough; if the service can be "spotty" and the "decor could use some updating", maxed-out shoppers respect it as that rare "affordable" option on Newbury Street (though it might seem "a bit overpriced" elsewhere).

Cilantro ⓜ *Mexican* | ▽ 18 | 18 | 18 | $35

Salem | 282 Derby St. (bet. Hawthorne Blvd. & Lafayette St.) |
978-745-9436 | www.cilantrocilantro.com

Salemites craving "flavorful", "upscale Mexican" cuisine and an "excellent tequila selection" say this "lovely little place" punctuated by exposed-brick walls and regional artwork does the trick; however, *enemigos* exclaim the "overpriced" fare "sounds better than it is."

CK Shanghai ⓜ *Chinese* | 22 | 13 | 18 | $28

Wellesley | 15 Washington St. (bet. Mica Ln. & River St.) | 781-237-7500 |
www.ckshanghai.com

Toting "great credentials", chef C.K. Sau "brings Chinatown to the 'burbs" at this Wellesley venture via his "delicious" Shanghainese cui-

sine featuring lots of "fantastic sauces" and "fresh veggies"; the strip-mall setting is "bland" and the interior is "cramped" and "noisy", but you can always "call in a take-out order" to "avoid the crowds."

☑ Clam Box of Ipswich *Seafood* | 26 | 10 | 16 | $22 |
Ipswich | 246 High St. (bet. Haverhill St. & Mile Ln.) | 978-356-9707
"Clams raise their hands to get fried" at this "legendary" "roadside attraction" in Ipswich, a "giant box-shaped" "shack" where "tender", "sweet" seafood is cooked till "golden" in "the lightest batter you've ever tasted"; there's one "heck of a long line" to order and another to get a seat (inside or out on the picnic tables), but "bivalve lovers" say it's "worth the wait"; N.B. BYO.

Clink *American* | 19 | 25 | 19 | $51 |
Beacon Hill | Liberty Hotel | 215 Charles St. (Cambridge St.) | 617-224-4004 | www.clinkboston.com
In an "ingenious" "building reuse", the old Charles Street Jail at the foot of Beacon Hill has been transformed into the Liberty Hotel's "stylish" New American where the "super cool" wash down "inventive" "small" entrees and "extremely small tapas" with "creative drinks" amid "old cell doors"; but it's too focused on "the wannabe seen, not foodies" complain "gimmick"-phobes who'd rather be "locked up" than pay "highway-robbery" prices for "average" taste and service.

☑ Clio/Uni *French* | 27 | 26 | 26 | $81 |
Back Bay | Eliot Hotel | 370A Commonwealth Ave. (Mass. Ave.) | 617-536-7200 | www.cliorestaurant.com
Within the "gracious confines" of the Back Bay's Eliot Hotel, this "tranquil enclave" continues to make foodies "swoon" over both the "bold, complex flavors" of chef Ken Oringer's "exceptional" New French fare ("with touches of molecular gastronomy") and the "heavy blow dealt to the wallet"; "more casual" yet just as "outrageously expensive", neighbor Uni does "spectacular" sashimi, and if a few find the staffers throughout to be "snooty", most cheer them as "professional" escorts to "ethereal" "heights of expectation fulfillment."

Club Cafe *American* | ▽ 18 | 18 | 18 | $33 |
(fka 209 Boston)
South End | 209 Columbus Ave. (Berkeley St.) | 617-536-0972 | www.clubcafe.com
Catering to a "captive gay audience" "for decades", this South End New American is "welcoming" to a "mixed crowd nowadays", which comes as much for the "solid", reasonably priced wares as they do for the "steady" social scene; the decor's a tad "dated" and the service occasionally comes "with attitude", but all in all, it's a "neighborhood joint" "everyone" "can count on."

Coda *American* | 22 | 20 | 22 | $29 |
South End | 329 Columbus Ave. (Dartmouth St.) | 617-536-2632 | www.codaboston.com
Though "small", this South End American "has plenty to offer": a "convenient", "genteel" setting (with a "tasteful, modern interior" marked

by "warm exposed brick" and "local art") "where you don't have to spend a fortune for a tasty meal"; tipplers toast the "beers galore", "well-made drinks" and "extensive wine list" with its "extremely helpful descriptions", while everyone appreciates the "no-attitude" staff.

Columbus Café *Eclectic* | 19 | 16 | 20 | $30

South End | 535 Columbus Ave. (Claremont Park) | 617-247-9001
"You always feel welcome" at this "unpretentious" South Ender where the "homey" dining room and "sunny patio" (a "great place to people-watch") are often packed with "symphony and Huntington Theatre-goers" munching on "tasty", "reasonably priced" Eclectic comfort dinners; the "knowledgeable" staff remains "calm, even when it's packed", which is the norm on weekends when brunch is the "draw."

🆕 Comfort Ⓢ *American* | - | - | - | M

Watertown | 5 Spring St. (Main St.) | 617-924-3220 |
www.eatcomfortfood.com
In chain-heavy Watertown, advocates of "the little guy" "would like to see this" new, "tucked-away" American "get off the ground", not least of all to support the "personable owner" and "helpful" staff; the "tasty", "reasonably priced" fare and casual atmosphere "both live up to the name", while live weekend music is a welcome embellishment.

Coolidge Corner Clubhouse ❶ *Pub Food* | 17 | 14 | 17 | $21

Brookline | 307A-309 Harvard St. (bet. Babcock & Beacon Sts.) |
617-566-4948
The "menus are entertainment in themselves", as the sandwiches are named after athletes at this "small" Brookline sports haven offering a "huge variety" of "basic", "bang-for-the-buck" American pub grub in "massive portions"; "noisy" parents cram "cheek-to-jowl" to get a gander at one of "several TVs" "during football season or any major" game, while their offspring peruse what is a "surprisingly large kids' menu for a bar."

🆉 Coriander Bistro Ⓢ Ⓜ *French* | 27 | 20 | 26 | $52

Sharon | 5 Post Office Sq. (bet. Billings & S. Main Sts.) | 781-784-5450 |
www.corianderbistro.com
The husband-and-wife chef-owners of this Sharon "gem" set a "special" tone by "making you feel like you're in their home" before plying you with "heaping plates" of "fabulous" French fare "executed with finesse" and paired with "well-chosen wines"; "wonderful" staffers lend "efficient" assists, and though it's "expensive", it's "worth every cent" to have a "restaurant of this caliber in the 'burbs."

Cornwall's ❶ *Pub Food* | 15 | 16 | 18 | $21

Kenmore Square | 654 Beacon St. (Commonwealth Ave.) | 617-262-3749
"Fun after work" or "before a game", this often "crowded" Kenmore Square "hangout" employs a "friendly staff" to oversee an "encyclopedic beer list" and "simple", "fine" British pub grub; those put off by the "stale" decor can focus instead on pool tables, dartboards and a "wall of classic American board games", which "stands waiting to entertain you on cold, rainy nights."

	FOOD	DECOR	SERVICE	COST

Cottage, The *Californian* — 19 | 21 | 19 | $31

Wellesley | 190 Linden St. (bet. Everett St. & Pine Tree Rd.) | Wellesley Hills |
781-239-1100 | www.cottagewellesley.com

An "import from La Jolla", this "delightful" Wellesley transplant serves
"true Californian cuisine" (starring "real-deal fish tacos") in a setting
"reminiscent of a Nantucket cottage", with "crisp white wood and
comfortable booths with pillows"; while it can be "laid-back" – with the
aid of "refreshing" cocktails and "gracious" staffers – singletons say
"don't go before 7 PM unless you want an upscale Chuck E. Cheese
experience": its "kid-friendliness" is off the charts.

Cottonwood Cafe ⬤ *Southwestern* — 18 | 17 | 17 | $30

Back Bay | 222 Berkeley St. (St. James Ave.) | 617-247-2225 |
www.cottonwoodboston.com

"It's all about the chips, dips and margaritas" (especially the latter)
at this "loud" and "crowded" Back Bay "after-work scene" serving
"satisfying" if "not memorable" Southwestern noshes "priced right";
the "decor has not changed in decades", but more interesting visu-
als can be found on the "nice patio in the summer" – "inconsistent
service", unfortunately, is perennial.

Court House Seafood Ⓢ *Seafood* — ▽ 22 | 9 | 16 | $18

East Cambridge | 498 Cambridge St. (6th St.) | Cambridge | 617-491-1213 |
www.courthouseseafood.com

It feels like a "neighborhood pizza place" ("paper plates", "no alcohol"), but this East Cambridge luncheonette dishes out "extremely
fresh", "well-prepared" seafood (the same owners run the "fish
market next door") at "wonderful-bargain" prices; a staff that
"keeps the line moving" "even when busy" is another plus – "ah, if
only it were open for dinner."

❷ Craigie on Main Ⓜ *French* — 27 | - | 25 | $64
(fka Craigie Street Bistrot)

Central Square | 853 Main St. (Allen St.) | Cambridge | 617-497-5511 |
www.craigieonmain.com

"Knowledgeable, serious" chef Tony Maws knows what his fans
want – "wildly inventive", "truly adventurous" French cuisine "emphasizing local ingredients", fashioned into "innovative presenta-
tions" and conveyed by "helpful, cheerful" servers – and now he
delivers it in Central Square, having moved from the old "tiny"
Harvard Square "basement" post-Survey; nervous Nellies who
"hope he can maintain the quality" in "bigger digs" most likely have
nothing to worry about, but dollar-watchers who "pray for lower
prices" shouldn't bet on it.

NEW Croma *Italian* — 19 | 19 | 18 | $30

Plymouth | The Village | 160 Colony Pl. (State Rd.) | 508-747-4456 |
www.cromaplymouth.com

"Gourmet" thin-crust pies are what this midpriced Plymouth parlor
is "known for", but it also does "Italian specialties" and "unique
cocktails" in "fine" fashion; the environs exhibit "modern" "flair"
and boast an "open-air feel during the summer."

	FOOD	DECOR	SERVICE	COST

Z Cuchi Cuchi ⊠ *Eclectic*   22 | 26 | 21 | $38

Central Square | 795 Main St. (Windsor St.) | Cambridge |
617-864-2929 | www.cuchicuchi.cc

"Pin-up waitresses" dressed in "flamboyant" "vintage" "costumes"
are just as "sexy" as the "decadent" "speakeasy" decor at this "over-
the-top" Central Square "hot spot"; "fun, flirty drinks" (props to the
"sassy mixologists") "kick off" many a "girls' night out", while "diverse" "international tapas" "designed to give you a food-gasm"
prove to be "fabulous" aphrodisiacs for "romantic evenings *à deux*."

Cygnet *American*   ▽ 21 | 22 | 22 | $42

Beverly | 24 West St. (Hale St.) | 978-922-9221 |
www.cygnetrestaurant.com

"Business meetings and quiet conversations" fill the "warm, relaxing"
dining room of this Beverly Farms American, but it's also a "recommended" choice for "elegant" parties too; "graceful", "helpful" servers
convey the somewhat expensive, "reasonably good" fare, while "professional" 'tenders "remember" what regulars drink in the "cozy" bar.

Daedalus *American*   17 | 19 | 18 | $28

Harvard Square | 45½ Mt. Auburn St. (bet. Bow & DeWolfe Sts.) |
Cambridge | 617-349-0071 | www.daedalusharvardsquare.com

"Let's face it", the main attraction of this pubby Harvard Square
"hangout" is its "beautiful roof deck" – so it's a good thing that the
American fare is "affordable", because it's "average at best"; the
"grad students and teaching assistants" who summer there say they
"wouldn't go out of their way" in winter, but they "always seem to
end up coming back because it's so damned convenient."

Daily Catch *Italian/Seafood*   24 | 11 | 17 | $35

North End | 323 Hanover St. (bet. Prince & Richmond Sts.) |
617-523-8567 ⊞

Seaport District | Moakley Federal Courthouse | 2 Northern Ave.
(Sleeper St.) | 617-772-4400
www.dailycatch.com

"Probably no bigger than your kitchen", this "garlic-scented" North
End storefront attracts "long lines" of folks waiting to pay "cash only"
for "amazing", "abundant" Italian seafood-and-pasta dishes "served
piping hot" "in the skillet they were cooked in", judiciously washed
down with "wine in juice glasses" (there are "no bathrooms"); the
larger Seaport District offshoot, boasting an "incredible view" from the
patio, is a "different experience" altogether, but it still "packs a punch."

NEW Daily Grill *American*   19 | 19 | 19 | $36

Back Bay | Prudential Ctr. | 105 Huntington Ave. (Bolyston St.) |
617-424-4400 | www.dailygrill.com

The Back Bay link of this ever-expanding national chain proffers a
"wide-ranging menu" of "consistently good" New American fare in an
"attractive setting" ("big booths, lots of dark wood, stately bar") that's
as suitable for a "casual" "business lunch" as it is for just "watching
the game"; in the long run, it's "nothing spectacular", but "large portions" and "decent prices" place it pretty much beyond reproach.

	FOOD	DECOR	SERVICE	COST

Dalia's Bistro & Wine Bar ◪ *American* ▽ 19 | 19 | 17 | $37

Brookline | 1657 Beacon St. (Winthrop Rd.) | 617-730-8040 |
www.daliasbistro.com

With the "right amount of subtle lighting" and "lots of good wines
that aren't offered everywhere", this "small", "pleasant neighborhood bistro" in Brookline is appropriate for a "romantic", moderately priced New American meal; its perpetual tranquility indicates
it's a "well-kept secret" – which it could remain say those who find
"nothing wrong, but nothing memorable."

Dalí Restaurant & Tapas Bar *Spanish* 25 | 24 | 23 | $39

Somerville | 415 Washington St. (Beacon St.) | 617-661-3254 |
www.dalirestaurant.com

Drop yourself "into a Dalí painting" when you drop into this "surreal"
Somerville Spaniard, an "endearingly kitschy, unabashedly romantic" tapas bar whose "amazing array" of "exquisite", "pretty pricey"
small plates comes from "gorgeous" staffers with "genuine"
"knowledge"; masses of "friends", "families", "dates" and "birthday
celebrations" keep the atmosphere "festive", and while that often
leads to "lines" to get in, "beautiful people" "wait it out" with the aid
of "awesome sangria."

Dalya's ◪ *American* 23 | 21 | 22 | $43

Bedford | 20 North Rd. (Rte. 62) | 781-275-0700 | www.dalyas.com

A "bit of sophistication" in Bedford, this New American attracts "ladies who lunch" and "romance"-seekers with its "homey" farmhouse setting ("like eating at a friend's home") and a "wide-ranging
menu" of "wonderful" fare "tastefully presented" by a "personable"
staff that "tries hard to please"; it's "a little spendy", but it's "dependable", which keeps locals "coming back."

dante *Italian* 24 | 22 | 22 | $48

East Cambridge | Royal Sonesta Hotel Boston | 40 Edwin H. Land Blvd.
(Cambridgeside Pl.) | Cambridge | 617-497-4200 |
www.restaurantdante.com

The "devastatingly delicious", "imaginative" Italian creations,
"lively wine list" and "assiduous" service at this "modern", "airy"
spot in East Cambridge's Royal Sonesta "exceed expectations for a
hotel restaurant", even though the "modest" food portions make it
somewhat "overpriced"; on the other hand, the "unbelievable
Sunday brunch" is a "value", especially on the "sublime" patio with
its "wonderful views of the Charles River."

Darwin's Ltd. *Coffeehouse/Deli* 24 | 14 | 15 | $13

Harvard Square | 148 Mt. Auburn St. (Brewer St.) | Cambridge |
617-354-5233

Harvard Square | 1629 Cambridge St. (bet. Roberts Rd. & Trowbridge St.) |
Cambridge | 617-491-2999

www.darwinsltd.com

Offering a bevy of "inventive", "superb" sandwiches, salads, pastries and "fabulous coffee", this Harvard Square deli duo incites "long
lines", especially at lunchtime (it's a bit "costly" for what it is, but

the "portions are hearty"); seating can be "hard to find" in the "loud, brick-walled rooms", so many customers ask the "knowledgeable" though sometimes "unfriendly" counter help to bag it for takeout.

Davide Ristorante *Italian*   ▽ 24 | 18 | 23 | $50

North End | 326 Commercial St. (bet. Battery & Clark Sts.) | 617-227-5745 | www.daviderestaurant.com

"Without a flashy/trendy environment", this North End basement draws clients celebrating "special occasions" or on "hot dates" solely via the promise of "good portions" of "classic Italian" cuisine in a "comfortable", "not jam-packed" setting – which is just a little too "drab" for some (not factoring in the "welcoming staff", of course).

Da Vinci ⧅ *Italian*   22 | 23 | 22 | $50

Park Square | 162 Columbus Ave. (Arlington St.) | 617-350-0007 | www.davinciboston.com

The "name befits the artistry of the chef-owner" applaud diners who've discovered this "charming", "warm" Park Square Italian where "wonderful pastas" are the "specialty" and the rest of the offerings are "presented beautifully" ("don't be surprised" if the toque "comes to your table to greet you personally"); though many find the prices "reasonable", dissenters deem them "expensive" for the portions.

⧅ Davio's *Italian/Steak*   25 | 24 | 24 | $55

Park Square | Paine Furniture Bldg. | 75 Arlington St. (Stuart St.) | 617-357-4810

NEW Foxboro | Gillette Stadium | 290 Patriot Pl. (Washington St., off Rte. 1) | 508-339-4810
www.davios.com

"Treat yourself" to a "fabulous" Northern Italian meal "presented with panache" by an "impeccable" staff at these "busy, noisy" and ultimately "awesome" steakhouse siblings: the "tasteful", "clubby" "see-and-be-seen" "famous-folk" magnet in Park Square and its new, "well-appointed" offshoot, an "instant" "top-choice" in Foxboro; the "expansive wine list" completes the experience – now, how about a "scholarship fund" to help pay for it?

Deep Ellum ☾ *Eclectic*   ▽ 18 | 17 | 19 | $25

Allston | 477 Cambridge St. (Brighton Ave.) | 617-787-2337 | www.deepellum-boston.com

There's "something for everyone" at this "cute, cozy", "grown-up" Allston address: a "deep" selection of "stellar beers", "fantastic cocktails" and inexpensive Eclectic "fun food" (try the "amazing pretzels") all doled out by "friendly" servers; inside gets "loud", while the "great" "deck out back" is a warm-weather sanctuary.

⧅ Delfino ⧄ *Italian*   27 | 17 | 24 | $37

Roslindale | 754 South St. (bet. Belgrade Ave. & Washington St.) | 617-327-8359 | www.delfinorestaurant.com

Regulars of this "casual" Roslindale Italian spot "treasure" its "generous portions" of "fresh and delightful" fare as much as they do the "accommodating" staff; indeed, the "drawbacks" of a "no-reservations policy" ("call ahead and put your name on the list"),

"long waits", "crowds", "noise" and "tight seating" are "small prices to pay", especially considering the "quite reasonable" tabs.

Delux Cafe ●⊠⇆ *Eclectic*   21 | 18 | 16 | $21

South End | 100 Chandler St. (Clarendon St.) | 617-338-5258

A "funky" "alternative" to some of "the pricier restaurants" in the South End, this "divey hole-in-the-wall" serves a "short menu" of "damn tasty" Eclectic eats to "posh" people, "hipsters", "bicycle messengers" and anyone else who digs a "crazy" space "festooned with Elvis memorabilia and Christmas lights year-round"; servers can become "distracted" "when it's crowded", but "great cocktails" and "not-your-average beers" provide "cheap" comfort – for which you must pay cash.

Deluxe Town Diner *Diner*   22 | 16 | 19 | $17

Watertown | 627 Mt. Auburn St. (Bigelow Ave.) | 617-926-8400 | www.deluxetowndiner.com

A "unique Watertown landmark", this "restored" diner's "interesting, adventurous" and "cheap" menu "goes far beyond greasy burgers and fries"; while it's "great all the time", weekend brunch is the real "scene", as boosters "brave" "lines out the door" (and then "uncomfortable" booths) for "amazing" pancakes and waffles "of all kinds", served in "sizable portions" by a "friendly, fun" staff.

Demos *Greek*   21 | 7 | 15 | $15

Waltham | 146 Lexington St. (Pond St.) | 781-893-8359
Watertown | 60-64 Mt. Auburn St. (Main St.) | 617-924-9660

As a "healthy alternative to traditional fast-food joints", these "crazy-busy" Waltham and Watertown drop-ins "can't be beat" for "ample servings" of "delicious" Greek classics at "rock-bottom prices"; those who can't get past the "bare-bones", "cafeteria-style" settings make it their "choice take-out destinations."

Devlin's *American*   20 | 21 | 19 | $30

Brighton | 332 Washington St. (Market St.) | 617-779-8822 | www.edevlins.com

Catering to a "young professional crowd", this "refined" "neighborhood spot" wins raves for an "interesting" menu of New American fare and "tasty designer drinks", as well as an "awesome patio" ("you'd never know you're sitting in the middle of Brighton"); inside, the "comfortable, contemporary" dining area is slightly "more formal" than the bar, which "can be loud and crowded", while "prompt", "friendly" servers are found throughout.

Dillon's *American*   16 | 16 | 15 | $24

Back Bay | 955 Boylston St. (Mass. Ave.) | 617-421-1818 | www.irishconnection.com

With a "nice patio" outside and "vintage oversized ceiling fans" and "big TVs" in, this Back Bay hang pulls in "happy-hour" crowds, "game-watchers" and dudes "looking for digits"; as far as the "typical" American grub goes, some's "enjoyable", some's "subpar" ("good pricing" though).

	FOOD	DECOR	SERVICE	COST

District ⓈⓂ *American* ▽ 17 | 25 | 18 | $36

Leather District | 180 Lincoln St. (bet. Beach & Kneeland Sts.) |
617-426-0180 | www.districtboston.com

"High class and tasteful all the way", this leather-and-birch lounge
lures after-workers and night owls to the sleepy Leather District for
"good" New American fare that's heavy on the small plates and reasonably priced; "the staff pulls everything together effortlessly",
particularly for the many "events" that are held here, but the whole
endeavor comes off as "a little pretentious" to some attendees.

Diva Indian Bistro *Indian* 22 | 20 | 16 | $27

Somerville | 246 Elm St. (Chester St.) | 617-629-4963 |
www.divabistro.com

Among Davis Square's Indian haunts, this Somervillean stands out
with a "contemporary space" in which to serve its "wonderful" cuisine
(don't skip the "giant", "crispy, delicious dosas"); surveyors split over
whether the tabs are "affordable" or comparatively "overpriced", but
most everyone agrees on the service issue: "slow", "brusque" and
dripping with "attitude" ("why?"); P.S. the "architecturally fascinating" lounge next door concocts "truly unique, scrumptious" cocktails.

NEW DJ's at the Garden *American* - | - | - | M

West End | 222 Friend St. (Valenti Way) | 617-723-3222 |
www.djsatthegarden.com

Sports fans cheer this West End bar/eatery as a "great place to watch
the game" on 25 HDTVs in multiple rooms while tackling a large menu
of "slightly upscale" yet moderately priced American grub; on non-
game days, frequent live bands score points from music lovers.

Dog Bar at 65 Main St. Ⓜ *American* ▽ 23 | 21 | 23 | $34

Gloucester | 65 Main St. (bet. Porter & Short Sts.) | 978-281-6565 |
www.dogbarcapeann.com

This "casual" Gloucester tavern serves a "delightful" assortment of
American classics in "cozy" digs marked by exposed brick and vintage-
looking photos; "friendly" servers deliver designer cocktails from
the bar, which "rocks" with "live music several nights a week."

Dok Bua *Thai* 24 | 11 | 20 | $17

Brookline | 411 Harvard St. (bet. Fuller St. & Naples Rd.) | 617-277-7087
"Welcome to Kitschville!"- this Brookline Thai is as known for its
"funky"/"fun" decor ("Christmas lights, travel posters", shelves from
its past "grocery-store" life) as it is for "delicious, plentiful" "lunch and
dinner specials" from an "encyclopedic menu with pictures of every
dish" and "unbeatable prices"; what's no joke is the "courteous" staff.

Dolphin Seafood *Seafood* 18 | 15 | 17 | $30

Harvard Square | 1105 Massachusetts Ave. (Remington St.) | Cambridge |
617-661-2937

Natick | 12 Washington St. (Rte. 135) | 508-655-0669
www.dolphinseafood.com

Taking folks "back to a simpler era in American seafood joints",
these "old-school" eateries with outposts in Harvard Square and

Natick (mostly) broil "big quantities" of "fresh fish" "without all the doctoring up"; if epicures dis the preparations as "boring" and the settings as "unimaginative", even they have to admit "at least it's cheaper" than the big chains.

Donatello *Italian*
24 | 19 | 21 | $48

Saugus | 44 Broadway/Rte. 1 (Rte. 95) | 781-233-9975 | www.donatellosaugus.com

"Right out of *The Sopranos*" and onto Saugus' strip-mall-heavy Route 1 comes this "nice surprise" offering "wonderful", "authentic" Italian fare in a setting that's "perfect for celebrations"; though the "prices are aggressive", not so the "accommodating" servers, "fun, chatty bartenders" and "low-pressure" ambiance.

Dong Khanh ⊅ *Vietnamese*
▽ 22 | 8 | 14 | $15

Chinatown | 81-83 Harrison Ave. (Kneeland St.) | 617-426-9410

"On a cold day when you want a hot bowl of noodle soup" or in summer when a cooling bubble tea or fruit smoothie is in order, join the "often crazy lines" for this Vietnamese "hole-in-the-wall" in Chinatown; the "decor needs a major overhaul" and "don't expect great service" – just be happy that the "solid" eats are "fresh, fast" and "cheap."

Don Ricardo's ⊠ *Brazilian/Peruvian*
▽ 23 | 14 | 26 | $24

South End | 57 W. Dedham St. (bet. Shawmut Ave. & Tremont St.) | 617-247-9249

A "hidden gem", this "reliable" spot serves "delicious", "authentic" Brazilian-Peruvian "treats" alongside "super sangria" at "significantly cheap" prices considering its South End address; the "lovely", "welcoming" staff makes it "feel like home", even though there's "not much atmosphere" to speak of.

Douzo ● *Japanese*
24 | 23 | 20 | $41

Back Bay | 131 Dartmouth St. (Stuart St.) | 617-859-8886 | www.douzosushi.com

"Everyday" sushi "classics are reinvented" at this Back Bay "sophisticate" whose "innovative" rolls befit the slightly "expensive" tabs and "trendy, modern" environs (design mavens can't help comparing it to a "West Elm" showroom); while you never know if you'll get a "responsive" or "underwhelming" server, you can usually "expect a bit of a wait" for a table, which goes quicker with "well-crafted cocktails" at the bar.

Doyle's Cafe *Pub Food*
15 | 18 | 18 | $21

Jamaica Plain | 3484 Washington St. (Williams St.) | 617-524-2345

Since 1882, this Irish pub "institution" has been "everyone's" Jamaica Plain "hangout", especially "politicians" who meet to deal among "townies, Sox fans", "famous and infamous faces staring down from the walls" and other "Boston lore decor"; the "stick-to-your-ribs" grub can be rather "undistinguished" (at "prices that haven't changed since your grandfather" was young), but the "substantial beer selection" is "outstanding."

	FOOD	DECOR	SERVICE	COST

NEW Drink *American*
| | - | - | - | M |

Seaport District | 348 Congress St. (bet. Farnsworth St. & Thomson Pl.) | 617-695-1806 | www.drinkfortpoint.com

With a "cool", "attractive" setting marked by a meandering wood-block bar and a "museumlike" display of mounted beetles, plus a "limited" yet "interesting" menu of "retro" American canapés by noted toque Barbara Lynch, this subterranean gastro-lounge brings "buzz" to an "iffy" stretch of the Seaport District; but with relatively "expensive" tabs for what amounts to "finger food" and rather "small drinks" (granted, they're concocted with "scientific flair" by "real pros"), for dollar-watchers, it fizzles when the check comes.

Z Duckworth's Bistrot Ⓜ *American*
| | 29 | 20 | 26 | $48 |

Gloucester | 197 E. Main St. (Plum St.) | 978-282-4426 | www.duckworthsbistrot.com

"Run, don't walk" to this "absolute gem in the most unexpected place" – Gloucester – for chef Ken Duckworth's "exceptional", seasonal New American fare "prepared with flair", featuring "entrees available in half portions" that can be paired with "excellent wines" "by the half glass", both "godsends for exploring" (and more "budget"-friendly to boot); the "casual" digs are "elbow-to-elbow" and often "noisy", but those are minor inconveniences for an experience to which "nothing on the North Shore compares."

Durgin-Park *New England*
| | 17 | 14 | 15 | $33 |

Faneuil Hall | Faneuil Hall Mktpl. | 340 N. Market St. (Congress St.) | 617-227-2038 | www.durgin-park.com

Famous for its "immense portions" of "New England favorites" like "tasty prime rib" and Indian pudding, this Faneuil Hall "blast" from 1826 is also "notable for surly", "sassy" waitresses who "put you in your place" (it also "prides itself" on "below-par decor" featuring "long tables" with "red-checked cloths"); yes, it's kind of an "over-priced" "tourist trap", but "everyone should go once", at least to "say you've done it."

Z East Coast Grill & Raw Bar *BBQ/Seafood*
| | 25 | 18 | 22 | $39 |

Inman Square | 1271 Cambridge St. (Prospect St.) | Cambridge | 617-491-6568 | www.eastcoastgrill.net

"The thrill of the Grill" is "still strong", as evidenced by the "wicked crowds" who "endure" "long waits" to "explore the world of heat" via Chris Schlesinger's "seriously hot BBQ" and "killer" "fresh seafood" at this "boisterous" Inman Square "classic"; a "seasoned staff" works the "zany" tropical-themed setting like a "well-oiled machine", delivering "cutting-edge cocktails" and checks that are only "slightly on the pricey side"; P.S. for the "ultimate" "fiery" "challenge", come for the regularly scheduled Hell Nights.

Z Eastern Standard ◑ *American/European*
| | 22 | 24 | 22 | $40 |

Kenmore Square | Hotel Commonwealth | 528 Commonwealth Ave. (Brookline Ave.) | 617-532-9100 | www.easternstandardboston.com

From a "wonderful breakfast" to a "casual, inexpensive" American lunch complemented by "intriguing", "innovative" cocktails (the

"mixologists are geniuses") to an "elegant, pricey" European dinner paired with "well-chosen wines", there's "something for everyone" at this "cavernous", "glamorous" Kenmore Square "grande cafe" with a "gorgeous marble bar", "high ceilings" and an "excellent heated patio"; always "buzzing", it's especially "noisy" on "game day" – "like the Gare du Nord filled with Sox fans."

East Ocean City *Chinese/Seafood* | 24 | 12 | 17 | $28 |

Chinatown | 25 Beach St. (bet. Harrison Ave. & Washington St.) | 617-542-2504 | www.eastoceancity.com

For fish "flapping one moment" in "tanks by the door", "delicately cooked and on your plate 10 minutes later", this "delicious" Cantonese canteen is the place in Chinatown; "locals" frequent it ("so you know it's good") for lunch and dinner, "bar-hoppers" are "forever indebted" to its "late hours" and "moderate" prices, and no one seems to mind the "brusque service" and "drab surroundings."

NEW Ecco *American* | - | - | - | M |

East Boston | 107 Porter St. (bet. Chelsea & Paris Sts.) | 617-561-1112 | www.eccoboston.com

Part restaurant, part nightlife hot spot, this affordable New American (with Latin and Asian influences) is a sexy addition to East Boston, offering a quiet dining room with black leather banquettes and a bar area that hops after-hours; N.B. the wall scrawled with sports-figure signatures is a leftover from the space's former occupant, Sablone's.

Eclano 🖾 *Italian* | ▽ 18 | 15 | 22 | $47 |

North End | 54 Salem St. (Cross St.) | 617-720-6001 | www.eclano.net

For a "classic visit to the North End", this trattoria gets all "the Italian dining basics right" in a "relaxing" (though sparsely decorated) dining room; too bad those who find the experience "leaves a little to be desired" calculate it's "overpriced."

Z Elephant Walk *Cambodian/French* | 23 | 20 | 20 | $36 |

Fenway | 900 Beacon St. (Park Dr.) | 617-247-1500
Porter Square | 2067 Massachusetts Ave. (bet. Hadley & Russell Sts.) | Cambridge | 617-492-6900
Waltham | 663 Main St. (Moody St.) | 781-899-2244
www.elephantwalk.com

"Still amazing after all these years", these triplets serve a "well-executed" menu (with many "lovely vegetarian options") of "mouth-watering" Cambodian and French fare – although the fact that it's "not fusion" per se, "rather two distinct cooking traditions", makes for a "strange concept" to some; the "handsome decor" "captures the imagination" of diners – that is, when they're not having to snag the "rushed, inattentive" members of the otherwise "professional" serving fleet.

El Oriental de Cuba *Cuban* | 24 | 14 | 19 | $17 |

Jamaica Plain | 416 Centre St. (S. Huntington Ave.) | 617-524-6464 | www.elorientaldecuba.com

"Justly famous" 'round Jamaica Plain, this "warm and welcoming" spot earns "institution" status thanks to its "huge portions" of

"amazing" Cuban cuisine offered at "low prices"; the "decor's nothing special", but there's plenty else to look at since it's "almost always filled to capacity."

El Sarape *Mexican* | 25 | 15 | 21 | $26 |

Braintree | 5 Commercial St. (Union St.) | 781-843-8005 | www.elsarape.com

South-of-the-border specialists say this Braintree cantina serves the "most authentic Mexican on the South Shore", with "zesty", "consistently amazing" preparations complemented by "dynamite margaritas" and "unreal sangria", all at reasonable rates; the "gracious staff" and occasional live music pleases, even when the colorfully "cliché decor" and heavy "weekend crowds" do not.

Emma's Pizza ⊠ *Pizza* | 24 | 13 | 18 | $18 |

Kendall Square | 40 Hampshire St. (Portland St.) | Cambridge | 617-864-8534 | www.emmaspizza.com

Kendall Square subjects hail this "queen" of "gourmet thin-crust pizzas", as she lets them eat "divine" pies topped with "creative combinations" of "inventive" ingredients for "reasonable prices"; but the "small space with only a handful of tables" makes them work for it ("be prepared to wait if you don't come early"), so many head instead for the "quick" "to-go counter."

Emperor's Garden *Chinese* | 21 | 13 | 14 | $20 |

Chinatown | 690 Washington St. (Kneeland St.) | 617-482-8898

Upon entering this "old theater" in Chinatown, dim sum lovers – including a heavily "Chinese clientele" – are "bombarded with a continuous flotilla of carts" manned by "nonchalant" staffers handing out the "remarkable" eats for "value" prices; the "shabby" setting "could definitely use a visit from HGTV", but with seating for roughly 800, "you can always get in" during the "crowded" weekend rush ("if you enjoy a meal in solitude, show up around dinnertime").

Equator *Eclectic/Thai* | ▽ 18 | 14 | 19 | $29 |

South End | 1721 Washington St. (Mass. Ave.) | 617-536-6386 | www.equatorrestaurantma.com

A "strange mix" of Thai standards, Italian pastas and steaks makes this South End eatery "hard to define", especially since everything's "average"; but "if you're in the area" for lunch or "the symphony", its "convenient" location, "efficient service" and "fairly reasonable prices" make it a "pleasant" option.

Erawan of Siam *Thai* | 22 | 23 | 20 | $26 |

Waltham | 469 Moody St. (High St.) | 781-899-3399 | www.erawanofsiam.net

"Wood carvings, decorative artwork" and traditional floor seating adds to the "charming" "authenticity" of this "spacious" Waltham Thai; the "reasonably priced", "well-prepared" fare comes "attractively presented" by "gracious", "receptive" staffers, mirroring their kitchen counterparts who "will accommodate 'Thai hot' if you ask for it – just be prepared for some serious heat."

	FOOD	DECOR	SERVICE	COST

NEW Erbaluce *Italian*

- | - | - | M

Park Square | 69 Church St. (Shawmut St.) | 617-426-6969 |
www.erbaluce-boston.com

"It's early in the game" for this "calm" Park Square Italian, but pre-
liminary word is its "ever-changing" fare is "flavorful" and "inventive", the wines are "well chosen" and the prices are "competitive";
service is mostly "friendly and informed", and while the proprietors
"didn't blow the budget" on the decor (cappuccino walls, terra-cotta
floors), the simple, "tiny" space feels "warm", thanks in part to
"views into the kitchen."

NEW Estragon ⊠ *Spanish*

- | - | - | M

South End | 700 Harrison Ave. (bet. E. Brookline & E. Canton Sts.) |
617-266-0443 | www.estragontapas.com

Authentic, moderately priced tapas are served at this South End
Spaniard from the former owner of Brookline's Taberna de Haro; its
sleek and sexy art deco-inspired setting features a small lounge
area with antique settees, a long bar and two large communal tables, and there's an affiliated gourmet shop next door.

Euno *Italian*

24 | 22 | 21 | $37

North End | 119 Salem St. (Cooper St.) | 617-573-9406 |
www.eunoboston.com

Tucked "away from the craziness of Hanover Street", this "intimate"
North Ender serves "tasty", "traditional" Italian cuisine at "affordable prices" in a "cute", brick-lined ground level with "windows that
open to the street" and a downstairs that feels "like dining in a private wine cellar"; words of caution for winter: while the "staff is accommodating", some report "having to wait" outside ("there's no
bar"), even with reservations.

⚡ EVOO ⊠ *Eclectic*

27 | 22 | 26 | $47

Somerville | 118 Beacon St. (Washington St.) | 617-661-3866 |
www.evoorestaurant.com

Devoted regulars say the "sophisticated" Eclectic fare with "great
emphasis on local ingredients" served at this "comfy", "urbane"
Somerville "gem" "scores every time", particularly with the assis-
tance of the "stellar" servers' "helpful" explanations of the "unique
combinations" and "wonderful wine" pairings; for "this caliber", the
prices are "completely reasonable", especially the "incredible-
bargain" three-course prix fixe, while the chef's tasting menu
(Monday–Thursday) is a "lovely splurge."

Exchange Street Bistro *Eclectic*

▽ 20 | 21 | 20 | $35

Malden | 67 Exchange St. (Main St.) | 781-322-0071 |
www.exchangestreetbistro.com

As "hip" and "modern" as any city venue, but without the
"Boston expense", this red-and-black Malden bistro attracts a
"great local crowd" for "delicious" "seasonal" Eclectic eats
brought by "pleasant", "accommodating" staffers; drivers appreciate that there's "lots of parking", while the driven toast the
"awesome martini bar."

	FOOD	DECOR	SERVICE	COST

Fajitas & 'Ritas *Tex-Mex*

16 | 14 | 14 | $20

Downtown Crossing | 25 West St. (bet. Tremont & Washington Sts.) | 617-426-1222 | www.fajitasandritas.com

"The young, the cheap and the hungry" habituate this "dark, dingy", "graffiti-splashed" Downtown Crossing Tex-Mexer (especially "after work") for "sizzling platters" of "inexpensive" fajitas and "huge pitchers" of "killer" margs; the staffers can swing from merely "spotty" to "appalling", but since they "don't even have to take your order" (you "fill out" a "checklist"), there's minimal interaction.

Fava ⓈⓂ *American*

25 | 20 | 24 | $48

Needham | 1027 Great Plain Ave. (bet. Chapel St. & Eaton Sq.) | 781-455-8668 | www.favarestaurant.com

"So warm and cozy" it's like getting "a big hug" reckon Needhamites of this "romantic hideaway" "tucked away" in an "old rail station" – and they return the favor by embracing its "ever-changing" menu of "inventive", "delightful" New American fare, no matter how "expensive" it is; add a "fantastic wine list" and "knowledgeable", "friendly" service to the mix, and it's no wonder they "can't get enough."

51 Lincoln *American*

23 | 20 | 22 | $49

Newton | 51 Lincoln St. (Columbus St.) | 617-965-3100 | www.51lincolnnewton.com

"A surprise in Newton Highlands", this "gem" vends "scrumptious" New American cuisine loaded with the "seasonal delights" and "innovation" ("you will never look at watermelon quite the same after you taste the grilled appetizer") of chef Jeffrey Fournier, also creator of the "beautiful" abstract artwork that bedecks the "inviting setting"; a vocal minority proclaims the experience "overrated", but most find it worth the "somewhat pricey" tabs.

Figs *Italian*

23 | 17 | 19 | $31

Beacon Hill | 42 Charles St. (bet. Chestnut & Mt. Vernon Sts.) | 617-742-3447
Charlestown | 67 Main St. (bet. Monument Ave. & Winthrop St.) | 617-242-2229
www.toddenglish.com

Todd English may no longer spend much time at his Beacon Hill and Charlestown "designer pizza" parlors, but his presence is felt in pies that feature "unusual ingredients and flavor combinations", supplemented by "amazing salads" and other "glorious" Italian eats; when the "cramped" environs get "loud and crowded", it can make the otherwise "thoughtful staff" seem "rushed" – which further irks folks who find the relatively "reasonable" tabs "overpriced for what you get."

Filippo Ristorante ⓈⓂ *Italian*

▽ 21 | 15 | 18 | $34

North End | 283 Causeway St. (Endicott St.) | 617-742-4143 | www.filipporistorante.com

"Within walking distance of the Boston Garden", this old-school Italian "on the far end of the North End" is a "great option prior to the game" – but it's also sort of a "cheesy" one due to its "overthought" in-

terior complete with ceiling frescoes; at least the "authentic", reasonably priced fare pleases, as do the "great wines" and service.

Finale ● *Dessert* | 23 | 20 | 20 | $23 |

Park Square | 1 Columbus Ave. (Park Plaza) | 617-423-3184
Harvard Square | 30 Dunster St. (bet. Mass. Ave. & Mt. Auburn St.) | Cambridge | 617-441-9797
Brookline | Coolidge Corner | 1306 Beacon St. (Harvard St.) | 617-232-3233
www.finaledesserts.com

"Dreams are made of" the "decadent" works of "gourmet" "art" whipped up at these "divine" desserteries where "chocoholics" "go with a big group" to create their own "buffet of deliciousness", coupled with "unusual coffees" and an "extensive" cordial selection ("small savory lead-ins" are also available, as are "yummy lunch sandwiches and salads"); while foes complain of "trying waits", "slow service" and "high prices", friends get the final say: "well worth" it, no matter any irritation.

Finz *Seafood* | 20 | 19 | 19 | $37 |

Dedham | 910 Washington St. (Fay Rd.) | 781-329-0097
Salem | Pickering Wharf | 76 Wharf St. (Derby St.) | 978-744-8485
www.hipfinz.com

With a "terrific" patio and "beautiful water views" in Salem, a "large", brightly colored, "open" feel in Dedham and "upbeat atmospheres" at both, these seafood siblings reel in cravers of "fresh", "creative" seafood; tough cookies call it "nothing exceptional" for tabs that are a smidge "pricey" (and with service that's merely "average"), but they can usually be swayed with the aid of "robust cocktails."

Fire & Ice *Eclectic* | 16 | 15 | 15 | $26 |

Back Bay | 205 Berkeley St. (St. James Ave.) | 617-482-3473
Harvard Square | 50 Church St. (bet. Brattle St. & Mass. Ave.) | Cambridge | 617-547-9007
www.fire-ice.com

A "fun", "interactive" concept to some, a "laughably fake" "take on Mongolian barbecue" to others, these Back Bay and Harvard Square "novelties" – "essentially buffets" where you choose Eclectic "meats, veggies and sauces", then watch "teenagers cook" them all on large, circular grills – are "often jammed" with "groups and families", making for "noisy, hectic" meals; since it's "all you can eat", it may seem "too expensive" if you don't "come hungry."

Firefly's *BBQ* | 20 | 16 | 18 | $25 |

Quincy | 516 Adams St. (bet. Alrick Rd. & Furnace Brook Pkwy.) | 617-471-0011
Framingham | Super Stop N' Shop Plaza | 235 Old Connecticut Path (Rte. 126) | 508-820-3333
Marlborough | 350 E. Main St. (Concord Rd.) | 508-357-8883
www.fireflysbbq.com

"Pretty darn good barbecue for a bunch of Yankees" reckon pit aficionados about these "hoppin'", "family-friendly" joints smoking up "enormous quantities" of "amazing ribs" and other "juicy meats" available with a "wide range of sauces" and "tasty sides"; the decor

and service are, in a word, "chain-y", but so is the "tremendous value"; P.S. "remember to get the red velvet cake" for dessert.

Fireplace, The *New England* | 21 | 21 | 20 | $40 |
Brookline | 1634 Beacon St. (Washington St.) | 617-975-1900 | www.fireplacerest.com

"Yes, there is a real live fireplace" at this "intimate", "friendly" Brookliner, but it's the "New England comfort food" featuring "innovative uses of local ingredients" that keeps it on the radar year-round; if "some dishes are just too convoluted" and "too pricey", "excellent wine tastings", "historical theme nights", regularly scheduled live music and other "interesting special events" "keep the community happy."

Five North Square *Italian* | 22 | 18 | 21 | $35 |
North End | 5 North Sq. (Prince St.) | 617-720-1050 | www.5northsquare.com

"Traditional, homelike", "a bit old around the edges" and "cramped at times", this nonetheless "pleasant" Italian exhibits exactly "what you'd like to see in a small, family-run place in the North End"; it also dishes out precisely what most crave in this part of town: "generous portions" of "rich" "red sauce" at moderate prices; P.S. "if you can get the table at the window overlooking the square", it can be "romantic."

Flash's ● *American* | 18 | 16 | 18 | $21 |
Park Square | 310 Stuart St. (Arlington St.) | 617-574-8888 | www.flashscocktails.com

"Nothing fancy" is offered at this Back Bay hangout, but for "after work or to just hang with friends" while scarfing down "quick, cheap" American fare (the "garlic fries are super-yum" – "just don't eat them on a date"), it's "lively and convenient"; like the rest of the staff, "the bartenders are all smiles and know their stuff", as is evident in "sure-bet signature cocktails" both "retro" and "imaginative."

Flat Iron Tapas Bar & Lounge *American* ▽ | 22 | 20 | 18 | $36 |
West End | Bulfinch Hotel | 107 Merrimac St. (Causeway St.) | 617-778-2900 | www.flatironboston.com

"Offering fresh twists on the genre", this "dark, sophisticated" New American tapas lounge with "limited seating" in a West End hotel pairs its "high-quality finger food" with "creative cocktails"; but the fact that the "small plates are smaller than usual" (and "pricey" to boot) steams some noshers, as does service that "needs to wake up."

Fleming's Prime Steakhouse *Steak* | 24 | 22 | 24 | $57 |
Park Square | 217 Stuart St. (bet. Arlington & Charles Sts.) | 617-292-0808 | www.flemingssteakhouse.com

"Not as stuffy" as the competition, this "inviting" chophouse chain purveys "classic" steaks and sides in "relaxed", "clubby" Park Square digs conducive to both "business and romance"; "low-profile" service and an "excellent wine-by-the-glass program" add to its allure, but since "everything's à la carte", be prepared for "high-end" tabs.

FOOD | DECOR | SERVICE | COST

Floating Rock ⌓ *Cambodian*

| - | - | - | I |

Revere | 144 Shirley Ave. (Nahant Ave.) | 781-286-2554

"Hard-core" Cambodian cuisine calls the adventurous to this "backwater storefront" near Revere Beach, where a "kind family" makes the fare "with a lot of care" amid "nonexistent decor"; there's "no liquor, but they do make a mean Thai iced tea" to counteract the "marvelous tiger tears" – "ask for them authentically hot" and be prepared yourself to be "brought to tears."

flora Ⓜ *American*

| 24 | 23 | 24 | $48 |

Arlington | 190 Massachusetts Ave. (Lake St.) | 781-641-1664 | www.florarestaurant.com

Having "done wonders" creating a "comfortable, modern space" out of a "former bank" (it "could be the one from *It's a Wonderful Life*"), this Arlington New American inspires more "revelations" in "inventive" "seasonal" fare "prepared with style and skill" and "inventive", "never-fussy service"; longtime customers calculate "prices are getting a bit high", but they're "balanced" by "great wine specials."

Florentine Cafe *Italian*

| 21 | 20 | 20 | $36 |

North End | 333 Hanover St. (Prince St.) | 617-227-1777 | www.florentinecafeboston.com

It's "too loud for an intimate conversation", and that's just how the "enthusiastic clientele" prefers things at this North End Italian known for its "happening bar scene" and "divine atmosphere" in the summer when "a wall of windows" "opens to the street"; but "reasonably priced", "well-prepared" "classic dishes" and "pleasant service" ensure it's much more than just a "fun place to see and be seen."

flour bakery & café *Bakery*

| 26 | 16 | 18 | $14 |

Seaport District | 12 Farnsworth St. (Congress St.) | 617-338-4333
South End | 1595 Washington St. (Rutland St.) | 617-267-4300
www.flourbakery.com

It's "hard to choose" from the "scrumptious" assortment of "impeccable" soups, salads and sandwiches served at these Seaport District and South End bakery/cafes, and it's just as "difficult to resist" the "moan-producing" pastries like "to-die-for homemade Oreos" and "sinful sticky buns"; the "overwhelming crowds", "cramped" digs and "besieged staff" can make joining the "never-ending lines" "daunting", so be sure to "bring your patience" – and a lot of dough ("it's a little pricey").

Forest Cafe *Mexican*

| 20 | 10 | 17 | $23 |

Porter Square | 1682 Massachusetts Ave. (Sacramento St.) | Cambridge | 617-661-7810 | www.theforestcafe.com

"Still amazing and exotic after all these years" aver advocates of this "shop-worn" "sports bar"/eatery thought of as a "pioneer" in "spicy", "seriously authentic" "regional Mexican" fare in its "easy-to-miss" location between Porter and Harvard squares; but detractors say it's "gone south", "cheap" tabs and drinks that "kick like a mule" notwithstanding.

Franklin, The *American*   26 | 20 | 21 | $35

NEW South Boston | 150 Dorchester Ave. (bet. 4th & 5th Sts.) |
617-269-1003

Franklin Café ◐ *American*

South End | 278 Shawmut Ave. (Hanson St.) | 617-350-0010

Franklin Cape Ann *American*

Gloucester | 118 Main St. (bet. Center & Hancock Sts.) | 978-283-7888
www.franklincafe.com

Some of "the best deals in town" are found in this "always crowded"
trio's "superb", "gourmet-at-a-bargain" New American comfort fare –
which only becomes "expensive" when "the bar tab racks up" with
"killer drinks" during the "endless wait" for a table ("no reservations"); the "cozy" South End "late-night gem" boasts a "dark, sultry
ambiance", the Gloucester branch is "larger" with a "little outdoor
deck", while the South Boston iteration opened post-Survey.

Frank's Steak House *Steak*   18 | 14 | 19 | $33

Porter Square | 2310 Massachusetts Ave. (Rice St.) | Cambridge |
617-661-0666 | www.frankssteakhouse.com

"Remember when we had sour cream on baked potatoes, blue
cheese dressing" on "iceberg lettuce" and steak that didn't "require
a home-equity loan"? – well, "the good old days" are alive and well
at this "reliable, reasonable" beefery in Porter Square that further
evokes "a bygone era" with its "gigantic", "no-frills" space and
weekend "lounge singer"; all in all, it's quite the "throwback"
"experience" – just "don't expect any wows."

NEW **Franky N the Boys** ⊄ *Burgers*   – | – | – | I

Brookline | 284 Washington St. (Harvard Sq.) | 617-739-7371

"For a cholesterol fix", Brookliners "stop in" to this retro red-and-
white newcomer and order off the "limited menu" of "great hand-
packed burgers", fries, shakes and soft drinks; there are "no-frills",
but with such "friendly service" and inexpensive prices, "what's
not to like?"

Z **FuGaKyu** *Japanese*   25 | 22 | 21 | $39

Brookline | 1280 Beacon St. (Harvard St.) | 617-738-1268 ◐
Sudbury | 621 Boston Post Rd./Rte. 20 (Horse Pond Rd.) | 978-443-1998
www.fugakyu.net

"A sushi-lover's dream", this "fin-tastic" Brookliner – with a "minimalist", cafe-style Sudbury offshoot – "always bustles" with "huge
crowds" sampling "innovative" rolls and other "high-quality"
"Japanese delicacies" listed on a "varied", "creative menu"; mostly "efficient" servers navigate two floors featuring a "flashy" lounge, "sushi
bar, private screened rooms and booths", and while it all "comes at a
price", it's "worth the expense" (conversely, "lunch is a steal").

Full Moon *American*   20 | 18 | 22 | $24

Huron Village | 344 Huron Ave. (bet. Chilton & Fayerweather Sts.) |
Cambridge | 617-354-6699 | www.fullmoonrestaurant.com

"Foodie adults" enjoy "sophisticated" New American fare and a
much-needed "glass of wine" while their "sippy-cup"-toting kids

"entertain" themselves with "toys, crayons and a play space" at this Huron Village "original" charging budget-friendly prices; "don't go" unless you can "tolerate hordes" of children the way the "continually cheery staff" can – for their patience, they "deserve early retirement."

▣ Galleria Umberto ⌧⌗ *Italian*   26 | 10 | 17 | $12

North End | 289 Hanover St. (bet. Prince & Richmond Sts.) | 617-227-5709
Newcomers are "dumbfounded by how delicious" and "astonishingly cheap" this "unique" North End "lunch-only" classic's "few items" are – most notably the "splendid" "thick-crust" pizza "blanketed with cheese" and "tangy fresh tomato sauce", "delicious" calzones and "amazing arancini" ("beautiful little deep-fried rice balls"); but if they don't "get there early", they're also stupefied by the "lines around the corner" – and the fact that "when it's out of food", "it closes."

Garden at The Cellar ⓜ *American*   25 | 17 | 20 | $33

Harvard Square | The Cellar | 991 Massachusetts Ave. (Dana St.) | Cambridge | 617-230-5880 | www.gardenatthecellar.com
"Tucked away a little outside Harvard Square", this "unassuming" "gem" offers a "varied" menu of "amazingly seasoned" New American fare made with "straight-from-the-farm" ingredients and served in portions that seem "huge" in light of the "moderate prices"; while the upstairs dining room splits surveyors ("comfortable" vs. "awkward and sterile"), everyone toasts the "great downstairs bar."

Gardner Museum Cafe ⓜ *American*   20 | 21 | 19 | $28

MFA | Isabella Stuart Gardner Museum | 280 Fenway (Palace Rd.) | 617-566-1088 | www.gardnermuseum.org
The "incredible" Gardner Museum "caters to all your senses", and its "lovely" New American midday cafe is "no exception"; "off a grand atrium", the "charmingly intimate", "relaxing" spot with a "glorious" garden proffers "light items" on a "brief menu" that offers "something for everyone" – and while it's "a bit pricey for lunch", it's "usually worth it."

Gargoyles on the Square ⓜ *American*   24 | 21 | 22 | $43

Somerville | 219 Elm St. (Grove St.) | 617-776-5300 | www.gargoylesonthesquare.com
"Always creative" and "sometimes sublime" cheer fans of the New American fare served at this "hip", "intimate" Davis Square spot where every "fairly priced" dish contains "an unusual ingredient" and "extraordinary flair"; a minority decries that the "over-ambitious" combinations "don't always work" while falling "short on value" – but at least they "outshine the strangely curtained decor"; P.S. don your "halter top" for the Sunday disco brunch – "the funnest!"

Gaslight Brasserie du Coin ◗ *French*   21 | 23 | 20 | $39

South End | 560 Harrison Ave. (Waltham St.) | 617-422-0224 | www.gaslight560.com
"Succulent" French brasserie cuisine comes for "surprisingly decent prices" – considering the "swanky" South End location – at this "hip,

fresh" Aquitaine sibling whose "classic", "elegant" decor looks imported from the "Left Bank"; "friendly, knowledgeable" staffers tend to the "lively" "hordes of young professionals" who truly appreciate that the "solid" wine *carte* offers both "great high- and low-end" selections; P.S. "gotta love the free parking!"

NEW G Bar & Kitchen ⊠ *American* ▽ | 21 | 23 | 18 | $55 |

Swampscott | 256 Humphrey St. (Blaney St.) | 781-596-2228 | www.gbarandkitchen.com

"Finally, some good food in 'the Swamp'" applaud early samplers of this newcomer's "interesting", "seasonal" American fare, which is served alongside "great drinks" in "warm, cozy", "sharp-looking" environs marked by a tiled floor, high ceilings and fancy chandeliers; it still needs to "work out kinks" in the service department, but on the whole, Swampscott suppers say it's "worth going back", even with such "expensive" pricing.

Geoffrey's Café ◑ *American* | 19 | 19 | 21 | $29 |

Roslindale | 4257 Washington St. (bet. Kittredge & Poplar Sts.) | 617-325-1000 | www.geoffreyscafebar.com

"Thank goodness it's back" cheer supporters of this muchtransplanted eatery, now a "welcoming" "neighborhood spot" in Roslindale, where "tasty", "satisfying" New American "comfortfood updates" are sold for "reasonable prices"; but "what really makes this place special" is the "patient, knowledgeable" staff, with "fun outdoor seating" coming in a close second.

NEW Ghazal Indian Cuisine *Indian* | - | - | - | M |

Jamaica Plain | 711 Centre St. (bet. Burroughs St. & Harris Ave.) | 617-522-9500 | www.ghazalboston.com

This affordable contemporary Indian in Jamaica Plain's former Café D space boasts a warm dining room with wood floors, granite tabletops and a portrait of the Taj Mahal; a classic Indian buffet at lunch gives way to a more romantic mood for dinner with candlelit tables, low lighting and wine.

Z Giacomo's ≢ *Italian* | 25 | 15 | 20 | $31 |

North End | 355 Hanover St. (bet. Fleet & Prince Sts.) | 617-523-9026
South End | 431 Columbus Ave. (bet. Dartmouth & W. Newton Sts.) | 617-536-5723

"Long lines" "form well before the evening opening" of this "cashonly" North End Italian "mainstay" where patient patrons are "blown away" by "rich, bold", "wonderful-value" pasta and seafood, paired with "inexpensive wines", before being "rushed out" to make way for the "people outside with their noses pressed against the glass"; the South End offshoot serves the same "scrumptious" fare in similarly "cramped", "frenetic" digs, but here it "takes reservations" (you'll still "wait").

Z Gibbet Hill Grill *New England/Steakhouse* | 24 | 26 | 25 | $45 |

Groton | 61 Lowell Rd. (Rte. 119) | 978-448-2900 | www.gibbethill.com

After driving through "rolling hills and small towns", travelers are delighted to come upon this "amazing" 100-year-old "wooden-post-

and-beam" Groton barn with "a central fireplace", serving "high-style" New England steakhouse fare amid "views of grazing cattle"; "attentive, timely" service and a "lively bar" also make it a "special" destination for "date night, a family outing" or a private party in rooms set in a silo.

Ginza *Japanese*   23 | 16 | 20 | $36

Chinatown | 16 Hudson St. (bet. Beach & Kneeland Sts.) | 617-338-2261
Brookline | 1002 Beacon St. (St. Marys St.) | 617-566-9688
www.bostonginza.com

"Nothing will surprise you" at these Brookline and Chinatown "mainstays", but all their patrons "care about" is that the sushi "never misses": it's "always fresh", "tasty" and presented in a "timely" fashion; the "environments lack" and some of the servers can be "intimidating", but as long as they continue to offer lunch "steals" and "very late dining" on weekends (till 3:30 AM on Hudson Street), they're bound to remain "stalwarts."

Glenn's Ⓜ *Eclectic*   ▽ 23 | 19 | 22 | $45

Newburyport | 44 Merrimac St. (Green St.) | 978-465-3811 |
www.glennsrestaurant.com

The "cozy", "dimly lit interior is rather nice", and the pervasively "pleasant" atmosphere even more so at this Newburyport spot to "chill out, munch out" on "wonderful" Eclectic eats and, on Sundays, veg out to "delightful" live jazz; those concerned the regular *carte* is "overpriced" join the "local crowd at the bar" "for a light dinner" via the "extensive appetizer menu."

Glory *American*   ▽ 21 | 19 | 19 | $46

Andover | 19 Essex St. (bet. Brooks & Central Sts.) | 978-475-4811 |
www.gloryrestaurant.com

"A treat" for locals and travelers "en route from NH to MA" alike, this "dark", "happening" Merrimack Valley venue serves "quality" (if "a bit overpriced, even for Andover") New American cuisine in a "romantic", "fireplace"-blessed dining room – which is often "invaded" by the "drunk", "young" singles who create a "real scene" in the lounge.

Golden Temple ⬤ *Chinese*   21 | 20 | 20 | $32

Brookline | 1651 Beacon St. (bet. University & Winthrop Rds.) |
617-277-9722 | www.healthyfreshfood.com

"High-quality" ingredients, "healthier" preparations and "costlier" tabs don't disguise the fact that this Brookliner serves "the Chinese food you grew up with" (read: "Americanized") – what you're really "paying extra" for is its "architecturally interesting design", something akin to the "belly of a fish" or "Thunderdome"; "aging high rollers" come early, while the "disco-fever"-afflicted arrive when it "turns into a nightclub", with a "bumping dance floor" and "terrific drinks."

Good Life Ⓩ *American*   17 | 17 | 16 | $27

Downtown Crossing | 28 Kingston St. (bet. Bedford & Summer Sts.) |
617-451-2622 | www.goodlifebar.com

If you take a seat in the somewhat "cramped" dining room ("with white cloths and roses on the tables") of this Downtown Crossing

American, you "have to remember it's a bar at heart" so as to not think it "a weird paradox" when "drunk after-workers spill" from its dueling lounges; the "gussied-up" "pub food" is "nothing to write home about", but it's "value" priced and "decent" enough for a business lunch.

Grafton Street Pub & Grill *American*   17 | 18 | 17 | $28
Harvard Square | 1230 Massachusetts Ave. (Holyoke St.) | Cambridge | 617-497-0400 | www.graftonstreetcambridge.com
"Young professionals and grad students" frequent this Harvard Square grill for "after-work" drinks and "quick" "pseudo-Irish" New American dinners that are a "notch above pub grub" (and "priced high for what you get"); you never know whether service will be "fine" or "sloppy", but the place is "always crowded" and "noisy", so it may be best to just come for the "preppy" "minglefest after 9 PM" – or in summer, when the "nice patio" and "large windows" open.

Grain & Salt *Indian/Pakistani*   - | - | - | M
Allston | 431 Cambridge St. (Denby Rd.) | 617-254-3373 | www.grainnsalt.com
A red-and-gold dining room with hardwood floors, tables draped in black and low-lit sconces sets a romantic, dramatic tone for this new Allston Indian-Pakistani eatery owned by a native of Mumbai; the modest prices seem even more so thanks to the nearby parking lot.

NEW Grand Chinatown *Chinese*   - | - | - | M
North Quincy | 21A-25 Billings Rd. (Hancock St.) | 617-472-6868
The owners of East Chinatown in North Quincy have opened this 'grander' Chinese around the corner, which serves authentic, mid-priced Cantonese fare in an expansive dining room; N.B. despite a full liquor license, it's beer-and-wine-only until it gets its sea legs.

Grapevine *American/Italian*   25 | 20 | 25 | $46
Salem | 26 Congress St. (Derby St.) | 978-745-9335 | www.grapevinesalem.com
"Wonderful for a celebration dinner", this "lively" Salem "destination" "always satisfies and sometimes inspires" with "superbly executed" New American fare flourishing "creative" Italian flair and paired with "fantastic wines"; if the eggplant-and-cranberry digs "have seen better days", they're "easily overlooked" in light of the "spirited" service and "real treat" of a warm-weather courtyard.

Grasshopper *Pan-Asian/Vegan*   20 | 10 | 16 | $19
Allston | 1 N. Beacon St. (Cambridge St.) | 617-254-8883 | www.grasshoppervegan.com
"Hard-core" vegans "delight" that this "mellow" Allston Pan-Asian even "exists", and they're further "delighted" to report the "extensive menu" boasts "innovative" combinations, "wonderful flavors" and "unbeatable value" (thus "excusing" the "low-budget decor"); confirmed carnivores, on the other hand, opine only a "die-hard tofu lover" could enjoy the "weird pseudo meats."

Great Bay ☒ *Seafood*
23 | 23 | 23 | $58

Kenmore Square | Hotel Commonwealth | 500 Commonwealth Ave. (Kenmore St.) | 617-532-5300 | www.gbayrestaurant.com

At this Kenmore Square "gem", chef/co-owner Michael Schlow imbues "ultrafresh" fin fare with a "host of unexpected flavors", creating "exciting", "*outré* concoctions that please the palate as well as the eyes" (they're "expensive but worth it"); the "beautifully designed" space includes a "trendy bar" where folks get "lively" over "inventive cocktails"; N.B. a post-Survey retool added more comfort to the interior and the menu, which may affect both the Decor and Food scores.

Green Briar *Pub Food*
▽ 17 | 16 | 18 | $21

Brighton | 304 Washington St. (Cambridge St.) | 617-789-4100 | www.greenbriarpub.com

Pay cheap tabs for Irish breakfasts on weekends or PM pub grub any day at this "authentic" Brighton "neighborhood spot" with brogue-sporting servers, live music, televised soccer and a "great back patio"; but even the "college kids and grads" for whom it's a home away from home wonder "why you would go here for anything other than drinking beer?"

Green Papaya *Thai*
20 | 12 | 19 | $24

Waltham | 475 Winter St. (2nd Ave.) | 781-487-9988

Don't let the "nondescript strip-mall" setting or "bland interior" "dissuade you from trying" this Waltham Thai – the "basic" dishes are "fresh", "tasty" and "fairly inexpensive", plus the cooks are "always willing to adjust to individual tastes"; "speedy service" keeps it "crowded" with "business" folk at lunch and take-out diners at dinner.

Green Street *New England*
24 | 19 | 22 | $31

Central Square | 280 Green St. (bet. Magazine & Pearl Sts.) | Cambridge | 617-876-1655

Sure, the "mind-blowing", "inventive cocktails" "get all the attention" ("and deservedly so" – you'll "wish you never wasted time with a Cosmo") at this Central Square spot, but the kitchen exudes a real "enthusiasm for food" with "fabulous", "reasonably priced" "New England-style comforts" (the "offal of the day" is "always a winner"); just "don't judge" it by its "divey" facade: the "intimate" interior's as "classy" as the staff is "friendly."

Greg's Restaurant ☒ *American/Italian*
▽ 19 | 11 | 19 | $24

Watertown | 821 Mt. Auburn St. (Belmont St.) | 617-491-0122

"Popular with the early-bird crowd", this "checkered tablecloth" Watertown "hangout" churns out "midcentury" Italian-American fare featuring "red sauce everywhere" and "durably coated fried food"; "great prices" and a "friendly" staff are two more reasons fans have been "going for 40 years", but honestly, the decor "could use some updating"; P.S. plant your tongue in cheek and hit the bar for "buckets" of "bright-orange 'cheese' dip" and "crackers" – an "amusing plus!"

	FOOD	DECOR	SERVICE	COST

Grezzo Ⓜ Vegan ▽ 23 | 21 | 23 | $42

North End | 69 Prince St. (Salem St.) | 857-362-7288 |
www.grezzorestaurant.com

"Holding its own" in Italian stronghold North End, this vegan venture presents "an innovative approach" to "raw, organic cuisine" with "tasty, nutritious" preparations that are as "beautiful to look at" as the "cozy, plush" surroundings, "colorful with oversized veggie and fruit paintings"; "knowledgeable" staffers add to an "interesting" (albeit "expensive") "new dining experience" – of course, the expected holdouts scoff "there's a reason cooking was invented."

Ⓩ Grill 23 & Bar Steak 25 | 24 | 24 | $66

Back Bay | 161 Berkeley St. (Stuart St.) | 617-542-2255 | www.grill23.com

"Just the right blend of old-world steakhouse" and "new-world trendy" goes into this "opulent" Back Bay "hall of famer" where "the usual suspects" – "suits", "Brahmins", "celebrities" – flock for "bigger-than-life portions" of "phenomenal" meats, "fabulous sides" and an "enormous wine list"; "exemplary service" is par for the course, as are "premium prices" and "noise" that "leaves with your ears ringing."

Grotto Italian 25 | 19 | 22 | $41

Beacon Hill | 37 Bowdoin St. (bet. Beacon & Cambridge Sts.) | 617-227-3434 | www.grottorestaurant.com

"If you're not careful" you might pass this "hidden jewel" in a Beacon Hill basement – so keep your eyes peeled, because its "indulgent" Northern Italian fare is "not to be missed", especially considering the "high quality-to-cost" ratio (the three-course prix fixe is a particularly "awesome" "bargain"); while some can't get past the "cramped" seating, most happily succumb to its "darkly lit", "ultraromantic" "charms" – with the help of "personal service" and "spectacular wines", of course.

Haley House Bakery Café Ⓩ American ▽ 24 | 16 | 20 | $13

Roxbury | 2139 Washington St. (Williams St.) | 617-445-0900 | www.haleyhouse.org

Have a "great breakfast" or lunch with a side of "instant karma" at this American cafe/"bakery with a heart" in Roxbury, which "turns lives around" by offering residents in need "training for culinary careers"; a "diverse" clientele appreciates that the "real treats" are made "using local, organic and seasonal produce" (props to the "rotating art displays" too), but that's just icing on a cake whose "service to the community is beyond belief."

Halfway Cafe Pub Food 17 | 11 | 18 | $19

Dedham | 174 Washington St. (VFW Pkwy.) | 781-326-3336 ☽
Watertown | 394 Main St. (Lexington St.) | 617-926-3595
NEW **Marshfield** | 1840 Ocean St. (Library Plz.) | 781-834-3040
Holbrook | 200 S. Franklin St. (bet. Adams St. & Technical Park Dr.) | 781-767-2900
Canton | Cobbs Corner Plaza | 95 Washington St. (Cobbs Corner) | 781-821-0944

(continued)
Halfway Cafe
Marlborough | 820 Boston Post Rd./Rte. 20 (bet. Farm &
Wayside Inn Rds.) | 508-480-0688 ❂
www.thehalfwaycafe.com

They're really "sports bars", but feel free to "take the kids" to these
"laid-back" "pub-grub" purveyors for "flavorful steak tips" (the "signature dish") and other reliable "cheap eats"; they're "nothing
fancy" – the decor's pretty much just "multiple televisions" and the
service is "typical" for a "family-friendly" chain – but "who can afford fancy all the time?"

Z Hamersley's Bistro *French* | 27 | 23 | 25 | $61 |

South End | 553 Tremont St. (Clarendon St.) | 617-423-2700 |
www.hamersleysbistro.com

"Maestro" Gordon Hamersley remains "very visible" at this "light,
airy" South End "institution", just as his "not-trendy", "seasonally
changing" country French fare "still lives up to its well-deserved reputation", particularly the "luscious" "signature roast chicken" (ru-
mored to trigger "out-of-body experiences"); the "top-notch" fare and
"superior service" command upper-tier pricing, but the "thoughtful
wine list" displays "some good buys."

Harry's Restaurant ❂▱ *Diner* | 20 | 10 | 18 | $24 |

Westborough | 149 Turnpike Rd./Rte. 9 (Lyman St.) | 508-366-8302 |
www.harrysrestaurant.com

"Everything a diner should be", this "small" "all-American" "riot" in
quiet Westborough plies an "eclectic mix of customers" with "great
breakfasts", plus "excellent" fried clams, "pies to die for" and other
inexpensive "greasy-spoon" plates; a "happy, homey" vibe pervades, and the "rapid" staffers keep it all flowing smoothly until the
AM ("go here for a good time late-night").

Haru ❂ *Japanese* | 20 | 21 | 19 | $40 |

Back Bay | 55 Huntington Ave. (Ring Rd.) | 617-536-0770 |
www.harusushi.com

"Prudential Mall masses" make this "very Zen" Back Bay outpost
(bamboo, slate, water features) of the NYC-based chain their choice
for "innovative, delicious maki" and nigiri, plus some "cooked"
Japanese fare, all offered at "prices on the high end of reasonable"; but
said tabs are "unwarranted" warn more discerning palates who judge
the sushi "so-so", the portions "small" and the service "a little slow."

Harvard Gardens ❂ *American* | 17 | 15 | 17 | $28 |

Beacon Hill | 316 Cambridge St. (Grove St.) | 617-523-2727 |
www.harvardgardens.com

More a "bar with food than a restaurant", this "dark" "meat market
for the Mass. General post-shift crowd" ("meet a doctor or nurse!")
serves American pub grub to soak up its "infused martinis" –
unfortunately, the fare's "generally a disappointment for the price"; it's
often "jammed", "making it hard to get around" for both patrons and
servers, the latter "doing their best under difficult circumstances."

Harvest *American*

| 25 | 22 | 23 | $53 |

Harvard Square | 44 Brattle St. (Church St.) | Cambridge | 617-868-2255 | www.harvestcambridge.com

A Harvard Square "institution for more than 30 years", this "oasis" "gracefully serves" "refined", "exquisitely prepared" New American cuisine with "local produce" to "Nobel Prize winners", "classy" "parents" and "employers wooing graduates" (read: "this is not a place to go slumming"); the "warm", "quietly elegant" setting, featuring a "lovely patio" and "stylish", "well-stocked" bar, furthers the feeling that the "pricey" tabs are "worth every penny."

Haveli *Indian*

| - | - | - | I |

Inman Square | 1248-1250 Cambridge St. (Prospect St.) | Cambridge | 617-497-6548

With "tapestry-covered walls" and other "fantastic" decor touches, this Inman Square Indian imparts "the true feeling of a haveli [private residence]", albeit quite a "romantic" one; "great deals" can be found throughout the "reliable, standard" menu, including a daily lunch buffet and "dinner specials that fill you up without emptying your wallet."

☑ Helmand *Afghan*

| 26 | 22 | 21 | $35 |

East Cambridge | 143 First St. (Bent St.) | Cambridge | 617-492-4646 | www.helmandrestaurantcambridge.com

"Who knew Afghani cuisine is so wonderful?" goes the common refrain from first-timers to this "exquisite" East Cambridge eatery where the "unusual, delicious" "food from another world" includes "plenty of vegetarian options" and "scrumptious bread" that comes from a "large oven in the center" of the "warm, romantic main room"; everything is "extremely well-priced" and "arrives quickly" – too fast to thwarted lingerers who feel the staff "can't wait to get you out."

Henrietta's Table *New England*

| 23 | 20 | 21 | $41 |

Harvard Square | Charles Hotel | 1 Bennett St. (Eliot St.) | Cambridge | 617-661-5005 | www.henriettastable.com

There's "always something new on the menu" at this hotel venue in Harvard Square, where the "hearty", "locally sourced" "comfort food" is "just like" "your New England grandmother" made – only "fancier" and "more expensive"; the ambiance in the "large, well-populated" "farmhouse-style" interior and "lovely patio" is forever "cheery", regardless of the "inconsistent" service; P.S. "don't miss the fabulous Sunday brunch."

Highland Kitchen *American*

| 23 | 19 | 21 | $31 |

Somerville | 150 Highland Ave. (Central St.) | 617-625-1131 | www.highlandkitchen.com

"The word is out!" – this relatively new "intimate joint" in "increasingly yuppified" Somerville offers "stellar", occasionally "triumphant" New American cuisine with "delicious" "Southern twists" for "reasonable" rates; indeed, it's "always crowded", especially with a "younger crowd" downing "funky cocktails" while programming the "groovy jukebox" in the bar – but somehow, "friendly service makes it seem less noisy."

	FOOD	DECOR	SERVICE	COST

NEW High Street Grill ⓜ *American/BBQ* | − | − | − | M |

North Andover | 25 High St. (Water St.) | 978-682-6363 | www.25high.net

Tucked away in a historic 19th-century mill in bucolic North Andover, this expansive contemporary spot co-owned by Chris Schlesinger (East Coast Grill) augments its midpriced BBQ with full American entrees; exposed beams and brick walls, plus a concrete bar, wood floors and sconces, lend an intimate, welcoming vibe to the interior, while a back deck keeps heat-seekers cool in the summer.

Hilltop Steak House *Steak* | 16 | 12 | 16 | $34 |

Saugus | 855 Broadway/Rte. 1 (Lynn Fells Pkwy.) | 781-233-7700 | www.hilltopsteakhouse.com

"Your very elderly relative's favorite" Saugus steakhouse – the one with the "seasonally attired" "plastic cows out front" – still draws "enormous volumes of people" who "don't mind" "waiting" for their tables to be called ("fawty-foah to Cah-son City!") before "being herded" to "huge" "theme rooms" with "out-of-date cowboy decor" for "big portions" of "value" beef; while many young 'uns will "never understand" its appeal, the "curious" admit it's "worth at least one trip."

Himalayan Bistro *Indian/Nepalese* | 24 | 17 | 22 | $26 |

West Roxbury | 1735 Centre St. (Manthorne Rd.) | 617-325-3500 | www.himalayanbistro.net

"For a change of pace", this West Roxbury "alternative" augments "fresh" Indian eats with "unique" "Nepalese specials", many delivering "quite a kick", all offering "good value"; the setting is "not enticing at all", but it's "quiet" and sufficiently "comfortable" thanks to "friendly" servers who clearly "take pride in serving their national fare."

Hi-Rise Bread Co. *Bakery/Sandwiches* | 24 | 14 | 14 | $14 |

Harvard Square | 56 Brattle St. (Church St.) | Cambridge | 617-492-3003 🏠

Huron Village | 208 Concord Ave. (Huron Ave.) | Cambridge | 617-876-8766

"Long lines" and "scant" seating don't deter Harvard Square and Huron Village hordes from these bakery/cafes' "innovative" sandwiches "piled high on heavenly fresh-baked bread" and "bursting with flavor" ("pricey" but almost "big enough for two meals"), plus "tasty soups" and "to-die-for pastries"; yes, "everything's delicious" – it's only the "grouchy", "snotty" counter help that "puts a bitter taste in your mouth."

Hot Tomatoes *Pizza* | 22 | 15 | 17 | $19 |

NEW Downtown Crossing | 45 Kingston St. (bet. Bedford & Otis Sts.) | 617-292-0233

North End | 261 North St. (Lewis St.) | 617-557-0033

The "small kitchen" of this "cute", "cramped" North End storefront "manages to produce incredible pizzas" with "fancy ingredients", "amazing soups and salads" and "innovative sandwiches" ("there's a sub to suit any taste bud"); some cost-assessors feel it's "expensive" for a deli, but "for the amount of food you get, it's a great value"; the lunch-only Downtown Crossing locale opened post-Survey.

	FOOD	DECOR	SERVICE	COST

House of Siam *Thai* — 24 | 17 | 19 | $27

South End | 542 Columbus Ave. (Worcester St.) | 617-267-1755
NEW **South End** | 592 Tremont St. (Dartmouth St.) | 617-267-7426
"Mouthwatering dishes" listed on a "menu so big, you get lost in it" are "served with a smile" "for reasonable prices" at these South End Thai "go-tos" for both eat-in and takeout; the Columbus Avenue "staple" "could use a spruce" (good thing it's "dimly lit"), while its slightly smaller Tremont Street sibling opened post-Survey.

House of Tibet Kitchen Ⓜ *Tibetan* — - | - | - | I

Somerville | Teele Sq. | 235 Holland St. (Broadway) | 617-629-7567
"What a find" marvel Somervilleans of this simple, "friendly", "reliable" restaurant when they first sample its "amazing, unique" Tibetan menu, which features "endless options for vegetarians" (it's also quite "comforting" in "cold weather"); "the portion sizes are just right", a real bonus considering how "cheap" it is.

Houston's *American* — 22 | 20 | 21 | $35

Faneuil Hall | Faneuil Hall Mktpl. | 60 State St. (Congress St.) | 617-573-9777 | www.hillstone.com
A "chain that doesn't feel like one", this "reliable" national franchise's Faneuil Hall outpost "clicks" thanks to a "pretty darn good" menu of "all-American comfort" items (including a notoriously "addicting spinach dip") and a "modern metropolitan" ambiance that brings in "mingling singles" and "consistent after-work crowds"; despite debate on the cost – "reasonable" vs. "overpriced" – most report "solid quality" here.

Hungry i, The *French* — 24 | 24 | 22 | $55

Beacon Hill | 71½ Charles St. (bet. Mt. Vernon & Pinckney Sts.) | 617-227-3524
"Many engagements have been sealed" at this "wildly romantic" "cove under Beacon Hill" with "cozy tables" next to three fireplaces, lots of "interesting nooks" and a "secret garden out back"; the "pricey", "outstanding country French fare" exhibits "innovation" while remaining "faithful to tradition", and the "attentive" servers can offer "good advice about" it to "serious foodies" who think it "has nothing to offer."

Ⓩ NEW Hungry Mother Ⓜ *American* — 27 | 22 | 25 | $41

Kendall Square | 233 Cardinal Medeiros Ave. (Binney St.) | Cambridge | 617-499-0090 | www.hungrymothercambridge.com
Settle in for some "high-end Southern comfort" at this "terrific" addition to Kendall Square, where a "small, innovative menu" of "elegant" New American cuisine gets a "Virginia spin" courtesy of "great", "dedicated" chef Barry Maiden (ex Lumière); but don't try it "without a reservation", because the "chic, homey" and "cramped" space is "already insanely busy" with folks keen on the "unique whiskey-based cocktails", "appreciable wine list" and "knowledgeable", "energetic staff."

☒ Icarus *American*

25 | 22 | 23 | $56

South End | 3 Appleton St. (bet. Arlington & Berkeley Sts.) | 617-426-1790 | www.icarusrestaurant.com

"A true classic", this South End "gem" from Chris Douglass is a "consistent performer" in the fields of New American fare ("delicious", "high quality"), service ("gracious", "knowledgeable") and live jazz (Thursday, Friday); while a few quibble the "somewhat stuffy", "fairly sleepy" "underground space" "needs a renovation" to justify such "pricey" checks, the majority counters "you get what you pay for."

☒ Il Capriccio ☒ *Italian*

27 | 22 | 25 | $58

Waltham | 888 Main St. (Prospect St.) | 781-894-2234 | www.ilcapricciowaltham.com

"Waltham's foodie paradise" "impresses" with "luxurious", "magical-at-times" Northern Italian cuisine ("don't miss" the "incredible" mushroom soufflé) – but it's "incomparable" sommelier Jeannie Rogers' "superb", "voluminous wine list" that really "makes the evening special"; some dub the setting a "cold", "tight" "maze", but most say it's "sophisticated", just like the "intelligent service" – "as you should expect for a restaurant in this [upper] price range."

Il Panino Express ⇗ *Italian*

23 | 12 | 17 | $15

North End | 264-266 Hanover St. (Parmenter St.) | 617-720-5720 | www.depasqualeventures.com

North Enders pop into this "little", "no-frills" stop for "quick", "cheap", "homemade Italian" bites like *bene* slices" and "hearty, tasty sandwiches"; the atmosphere's strictly "cafeteria", but it's "nicer" on a "summer night when they open the windows."

Imperial Seafood House ◐ *Chinese/Seafood*

▽ 24 | 11 | 17 | $27

Chinatown | 70 Beach St. (Edinboro St.) | 617-426-8439

"Lots of variety" of "dim sum, shellfish" and other Chinese eats boasting "so much flavor" are served in "copious" portions by an "accommodating" if "not overly friendly" staff at this Chinatown spot; there's "no atmosphere, but you don't go for atmosphere" – you go for a cheap-to-moderately priced meal, especially late at night.

Incontro ◐ *Italian*

22 | 22 | 17 | $43

Franklin | 860 W. Central St. (Forge Pkwy.) | 508-520-2770 | www.incontrorestaurant.com

The folks behind this Franklin Italian have done a "beautiful job fixing up an old mill", outfitting it with a "modern, comfortable" downstairs dining area (it gets "noisy", so "ask for one of the round banquettes" for "a more intimate meal") and a "funky" "see-and-be-seen" bar with billiards upstairs; the fare, especially the wood-fired pizza, is also "superb" (if "a bit pricey for the area") – it's just service that "needs work."

Independent *American*

18 | 19 | 16 | $30

Somerville | 75 Union Sq. (Washington St.) | 617-440-6022 | www.theindo.com

"Two environments – one for eating" a "diverse menu" of "dependable", "occasionally innovative" New American "pub standards"

and some "serious entrees" ("alright for the price"), and "one for drinking" an "excellent selection of craft beers and classic cocktails" – define this Somerville hangout; the service is somewhat "erratic", but the crowd makes it "an oasis of conviviality."

India Pavilion *Indian*

∇ 20 | 13 | 16 | $24

Central Square | 17 Central Sq. (Western Ave.) | Cambridge | 617-547-7463 | www.royalbharatinc.com

"Central Square has no shortage of Southwest Asian" eateries, but this "old reliable" "makes a name for itself" with "pretty generous portions" of "typical", "traditional" Indian fare at "modest" prices; area workers deem it easy "to grab lunch with coworkers", despite having to occasionally "flag down" service (and that it "could use new decor").

India Quality *Indian*

24 | 15 | 21 | $23

Kenmore Square | 484 Commonwealth Ave. (Kenmore St.) | 617-267-4499 | www.indiaquality.com

"Despite its dreary location" in a "cramped" "Kenmore Square basement", this Indian "obsesses" "curry lovers" with its "generous portions" of "out-of-this-world", "value"-priced "staples", all of which "can be tailored to mild, medium or hot"; "quick" "service with a smile" is another reason it has so many "regular customers."

Isabella *American*

24 | 20 | 22 | $40

Dedham | 566 High St. (bet. Eastern Ave. & Washington St.) | 781-461-8485 | www.isabellarestaurant.com

You can really "taste the fresh ingredients" in the "imaginative" New American cuisine created at this Dedham "keeper" whose "high quality" is even more notable for its "reasonable prices"; a reputation as an "oasis of sophistication" is bolstered by "elegant yet casual" environs, characterized by a "nice mural of Isabella Stewart Gardner" and an "accommodating" staff that "always makes you feel welcome."

Island Hopper *Pan-Asian*

19 | 17 | 18 | $24

Back Bay | 91 Massachusetts Ave. (bet. Commonwealth Ave. & Newbury St.) | 617-266-1618 | www.islandhopperboston.com

What a "great idea" marvel "deal"-seekers who happen upon this "solid" Back Bay bastion of all things Pan-Asian – Malaysian, Singaporean, Vietnamese, Thai, Chinese (including "hard-to-find Hainanese dishes") and others – where "quick", "friendly" meals are the norm since it's "usually not crowded"; but "be wary of a restaurant that tries to squeeze in too many cuisines" warn detractors who also shun "cheesy" "island" decor.

⧉ Ithaki
Mediterranean Cuisine Ⓜ *Mediterranean*

26 | 21 | 24 | $43

Ipswich | 25 Hammatt St. (Depot Sq.) | 978-356-0099 | www.ithakicuisine.com

Ipswich Greek groupies tell their Boston counterparts it's "definitely worth the trek" for this "sophisticate's" "expertly prepared and presented", "modern" Med cuisine; they further point toward the "gra-

cious", "attentive" service and "lovely" fresh-flower-festooned environment as reasons it's not only a "guaranteed positive experience", but deserving of the "expensive" cost.

Ivy Restaurant *Italian* 20 | 20 | 17 | $35

Downtown Crossing | 49 Temple Pl. (bet. Tremont & Washington Sts.) | 617-451-1416 | www.ivyrestaurantgroup.com

"Come with friends and share" this "stylish", "loud" Downtown Crossing spot's "delicious, interesting" Italian tapas while perusing the "nice range" of vini priced under $30 (it "falls short for wine snobs", but it's a "great value" to everyone else) and the "young", "scantily clad crowd clustered at the bar"; but "make sure to leave enough time for the relaxed" servers – "just eye candy apparently", when they're "rude."

Jacob Wirth *American/German* 17 | 18 | 17 | $28

Theater District | 31-37 Stuart St. (bet. Tremont & Washington Sts.) | 617-338-8586 | www.jacobwirth.com

One of the Theater District's longest-running attractions, this "landmark" 1868 "beer hall" stars "saucy" servers and "the only authentic German menu in Boston" (tempered with some "less hearty" New American fare, none of it overpriced); ok, it may be wholly "mediocre" and a smidge "shabby", but it's "interesting" from a "historical" perspective, plus the brew list is "a thing to behold", as is the "amazing Friday night sing-along."

Jae's *Pan-Asian* 20 | 16 | 18 | $31

South End | 520 Columbus Ave. (Concord Sq.) | 617-421-9405
Brookline | 1223 Beacon St. (St. Paul St.) | 617-739-0000
www.jaescafe.com

With an "interesting menu" of "dependable sushi" and other Japanese offerings, "spicy Thai" and "traditional Korean fare", this Brookline and South End duo "satisfies" all sorts of Pan-Asian hankerings in one fell swoop and for a "reasonable price"; the fact that it "could use some sprucing" doesn't keep the "crowds" away, which in turn leads to occasionally "slow service"

Jake's Dixie Roadhouse *BBQ* 17 | 13 | 16 | $25

Waltham | 220 Moody St. (bet. Main & Pine Sts.) | 781-894-4227 | www.jakes-bbq.com

"BBQ, blues and beer" are what this "real roadhouse" in Waltham is all about, and its "grubby"-"comfy" atmosphere proves a fitting setting for "good" live music and "different regional" styles of cheap, "mediocre" 'cue served in "big portions"; to say it's "so loud" is an understatement, which is why it works "better as a bar scene."

James's Gate Ⓜ *American/Irish* ▽ 16 | 16 | 18 | $23

Jamaica Plain | 5-11 McBride St. (South St.) | 617-983-2000 | www.jamessgate.com

This "cozy" "place to hang" employs an "Irish-accented staff" that tends a "blazing fire in the winter" as it vends "unpretentious, satisfying" pub grub and "copious" amounts of beer in the bar (there's also a patio come summer); the separate dining room boasts its own "charm

and character", but a few foodies conclude that ordering from its seemingly "more upscale" American menu could be a "mistake."

Jamjuli *Thai*   19 | 16 | 18 | $24

Newton | 1203 Walnut St. (Centre St.) | 617-965-5655 | www.jamjuli.com
"Darn reliable", "quick" Thai for "reasonable prices" makes this "easy-to-drive-past" Newton spot a stop, and while its flavor may be "run-of-the-mill" (despite a "strong range of selections"), you can always "ask" the "friendly people" who work there "to increase the spice" – who knows, that might also make up for the setting's "lack of warmth."

Jasmine Bistro Ⓜ *French/Hungarian*   ▽ 24 | 16 | 25 | $39

Brighton | 412 Market St. (Washington St.) | 617-789-4676
The "extremely personable" family that operates this "cozy" Brighton "treasure" "treats you like one" of its own while plying "spectacular" renditions of "multiple cuisines": French, Middle Eastern and "true Hungarian" ("hard to find in Boston"); it's argu-able that "home cooking shouldn't cost this much", but to the loyal regulars who make it a "destination", it "never disappoints."

Jasper White's Summer Shack *New England*   21 | 14 | 18 | $37

Back Bay | 50 Dalton St. (Boylston St.) | 617-867-9955
Huron Village | 149 Alewife Brook Pkwy. (Cambridge Park Dr.) | Cambridge | 617-520-9500
www.summershackrestaurant.com
Have an "adult meal" of "fresher-than-fresh" "New England sea-food" like "to-die-for clam bakes" while the kids nosh on "great corn dogs" ("if you don't come with a toddler, you're in the minority") at these "noisy" "airplane hangars" in the Back Bay and near Huron Village whose "campy" "decor conjures the coast" with "sticky" "picnic benches and paper tablecloths"; but the fact that it's "prob-ably the most expensive 'shack' you'll ever visit" rankles "pooh-poohing foodies" who call it "completely unremarkable."

Jer-Ne *American*   20 | 22 | 20 | $54

Theater District | Ritz-Carlton Boston Common | 10 Avery St. (Tremont St.) | 617-574-7176 | www.ritzcarlton.com
"Pretty laid-back" for the upscale Ritz-Carlton Boston Common, this stylish, loungey eatery – in which "modern art" hangs below "soaring ceilings" – is a place to go "if you want to sit quietly at a bar and en-joy" "great drinks and snacks" in the Theater District; as for the New American meals, though "elegant", they're too "uninspired" to com-mand checks for which "you need to jer-ne for more money."

NEW Jerusalem Pita *Israeli*   - | - | - | M

Brookline | 10 Pleasant St. (bet. John & Waldo Sts.) | 617-739-2400
There's an uptown urban feel to this small Brookline arrival that im-ports pita and spices for its midpriced kosher Israeli fare, including shawarma, falafel and grilled meats; guests can cozy up to the gran-ite bar for a glass of wine or beer or sit at tables surrounded by mu-rals and shimmering hanging lights.

	FOOD	DECOR	SERVICE	COST

Jimmy's Steer House *Steak*
20 | **16** | **20** | **$27**

Arlington | 1111 Massachusetts Ave. (Quincy St.) | 781-646-4450 | www.jimmysarlington.com
Saugus | 114 Broadway (bet. Rte. 129 & Walnut St.) | 781-233-8600 | www.jimmyssaugus.com

"Older folks and families" "mob" these "not-fancy" Arlington and Saugus "standby" steakhouses for "fair-sized portions" of "consistent" beef that, while "not prime", lies "as close as you can come" for such "modest costs"; "you might need to wait" for a table, although the "harried staff" does its best to get the early birds "home by 6 PM."

Joe's American Bar & Grill *American*
16 | **16** | **17** | **$29**

Back Bay | 279 Dartmouth St. (Newbury St.) | 617-536-4200
North End | 100 Atlantic Ave. (Commercial Wharf) | 617-367-8700
Braintree | South Shore Plaza | 250 Granite St. (I-95, exit 6) | 781-848-0200
Dedham | 985 Providence Hwy. (bet. Rtes. 1 & 128) | 781-329-0800
Peabody | Northshore Mall | 210 Andover St./Rte. 114 (Rte. 128) | 978-532-9500
Woburn | 311 Mishawum Rd. (Commerce Way) | 781-935-7200
Hanover | Merchants Row | 2087 Washington St./Rte. 53 (Rte. 123) | 781-878-1234
Franklin | 466 King St. (Union St.) | 508-553-9313
Framingham | Shoppers World | 1 Worcester Rd./Rte. 9 (bet. I-90 & Rte. 30) | 508-820-8389
www.joesamerican.com

"When in doubt, go to Joe's" for "large portions" of "decent-value" "straight American" chain fare (a "step up from bar food" and "reliable"); it's "noisy" and the "decor is kind of generic"/"corporate", but many branches' "outdoor seating" – especially those in the Back Bay and North End, where they come "for a fraction of the cost" of their neighbors – are "crowd-pleasing" "pluses."

Joe Tecce's *Italian*
19 | **17** | **18** | **$36**

North End | 61 N. Washington St. (Cooper St.) | 617-742-6210 | www.joetecces.com

"For a taste of old-school Italian" "red sauce", head to this "North End institution" where "accommodating" servers bring it in "huge portions" for "reasonable prices"; "every square inch is decorated" with grapes, "urns, mosaics and statues", and though quite a few peg it as a "tacky cliché", still "it's been around so long, you have to pay it some respect – but not very often."

John Harvard's Brew House ❂ *Pub Food*
16 | **16** | **17** | **$25**

Harvard Square | 33 Dunster St. (bet. Mass. Ave. & Mt. Auburn St.) | Cambridge | 617-868-3585
Framingham | Shoppers World | 1 Worcester Rd./Rte. 9 (bet. I-90 & Rte. 30) | 508-875-2337
www.johnharvards.com

The "inexpensive" American pub grub's merely "mediocre", but the "brewed on-site beers" are "terrific" at this "casual gathering place" for "tourists and students" in Harvard Square and its offshoot, "the salvation of suburbanites who don't have much

choice" in Framingham; "lots of TVs" distract "sports-watchers" from the "inconsistent service."

Johnnie's on the Side *Eclectic* ▽ 17 | 18 | 19 | $32
West End | 138 Portland St. (Causeway St.) | 617-227-1588 | www.johnniesontheside.com

A "fun place to meet a bunch of friends" "near the Boston Garden", this West End hangout – a high-ceilinged, "open" room filled with sports-and-movie memorabilia – gets "extremely loud" on event nights; the "wide variety" of moderately priced Eclectic fare is "nothing special", but the fact that it exhibits some "fancy" aspirations leaves critics wondering "what this place is trying to be."

Johnny D's Uptown Ⓜ *American* 19 | 15 | 17 | $24
Somerville | 17 Holland St. (College Ave.) | 617-776-2004 | www.johnnyds.com

"Great" live music "every night of the week" is "definitely the draw" to this Somerville "icon" with "record covers on the walls" and service that swings between "friendly" and "obnoxious"; the "reasonably priced" American pub fare is strictly "concomitant", except at the "crowded, loud" and "awesome weekend" jazz brunch when "slow-cooked oatmeal" and other AM alimentation "stand out."

Johnny's Luncheonette *Diner* 18 | 14 | 17 | $19
Newton | 30 Langley Rd. (bet. Beacon & Centre Sts.) | 617-527-3223 | www.johnnysluncheonette.com

"Gigantic portions" of "retro" American diner food – especially all-day "breakfast items beyond belief" – "at affordable prices" incite "long lines at peak times" for this "cool little '50s-style" "staple" in Newton Center; it's so packed and "noisy" with "multigenerational crowds", you shouldn't be surprised if you have to "chase the staff for everything."

José's *Mexican* 19 | 16 | 20 | $20
Huron Village | 131 Sherman St. (bet. Rindge Ave. & Walden St.) | Cambridge | 617-354-0335 | www.josesmex.com

Lots of tequila buffs consider it "worth the schlep" to this "colorful, slightly rickety" Mexican "on a quiet street" near Huron Village because it always "feels like a party", helped no doubt by "second margaritas that always [seem] way stronger than the first"; as for the fare, it's "reliable", "cheap" and plentiful, if "a tad underspiced."

Joshua Tree *Pub Food* 15 | 14 | 15 | $21
Allston | 1316 Commonwealth Ave. (bet. Griggs & Redford Sts.) | 617-566-6699 | www.joshuatreeallston.com
Somerville | 256 Elm St. (Davis Sq.) | 617-623-9910 | www.joshuatreesomerville.com

"Younger" folks, including "lots of students", descend on these Allston and Somerville sports bars for their "tons" of "high-def flat-screens"; "as a side" to the "excellent beers", the "basic", inexpensive pub grub does the trick, but "as a main meal", it "leaves much to be desired", just like service that "isn't always the quickest."

JP Seafood Cafe *Japanese/Korean*   23 | 15 | 20 | $26

Jamaica Plain | 730 Centre St. (Harris Ave.) | 617-983-5177 |
www.jpseafoodcafe.com

A "solid choice for no-nonsense", "high-quality sushi", this "reliable"
Jamaica Plain Japanese also offers "moderately priced" Korean barbecue delivered by a "welcoming" staff; the "casual, kid-friendly", "fish-
themed" digs can feel like a "noisy" "school cafeteria", which leads
non-parents to decree "all in all, it's probably better for takeout."

Z J's at   26 | 26 | 23 | $44
Nashoba Valley Winery M *American*

Bolton | 100 Wattaquadock Hill Rd. (Berlin Rd.) | 978-779-9816 |
www.nashobawinery.com

"You'll think you're in a farmhouse in Normandy" at this Bolton hill-
top "romantic" with "breathtaking" views of "aromatic orchards" –
even though the "delicious", "adventurous" fare, featuring "produce
grown on the premises", is all (New) American; the "wonderful"
staff does "an excellent job pairing the food with the vineyard's own
fruit wines", and while the cost is "high", the portions make it "a
value"; P.S. bring "a group for brunch" on the "beautiful" patio, "come
early for apple picking" and remain for *vin* "tastings afterward."

Jumbo Seafood *Chinese/Seafood*   23 | 15 | 18 | $28

Newton | 10 Langley Rd. (Centre St.) | 617-332-3600 |
www.jumboseafoodrestaurant.com

New Jumbo Seafood ● *Chinese/Seafood*

Chinatown | 5 Hudson St. (bet. Beach & Kneeland Sts.) | 617-542-2823 |
www.newjumboseafoodrestaurant.com

When it comes to Cantonese fare, this separately owned pair is "a
step above most" (and "a bit more expensive", but "worth it")
thanks to "fresh seafood" you "choose from a tank", supplemented
by "well-prepared" dim sum at weekend brunch; with "white tablecloths and high-definition TVs" "over the bar", the Newton location
sports more of a "modern feel" than the "basic", "cramped"
Chinatown original, while both offer "adequate service."

NEW Jury Room, The Z *American*   ∇ 19 | 17 | 17 | $37

Quincy | 39 Cottage Ave. (Hancock St.) | 617-328-7234 |
www.thejuryroom.us

In the case of this newcomer across from the Quincy courthouse, the
defense argues that the staff is "friendly and helpful", the environment
pleasant (particularly the orange bar, which often hosts live music)
and the American fare "enjoyable", "once you get past the cutesy"
trial-themed menu; but "it's a bit pricey for the neighborhood"
counters the prosecution, which also wants to throw the book at
"so-so service" and the "drab" eggplant-colored dining room.

Karoun Z M *Armenian/Mideastern*   22 | 18 | 21 | $34

Newton | 839 Washington St. (Walnut St.) | 617-964-3400 |
www.karoun.net

"It's all about the belly dancing" say Newtonians who frequent this
"family-run" establishment's "amazing" weekend shows – but it's

also "reliable" for a "kebab fix", as the midpriced Middle Eastern fare, coupled with "authentic Armenian" dishes, "never disappoints"; "the decor could use a bit of modernizing", while the staff is dependably "lovely and welcoming."

Kashmir *Indian*   23 | 19 | 19 | $32

Back Bay | 279 Newbury St. (Gloucester St.) | 617-536-1695 | www.kashmirrestaurant.com

As "classy" and "civilized" as the Back Bay itself, this venue offers "brilliant" Indian cuisine in a "well-decorated" interior where "there's almost never a wait" (because everyone knows the "outdoor seats in nice weather are the way to go"); it's "a bit pricey" for the genre, but it "costs more because it's on Newbury Street" – indeed, the "lunch buffet is the only bargain", but it's "a magnificent one."

Kathmandu Spice *Nepalese*   22 | 16 | 19 | $24

Arlington | 166 Massachusetts Ave. (Lake St.) | 781-316-1755 | www.kathmanduspice.com

"Easily one of the more interesting restaurants in Arlington", this eatery offers "reasonably priced" Nepalese fare featuring a "nice variety of vegetarian and meat dishes", "unusual textures and spices" and "outside influences", especially from "India and Tibet"; the "great" "deal" lunch buffet in particular often draws "noisy crowds" to the "dreary, dull" digs, which the "warm staff" does its best to offset.

Kayuga ◐ *Japanese/Korean*   ▽ 24 | 15 | 20 | $31

Brookline | 1030 Commonwealth Ave. (Babcock St.) | 617-566-8888

Kayuga II *Japanese/Korean*

NEW **Arlington** | 444 Massachusetts Ave. (Medford St.) | 781-648-7878

"Unpretentious", "satisfactory" Japanese and Korean eats, including low-priced sushi, and late hours make this spot a destination for students in Brookline, nondescript atmosphere notwithstanding; meanwhile, its offshoot, a "delightful addition to the growing Arlington restaurant scene", adds Chinese and Thai dishes to the mix while keeping the portions "generous" and the prices "fair."

Kaze ◐ *Japanese*   23 | 16 | 16 | $26

Chinatown | 1 Harrison Ave. (Essex St.) | 617-338-8283 | www.kazeshabushabu.com

"Great for a date", "healthy eating" or to just "show off your boiling skills", this Chinatown "change of pace" offers "a nice range of ingredients and broths" to do shabu-shabu, Japan's more wholesome version of fondue; the "clean, modern", "spacious" space loses points for a "garish" facade, but it matters not to seekers of "fun" "without breaking the bank."

Kebab Factory *Indian*   24 | 16 | 19 | $22

Somerville | 414 Washington St. (Beacon St.) | 617-354-4996 | www.thekebabfactory.net

"Both the skewered and non-skewered" Indian dishes at this "tiny", "distinctive" Somerville spot come "innovatively presented" with "adventurous" "spins" via "friendly, attentive" servers; the some-

what industrialized "decor does little" to attract, but the "nice prices" and "oh-so-yummy lunch buffet" "blow [folks] away."

Khao Sarn Cuisine *Thai*   24 | 20 | 21 | $29

Brookline | 250 Harvard St. (Beacon St.) | 617-566-7200 | www.khaosarn.com

"Exotic" for Brookline, the Northern Thai cuisine offered at this "comfortable" storefront is "delicious, fresh" and "fills your belly without emptying your wallet"; takeout is as "pleasant" as eating in the "elegant, minimalist setting", which features a full bar where "capable", "attentive" servers procure "luscious mango martinis and delicious mai tais."

King & I *Thai*   22 | 14 | 21 | $24

Beacon Hill | 145 Charles St. (Cambridge St.) | 617-227-3320 | www.kingandi-boston.com

"Year after year", this "classic Thai" "in the heart of Beacon Hill" doles out "generous portions" of "inexpensive", "fresh and de-licious" fare, which is "prepared to your taste" "fast" by "friendly" servers; patrons who shun "fairly small" spaces with "unremarkable decor" "stick to takeout."

KingFish Hall *Seafood*   22 | 20 | 20 | $46

Faneuil Hall | Faneuil Hall Mktpl. | 188 Faneuil Hall Marketplace (Chatham St.) | 617-523-8862 | www.toddenglish.com

"Due to its Faneuil Hall location", this "large place" is "filled with tourists", but locals get "reeled in" too due to "Todd English's mas-tery of seafood" with "delicious twists", which "friendly, efficient" servers deliver alongside "fun cocktails" on two "noisy" floors with "riotous clam-shaped booths", a "splendid patio" and "terrific raw bar"; if only it weren't "such a hit on the wallet."

Kingston Station ❂ *French*   20 | 18 | 19 | $29

Downtown Crossing | 25 Kingston St. (bet. Bedford & Summer Sts.) | 617-482-6282 | www.kingstonstation.com

"Short money" gets Downtown Crossing lunch-goers and after-workers "solid" French fare, "inventive drinks" and "unpretentious wines" from a "focused list" ("love that it serves by the glass, half-carafe, full-carafe" or bottle) at this "laid-back" bistro; though the "cool" decor's tiled surfaces make a "noisy" first impression, the "personable" staff engenders the intended "cozy atmosphere."

KO Prime *Steak*   24 | 22 | 23 | $66

Downtown Crossing | Nine Zero Hotel | 90 Tremont St. (Bosworth St.) | 617-772-0202 | www.koprimeboston.com

"Ken Oringer has outdone himself" at his "exciting" "nontraditional steakhouse" in Downtown Crossing's "boutique-y Nine Zero Hotel", which "delivers what the masses expect" ("handsome presenta-tions" of "amazing" beef) alongside more "cutting-edge" fare (the "chef likes to use all of the animal", so expect plenty of offal); the "sexy scene", "plush" environs, "trendy" cocktail "concoctions" and "beautiful", "young" crowd are expectedly "over the top" – is it any wonder the prices are "sky high" too?

Koreana *Japanese/Korean*   21 | 14 | 17 | $30

Central Square | 154 Prospect St. (Broadway) | Cambridge | 617-576-8661 |
www.koreanaboston.com

An "authentic" "grill-your-own" Korean barbecue experience awaits at this spot between Central and Inman Squares, where the "intense, exotic flavors" of "incredible marinades" and "interesting sides" can be coupled with hot pots and sushi; despite "nothing-special decor", it's usually "lively" with "students" for whom "fair prices" trump "mediocre service."

Kouzina ⊠Ⓜ *Greek/Mediterranean*   23 | 16 | 21 | $37

Newton | 1649 Beacon St. (Windsor Rd.) | 617-558-7677

"Such a prize" is this storefront's "consistently delicious", "fairly priced" Greek and Mediterranean fare (with "some innovative takes") and "personalized service" that fans "don't want anyone else to know about it"; but it's obviously too late since the "tiny" space located in Newton's Waban neighborhood with "very close" tables "fills up fast" despite the promise of "noise", "uncomfortable seating" and "drafts when the door opens" in winter.

Kowloon ⬤ *Pan-Asian*   17 | 17 | 15 | $26

Saugus | 948 Broadway/Rte. 1 (Main St.) | 781-233-0077 |
www.kowloonrestaurant.com

"Gloriously tacky", this "huge", "always packed" 1950 Saugus "institution"/"food factory"/exercise in "frivolity" offers the "spectacle" of "throwback Polynesian decor" (like a "tiki party" on "acid"), plus a "dizzying array" of Pan-Asian fare; but it's "rather greasy" say foodies who are "amazed" what people "drunk" on "scorpion bowls" will "put in their mouths"; P.S. weekend music and "comedy shows upstairs" make for complete nights of "entertainment."

🆉 La Campania ⊠Ⓜ *Italian*   28 | 25 | 26 | $59

Waltham | 504 Main St. (bet. Cross & Heard Sts.) | 781-894-4280 |
www.lacampania.com

For a "special" "event", "reserve well in advance" for this "sublime" Waltham "experience" where "wonderfully flavorful, well-plated and inventive Italian cuisine" is conveyed by "exquisite, unobtrusive" staffers in a "charmingly rustic", "romantic" dining room; a "stellar wine list" completes the nearly "flawless package", and though you may be "surprised at how expensive" it is, this is one "splurge" that's "worth every penny."

La Cantina Italiana *Italian*   ∇ 20 | 13 | 19 | $24

Framingham | 911 Waverly St. (Winter St.) | 508-879-7874 |
www.golacantina.com

"Huge plates of pasta like your nona used to make" are the linchpins of the "hearty" "old-time Italian" menu that's been drawing Framingham "parm fans" to this kitchen for more than 50 years; because the proprietors "don't gouge you" and "treat you like family", "seniors" and folks with "kids" just grin and bear the "less than desirable" decor.

La Casa de Pedro *Venezuelan*   21 | 20 | 20 | $31

Watertown | 343 Arsenal St. (School St.) | 617-923-8025 |
www.lacasadepedro.com

"Pedro himself" "keeps a close eye" on the "spicy", "scrumptious",
"reasonably priced" Venezuelan vittles (featuring lots of "memorable meat dishes") and "potent mojitos" served at his "bustling",
"cavernous" Watertown *casa*; the "bright", "colorful" interior ("you
have to see the palm trees") hosts "fun" live music Thursday-
Saturday, while the patio is a "great place to sit" in the summer.

La Famiglia Giorgio *Italian*   23 | 14 | 22 | $27

North End | 112 Salem St. (bet. Cooper & Prince Sts.) | 617-367-6711 |
www.lafamigliagiorgio.com

"Go on an empty stomach" and down as much of the "ridiculously enormous portions" of "hearty" "red-sauce Italian" as you
can at this "family-style" "strong value" in the North End; the
mural-bedecked digs are "too crowded and noisy" for some, but
the "friendly, efficient" staff "knows how to make customers feel
right at home."

La Galleria 33 *Italian*   ▽ 26 | 22 | 22 | $40

North End | 125 Salem St. (Prince St.) | 617-723-7233 |
www.lagalleria33.com

"Huge portions" of "fine Italian cuisine" are offered for prices that
most consider "reasonable" at this venue with a "hot location" in the
North End; the service is as "relaxed" as the setting, a "pretty room"
with an open kitchen, French doors and exposed brick that peeks
from behind large-scale art pieces.

Lala Rokh *Persian*   23 | 21 | 22 | $43

Beacon Hill | 97 Mt. Vernon St. (Cedar St.) | 617-720-5511 |
www.lalarokh.com

"Exotic" yet "subtle flavors" born of "unusual ingredients" are the
hallmarks of the "refined" Persian cuisine offered at this Beacon Hill
destination – and it's elevated to a "ceremonial level" via "professional, eager" staffers that "guide diners through the sophisticated
menu"; most agree the "intimate", "subdued" setting abets "romance", while a cadre of critics admit to being "a little underwhelmed" in the wake of such "high expectations", calculating you
must be "paying for the address."

La Morra *Italian*   24 | 20 | 23 | $47

Brookline | 48 Boylston St. (bet. Cypress St. & Harvard Ave.) |
617-739-0007 | www.lamorra.com

"Give us more of La Morra" beg Brookline Villagers of this "upscale
neighborhood" "charmer" (with an "odd location" "on the high-
way"), not least of all because its "superb" Northern Italian entrees,
"yummy small plates" and "wonderful wine selection" are "fairly
priced" for the "high quality"; "hands-on owners" patrol the "warm",
"rustic" "multilevel environment" (admittedly, it "can be noisy"),
ensuring that the "informal yet gracious" servers "hustle"
when need be.

	FOOD	DECOR	SERVICE	COST

Lam's *Thai/Vietnamese* — 21 | 15 | 20 | $24

Newtonville | 825 Washington St. (Walnut St.) | 617-630-5222 |
www.lamsrestaurant.com

Newton "families" "keep coming back" to this "relaxing" "pleaser"
because they "know what they're going to get every time": Thai and
Vietnamese fare "deliciously prepared" with "colorful, fresh ingredients" by a "charming", "friendly" staff; as for the "modest surroundings", they just don't matter vis-à-vis the "fairly inexpensive" tabs.

L'Andana *Italian* — 25 | 24 | 23 | $55

Burlington | 86 Cambridge St. (Arlington Rd.) | 781-270-0100 |
www.landanagrill.com

"Suburban foodies" turn up at this "vibrant" Burlington sophomore
from chef-owner Jamie Mammano (Mistral, Sorellina, Teatro) for
"fancy", wood-grilled Italian dishes presented in rustic, "barnlike"
digs; the "cavernous" setting may "take away from some of the inti-
macy" and prices can be "out of sight", but most find it an "excellent
option" when you "don't want to drive into the city."

Landing, The *American* — ▽ 16 | 21 | 20 | $36

Manchester-by-the-Sea | 7 Central St. (School St.) | 978-526-7494 |
www.thelandingat7central.com
Marblehead | 81 Front St. (State St.) | 781-631-1878 |
www.thelandingrestaurant.com

These "picturesque" venues in Manchester-by-the-Sea and
Marblehead are dining "staples", offering "standard" American comfort chow for "reasonable" sums; while the "old-school" cooking "may
not approach the quality found in Boston's greatest restaurants", "fun
locations", "water views" and "good bar scenes" compensate.

La Paloma Ⓜ *Mexican* — 21 | 15 | 19 | $24

Quincy | 195 Newport Ave. (Hobart St.) | 617-773-0512 |
www.lapalomarestaurant.com

With help from a "friendly, efficient" staff, this "festive" cantina
brings a south-of-the-border groove to Quincy via "authentic tasting" Mexicana and "fantastic" margaritas; despite "tacky decor",
"long lines" and "strip-mall" atmospherics, those who "like it hot"
dub it a "good cheap-eats destination."

La Summa *Italian* — ▽ 22 | 18 | 22 | $35

North End | 30 Fleet St. (bet. Atlantic Ave. & Hanover St.) | 617-523-9503
For "no-frills", "reasonably priced" Southern Italian dining, you can't
go wrong at this "old-world" North Ender where a "friendly" crew
ferries "good-sized portions" in a "warm" room that's "like being at
your grandmother's"; snobs sneer it's "second tier", yet admit the
chow is "solid" – and "you'll always leave full."

Laurel *American* — 20 | 18 | 20 | $34

Back Bay | 142 Berkeley St. (Columbus Ave.) | 617-424-6711 |
www.laurelgrillandbar.com

Though the New American food "looks expensive", the pricing is actually "decent" at this "nonpretentious spot" that's "definitely a switch"

| | FOOD | DECOR | SERVICE | COST |

from the usual in the Back Bay; some say the menu and setting are beginning to "show their age", but most laud it for the "generous" portions, "aim-to-please" service and "relaxed, peaceful" air.

NEW Lavender Asian Cuisine & Bar *Asian* — | — | — | I

Sudbury | Sudbury Plaza | 519A Boston Post Rd. (Rte. 20) | 978-579-9988 | www.lavenderasiancuisine.com

Fresh ingredients are the hallmark of this suburban arrival inside the Sudbury Plaza shopping center, serving inexpensive, MSG-free Asian cuisine, including Chinese, Thai, Malaysian and Japanese (*sans* sushi); its carpeted dining room features white-clothed tables, a Great Wall of China illustration and a resplendent blue-pearl-topped bar.

La Verdad *Mexican* 22 | 14 | 15 | $27

Fenway | 1 Lansdowne St. (Ipswich St.) | 617-421-9595 | www.laverdadtaqueria.com

Fans of "amazing" Mexican chow "on the cheap" cheer Ken Oringer's "bright spot in the Fenway", vending "authentic" street eats in a dining room and via the taqueria's take-out counter; cynics nix "teeny-tiny" portions, "uneven" service and "way too loud" acoustics – especially "when the Sox are in town" – but agree that the "great tequila list" knocks it out of the park.

La Voile 23 | 23 | 22 | $55
Boston Brasserie *French/Mediterranean*

Back Bay | 259 Newbury St. (bet. Fairfield & Gloucester Sts.) | 617-587-4200 | www.lavoileboston.net

"Real French waiters" with "Cannes-do" attitudes serve "outstanding" Gallic coastal classics (as well as Mediterranean dishes that are "true to their origins") at this *très belle* Back Bay room with a "sailing theme"; sure, it's a bit "pricey" and many "wish it were easier to get a table", but overall it's a "wonderful" "brasserie translation."

Left Bank *American* ▽ 21 | 20 | 20 | $66

Tyngsboro | Stonehedge Inn | 160 Pawtucket Blvd. (Rte. 113) | 978-649-4400 | www.stonehedgeinnandspa.com

Somewhat "more casual" than its predecessor, Silks, this "reinvented" New American in Tyngsboro's Stonehedge Inn "continues its tradition" of "leisurely dining" with a "creative" menu paired with an "extensive wine list"; but with such "high prices", it may be more appropriate for "special occasions" and "romantic" trysts.

Z Legal Sea Foods *Seafood* 22 | 18 | 20 | $41

Back Bay | Copley Pl. | 100 Huntington Ave. (bet. Dartmouth & Exeter Sts.) | 617-266-7775
Back Bay | Prudential Ctr. | 800 Boylston St. (Fairfield St.) | 617-266-6800
Park Square | 26 Park Plaza (Columbus Ave.) | 617-426-4444 ◑
Waterfront | Long Wharf | 255 State St. (Atlantic Ave.) | 617-227-3115
Harvard Square | 20 University Rd. (Eliot St.) | Cambridge | 617-491-9400
Kendall Square | 5 Cambridge Ctr. (bet. Ames & Main Sts.) | Cambridge | 617-864-3400
Braintree | South Shore Plaza | 250 Granite St. (I-95, exit 6) | 781-356-3070
(continued)

(continued)

Legal Sea Foods

Chestnut Hill | Chestnut Hill Shopping Ctr. | 43 Boylston St. (Hammond Pond Pkwy.) | 617-277-7300

Peabody | Northshore Mall | 210 Andover St./Rte. 114 (Rte. 128) | 978-532-4500

Framingham | 50-60 Worcester Rd./Rte. 9 (bet. Concord & Speen Sts.) | 508-766-0600

www.legalseafoods.com

Additional locations throughout the Boston area.

"Chain shmain!" – this seafood "institution" again earns Boston's Most Popular restaurant title not (only) due to its "ubiquity", but because of its "consistent" delivery of "guaranteed-fresh, well-prepared" fish, from the "basic" to the "ambitious", plus a "surprisingly decent wine list"; the "big, bustling" settings swing from "plain-Jane" to "upscale" ("service varies" too), and while even admirers admit it's "perhaps a little overpriced", it's "worth it" for such "quality."

Le Lyonnais Ⓜ *French*

▽ 23 | 18 | 23 | $42

Acton | 416 Great Rd./Rte. 2A (Rte. 27) | 978-263-9068 | www.lelyonnaisacton.com

The "pleasant setting" for this "quaint" Acton bistro is a "well-appointed", circa-1850 house where "classic" Gallic cuisine reminiscent of "the France of yesterday" is served for "reasonable" prices; while the "cozy" mood and "good service" make it an "old standby" for some, others report "dated ideas" that yield "uninspired" fare.

Le's *Vietnamese*

21 | 13 | 16 | $17

Allston | 137 Brighton Ave. (Harvard Ave.) | 617-783-2340

Harvard Square | 35 Dunster St. (Mt. Auburn St.) | Cambridge | 617-864-4100

Chestnut Hill | Atrium Mall | 300 Boylston St. (Florence St.) | 617-928-0900

www.lesrestaurant.com

"Amazing bargains" "under any name", these Vietnamese siblings – once known as Pho Pasteur – offer "giant bowls" of pho "with all the fixin's" plus other "traditional dishes" for "college budget" tabs; despite "bland" decor and "spotty" (albeit "lightning fast") service, they're "reliable" choices for a "quick" bite.

Ⓩ L'Espalier *French*

28 | - | 28 | $95

Back Bay | 774 Boylston St. (bet. Exeter & Fairfield Sts.) | 617-262-3023 | www.lespalier.com

"An extraordinary culinary adventure" awaits at this Back Bay "legend" where the "unforgettable textures, flavors and scents" of its "inventive" New French cuisine – once again "soaring above the rest" to earn Boston's No. 1 Food rating – are "matched" to "world-class wines" by "extremely well-informed", "never stodgy" staffers; post-Survey, it moved into "more spacious", "modern" digs connected to the Mandarin Oriental, and while "the jury's out as to how it translates" ("can a hotel have the warmth and charm of the old brownstone?"), "as long as" "genius" chef Frank McClelland is "in the kitchen", longtime fans with "fat wallets" will "be in the dining room."

Les Zygomates 🗷 *French/Mediterranean*   22 | 20 | 20 | $44

Leather District | 129 South St. (Essex St.) | 617-542-5108 |
www.winebar.com

Imagine "Paris at South Station" at this "relaxed yet upscale"
Leather District bistro where "classic" French-Med dishes "done
with panache" are served by "welcoming" staffers in "brick-and-
beam"-lined digs; "good value", "great live jazz" and "interesting
wines by the glass" further make it a "treasure."

Lexx *American*   17 | 18 | 17 | $37

Lexington | 1666 Massachusetts Ave. (bet. Grant St. & Wallis Ct.) |
781-674-2990 | www.lexx-restaurant.com

With its "homey" bar, "pleasant atmosphere" and "dependable"
cooking, this somewhat "upscale" New American is a "solid" alternative to the sea of "chain restaurants" in Lexington; while "not bad for a
suburban place", locals shrug it's "safe if somewhat boring", citing
"spotty service" and "above-average prices for just average food."

Lil Vinny's Ristorante *Italian*   ▽ 20 | 13 | 19 | $30

Somerville | 525 Medford St. (Broadway) | 617-628-8466 |
www.lilvinnys.com

"Home-cooked" Southern Italian fare, a "warm" vibe and "friendly"
service make this "family-run" Somerville "red-sauce" specialist a
"nice neighborhood" option (it's a sibling of the popular Vinny's at
Night); given its "small" dimensions and "good value for the
money", don't be surprised by a "busy" scene on weekends.

Limoncello *Italian*   22 | 19 | 21 | $42

North End | 190 North St. (Richmond St.) | 617-523-4480 |
www.ristorantelimoncello.com

This North End Italian on the Freedom Trail "feels like home", with
its "welcoming" atmosphere and "entertaining" staffers, and boasts
an "interesting" back story – the place was bankrolled from lotto
winnings; though a minority finds things a bit "ordinary", they admit
the food arrives in "generous portions" and the "large" dining room
"accommodates groups" easily.

LiNEaGe 🅼 *American*   23 | 20 | 23 | $45

Brookline | Coolidge Corner | 242 Harvard St. (Beacon St.) | 617-232-0065 |
www.lineagerestaurant.com

Brookline's Coolidge Corner is home to this neighborhood "hideaway", a "top-notch" destination for "seasonal", "farm-fresh" New
Americana (though insiders hint it's "best for fish"); sure, it may be
"a bit on the expensive side", but "informative" service, a "warm"
setting and a "cool crowd" make for "always pleasant" dining;
P.S. the butterscotch pudding is "not to be missed."

Little Q Hot Pot ● *Mongolian*   ▽ 25 | 14 | 23 | $21

Quincy | 1585 Hancock St. (Revere Rd.) | 617-773-5888 |
www.littlequsa.com

"Hands-on" diners in the mood to "cook their own food" turn up at this
Quincy hot-pot spot where the "exotic" Mongolian/Chinese offerings

are both "delicious" and "addictive"; despite decor that "leaves a little to be desired", this "really cool concept" can be a "great date option" given its "fun" vibe, "helpful" staff and cheap tabs.

NEW Littlest Bar, The *Pub Food* — | — | — | I

Financial District | 102 Broad St. (Wharf St.) | 617-542-8469
This legendary watering hole, once tucked inside a shoebox of a space in Downtown Crossing, has moved into not-so-little digs in the Financial District and added American pub grub (lunch and dinner) to go with the nearly dozen beers on tap; the handsome wood bar is adorned with two TVs, though the overall effect is still cozy.

Living Room, The ● *American* 15 | 19 | 15 | $29

Waterfront | 101 Atlantic Ave. (Richmond St.) | 617-723-5101 | www.thelivingroomboston.com
A no-brainer for "after-work drinks", this "yuppie" Waterfront lounge-cum-eatery is better known for its "great nightlife" scene – so long as you're "under 25" – than its "subpar" New American grub; indeed, sluggish service and "small portions for big prices" lead many to sigh it "could be so much better."

NEW Local, The *American* — | — | — | M

West Newton | 1391 Washington St. (Elm St.) | 617-340-2160
This West Newton gastropub promises to live up to its name with New England–brewed beers on tap and sustainable, moderately priced New American comfort food; sleek and open yet invitingly dark, it's the kind of upscale watering hole where you can settle into the dining room for a meal or catch a game on TV at the bar.

Locke-Ober ☒ *American/Continental* 24 | 25 | 24 | $66

Downtown Crossing | 3 Winter Pl. (bet. Tremont & Washington Sts.) | 617-542-1340 | www.lockeober.com
"Important" dining lives on at this Downtown Crossing "institution", a circa-1875 "trip back in time" that "lives up to its reputation" as a perennial "business" and "special-occasion" dinner destination; "classic clubroom" looks and "old-world service" set the tone for the "reimagined" Continental classics and "creative" New American dishes by chef Lydia Shire, and the overall "outstanding" quality leads "blue bloods" to declare it's "still a grande dame" – despite a few rumbles that it "could be better for the prices charged."

Longfellow's Wayside Inn *New England* 18 | 24 | 21 | $38

Sudbury | Longfellow's Wayside Inn | 72 Wayside Inn Rd. (Rte. 20) | 978-443-1776 | www.wayside.org
Set in what is billed as America's oldest continuously operating inn, this "historic jewel" in Sudbury transports you to "Colonial Massachusetts" with its ultra-"traditional" New England menu and "time-warp" decor ("rustic tables, uneven floors"); granted, it's "not the place for haute cuisine", but the food is "solid Yankee" all the way and its "gorgeous grounds" and "homey service" make it a "family" destination if nothing else.

FOOD DECOR SERVICE COST

L'Osteria *Italian* 23 | 16 | 21 | $34

North End | 104 Salem St. (Cooper St.) | 617-723-7847 | www.losteria.com
This longtime North End staple "hasn't changed a bit", plating "plentiful" portions of "classic", "honest" Italian food in a setting that's "fine for families" and "large groups" (but "not romantic enough for a date"); a "jovial" mood, "great prices" and "wonderful husband-and-wife" owners have fans purring this one "fits like an old slipper."

Lotus Blossom *Chinese/Japanese* 22 | 21 | 21 | $30

Sudbury | 394 Boston Post Rd./Rte. 20 (Station Rd.) | 978-443-0200 | www.lotuscuisine.com
Sudbury diners in search of "upscale Chinese" head to this "popular" spot offering a "varied", "Westernized menu" alongside sushi; "pleasant" service and "tasteful" decor compensate for "long waits" on weekends and the fact that it's "a bit pricey" for the genre.

LTK *Eclectic* 20 | 19 | 17 | $37

Seaport District | 225 Northern Ave. (D St.) | 617-330-7430 | www.ltkbarandkitchen.com
"Definitely different" and "more edgy" than its parent, Legal Sea Foods, this Seaport District Eclectic aims for a "younger demographic" with an "expansive menu" of "innovative" dishes with an Asian influence; it's "loud but fun" and particularly "great before a show at the nearby Bank of American Pavilion", but "overworked" staffers and "noisy" acoustics lead some to report "hit-or-miss" experiences – still, supporters say "that's why it's a test kitchen."

Lucca ● *Italian* 25 | 22 | 22 | $50

North End | 226 Hanover St. (Richmond St.) | 617-742-9200 | www.luccaboston.com
This "sleek" yet "comfortable" North End Northern Italian is just the place for an "upscale night out" with a "wonderful", "not-your-standard-red-sauce" menu, "exceptional service" and a "prime" Hanover Street location (the "front windows are great for people-watching"); it's "noisy upstairs, more romantic downstairs", but wherever you wind up, it's fairly "pricey."

Lucky's Lounge *American* 18 | 20 | 17 | $27

Seaport District | 355 Congress St. (A St.) | 617-357-5825 | www.luckyslounge.com
A Fort Point Channel "hideout" with a "very '50s" vibe, this Seaport "retro lounge" serves "delicious" American comfort grub for a "reasonable price" – "if you can find it" (there's "no sign" and it's "subterranean"); still, "twentysomething" fans say it's "not about the food", rather the "late-night" scene, "cocktails-are-king" mood and live entertainment, including Sunday night's "Sinatra" homage.

☑ Lumière *French* 27 | 23 | 26 | $57

Newton | 1293 Washington St. (Waltham St.) | 617-244-9199 | www.lumiererestaurant.com
Demonstrating "what can be done with a few exceptional ingredients", Michael Leviton's West Newton "destination restaurant" of-

fers an "ever-changing" menu of "consistently superb" New French dishes with an "emphasis on local produce" (you can "feel the love with each bite"); the "classy white", "modernist" setting, "impeccable" service and "quiet" sophistication make it a natural for "special-occasion" dining, and even though it's "a little dear" pricewise, it "never fails to please."

Lyceum Bar & Grill *American*   23 | 21 | 21 | $39

Salem | 43 Church St. (Washington St.) | 978-745-7665 | www.lyceumsalem.com

Housed in the "historic", circa-1843 building from which Alexander Graham Bell made the first telephone call, this "consistent" Salem "classic" keeps the trade brisk thanks to "fresh", "first-rate" cooking and a particularly "great brunch"; "wonderful" staffers, "well-spaced tables" and a "welcoming atmosphere" have made it a "solid" destination for over 20 years.

Machu Picchu *Peruvian*   19 | 13 | 15 | $24

Somerville | 25 Union Sq. (Stone Ave.) | 617-623-7972
Somerville | 307 Somerville Ave. (bet. Hawkins St. & Warren Ave.) | 617-628-7070
www.machupicchuboston.com

Transporting you from Somerville to "Lima", these "garlicky" "gems" are celebrated for their "terrific" Peruvian dishes, most notably "amazing" rotisserie chickens; ok, their interiors are "not the prettiest" things around, but "fun atmospheres" and "affordable" tabs serve as distractions.

Maddie's Sail Loft *New England/Seafood*   ▽ 18 | 18 | 18 | $25

Marblehead | 15 State St. (bet. Front & Washington Sts.) | 781-631-9824 | www.maddiessailloft.com

This "classic sailing bar" – a "Marblehead staple" since 1946 – is a "spirited" "holdout" from the town's "pre-boutique" era, populated by "locals" who drink in the downstairs pub and nosh on New England seafood in the upstairs dining room; fans say this "unique maritime experience" has benefited from "new ownership", i.e. "better service" and "improvements overall."

Maggiano's Little Italy *Italian*   19 | 18 | 19 | $33

Park Square | 4 Columbus Ave. (bet. Boylston & Stuart Sts.) | 617-542-3456 | www.maggianos.com

You almost "expect to see Sinatra walk in behind you" at this "1940s-esque", checkered-tablecloth chain where "monster portions" of "red-sauce" Italiana are dished out in "enjoyably hectic" Park Square surroundings; some dub it a "mixed bag", citing a "mass-production", "quantity-trumps-quality" approach, but fans tout this "crowd-pleaser" as a "big night out" for "not a lot of money."

Mamma Maria *Italian*   25 | 22 | 23 | $54

North End | 3 North Sq. (Sun Court St.) | 617-523-0077 | www.mammamaria.com

Ignore the "hokey name": this North End Northern Italian is one "classy" joint, an "upscale", "special-occasion" magnet whose "ro-

mantic" environs (a series of "small rooms") are spread throughout a "beautiful old townhouse"; it's known for "inventive twists" on classic dishes, "lovely service" and "valet parking", and in spite of some "steep pricing", it's consistently "mobbed on weekends" – "reservations are only estimates" here.

Mantra ☒ *French/Indian* | 18 | 21 | 16 | $47 |

Downtown Crossing | 52 Temple Pl. (bet. Tremont & Washington Sts.) | 617-542-8111 | www.mantrarestaurant.com

Fusing "Indian food with French preparation" techniques, this Downtown Crossing hybrid "tries hard" but unfortunately "doesn't quite meet expectations" – and is "expensive" to boot; still, the atmosphere is "hip", the crowd "young" and the decor "fabulous" (a "clever" reworking of a former bank building), making the sometimes "nonexistent" service more bearable.

Marco Cucina Romana Ⓜ *Italian* | 26 | 21 | 25 | $47 |

North End | 253 Hanover St., 2nd fl. (bet. Cross & Parmenter Sts.) | 617-742-1276 | www.marcoboston.com

"Literally a level above the competition", this "charming" North Ender – "tucked away on the second floor of a building on busy Hanover Street" – is "worth climbing a flight of stairs" for a taste of the "hearty", "real-deal" Northern Italian cooking of chef Marc Orfaly (Pigalle); "informative" service and a "cozy", "intimate" vibe enhance its allure, but the space is "small", so "reservations are essential."

Mare *Italian* | 26 | 21 | 22 | $51 |

North End | 135 Richmond St. (North St.) | 617-723-6273 | www.mareorganic.com

A "top-notch" mix of "imaginative seafood" and dishes assembled from mostly "organic" ingredients makes this "modern" Italian rather "unusual for the North End"; "attentive" service, "trendy" atmospherics and an "all-too-cool" setting (including "full-length windows" that open up to the street in the summertime) help justify the rather "expensive" outcome.

NEW Market ☒ *American* | ∇ 16 | 16 | 17 | $46 |

Financial District | 21 Broad St. (Water St.) | 617-263-0037 | www.mktboston.com

From chef Rene Michelena comes this "upscale" Financial District newcomer featuring a New American menu presented in a four-story space offering everything from a candlelit lounge to a "roof deck" with a retractable top; early visitors say it's "still working out the kinks", which helps explain the "quiet" mood and sometimes "lackluster" feel.

NEW Marliave *Continental/Italian* | ∇ 22 | 17 | 19 | $39 |

Downtown Crossing | 10 Bosworth St. (Tremont St.) | 617-422-0004 | www.marliave.com

After a lengthy closure, this "historic" Downtown Crossing duplex originally founded in 1885 has been restored by a "new owner", who's given the Italian menu a more Continental twist; the "classy"

upstairs dining room offers a view and a "splurge"-worthy prix fixe menu, while downstairs is "more casual" with lower prices and an "amazing" bar serving Prohibition-era cocktails.

Martsa's on Elm Ⓜ *Tibetan*

▽ 21 | 16 | 20 | $20

Somerville | 233A Elm St. (Grove St.) | 617-666-0660

"Bargain" tabs draw fans to this Tibetan in Somerville's Davis Square, a "small" but "cute" showcase for a "delicious" cuisine that's "in a league all its own"; "nice" staffers keep the mood "lively and fun", while the "ample" lunch buffet is a "fantastic way to sample the range of savory dishes."

Mary Chung ⊄ *Chinese*

21 | 8 | 18 | $20

Central Square | 464 Massachusetts Ave. (Central Sq.) | Cambridge | 617-864-1991

"Like Chinatown in Cambridge", this "cash-only" Central Square "cult" Chinese is an "icon to MIT students" thanks to a menu that aspires to "spicy greatness" for "unbeatable bargain" tabs; while it's decidedly "low on atmosphere" (verging on "dreary"), patrons "keep coming back" for "excellent" weekend dim-sum as well as "house specialties" that you "won't find on other menus."

Masa *Southwestern*

23 | 21 | 20 | $38

South End | 439 Tremont St. (Appleton St.) | 617-338-8884

NEW Woburn | 348A Cambridge Rd. (Rte. 3/3A) | 781-938-8886

www.masarestaurant.com

"Change-of-pace" seekers who "aren't afraid of some kick" tout this "upscale" South Ender purveying Southwestern fare rife with "bold", "exotic" flavors and washed down with "great margaritas of all shapes and sizes" (indeed, the place is a veritable "tequila-lover's dream"); "lively" goings-on at the bar and "reasonable prices" make up for the generally "accommodating" though occasionally "spotty" service; N.B. the Woburn offshoot opened post-Survey.

Masala Art *Indian*

23 | 21 | 20 | $33

Needham | Needham Ctr. | 990 Great Plain Ave. (Chestnut St.) | 781-449-4050 | www.masala-art.com

"Ambitious" is the word for this "classy" Needham Indian, dishing out "flavorful" chow (and a "crowd-pleasing" lunch buffet) in a "funky cool" space that's "more beautiful" than the norm for the genre; a "relaxed atmosphere" and "friendly" service keep the trade brisk, while the Spice Bar, a variation on the "chef's table" concept, offers "interesting" interactive cooking sessions.

Ma Soba *Pan-Asian*

20 | 19 | 17 | $31

Beacon Hill | 156 Cambridge St. (Hancock St.) | 617-973-6680 | www.masobaboston.com

"Neighborhood sushi" for the "Beacon Hill crowd" sums up the scene at this Pan-Asian, a "standby" offering "good-value" lunch boxes and "windows that slide open in warmer weather"; though surveyors split on the food quality ("creative" vs. "unremarkable"), there's general agreement that "service can be slow" when the place is crowded, especially "before Celtics games."

Masona Grill Ⓜ *American/Peruvian*

25 | 18 | 23 | $38

West Roxbury | 4-6 Corey St. (Centre St.) | 617-323-3331 |
www.masonagrill.net

Fairly "exotic" for "white-bread West Roxbury", this "adorable little"
spot features an "imaginative" kitchen that fuses New American
and Peruvian flavors into especially "delicious" dishes; it's brought
to you by the owner of the former Claremont Cafe, and the "homey"
environs and "excellent" service leave fans "never disappointed."

Massimino's Cucina Italia *Italian*

23 | 17 | 21 | $33

North End | 207 Endicott St. (Commercial St.) | 617-523-5959 |
www.massiminosboston.com

A "tiny place with heart", this "unpretentious" red-sauce Italian "off
the main drag in the North End" has "loads of character", starting
with its "talkative" staff; a "feel-like-family" vibe and "delectable"
grub plated in "huge" portions may be reasons why it's becoming increasingly "full of tourists."

Matt Murphy's Pub ⊘ *Pub Food*

22 | 18 | 19 | $26

Brookline | 14 Harvard St. (bet. Kent St. & Webster Pl.) | 617-232-0188 |
www.mattmurphyspub.com

The "staff gets to know the locals" at this "real-deal" Irish pub in
Brookline Village where "hearty" grub (including some "amazing
homemade ketchup") is slung in a "comfortable" setting; it may be "a
little more expensive than the standard" and that "cash-only" policy
is a drag, but "live music" keeps the "loud" crowds content.

Maurizio's *Italian*

25 | 17 | 23 | $42

North End | 364 Hanover St. (Clark St.) | 617-367-1123 |
www.mauriziosboston.com

"Authentic Sardinian" dishes distinguish this Italian "treasure" in
the North End from the pack, while the "well-thought-out" menu,
"reasonable prices" and "helpful" service keep it "popular" (and
"noisy"); despite "not much atmosphere" and "limited seating",
supporters insist this "tiny place" has a "big impact."

🆕 Max & Dylans Kitchen & Bar *American*

- | - | - | M

Charlestown | 1 Chelsea St. (City Sq.) | 617-242-7400
Downtown Crossing | 15 West St. (bet. Tremont & Washington Sts.) |
617-423-3600
www.maxanddylans.com

Downtown Crossing welcomes this "awesome little place" (named
after the owners' sons) serving upscale yet moderately priced
American bar food in sleek environs that incorporate two bars –
upstairs and down – TVs, hardwood floors and glowing faux votives on
the tables; the Charlestown sibling is a similar neighborhood spot.

Max Stein's 🅱 *Steak*

18 | 21 | 19 | $46

Lexington | 94 Hartwell Ave. (Cross St.) | 781-402-0033 |
www.maxsteins.com

"Older, well-dressed" types frequent this "fancy" Lexington steakhouse set in "dark" digs that look like a "1940s supper club"; though

the menu's "solid", picky eaters find it too "vanilla" and "overpriced for the quality received", yet the atmosphere is "relaxing" and there's also a "nice bar" for "after-work" tippling.

☑ Maxwell's 148 ⑤ Ⓜ *Asian Fusion/Italian*   26 | 24 | 27 | $54

Natick | 148 E. Central St. (Rte. 135) | 508-907-6262 | www.maxwells148.com

"Attention to detail" is the thing at this "sophisticated" destination in Natick whose "diverse menu" is a blend of "top-notch" Asian fusion and Northern Italian dishes, paired with a "wine list that's the equal of the food"; "extraordinary" service and "high-end pricing" come with the territory, but "don't be deceived" by its "unassuming" strip-mall exterior: this is a "place to dine and to linger."

McCormick & Schmick's *Seafood*   21 | 19 | 20 | $46

Faneuil Hall | Faneuil Hall Mktpl. | N. Market Bldg. (North St.) | 617-720-5522

Park Square | Park Plaza Hotel | 34 Columbus Ave. (Charles St.) | 617-482-3999

www.mccormickandschmicks.com

An "endless menu" that "changes daily depending on what's freshly caught" reels folks into this seafood chain where the fish is "fresh" and the atmosphere "clubby", both at the Park Square locale, which is well-situated for a "dash to the theater", and the Faneuil Hall outpost, offering a "pleasant" patio; some protest "kind-of-costly" tabs, but so long as you have an "expense account" (or come for the "fantastic happy-hour" deals), the "unsurpassed variety" can't be beat.

Mela *Indian*   24 | 20 | 20 | $29

South End | 578 Tremont St. (bet. Public Alley 701 & Union Park) | 617-859-4805

"Upmarket" Indian grub comes to the South End via this "stylish" eatery that whips up "tasty", "well-prepared" meals in a "modern" setting; those seeking something "quick" for lunch tout the "great deal" buffet, but no matter when you show up, the "attentive" staff "won't let your glass run dry."

Ⓝ️Ⓔ️Ⓦ️ Melting Pot *Fondue*   20 | 18 | 19 | $44

Park Square | 76 Arlington St. (Columbus Ave.) | 617-357-7007

Bedford | 213 Burlington Rd. (Network Dr.) | 781-791-0529

Framingham | 92 Worcester Rd. (Under Prince Way) | 508-875-3115

www.meltingpot.com

"Change-of-pace" mavens and "do-it-yourself" types are fond of this "novel" fondue franchise for its "interactive" approach, i.e. the chance to "cook your own dinner"; the "long, slow meals" make it appropriate for "first dates" or "large crowds", and although the morsels are "tasty", you'll "end up spending a lot of money" for them.

Merchants Row *New England*   - | - | - | M

Concord | Colonial Inn | 48 Monument Sq. (Rte. 62) | 978-369-2373 | www.concordscolonialinn.com

"Stick-to-your-ribs Yankee cooking" (think New England favorites like wild game and "classic prime rib") is yours as this "solid" dining

room housed in Concord's historic Colonial Inn, a "wonderful place to rest your feet after traveling the revolutionary paths"; it's got special appeal for history-minded "grandmas and grandpas" who enjoy olde-fashioned service by "kind tavern maids."

Merengue *Dominican*

-	-	-	I

Roxbury | 156 Blue Hill Ave. (Clifford St.) | 617-445-5403 | www.merenguerestaurant.com

Authentic Dominican comfort fare at "outstanding-value" tabs is the draw at this longtime Roxbury dining room that's festooned with colorful native art; even though the staff seems to operate on "island time", no one minds with food this "amazing."

☒ Meritage Ⓜ *American*

27	27	26	$68

Waterfront | Boston Harbor Hotel | 70 Rowes Wharf (High St.) | 617-439-3995 | www.meritagetherestaurant.com

"Fabulous harbor views" are only part of the package at this "special" Waterfront "wine-lover's paradise" via chef Daniel Bruce, whose "innovative" New American dishes are available in "small and large" portions ("enabling those with smaller appetites to sample more") and designed to be paired with a "perfect" selection of "terrific" vini; true, it's "expensive, but totally worth it" given the "polished service", "sumptuous surroundings" and overall "exquisite dining experience."

Met Bar & Grill *American/Steakhouse*

21	20	19	$37

Natick | Natick Collection | 1245 Worcester St. (Speen St.) | 508-651-0003 | www.metbarandgrill.com

A "great spin-off" of the Metropolitan Club, this American steakhouse in the "swanky Natick Collection" is "not your standard mall restaurant", what with its "slick cocktails" and "sleek, dark-wood" setting; sure, the steaks are "terrific" but the "make-your-own burger bar" verges on the "life-altering" (the "condiment options" alone are "dizzying"), leaving "small portions" and "high prices" as the only drawbacks.

Metro 9 Steak House *Seafood/Steakhouse*

19	20	18	$44

Framingham | 30 Worcester Rd. (Shoppers World Dr.) | 508-620-9990 | www.metro9steakhouse.com

"Stick with the basics" for the best results at this "traditional" Framingham surf 'n' turf specialist festooned with all the classic men's club accoutrements including "big booths for conversation"; maybe the "food isn't quite at the level of the chain steakhouses", but the good news is that the "prices aren't either."

Metropolis Cafe *Eclectic*

23	19	20	$37

South End | 584 Tremont St. (bet. Clarendon & Dartmouth Sts.) | 617-247-2931

"It's a squeeze but worth it" at this "casually bustling" South End cafe, a "locals' spot" that's "always reliable" for "delicious" Eclectic eats for "lower-than-expected" dough; the "tightly packed" tables right out of a "cramped Parisian bistro" are a perfect fit with the "equally European service" – "just hope your waiter remembers you"; P.S. "brunch is when it really shines."

	FOOD	DECOR	SERVICE	COST

Metropolitan Club *Steak*   21 | 21 | 20 | $49

Chestnut Hill | 1210 Boylston St. (Hammond St.) | 617-731-0600 |
www.metclubandbar.com

Bringing a "cool urban vibe to the suburbs", this "swanky" Chestnut
Hill chop shop offers "terrific" steakhouse standards along with
some "sophisticated" twists on New American classics; while its
"young, professional" crowd and "hopping" bar scene get mixed
marks ("hip" vs. "pretentious"), there's consensus on the "inconsistent" service and "pricey" pricing.

Middle East, The ● *Mideastern*   17 | 15 | 17 | $20

Central Square | 472-480 Massachusetts Ave. (Brookline St.) |
Cambridge | 617-492-9181 | www.mideastclub.com

"Cheap and tasty" sums up the sustenance at this Central Square
Middle Eastern "landmark", but the mainly Lebanese menu plays
second fiddle to "three music venues" that are part of the
"community-oriented" complex; "fantastic bands", belly dancers, a
"young crowd", "grumpy" service and "funky, down-home" decor
are all part of the package.

Middlesex Lounge ●▨ *Eclectic*   ▽ 17 | 17 | 16 | $22

Central Square | 315 Massachusetts Ave. (Blanche St.) | Cambridge |
617-868-6739 | www.middlesexlounge.com

"Better known as a place to get a groove on", this "popular" night-
club/eatery in Central Square ("owned by Miracle of Science next
door") attracts party animals more bent on "dancing and drinking"
than dining, even though the Eclectic small plates on offer are "better than your typical pub food"; the cocktails may be "a step above"
the norm, but the "snarky" service, "knee-high tables" and "limited"
menu are less memorable.

Midwest Grill ● *Brazilian/Steak*   20 | 13 | 18 | $32

Inman Square | 1124 Cambridge St. (bet. Elm & Norfolk Sts.) | Cambridge |
617-354-7536

Brace yourself for a "food coma" after a visit to this "fun" Inman
Square Brazilian rodizio, where the $24.95 "all-you-can-eat-meat"
deal draws gluttons with "bottomless pit appetites"; an "unlimited
food bar" buffet offsets the "tightly packed tables", but the "endless
skewers" of beef get mixed response: "tender and tasty" vs.
"average – you get what you pay for."

Miel ● *French*   21 | 22 | 22 | $52

Waterfront | InterContinental Boston | 510 Atlantic Ave.
(Congress St.) | 617-217-5151 |
www.intercontinentalboston.com

Open "24/7" – a rarity for Boston – this "high-end" Waterfront
brasserie in the InterContinental hotel "pleases the palate" with
a "fine" array of "French country" dishes drawn from the
Côte d'Azur region, served in "posh", "power lunch"-ready environs; nature lovers love its "beautiful" outdoor patio, but even
though the "view is priceless", some say the tabs are "too pricey
for what you get."

	FOOD	DECOR	SERVICE	COST

Mifune   *Chinese/Japanese*   ▽ 20 | 16 | 21 | $27

Arlington | 303 Broadway (Mass. Ave.) | 781-641-2388 |
www.mifunearlington.com

This Arlington venue is just the ticket "when you're not sure what you're hankering for" given a menu that offers a variety of Chinese-Japanese items, plus a "solid" sushi bar; "reasonable prices" (the "lunch menu is a particular value") make it especially "family-friendly."

Mike's City Diner ⊄ *Diner*   20 | 13 | 18 | $17

South End | 1714 Washington St. (E. Springfield St.) | 617-267-9393

"Good neighborhood energy" abounds at this "quintessential greasy spoon" in the South End where "substantial" diner classics are "served fast" in a "small", "hole-in-the-wall" setting brimming with "tons of character"; "cheap" prices, "heaping" portions and "fun people-watching" account for the "long lines"; N.B. breakfast and lunch only.

Miracle of Science Bar & Grill ● *Pub Food*   19 | 17 | 17 | $19

Central Square | 321 Massachusetts Ave. (State St.) | Cambridge |
617-868-2866 | www.miracleofscience.us

"Geek chic" is alive and well at this "laid-back" Central Square "techie" magnet near MIT that lures in everyone from "grad students" to "Internet millionaires" with its "unfussy" New American grub and "to-die-for" burger selection; the "lab stool" seating, "high-IQ vibe" and "periodic-table-of-the-elements menu" help take your mind off the "slow service."

Mission Bar & Grill ● *Pub Food*   19 | 18 | 17 | $23

MFA | 724 Huntington Ave. (Tremont St.) | 617-566-1244 |
www.themissionbar.com

"Affordable", "upscale tavern food" that's a "step up from standard pub grub" is dispensed at this "low-key" Brigham Circle bar and grill near the MFA; it's catnip for "after-work crowds of doctors and nurses", so "wear your scrubs to fit in."

☑ Mistral   *French/Mediterranean*   27 | 26 | 25 | $65

South End | 223 Columbus Ave. (bet. Berkeley & Clarendon Sts.) |
617-867-9300 | www.mistralbistro.com

Regulars "dress to impress" at this "wow"-inducing South End bastion of "sophistication" that's "still one of the hottest tickets in town" thanks to chef Jamie Mammano's "delectable" French-Med menu; given the "stylish", high-ceilinged setting (with "lighting that makes everyone glow"), "smooth-as-silk" service, "elite", "power-broker" following and "mortgage payment"–worthy price tags, this is "fine dining" personified – "noisy" acoustics notwithstanding.

M.J. O'Connor's ⊠ Ⓜ *Pub Food*   - | - | - | I

Park Square | 27 Columbus Ave. (Arlington St.) | 617-482-2255
NEW Seaport District | Westin Boston Waterfront Hotel |
425 Summer St. (D St.) | 617-443-0800
www.mjoconnorsboston.com

A handsome dark-wood bar imported from Ireland provides the central gathering place at this budget-friendly American pub grub spot

that's been a Park Square staple for years, while a second location has opened in the Westin Boston Waterfront.

Montien *Thai*
23 | 17 | 20 | $27

Theater District | 63 Stuart St. (Tremont St.) | 617-338-5600
Inman Square | 1287 Cambridge St. (Prospect St.) | Cambridge | 617-868-1240
www.montien-boston.com

These Thai options vend "solid" chow for "inexpensive" tabs; speedy service makes the Inman Square branch a "reliable" stop "when short on time", while the "good bet" Theater District outpost also offers a "diverse" assortment of "reasonably priced" sushi.

Mooo . . . *Steak*
24 | 24 | 25 | $69

Beacon Hill | XV Beacon Hotel | 15 Beacon St. (bet. Bowdoin & Somerset Sts.) | 617-670-2515 | www.mooorestaurant.com

Ignore the "ridiculous name": this "popular-as-all-get-out" Beacon Hill steakhouse draws "politicos" and assorted "chic" types with its "excellent" chops, "spiffy" service and "hip", cow-centric decor (that's a bit "less manly" than the genre norm); it's best enjoyed "on someone else's tab", however, given the "breathlessly expensive" pricing, but overall, mooost rate it a "great dining experience from start to finish."

Morse Fish *Seafood*
▽ 21 | 5 | 19 | $16

South End | 1401 Washington St. (Union Park) | 617-262-9375

"Fresh fish, stale space" sums up the scene at this "simple" South End eatery/market slinging "value-priced" seafood prepared any way you like it – "so long as that's fried or broiled"; Styrofoam dishware and "nil decor" to the contrary, the "unpretentious" joint draws a mixed crowd of "urbanites, hipsters and policemen."

☑ Morton's The Steakhouse *Steak*
25 | 22 | 24 | $66

Back Bay | Exeter Plaza | 699 Boylston St. (Exeter St.) | 617-266-5858
Seaport District | World Trade Center East | Two Seaport Ln. (bet. Congress St. & Northern Ave.) | 617-526-0410
www.mortons.com

"Consistency abounds" at this "can't-go-wrong" steakhouse chain pairing "well-prepared" chops that "hang off the plate" with "seriously powerful martinis" in a Back Bay "basement" and a "jumping" Seaport District locale; "arm-and-a-leg" pricing comes with the territory, along with a "Saran-wrapped presentation" of raw meats (accompanied by an instructional "recitation" by the waiter) – a "shtick" that many find "tired."

Mother Anna's *Italian*
21 | 14 | 19 | $30

North End | 211 Hanover St. (Cross St.) | 617-523-8496 | www.motherannas.com

In the North End since 1937, this longtime "locals' spot" vends "solid red-sauce" Italian fare in a "relaxing", "not-fancy" milieu; while the "basic" cooking is "not a standout", "excellent" pricing and "great patio seating" help explain why it's "been around forever."

Mount Blue *Eclectic*   ▽ 18 | 18 | 18 | $41

Norwell | 707 Main St. (Central St.) | 781-659-0050 | www.mountblue.com
Though most diners have "yet to see Steven Tyler here" (it was formerly owned by "members of Aerosmith"), this Norwell eatery still attracts rock groupies with "great live music" and a hopping bar scene, if not for the Eclectic eats: "sometimes great, sometimes average" and always pricey.

Mr. Bartley's Burger Cottage 🗷🖭 *Burgers*   24 | 13 | 15 | $16

Harvard Square | 1246 Massachusetts Ave. (Plympton St.) | Cambridge | 617-354-6559 | www.mrbartley.com
"Doing it right forever" (or at least since 1961), this "perennial" Harvard Square patty palace is renowned for "big, juicy" burgers "named after celebrities and politicians" and washed down with "dreamy shakes"; despite "no bathroom", a "cash-only" policy, "crazy-busy" atmospherics and "rough 'n' ready" decor recalling the "dorm room of a poster-crazed college student", all are more than content to "go with the flow" here.

Mr. Crepe *French*   18 | 12 | 15 | $13

Somerville | 51 Davis Sq. (bet. Elm St. & Highland Ave.) | 617-623-0661
This Davis Square "college hangout" specializes in "massive" French crêpes in sweet and savory iterations that are "tasty" to some, "unimpressive" to others; "cheap" pricing can result in "long waits" and a "zoo"-like "weekend rush", while "Ikea"-inspired decor reflects the "relaxed" surroundings.

Mr. Sushi *Japanese*   21 | 14 | 19 | $28

Arlington | 693 Massachusetts Ave. (bet. Central & Water Sts.) | 781-643-4175
Brookline | 329 Harvard St. (Babcock St.) | 617-731-1122
"Inauspicious name" to the contrary, proponents praise the "reliably fresh" sushi at this "efficient" Japanese duo that manages to get the job done with "no frills" (and "you rarely have to wait"); they may suffer from "no decor" and "dumbed-down" menus, but they're popular for a simple reason: the "price is right."

MuLan Taiwanese Cuisine 🖬 *Taiwanese*   23 | 11 | 17 | $19

Kendall Square | 228 Broadway (Clark St.) | Cambridge | 617-441-8813
Popular with "MIT students" and curiosity seekers, this "different" Kendall Square venue specializes in "authentic Taiwanese" fare as well as some "unusual" Chinese dishes; the "typical looking" storefront setting is "not for a romantic meal or special night out", but "cheap" tabs and "friendly" service keep regulars regular.

Muqueca 🖬 *Brazilian*   24 | 13 | 19 | $21

Inman Square | 1093 Cambridge St. (Elm St.) | Cambridge | 617-354-3296 | www.muquecarestaurant.com
"Tiny, unassuming" and "ridiculously tasty", this Brazilian "foodie dive" near Inman Square is "always crowded" with "adventurous eaters" for a "good reason": instead of the "typical meat-oriented menu" common to the genre, it specializes in seafood and "signa-

ture stews big enough to share"; prices are more than "affordable", and though they serve "no booze", the "flavorful" chow is "worth staying sober for."

Myers + Chang *Pan-Asian*   23 | 19 | 20 | $34

South End | 1145 Washington St. (E. Berkeley St.) | 617-542-5200
Pan-Asian dining goes "trendy" at this "chic diner" in the South End from restaurateur Christopher Myers, where "fashionable" folks dig into chef Joanne Chang's "modern" Chinese, Thai and Vietnamese specialties; sure, it's "loud" and the "family-style small-plates" approach means the "bill can add up quickly", but ultimately most say this eating "adventure" is one "highly entertaining experience."

Naked Fish *Nuevo Latino/Seafood*   19 | 18 | 19 | $34

Waltham | 455 Totten Pond Rd. (3rd Ave.) | 781-684-0500
Billerica | 15 Middlesex Tpke. (Bedford St.) | 978-663-6500
Lynnfield | 215 Broadway/Rte. 1 (bet. Carpenter & Daly Rds.) | 781-586-8300
Framingham | 725 Cochituate Rd. (Speen St.) | 508-820-9494
www.nakedfish.com
For an "interesting change from the usual", check out this "unique" suburban mini-chain specializing in "Cuban-inspired seafood" and cocktails, jazzed up by "hopping" after-work bar scenes; although it's "above average" overall for "strip-mall" dining, critics carp that the "workmanlike" food is "inconsistent", the atmosphere "corporate" and the staff "overworked" – nevertheless, the pricing "won't break the bank."

Namaskar *Indian*   ▽ 23 | 19 | 22 | $24

Somerville | 236 Elm St. (Chester St.) | 617-623-9911 | www.namaskar-cuisine.com
Often "overlooked" despite a location "in the heart of Davis Square" in Somerville, this "reliable" spot turns out "authentic", "unfailingly good" Indian fare – including some "hard-to-find regional dishes" – that may "singe your taste buds and make you sweat" ("be careful how you order"); "friendly service" and moderate pricing complete the "tasty" picture.

Navy Yard Bistro & Wine Bar *American*   23 | 18 | 22 | $35

Charlestown | 1 First Ave. (6th St.) | 617-242-0036 | www.navyyardbistro.com
"Neighborhood restaurants" don't get much more "cozy" than this Charlestown bistro that's praised for "well-prepared" New Americana and for tabs that "won't bankrupt you"; though it can be "hard to find" ("hidden" away in the Navy Yard), this "perfect little find" stands out in an area that "lacks choices."

Nebo ◑ ▣ *Pizza*   21 | 19 | 20 | $30

North End | 90 N. Washington St. (Thacher St.) | 617-723-6326 | www.neborestaurant.com
"Close to the Boston Garden", this "hip" North End pizza purveyor is a "great spot to grab a quick bite before or after a game" given its "delish" thin-crust pies and "wonderful" homemade pastas "based

on the owners' mothers' recipes"; slick modern looks and a "good selection of wine" add to its upscale feel.

Neighborhood Restaurant & Bakery ⊅ *Portuguese*

▽ 23 | 12 | 15 | $14

Somerville | 25 Bow St. (bet. Somerville Ave. & Summer St.) | 617-623-9710

There's no need to "eat again all day" after hunkering down at this Portuguese cafe famed for "value" dining, especially its "enormous breakfasts" where the portions are so "plentiful" that the omelets practically "come with a side of eggs"; "spotty service" and "hole-in-the-wall" decor are forgotten in warm weather, when a patio seat under a grape trellis is "pleasant" indeed; N.B. lunch is served also, but not dinner.

☑ Neptune Oyster *Seafood*

27 | 20 | 22 | $42

North End | 63 Salem St. (Cross St.) | 617-742-3474 | www.neptuneoyster.com

"Escape the typical Italian fare in the North End" at this "sardine"-sized, perennially "packed" seafooder famed for its "magnificent" raw bar selection and "vaunted hot lobster roll", served in a "little-bit-of-Paris" setting; the "cramped conditions" aren't helped by the "no-reservations" policy, so savvy shuckers snag seats by "arriving early" and "checking their bank account" before digging in (it's on the "pricey" side).

NewBridge Cafe ⊅ *American*

24 | 7 | 16 | $20

Chelsea | 650 Washington Ave. (Woodlawn Ave.) | 617-884-0134 | www.newbridgecafe.com

Ok, it's "not fine dining", but this "longstanding" Chelsea "dive", a former barroom turned eatery, offers "basic" American comfort grub at a "basic price" and is renowned for its signature steak tips, "marinated and grilled to perfection"; downsides include so-so service and "fuhgeddaboudit" decor ("don't use the bathroom"), but those "cheap" tabs are fine as is.

New Ginza *Japanese*

24 | 18 | 21 | $37

Watertown | 63-65 Galen St. (Aldrich Rd.) | 617-923-2100 | www.newginza.net

The sushi is "sublime" at this Watertown Center Japanese, a "reliable" destination for "excellent" raw fish as well as "top-notch" traditional cooked specialties, all ferried by a "gracious", "energetic" crew; the blond wood-lined setting is "pretty", the vibe "pleasant" and the pricing "reasonable (for sushi)" – no wonder it's "always packed."

New Jang Su BBQ ◪ *Korean*

▽ 23 | 11 | 19 | $26

Burlington | 260 Cambridge St. (Arthur Woods Ave.) | 781-272-3787

"Adventuresome" types and do-it-yourselfers tout this "authentic" Burlington Korean where a "wide selection of quality BBQ" is cooked on a "grill in the center of your table" (small fries "love the drama"); it "doesn't look like much from the outside" – or inside, for that matter – but "attentive staffers" and "affordable prices" are ample distractions.

New Mother India Ⓜ *Indian* | 22 | 15 | 19 | $30

Waltham | 336 Moody St. (Gordon St.) | 781-893-3311 | www.newmotherindia.com

A "great beer selection" distinguishes this "pleasant" Waltham Indian from the rest of the pack, though fans report that its "high-quality" cooking is just as "satisfying"; lunchtime takes an "all-you-can-eat approach" via an "excellent buffet" and prices are "reasonable", leaving only service as a matter of debate: "polite" vs. "incompetent."

New Shanghai *Chinese* | 16 | 10 | 16 | $24

Chinatown | 21 Hudson St. (Kneeland St.) | 617-338-6688

Not "your usual Chinese", this Chinatownie offers a "great mix of spicy and mild" Shanghainese fare that's "cheap" and "reliable" albeit rather "Americanized"; though slipping ratings suggest it's "disappointing compared to a few years ago", fans report the "lunch specials rock."

9 Tastes *Thai* | 20 | 14 | 18 | $19

Harvard Square | 50 JFK St. (Mt. Aubrun St.) | Cambridge | 617-547-6666 | www.9taste.com

"Reliable", "tasty" and "cheap" "Thai standards" "do the trick" for the hungry, "frugal students" who frequent this Harvard Square basement; it's "a bit crowded" and the "decor is unimaginative", but the "friendly" servers do their best to get everyone in and out "fast."

No Name *New England/Seafood* | 19 | 10 | 15 | $27

Seaport District | 15½ Fish Pier (Northern Ave.) | 617-338-7539

Like the name suggests, this "no-frills" "ramshackle hut" in the Seaport District supplies "no-fuss, no-muss" dining with "no atmosphere" and "no-nonsense" service, just "simply prepared" New England seafood at "true-delight prices"; like everything else here, the "noisy", "touristy" crowd is "casual to the nth degree."

Ⓩ No. 9 Park Ⓢ *French/Italian* | 28 | 24 | 27 | $75

Beacon Hill | 9 Park St. (bet. Beacon & Tremont Sts.) | 617-742-9991 | www.no9park.com

Barbara Lynch still "dazzles" at her "jewel box"–esque Beacon Hill flagship where "movers and shakers" for whom "money is no object" "celebrate in style" with "elegant", "intriguing" French-Italian creations that "marry unexpected tastes and textures" with "decadent, heavenly" results; if the "smaller-than-small portions" are occasional balloon-bursters, the "savvy", "polished" "service team" and "superior" bartenders ("mixology is an art here", as is wine selection) "heighten the experience" – right on up to "cloud 9."

Noodle Street *Pan-Asian* | ▽ 19 | 11 | 16 | $15

Boston University | 627 Commonwealth Ave. (bet. Granby & Sherborn Sts.) | 617-536-3100 | www.noodlestreet.com

Those who like it "hot 'n' healthy" tout this "deelish" Pan-Asian noodle shop near B.U. for its encyclopedic (verging on "confusing") menu that allows you to "customize" your meal with lots of "flavorful" choices; "students" naturally show up since it's so "inexpensive", and they don't mind "nothing-fancy" decor and middling service.

	FOOD	DECOR	SERVICE	COST

No. 1 Noodle House *Pan-Asian*

| 18 | 7 | 15 | $17 |

Newton | 51 Langley Rd. (bet. Beacon & Union Sts.) | 617-527-8810

This "simple" Pan-Asian purveyor in Newton Centre may supply "no frills or thrills" on the menu, but it does provide "decent stir-fry" and "huge bowls of noodle soup" for "cheap" tabs – and the service is "quick"; what with the "hole-in-the-wall" looks, it's probably best for "takeout."

North Street Grille ⓜ *American*

| ▽ 23 | 11 | 15 | $23 |

North End | 229 North St. (Lewis St.) | 617-720-2010

"Everything you could ever want" in a brunch (except for the weekend "lines") is yours at this North End American offering a "wide variety" of options at the "prices you want to pay"; while dinner is more of a "low-key" event, it's equally "delicious", making the "slow" service and "nothing-to-write-home-about" decor easier to swallow.

⼄ Not Your Average Joe's *American*

| 18 | 16 | 18 | $26 |

Arlington | 645 Massachusetts Ave. (Pleasant St.) | 781-643-1666
Lexington | Lexington Ctr. | 1727 Mass Ave. (Edison Way) | 781-674-2828
Needham | 109 Chapel St. (bet. Great Plain Ave. & May St.) | 781-453-9300
Watertown | 55 Main St. (Church St.) | 617-926-9229
Newburyport | Firehouse Ctr. | 1 Market Sq. (State St.) | 978-462-3808
Beverly | Commodore Plaza | 45 Enon St. (bet. Hoover Ave. & Lincoln St.) | 978-927-8950
Methuen | The Loop | 90 Pleasant Valley St. (Milk St.) | 978-974-0015
Randolph | 16 Mazzeo Dr. (West St.) | 781-961-7200
Dartmouth | 61 State Rd. (bet. Slocom Rd. & Suffolk Ave.) | 508-992-5637
www.notyouraveragejoes.com
Additional locations throughout the Boston area

"Fun for a night away from the stove", this "spirited" local chain and its "down-to-earth" staff serve up "reasonably priced" American comfort chow from an "enormous", "something-for-everyone" menu (be warned: its focaccia and dipping oil starter is "addictive" and "could be an entire meal"); picky eaters find it "a bit out of the corporate playbook", but most label it an "easy" choice for "solid" grazing.

Novel ⓩ *American*

| - | - | - | M |

Back Bay | McKim Bldg., Boston Public Library | 700 Boylston St. (Dartmouth St.) | 617-859-2251 | www.bpl.org

A "beautiful room" festooned with chandeliers and rotating artwork is the setting for this weekdays-only cafe in the Boston Public Library, where the "simple", midpriced New American menu features select lunchtime choices that "somehow seem to please everyone"; there's also a "tempting" afternoon high tea when you're in the mood for "peaceful refinement."

⼄ Oak Room *Steak*

| 25 | 27 | 26 | $65 |

Back Bay | Fairmont Copley Plaza | 138 St. James Ave. (bet. Dartmouth & Trinity Sts.) | 617-267-5300 | www.theoakroom.com

"Very old and very Boston", this "elegant" Back Bay "grande dame" is a "throwback to the glory days of formal fine dining", offering "superb" steakhouse fare and "expert traditional service"; cushy "leather chairs" and acres of "wood paneling" embellish its "regal"

feel, and though modernists scoff it's "stuffy", proponents say this "classy joint" is more than "worth the impact on your wallet."

Oceana *American/Seafood*   24 | 21 | 20 | $47

Waterfront | Boston Marriott Long Wharf | 296 State St. (Atlantic Ave.) | 617-227-3838 | www.oceanaatlongwharf.com

"Harbor views" and "tasty" food sum up this "pleasurable" Waterfront New American in the Marriott Long Wharf, a nautically themed dining room offering a "complex" menu emphasizing seafood; indeed, it "should be busier" even though it's "not inexpensive" (insiders say the Sunday brunch offers real "bang for the buck").

Oceanaire Seafood Room *Seafood*   24 | 24 | 23 | $57

Financial District | 40 Court St. (Congress St.) | 617-742-2277 | www.theoceanaire.com

"So good, it's hard to believe it's a chain", this "exceptional" seafood franchise's Financial District outpost features "all the exuberance of a steakhouse in a fish house", starting with its "bountiful menu" and "fine wine list"; the "incredible" setting in a "defunct bank", "happening" bar scene and "big prices" reflect the overall "classy" mood.

Oga's *Japanese*   26 | 20 | 21 | $42

Natick | 915 Worcester St./Rte. 9 (Rte. 27) | 508-653-4338 | www.ogasnatick.com

"Even visitors from Japan are impressed" by the "artfully presented" sushi at this Natick "surprise" incongruously set in a "not particularly scenic" suburban strip mall; given the "sublime" raw fish, "unusual rolls" and "creatively interpreted Japanese dishes", no one is bothered by the "generic decor", while "friendly" service, "easy parking" and a "great sake menu" blunt the rather "pricey" tabs.

Z Oishii M *Japanese*   27 | 17 | 21 | $55

Chestnut Hill | 612 Hammond St. (Boylston St.) | 617-277-7888
Sudbury | Mill Vill. | 365 Boston Post Rd./Rte. 20 (Concord Rd.) | 978-440-8300

Z Oishii Boston ● M *Japanese*

South End | 1166 Washington St. (E. Berkeley St.) | 617-482-8868 | www.oishiiboston.com

"Pristine" "flavors come shining through" thanks to "chefs who care about the fundamentals" at this "sublime" sushi set that provides "aesthetic" as well as "culinary treats" with "fantastical", "innovative presentations"; the staffers can be "quite helpful" in their "recommendations" at all locations, whether at the original Chestnut Hill "shoebox" ("always a wait", "expensive"), the more "modern" Sudbury branch (less "frenetic", "expensive") and the "hoity-toity" South End offshoot ("dark, romantic", "insanely expensive").

Z Oleana *Mediterranean*   28 | 23 | 25 | $52

Inman Square | 134 Hampshire St. (bet. Elm & Norfolk Sts.) | Cambridge | 617-661-0505 | www.oleanarestaurant.com

"Attention to detail" is the hallmark of this "compelling" Inman Square "foodie attraction", where a "coveted reservation" allows the opportunity to sample chef-owner Ana Sortun's "unrivaled" Arabic-

Mediterranean cooking (and simultaneously get an "education in spices" from the "enthusiastic" staffers); though seating is a little "cramped" and the pricing decidedly "upscale", diehards declare "there's no other restaurant like it"; P.S. a meal on the "first-come, first-served" patio is as "close to heaven" as you'll find in these parts.

Olecito ⊄ *Mexican* | 24 | 21 | 21 | $31 |

Inman Square | 12 Springfield St. (Cambridge St.) | Cambridge | 617-876-1374

Olé Mexican Grill *Mexican*

Inman Square | 11 Springfield St. (Cambridge St.) | Cambridge | 617-492-4495 | www.olegrill.com

"Fine Mexican dining" is yours in Inman Square via this "not typical" cantina where the "well-executed classic dishes" (including "addictive guacamole prepared tableside") are "*elegante* and *picante*" and served in a "charmingly authentic setting"; for those who think it's a little too "pricey", across-the-street offspring Olecito offers "great takeout" prepared "in a flash."

NEW Olivadi Restaurant *Italian* | - | - | - | M |

Norwood | 32 Guild St. (Central St.) | 781-762-9090 | www.olivadirestaurant.com

Regional Italian classics with contemporary twists make up the mid-priced menu at this "nice new spot" in Norwood Center; wood and tile floors, sun-colored walls and exposed brick impart a Tuscan ambiance to the "big seating area", while a granite chef's table overlooks the main draw – a semi-open kitchen with a wood-burning pizza oven.

Z Olives *Mediterranean* | 25 | 22 | 23 | $57 |

Charlestown | 10 City Sq. (Main St.) | 617-242-1999 | www.toddenglish.com

A "longstanding" Charlestown "favorite", this "flagship" of the Todd English empire is "still the place to go" for "top-notch" Mediterranean meals that are "as magnificent to look at as they are to eat"; a "warm" setting and "congenial" service keep the mood "vibrant", although a few sniff it's too "expensive" and "coasting on its reputation."

OM Restaurant & Lounge *American* | 19 | 23 | 17 | $46 |

Harvard Square | 92 Winthrop St. (JFK St.) | Cambridge | 617-576-2800 | www.omrestaurant.com

"Style" is the watchword at this "trendier-than-thou" Harvard Square lounge-cum-restaurant offering "classy" New Americana with an "Asian flair" served in a "beautiful" setting with a distinct "nightclub" vibe; though the "exotic" cocktails are "amazing" and the scene "happening", critics cite "pretentious service" and food that's "overpriced and underportioned."

Orinoco: A Latin Kitchen ⊠ *Venezuelan* | 25 | 19 | 21 | $30 |

South End | 477 Shawmut Ave. (W. Concord St.) | 617-369-7075
NEW Brookline | 22 Harvard St. (Webster St.) | 617-232-9505
www.orinocokitchen.com

"Homey" and "unassuming", this "laid-back" South Ender draws "crowds" thanks to its "vibrant", "gently priced" Venezuelan eats

(including "mouthwatering" empanadas and "to-die-for" arepas), so be prepared for "long waits" and a "tight squeeze"; fortunately, the new Brookline Village location "takes the heat off" with somewhat "bigger" digs, plus a "full bar."

Orleans *American/Italian* | 17 | 17 | 16 | $32 |

Somerville | 65 Holland St. (Wallace St.) | 617-591-2100 | www.orleansrestaurant.com

More "pickup joint" than fine-dining destination, this Davis Square bar/eatery offers "decent" Americana by day and a more Italian-focused menu after dark; the "loud" acoustics, "hit-or-miss" service and "mediocre-to-pretty-good" grub may be a drag, but the "college" crowd is more intent on sucking down "fun cocktails" to care.

NEW Orta M *Italian* | - | - | - | I |

Hanover | 75 Washington St./Rte. 53 (Columbia Rd.) | 781-826-8883 | www.ortarestaurant.com

Though named for a lake in Italy's Piedmont region, this trattoria near Hanover in Pembroke from longtime chef and restaurateur Jimmy Burke (ex Allegro, Tuscan Grill) was inspired by a trip to Naples; the affordable menu specializes in Neapolitan pizza, pasta and entrees, while the setting offers ochre walls, an Italian-tile floor and a brick oven in the dining room.

Osushi *Japanese* | 23 | 21 | 20 | $44 |

Back Bay | Westin Copley Pl. | 10 Huntington Ave. (Dartmouth St.) | 617-266-2788 | www.osushirestaurant.com

"Small" and "sexy", this "luxe" Japanese set in a Back Bay hotel "shopping center" purveys "fresh", "artfully prepared" rolls and other "inventive" plates, supplemented by a "large sake menu"; fashionably "dim lighting" ("bring a flashlight") and "Asia-modern" decor enhance its "trendy" vibe, but don't forget to bring a "fat wallet" – it's on the "expensive" side.

Other Side Cafe ● *Sandwiches* | 19 | 15 | 14 | $18 |

Back Bay | 407 Newbury St. (Mass. Ave.) | 617-536-8437

Definitely "not for the afternoon tea set", this "funky, grungy" Back Bay cafe metes out "oversized portions" of "delicious, healthy" and "inexpensive" sandwiches, salads and soups, of which there are "lots of vegan and vegetarian options"; the target market? – "cool indie kids" and bike "couriers" who "don't mind loud music" and "slow service" by "annoyed" "tattooed" people, especially when vegging on the patio.

Out of the Blue M *Seafood* | 22 | 16 | 19 | $31 |

Somerville | 215 Elm St. (Grove St.) | 617-776-5020 | www.outofthebluerestaurant.com

For "excellent value, right in Davis Square", Somerville seafood-cravers come to this "casual and family-friendly" "charmer" offering "simple, fresh" fish with Italian and New England influences; items from land "do not disappoint" either, and when one factors in the "generous portions" and the "nice people" who bring them, it's understandable why it "gets crowded."

Oxford Spa *Sandwiches* 21 | 12 | 15 | $12

Porter Square | 102 Oxford St. (Crescent St.) | Cambridge | 617-661-6988
"Everything you expect from a locally owned, high-end" breakfast and lunch stop is found at this spot near Porter Square: "excellent housemade pastries", "fresh", "consistently delicious sandwiches" and "slight overpricing"; the counter-serve space is "cozy" if heavy with the "general air of student grubbiness" – or maybe that's just the "hit-or-miss servers"?

⊠ o ya ⊠Ⓜ *Japanese* 28 | 23 | 26 | $112

Leather District | 9 East St. (South St.) | 617-654-9900 | www.oyarestaurantboston.com
"Oh yeah", "the accolades are warranted!" – this "tiny" Leather District firehouse-turned–"sleek" izakaya provides culinary "transcendence" via "wildly creative Japanese-fusion morsels" bursting with "extraordinary" "flavors not found elsewhere"; "put yourself in the capable hands" of the "enthusiastic" staff by ordering the "knockout omakase" – but bear in mind those 15 courses yield about "17 bites of food", which causes the "still hungry" to cry "o ya gotta be kidding me" when handed the "mortgage payment"–worthy, "nosebleed"-triggering bill.

Pagliuca's *Italian* 22 | 15 | 19 | $35

North End | 14 Parmenter St. (Hanover St.) | 617-367-1504 | www.pagliucasrestaurant.com
No "modern concoctions" are made at this North Ender, just "straight-up, authentic" Southern Italian red-sauce classics – and that's just what its "ton of local regulars" prefer; though "not the place for a romantic dinner" (the "homey", "cozy" setting's "low ceilings" can make it "feel quite cramped"), it does boast large "windows that open to the street", plus "value" prices on both food and wine.

Palm, The *Steak* 23 | 19 | 23 | $63

Back Bay | Westin Copley Pl. | 200 Dartmouth St. (bet. St. James Ave. & Stuart St.) | 617-867-9292 | www.thepalm.com
"Fred Flintstone would love" the "insanely large portions" of "well-prepared meat" and "memorable sides" hauled by "smooth servers" at this Back Bay link of the "reliable" steakhouse chain; however, it's "business" types who keep it "bustling" – after all, they're the ones with the "expense accounts"; P.S. quite a few design-mavens declare the "tacky decor" "has got to change."

Panificio *Italian* 19 | 15 | 15 | $20

Beacon Hill | 144 Charles St. (bet. Cambridge & Revere Sts.) | 617-227-4340 | www.panificioboston.com
"Home-cooked goodness" comes out of the kitchen of this "rustic", "relaxed" Italian bakery/cafe in Beacon Hill purveying "plentiful breakfast options", "reliable sandwiches", soups, salads and pizzas for lunch and "dinner specials" that are "great for take-out"; whether it's all "reasonable" or "overpriced" is a point of contention, but nearly everyone has issues with the "sourpusses" behind the counter.

	FOOD	DECOR	SERVICE	COST

Paolo's Trattoria *Italian*   ▽ 21 | 18 | 19 | $36

Charlestown | 251 Main St. (Lawnwood Ave.) | 617-242-7229 |
www.paolosboston.com

"A boon for Charlestown dwellers" not in the mood to "schlep across the bridge" for Italian fare, this "great neighborhood joint" "consistently satisfies" with an "affordable", "diverse menu" and "nice wines"; the "cozy" setting "can get noisy" due to "high ceilings, brick walls" and tightly spaced tables, but when it's quiet, it's the "perfect date spot."

Papa Razzi *Italian*   18 | 17 | 19 | $33

Back Bay | 271 Dartmouth St. (bet. Boylston & Newbury Sts.) |
617-536-9200
Chestnut Hill | The Mall at Chestnut Hill | 199 Boylston St.
(Hammond Pond Pkwy.) | 617-527-6600
Hanover | Merchants Row | 2087 Washington St./Rte. 53 (Rte. 123) |
781-982-2800
Framingham | 155 Worcester Rd. | 508-848-2300
Wellesley | 16 Washington St. (Rte. 128, exit 21) | 781-235-4747
Burlington | 2 Wall St. (Rte. 3A) | 781-229-0100
Concord | 768 Elm St. (Concord Tpke./Rte. 2) | 978-371-0030
www.paparazzitrattoria.com

"Everyone can find something" on the "solid", "reasonably priced" ("for the most part") menu proffered at this "quick and efficient", "kind of slick" and "noisy" Italian chain, which means it "works for a family dinner, a business lunch", a night out with "girlfriends" or as a "fill-in" for the "undecided"; just "don't expect to eat anything that actually tastes like it was cooked in Italy" and you too will "be happy."

Paramount *American*   23 | 16 | 17 | $20

Beacon Hill | 44 Charles St. (Mt. Vernon St.) | 617-720-1152 |
www.paramountboston.com

"Even with a hangover", it's worth the additional "pain" of having to "wait" on "huge" though "quickly moving" "lines" to get a "trayful" of "delicious and cheap" American breakfast at this "small", "crazy" cafeteria-cum-diner in Beacon Hill (not to worry, "a table magically opens by the time you need it"); at night, it "transforms" into a candlelit, table-service spot for "inspired dinners" – but it's "not as much fun" as the daytime.

Paris Creperie *French*   22 | 12 | 16 | $12

Brookline | 278 Harvard St. (Beacon St.) | 617-232-1770

"A mind-boggling variety of delicious sweet and savory crêpes" is churned out in this "tiny" Coolidge Corner "hole-in-the-wall"; there's "always a wait" – partially because the "cute hipster" staffers really "take their time" – and the "hodgepodge seating" is "limited", but "if you aren't in a rush" and don't mind "eating while strolling", you're guaranteed a "tasty, cheap" "bite."

Parish Cafe ◗ *Sandwiches*   22 | 14 | 18 | $23

Back Bay | 361 Boylston St. (bet. Arlington & Berkeley Sts.) | 617-247-4777 |
www.parishcafe.com

Boosters of this "interesting concept" in the Back Bay admit to "falling deeper in love" each time they try a new "upscale sandwich"

made from "unique" recipes by almost "every famous chef in town", all paired with "specialty cocktails" that "follow the same blueprint"; a "knowledgeable staff" monitors the "hectic, loud" (and "not impressively decorated") interior, while patio-dwellers have "fun people-watching" while debating whether the fare is "inexpensive" or "pricey for what it is."

Parker's *New England* | 22 | 24 | 24 | $49 |

Downtown Crossing | Omni Parker House | 60 School St. (Tremont St.) | 617-227-8600 | www.omniparkerhouse.com

For a "classy" taste of "classic Boston", hit this "historic spot" in a "beautiful" Downtown Crossing hotel, a "stately", "storied room" where Parker House rolls and Boston cream pies were invented and continue to "live up to their reputations"; though the rest of the New England menu may be merely "ok" (some ingenuity-seekers are flat-out "bored"), "old-world" experiences like this and their accompanying "admirable service" "seem to be disappearing", so enjoy it while it lasts – it's "well worth the money."

Passage to India *Indian* | ▽ 20 | 15 | 20 | $28 |

Porter Square | 1900 Massachusetts Ave. (Somerville Ave.) | Cambridge | 617-497-6113
Salem | 157 Washington St. (Rte. 114) | 978-832-2200
www.passageindia.com

These separately owned Indian eateries provide equally "awesome flavors", "pleasant atmospheres" and "friendly service", with an added "touch of Colonial class" at the Salem spot courtesy of an English co-proprietor; "great lunch buffets" beckon in the daytime, while "nice, quiet", midpriced dinners can be had when they're not "packed."

Peach Farm ◑ *Chinese/Seafood* | 25 | 7 | 16 | $23 |

Chinatown | 4 Tyler St. (Beach St.) | 617-482-3332

"Don't be turned off" by the "dingy", "cavelike" setting of this often "noisy" and "packed" Chinatown "cellar" – "your mouth will thank you for every bite" of its "hearty", "authentically prepared" Cantonese fare, "especially the seafood", which is "brought to your table still flapping in a bucket for your inspection" (slightly elevating otherwise "so-so service"); the penny-wise appreciate that the rates are "super-affordable", while post-partyers are grateful that it's open until 3 AM.

Peking Cuisine *Chinese* | ▽ 21 | 17 | 23 | $25 |

Newton | 870 Walnut St. (Beacon St.) | 617-969-0888

Newtonites know to hit this "friendly neighborhood Chinese" joint in a "little strip mall" for "consistent", inexpensive fare the whole family can get into; indeed, it's got a slew of "regular customers" who appreciate that the "nice people who work there" always remember them.

Pellana *Steak* | ▽ 26 | 21 | 21 | $64 |

Peabody | 9 Rear Sylvan St. (bet. Andover & Endicott Sts.) | 978-531-4800 | www.pellanasteakhouse.com

A "deceiving location" in a "suburban strip mall" masks the "elegant oak-paneled room within" at this "great steakhouse" in Peabody,

	FOOD	DECOR	SERVICE	COST

where "yummy" beef is served "with all the usual trimmings"; "nice" servers are appropriate guides for "special occasions", but even so, it may be "a little expensive for the neighborhood."

Pellino's *Italian* - | - | - | M

Marblehead | 261 Washington St. (bet. Atlantic Ave. & Pleasant St.) | 781-631-3344 | www.pellinos.com

Many Marblehead "families" "count on" this "cozy", "quiet spot" for moderately priced Tuscan dinners featuring "perfectly cooked pastas, delicious sauces" and the like, all brought by "hard-working", "personable" staffers.

Penang *Malaysian* 22 | 17 | 17 | $24

Chinatown | 685 Washington St. (Kneeland St.) | 617-451-6373 | www.penangusa.com

"Still yummy" "after all these years", this "casual" Chinatown eatery's "addictive Malaysian fare" is an "excellent value" and sometimes "spicier than expected" – when they "warn" you on the menu to "ask the waiter" before ordering, "they're serious!"; the bamboo-heavy environs, which some deem as "interesting" and others "quite odd", can get "loud" and "overcrowded at peak hours", but service is usually "very fast" (bordering on "pushy").

Persephone ☒ *American* 25 | 22 | 25 | $49

Seaport District | Achilles Project | 283 Summer St. (Melcher St.) | 617-695-2257 | www.achilles-project.com

"Another hit" from Michael Leviton (Lumière), this "interesting" "experiment" in the Seaport District's "edgy" Fort Point Channel area delivers "familiar yet new and deliciously done" New American small and large plates emphasizing "fresh, local ingredients" in "a lively, unusual" "urban industrial" room "behind a clothing boutique"; adding to the "excitement" is a "trendy" bar where one can "play Wii" while sampling "amazing", "unique" cocktails, making for "quite an experience" that's "well worth" the "expensive" tabs.

☒ Petit Robert Bistro *French* 24 | 20 | 22 | $39

Kenmore Square | 468 Commonwealth Ave. (Charlesgate W.) | 617-375-0699

South End | 480 Columbus Ave. (Rutland Sq.) | 617-867-0600

NEW Needham | 45 Chapel St. (Highland Ave.) | 781-559-0532 www.petitrobertbistro.com

"Almost perfect replicas of French bistros" can be found at these "unpretentious", "cozy" sibs in Kenmore Square and the South End, where "authentic" "comfort fare for Francophiles" is paired with "suitable wines"; "respectful service" from "accented" staffers earn cheers, but it's the "great bang for the buck" that really gets fans to cry "*c'est magnifique!*"; P.S. suburbanites are "excited for the Needham location", which opened post-Survey.

P.F. Chang's China Bistro *Chinese* 19 | 19 | 18 | $32

Back Bay | Prudential Ctr. | 800 Boylston St. (Fairfield St.) | 617-378-9961

Theater District | Transportation Bldg. | 8 Park Plaza (bet. Boylston & Stuart Sts.) | 617-573-0821

(continued)

P.F. Chang's China Bistro
NEW Peabody | 210 Andover St. (Sylvan St.) | 978-326-2410
NEW Natick | Natick Collection | 1245 Worcester St. (Speen St.) |
508-651-7724
www.pfchangs.com

Expect "major hustle-bustle" at this "noisy" Chinese chain with Back
Bay and Theater District branches where the "sanitized", "mass-
produced" menus "aren't really authentic" yet do "appeal to most palates" (when in doubt, the "lettuce wraps rule"); no one minds the
"spotty" service and "ersatz" Sino decor since they "have the formula
down" – starting with "nothing-fancy" prices and an overall "fun" vibe.

Phoenicia *Lebanese* ▽ 21 | 13 | 19 | $24
Beacon Hill | 240 Cambridge St. (Blossom St.) | 617-523-4606
"Don't let the bland decor put you off" this family-owned business
whose "fabulous" Lebanese comestibles deliver a "delicious"
"change of pace" to Beacon Hill for "value" tabs; indeed, it's "not a
place to bring a date", so ask the "friendly, helpful" staffers to pack
it to go, "then enjoy a picnic along the Charles."

Pho Hoa *Vietnamese* ▽ 22 | 9 | 15 | $14
Chinatown | 17 Beach St. (Washington St.) | 617-423-3934
Dorchester | 1356 Dorchester Ave. (Kimball St.) | 617-287-9746
North Quincy | 409 Hancock St. (Billings Rd.) | 617-328-9600
www.phohoa.com

"True to the name, the pho is the star" at these separately owned,
"family-friendly" eateries, which "hit the spot" for "authentic"
Vietnamese "comfort food" served in "generous portions" and at "fantastic prices"; because they're "spacious", they're usually "not nearly
as packed" as others of their ilk, allowing for "fast", "easy in and out."

Pho Lemongrass *Vietnamese* 20 | 15 | 18 | $24
Brookline | 239 Harvard St. (Webster St.) | 617-731-8600 |
www.pholemongrass.com

"On a cold winter evening", Brookliners "go with the pho" at this "totally affordable" Coolidge Corner canteen whose "varied menu" of
"finely flavored and seasoned" Vietnamese eats, "friendly", "quick
service" and "pleasant environment" make it "interesting to return
to time and time again."

NEW Pho n' Rice *Thai/Vietnamese* - | - | - | I
Somerville | 289 Beacon St. (Sacramento St.) | 617-864-8888 |
www.phonrice.com

After Zoe's in Somerville moved across the street, it was replaced by
this quaint Thai-Vietnamese cafe serving dozens of soup, noodle
and rice dishes at budget-friendly prices; the simple decor (and lack
of a liquor license) keeps the pho-cus on the food.

Pho Pasteur *Vietnamese* 23 | 10 | 16 | $18
Chinatown | 682 Washington St. (Beach St.) | 617-482-7467
Reports that the "spicy, sweet", "amazing pho" ladled out at this
Chinatown Vietnamese can "cure the common cold" are unsubstan-

...ᵗᵉᵈ, ᵇut "ridiculously cheap" prices for "huge portions" of its "fantastic" fare are guaranteed; just "look past the dingy dining room" and "admire the efficiency" of the staff as it "shuttles people in and out" of the "always bustling" space.

Pho République ● *Pan-Asian*

21 | 21 | 20 | $33

South End | 1415 Washington St. (Union Park) | 617-262-0005 | www.phorepublique.net

"Funky, flavorful and fun", this "chic" South Ender employs a "quirky staff" to deliver "huge portions" of "designer Vietnamese" and Pan-Asian dishes in a "cool" (some say "overdone"), "dimly lit" environment marked by a "big gong" and other "eccentric" decor; the "great bar" "tends to be boisterous", but after just one "exotic cocktail", you'll be "lively" too.

Piattini *Italian*

23 | 18 | 20 | $35

Back Bay | 226 Newbury St. (bet. Exeter & Fairfield Sts.) | 617-536-2020 | www.piattini.com

The "adorable below-street-level" dining room proves a "private", "pleasant" "place for a quiet, intimate" meal, while the patio provides a "beautiful" spot to Back Bay "people-watch" at this "cozy" establishment dishing out nearly "perfect little plates" of Italian victuals paired with "unusual flights of wine at a great price" – which is welcome news considering the nibbles "do add up in terms of cost", especially if you're hungry.

Picante Mexican Grill *Californian/Mexican*

19 | 13 | 18 | $14

Central Square | 735 Massachusetts Ave. (bet. Inman & Prospect Sts.) | Cambridge | 617-576-6394 | www.picantemex.com

Spanning "several degrees of spicy, from mild to super-hot", the "awesome salsa bar" at this "reliable, cheap" Central Square stop really peps up its Californian-influenced Mexican grub; on the other *mano*, "cheesy decorations" bring the already "grubby setting" down, but "if you can ignore" it, you'll "be happy" – especially if you close your eyes and get it to go.

Picco *Dessert/Pizza*

22 | 16 | 18 | $25

South End | 513 Tremont St. (Berkeley St.) | 617-927-0066 | www.piccorestaurant.com

What a "brilliant idea!" – this "cute", "high-end" South End parlor specializes in "crunchy yet melt-in-your-mouth" "wood-fired pizzas" "with interesting toppings" and "gourmet ice cream made in-house", plus there's a "fun selection" of beer and wines; the only thing "needing improvement is the service", which can be "slow" and "not always nice", and obviously you should "expect a lot of parents with kids . . . little kids . . . loud little kids."

Piccola Venezia *Italian*

22 | 18 | 20 | $31

North End | 263 Hanover St. (bet. Cross & Richmond Sts.) | 617-523-3888 | www.piccolaveneziaboston.com

Doing the "North End on a budget"? – nourish yourself at this "cozy", "old-school Italian" whose "huge servings" of "tasty", "traditional" victuals help it to "endure" "in a neighborhood with no shortage of

good restaurants"; locals find "value" too, testifying it's "a nice place to go for a quick bite before a game" or just "lingering with friends."

Piccolo Nido ☒ *Italian* ▽ 24 | 19 | 25 | $37

North End | 257 North St. (Lewis St.) | 617-742-4272 |
www.piccolonido.com

Slightly separate from "the main action in the North End", this "little nest", as it translates, is owned by a "neighborhood personality" ("gotta love him") who provides "attentive" staffers and "unfailingly reliable", "traditional Italian" fare for "reasonable prices" – all of which, in turn, guarantees "cheerful, pleasant" evenings.

Pie Bakery & Café *American/Dessert* 18 | 14 | 15 | $14

Newton | 796 Beacon St. (Centre St.) | 617-332-8743 |
www.piebakeryandcafe.com

Newtonians have "fun" coming to sample the "sweet and savory" pies, plus other light American fare, baked at this "small" cafe featuring "a counter where you can watch the kitchen in action"; however, some leave "unimpressed" by goods they deem "pricey" for being "ok but not great", while others go away "disappointed" because someone at the counter was "kind of mean" to them.

Pierrot Bistrot Français ☒ *French* 24 | 19 | 24 | $42

Beacon Hill | 272 Cambridge St. (Anderson St.) | 617-725-8855 |
www.pierrotbistrot.com

"Reminding" Beacon Hill folk of "a neighborhood bistro in Paris", this corner establishment supplies "wonderful, authentic", "old-fashioned French cooking" alongside "complementary wines", about which the "friendly owner and staff" make "helpful recommendations"; "decent prices" sweeten the deal, and while there aren't many fans of the "clown pictures everywhere", "exposed brick provides warmth to the intimate room."

Pigalle ☒ *French* 26 | 22 | 24 | $59

Theater District | 75 Charles St. S. (bet. Stuart St. & Warrenton Pl.) |
617-423-4944 | www.pigalleboston.com

"Hidden on the quieter side of Charles Street", this "cozy, elegant" Theater District destination touts a "tour de force" in Marc Orfaly's "marvelous" French fare with an "inventive" "edge"; a "romantic ambiance" is abetted by "service that makes you feel wonderfully pampered" (not to mention "terrific wines"), and while dollar-watchers calculate it's "pricey for what you get", their "innovation"-backing counterparts deem it "well worth every cent."

Pizzeria Regina *Pizza* 24 | 12 | 14 | $17

Back Bay | Prudential Ctr. | 800 Boylston St. (Ring Rd.) |
617-424-1115
Leather District | South Station | Grand Concourse (Essex St.) |
617-261-6600
Faneuil Hall | Faneuil Hall Mktpl. | 226 Faneuil Hall Mktpl. (Congress St.) |
617-742-1713
North End | 11½ Thacher St. (Margin St.) | 617-227-0765

(continued)

FOOD DECOR SERVICE COST

(continued)

Pizzeria Regina

Braintree | South Shore Plaza | 250 Granite St. (I-95, exit 6) | 781-848-8700

Medford | 44 Station Landing (Revere Beach Pkwy.) | 781-306-1222

Kingston | Independence Mall | 101 Independence Mall Way (Raboth Rd.) | 781-585-6444

Burlington | Burlington Mall | 1131 Middlesex Tpke. (Rte. 128) | 781-270-4212

Auburn | Auburn Mall | 385 Southbridge St. (Auburn St.) | 508-721-0090

Marlborough | Solomon Pond Mall | 580 Donald Lynch Blvd. (River Rd. W.) | 508-303-6999

www.pizzeriaregina.com

Additional locations throughout the Boston area

"Stick to the original" when craving this familiar name's "real-deal" pizza, because the "humble", "slightly grungy" North End address is where the "ancient wood-burning oven" resides – just look at the "droves" "waiting" on "long lines" for the "amazing", "gooey" goods, which are brought by "waitresses as crusty as the pies"; the other locations, mostly set in "food courts", are "nothing in comparison."

Plaza III –
The Kansas City Steakhouse *Steak*

21 | 19 | 21 | $53

Faneuil Hall | Faneuil Hall Mktpl. | 101 S. Market Bldg. (Merchants Row) | 617-720-5570 | www.plazathreeboston.com

"For that manly meat experience" in Faneuil Hall, nearby business folk "take clients" to this "high-end" steakhouse with a somewhat "low-key atmosphere" to wheel and deal over "huge, crusty" cuts they ascertain "stand up to competition well"; nah, counter detractors, "compared to others, this place is nothing special."

Pleasant Cafe ● *American*

▽ 18 | 8 | 15 | $21

Roslindale | 4515 Washington St. (Beech St.) | 617-323-2111 | www.pleasantcafe.com

While this Roslindale "neighborhood hangout for beer, pizza" and other American grub dates back to the 1940s, it seems like "it's been there since the world was created", with prices and "waitresses that haven't changed since then" either; indeed, it was, is and, hopefully, will be "always fun", whether for eating in the vinyl booths, "taking out" or "sitting in the bar and watching the Sox."

Polcari's *Italian*

17 | 16 | 17 | $28

Woburn | 309 Montvale Ave. (bet. Central & Washington Sts.) | 781-938-1900

Saugus | 92 Broadway/Rte. 1 (Walnut St.) | 781-233-3765

www.polcaris.com

"Large servings for big families with big appetites" is the stock in trade of this "old reliable" in Saugus and Woburn dishing out "everyday" "red-sauce" Italian "as well as Pizzeria Regina pizza" in "gaudy" checked-tablecloth surroundings; even discerning palates who peg it merely "mediocre" begrudgingly admit "it'll do in a pinch" – or at least in a credit crunch.

Pomodoro ⊘ *Italian* | 24 | 18 | 21 | $37 |

North End | 319 Hanover St. (bet. Prince & Richmond Sts.) | 617-367-4348 Ⓜ

Brookline | 24 Harvard St. (Washington St.) | 617-566-4455

"Noisy, small and hard to get a seat in", this "rustic" North Ender vends the same "skillfully prepared but simple Italian cooking" with "fresh ingredients" and "red sauce to dream about" as its "sophisticated but homey" Brookline Village offshoot, which diverges with "bigger", hence more "relaxing", digs; service "can vary from perfect to unfriendly", while the cash-only policy always "irritates, considering some entrees are north of $20."

Ponzu *Asian Fusion* | ▽ 23 | 18 | 20 | $32 |

Waltham | 286 Moody St. (Gordon St.) | 781-736-9188 | www.theponzu.com

"Wow", "what a great surprise" marvel first-timers to Waltham's "best-kept secret", which harbors a "large variety" of "contemporary" Asian fusion small and large plates prepped in "clever", "flavorful" ways by "friendly sushi chefs" and servers; opinions on the decor veer from "nice" to "uninspiring", but since it's "best enjoyed with a group", it's usually "fun" either way.

Pops *American* | 22 | 20 | 19 | $35 |

South End | 560 Tremont St. (Clarendon St.) | 617-695-1250 | www.popsrestaurant.net

"Fun food with flair" flies out of the kitchen of this "adorable" South End New American whose "sophisticated twists on comfort" fare seem even more "scrumptious" for being "pretty reasonably priced, given the trendy neighborhood"; the "bold", "classy" yet "quirky" space gets "cramped" but "not uncomfortable", unless you're saddled with one of the "arrogant and indifferent" members of the otherwise "professional" staff.

Porcini's *Mediterranean* | 22 | 17 | 22 | $37 |

Watertown | 68 School St. (Arsenal St.) | 617-924-2221 | www.porcinis.com

At this Watertown haunt, a "nondescript", somewhat "foreboding exterior" sheaths a slightly "dark" dining room that could use "some updating" – but "the real reason you go out to eat" is the food, and surveyors say the Mediterranean meals are not only "terrific" here, but "fair priced" to boot; an "outgoing" staff adds "warmth" to the proceedings, especially at the "friendly bar", which is "worth a stop even if you don't have to wait for a table."

🄩 Prezza *Italian* | 27 | 22 | 24 | $57 |

North End | 24 Fleet St. (Moon St.) | 617-227-1577 | www.prezza.com

"Not your typical North End" eatery, this "classy" spot puts a "unique", even "edgy" spin on Italian with "flavorful" results quite different from "typical red-sauce fare"; a "vast wine list", "helpful, charming" staff and "stylish", "intimate", "quite romantic" setting add to a night out that's a "heavenly" "treat" – "when you can afford it."

	FOOD	DECOR	SERVICE	COST

Prose ☒Ⓜ *American*
▽ 24 | 14 | 14 | $37

Arlington | 352A Massachusetts Ave. (Wyman Terrace) | 781-648-2800

A true "labor of love", this "tiny", "nondescript" Arlington eatery is known for a chef-owner "who is also [often] the waitress, quite opinionated" and, truth be told, sometimes "a bit curt" – but any perceived hassles are "worth it" for her "seasonal", "inventive" and "reasonably priced" New American cuisine featuring "lots of locally produced ingredients"; since "everything is cooked from scratch", "service is quite slow" ("she does warn you"), "but if you've got the time", the fare is "sublime."

Publick House, The *Pub Food*
21 | 20 | 17 | $28

Brookline | 1648 Beacon St. (Washington St.) | 617-277-2880

"A beer snob's dream", this Brookline tavern serves an "extraordinary selection" of "rare" brews "served in brand-appropriate glasses" alongside "hefty portions" of "awesome" Belgian *cuisine à la bière* (the "standout" being "mind-blowing mac 'n' cheese" "mixed with whatever your little heart desires"); there's a "maddening" "line out the door almost every night", hence the "slow" service, but once you get their attention, the staffers give "excellent recommendations."

Punjab *Indian*
25 | 21 | 19 | $27

Arlington | 485 Massachusetts Ave. (Medford St.) | 781-643-0943 | www.punjabarlington.com

"After being luxuriously renovated", this Arlingtonian's "classy" "new space means even more folks can enjoy" what many consider "the crown jewel of Indian food in the 'burbs", as it brims with "aromatic", "distinctive spices and flavors"; indeed, the cuisine – not to mention the "yummy cocktails" and "reasonable prices" – makes up for" service that's sometimes "ok" but often "offhand" and "disjointed."

Punjabi Dhaba ●🖛 *Indian*
24 | 7 | 14 | $12

Inman Square | 225 Hampshire St. (Cambridge St.) | Cambridge | 617-547-8272 | www.royalbharatinc.com

Like a Punjabi "roadside diner" transported to Inman Square, this "not-very-attractive" "two-story shack" is a "mecca" for "authentic, tasty" "Indian street food" offered "at its greasy best" for "minuscule prices"; it's basically "self-serve" and "by no means fast", but at least there's a "continuous loop" of "loud" "Bollywood" musicals to keep you occupied as you "wait" on the "insane lines"; P.S. there is "limited" seating, but really, "take it home."

Punjab Palace *Indian*
24 | 15 | 21 | $23

Allston | 109 Brighton Ave. (bet. Harvard & Linden Sts.) | 617-254-1500 | www.punjabpalace.com

"Bollywood videos playing on large-screen TVs" notwithstanding, this Allston subcontinental is somewhat "posher" (and larger) than India Quality, it's Kenmore Square sibling; what's similar is the fare: "flavorful", "wonderful curries" and more sold for a "steal" in "generous portions" whose spiciness the "attentive servers" will "adjust according to your preferences."

Purple Cactus Burrito & Wrap Bar *Eclectic/Mexican*

▽ 21 | 14 | 21 | $10

Jamaica Plain | 674 Centre St. (Seaverns Ave.) | 617-522-7422 | www.thepurplecactus.com

"Get a fast Mex fix without the guilt" at this Jamaica Plain "week-night staple" that puts Eclectic, "healthy" spins on its burritos wraps, salads and fresh-fruit smoothies in "small, colorful", counter-serve surroundings "with a few tables"; unfortunately, some spice-aholics deem the offerings "too bland."

Qingdao Garden *Chinese*

24 | 5 | 15 | $18

Porter Square | 2382 Massachusetts Ave. (bet. Dudley & Harvey Sts.) | Cambridge | 617-492-7540 | www.qingdao-garden.com

"Skip the Americanized stuff and dive into" the "amazing home-made dumplings", "outstanding Northern Chinese dishes" and all-day weekend dim sum that "grace the menu" at this "unique in the best sense" Porter Square eatery; service can either be "ultrahelp-ful" or "atrocious", and the setting "doesn't look like much" – "but who cares" with such low prices?

❷ Radius ⌧ *French*

26 | 25 | 25 | $69

Financial District | 8 High St. (bet. Federal & Summer Sts.) | 617-426-1234 | www.radiusrestaurant.com

Michael Schlow's "rarefied" Financial District "masterpiece" deliv-ers "imaginative, edgy, impeccably prepared" New French fare and "divine wines" – with the aid of "knowledgeable", "attentive" servers – to a "debonair clientele" in a "dramatic", "handsome", "circular" room (the only issue there: "tables are crowded on top of each other"); the across-the-board "artistry" "helps mitigate the sticker shock", especially felt by complainers of portions that are "at times woefully small."

Rami's ⍩ *Mideastern*

23 | 7 | 15 | $13

Brookline | 324 Harvard St. (Babcock St.) | 617-738-3577

"Close your eyes when you bite into" the "far-out falafel" sold at this "hole-in-the-wall" "Brookline bargain" and "you're transported to Israel"; the shawarma and other Middle Eastern "fast food" are equally "lick-your-fingers good" – just don't let the sometimes "grumpy" service from the "dry-humored staff" and "small, crowded" dining room get you down; P.S. being a kosher establish-ment, it's "closed on the Sabbath."

Rani *Indian*

20 | 19 | 17 | $28

Brookline | 1353 Beacon St. (Harvard St.) | 617-734-0400 | www.ranibistro.com

With "enough diversity to make it stand out", this Indian establish-ment serves not just the "traditional Northern fare", but "interesting and delicious regional cuisine", of which the Hyderabadi dishes par-ticularly "should be tried"; "service is spotty", but the atmosphere is relatively "upscale" – which is why it's "a little pricier than some" of its competitors.

Rattlesnake
Bar & Grill ● *South American/Southwestern*

| 12 | 15 | 15 | $25 |

Back Bay | 384 Boylston St. (bet. Arlington & Berkeley Sts.) | 617-859-8555 | www.rattlesnakebar.com

Attracting "nearby office workers as well as students", the "biggest appeal" of this "popular place to hang" is a "cool roof deck": even though the "views aren't exactly stellar", it's still considered "one of the hidden treasures" of the Back Bay; drinks like sangria and margaritas are for the most part "great", unlike the South American–Southwestern fare, whose "froufrou" aspirations turn out "mediocre at best" (ditto the "aloof staff").

Redbones BBQ ● *BBQ*

| 22 | 14 | 18 | $23 |

Somerville | 55 Chester St. (Elm St.) | 617-628-2200 | www.redbones.com

"Bring your elastic pants" to Davis Square's "reasonably priced" "hog heaven", because its "addictive", "succulent", "sauce-covered" BBQ is served in "massive portions" and paired with "tons of beers" ("spin the wheel" "if you can't decide"); the "utilitarian" "roadside-diner" decor is "funkier" in the basement bar ("decked out voodoo style"), while staffers are "efficient" in helping the "huge crowds" "gorge" and "stagger out the door" "satisfied"; P.S. a shout-out to the "bicycle valet": "sooo cute!"

Red Fez ● *Mideastern*

| 18 | 18 | 16 | $35 |

South End | 1222 Washington St. (Perry St.) | 617-338-6060

Though "conventional", the "decent variety" of Middle Eastern fare offered at this South End haunt is "well priced" and "tasty", and it adequately soaks up the "yummy drinks" (like a Tang-rimmed martini); the decor – "a mix of bold and muted colors" among Moroccan accoutrements – abets a "festive" vibe, but it's too bad "marginal service" can kill the buzz; P.S. a "huge patio", weekend live music and belly dancing and "free parking" are "pluses."

Red House ⓜ *Eclectic*

| 20 | 21 | 20 | $39 |

Harvard Square | 98 Winthrop St. (bet. Eliot & JFK Sts.) | Cambridge | 617-576-0605 | www.theredhouse.com

With a "cozy fireplace in the bar for cold evenings", a "tiny but so wonderful patio for the warm months" and a variety of "private", "romantic" dining rooms, this "charming" Harvard Square Eclectic in a "cute old house" with "sloped ceilings and winding stairs" "nurtures" its supporters whatever the weather; the "genteel" vibe carries over to the fare, much of it offered in half portions (still "quite plentiful") and all "balancing predictability with innovation" "without steep pricing."

Redline ⓩ *American*

| 17 | 14 | 15 | $25 |

Harvard Square | 59 JFK St. (bet. Eliot & Winthrop Sts.) | Cambridge | 617-491-9851 | www.redlinecambridge.com

"Grad students" in particular come to this "clubby", "cozy" Harvard Square spot for a "one-stop evening" where they fill up on "informal", "right-priced" New American eats and either chill out with "sporting events on TV" or get down to "live music" and DJs; just

	FOOD	DECOR	SERVICE	COST

"don't expect much" from the menu and you'll have a better chance of "leaving with a sense of fulfillment."

Red Rock Bistro *American* | 20 | 21 | 18 | $38

Swampscott | 141 Humphrey St./Rte. 129 (Redington St.) | 781-595-1414 | www.redrockbistro.com

When it comes to Swampscott restaurants, "you can't beat the setting" of this "high-profile location" "overlooking the ocean" with "beautiful views of the Boston skyline" ("ask for a table outside or by a window"), while the seafood-heavy New American menu holds its own with many "brilliant" preparations and "large portions"; the rest of the experience wildly diverges between "moderate" and "rip-off" pricing, "loud" and "quiet" atmospheres, and "pleasant" and "snooty service."

Red Sky ● *American* | ▽ 18 | 22 | 20 | $30

Faneuil Hall | 16 North St. (Congress St.) | 617-742-3333 | www.redskyboston.com

An "alternative" to the Faneuil Hall usual, this "chic, classy" hangout offers a "reasonably priced" menu of New American fare for "elegant" lunches, dinners and "late-night dining" amid "loud music, hip people" and an "awesome bar atmosphere"; yes, despite its daytime hours, it really is a "nightclub", but it's "not stuck-up" in any way.

Rendezvous *Mediterranean* | 26 | 19 | 24 | $47

Central Square | 502 Massachusetts Ave. (Brookline St.) | Cambridge | 617-576-1900 | www.rendezvouscentralsquare.com

Central Square suppers "pray to the altar" of "restaurateur par excellence" Steve Johnson at his "whopper" of a "casual" restaurant, a "jazzed-up" "former Burger King" where he "creatively combines" "locally sourced ingredients" to yield "glorious, distinctive" Mediterranean fare ("quite well priced", just like the "fantastic wine list"); "friendly, helpful service" keeps the "comfort level high", especially during Sunday's prix fixe service, featuring the same "wonderful food for a little less cash."

Restaurante Cesaria Ⓜ *Cape Verdean* | - | - | - | 1

Dorchester | 266 Bowdoin St. (bet. Hamilton & Quincy Sts.) | 617-282-1998 | www.restaurantecesaria.com

"If you are willing to travel to Dorchester to find it", this colorful cafe offers the unique tastes of Cape Verdean fare, an exotic mixture of Portuguese and West African cuisines; inexpensive prices help to make it "worth the trip", while weekend musicians from the homeland merit sticking around a while.

Ⓩ Rialto *Italian* | 26 | 25 | 25 | $63

Harvard Square | Charles Hotel | 1 Bennett St. (Eliot St.) | Cambridge | 617-661-5050 | www.rialto-restaurant.com

Breathing "new life" into a "fantastic forbearer", culinary "goddess" Jody Adams has not only "beautifully renovated" her "formal" Harvard Square establishment to more "modern", "stylish" effect, but has "shifted" to "regional Italian specialties", working with "creative", "incredible combinations" of "the freshest ingredients" that

"layer flavor after flavor"; like the menu, the "impressive wine list" contains several "wallet-busters", so "bring the wealthy in-laws" and succumb to the "savvy suggestions" of the staffers, "exemplars of stellar service" all.

Rincon Limeno *Colombian/Peruvian* — | — | — | I

East Boston | 409 Chelsea St. (Shelby St.) | 617-569-4942

Though the translation of its name would have you believe it's a 'corner of Lima', this casual East Boston eatery augments its "delicious Peruvian food" with authentic Colombian fare, of which "amazing", "fresh ceviche" is the star, all of it served in heaping piles; though the colorful environs are tiny, "great service", not to mention "cheap" bills, helps to attracts entire families.

NEW Ristorante Damiano ◐ *Italian* — | — | — | M

North End | 307 Hanover St. (Wesley Pl.) | 617-742-0020 | www.ristorantedamiano.com

Small plates of moderately priced Italian cuisine are served at this intimate North End arrival with exposed brick and gold-tone walls hung with family photos of the Sicilian owner; guests can sip wine and unwind while watching the chefs work in the open kitchen, or get a closer view of the action at the chef's table.

Ristorante Fiore *Italian* 21 | 21 | 19 | $40

North End | 250 Hanover St. (bet. Cross & Parmenter Sts.) | 617-371-1176 | www.ristorantefiore.com

"Good luck getting a table" on this "staple of any North End restaurant tour's" "rocking roof deck", which along with the "street-level patio" is one of "two outdoor dining options" providing a respite from the often "chaotic", "cozy" interior; "although nothing phenomenal", the "old-time" Italian fare is "consistently good" and "not too pricey", while the "wine selection is quite extensive" and the "chatty" "service is more hit than miss."

Ristorante Lucia *Italian* 21 | 16 | 19 | $40

North End | 415 Hanover St. (Charter St.) | 617-367-2353 | www.luciaboston.com

Winchester | 5-13 Mt. Vernon St. (bet. Main & Washington Sts.) | 781-729-0515 | www.luciaristorante.com ◐

"Old timey" to the hilt, this North End and Winchester duo offers Italian "the way it used to be", with all the "usual offerings", "fresh ingredients" and "good wine" pairings; if sometimes it takes a while for the staff to "notice you", at least the Sistine Chapel-inspired "frescoes provide visual entertainment while you wait" in otherwise "tired" digs.

Ristorante Marcellino Ⓜ *Italian* ▽ 16 | 15 | 16 | $39

Waltham | 11 Cooper St. (Pine St.) | 781-647-5458 | www.marcellinorist.com

Friends of this "old-school" Waltham "hideaway" tout its "often terrific", "traditional" Southern Italian cuisine, which is brought to table by a "knowledgeable staff"; foes, however, cite occasionally "rude" servers and a "price-to-quality ratio" that "just

isn't there" as reasons it should either "lower" the tabs or try out some "fresh ideas."

Ristorante Toscano *Italian*   24 | 23 | 22 | $53

Beacon Hill | 41-47 Charles St. (bet. Chestnut & Mt. Vernon Sts.) | 617-723-4090 | www.toscanoboston.com

"Congratulations" are in order, as the new management of this Beacon Hill Italian spot has "much improved" it with "beautiful" "freshened" wood-and-leather decor and "revitalized" "upmarket" fare featuring "tasty" "tributes to authentic Florentine recipes"; mostly "doting" servers offer "terrific advice" on the "great wines", and although it's "pretty pricey", "the clientele can handle it."

Ristorante Villa Francesca ● *Italian*   ▽ 19 | 18 | 19 | $41

North End | 150 Richmond St. (Hanover St.) | 617-367-2948 | www.ristorantevillafrancesca.com

An "attractive setting" (tin ceilings, brick archways, "windows open in the summer"), "knowledgeable, attentive" service and red-sauce "classics done well" lure North End sight-seers to this caffe "off the hustle and bustle of Hanover Street"; however, some connoisseurs caution that those "passionate" about big Italian flavors may find it too "ordinary" "for the money charged."

Riva *Italian*   ▽ 26 | 19 | 24 | $44

Scituate | 116 Front St. (Otis Pl.) | 781-545-5881 | www.rivarestaurant.net

"New owners continue the same tradition of outstanding" dining at this harborside "jewel" in Scituate, whose "small quarters" foodies continue to "jam" for an "extensive menu" of "yummy" Italian cuisine with "pizzazz"; likewise, the "engaging, energetic" staff remains "constantly on alert to answer any questions" that may arise.

Rocca *Italian*   24 | 24 | 21 | $48

South End | 500 Harrison Ave. (Perry St.) | 617-451-5151 | www.roccaboston.com

This South Ender "intrigues" as much with its "refreshing approach to Italian cooking" – namely "terrific", "artfully presented" Ligurian specialties – as it does with "interesting cocktail variants", an "impressive wine list" and a "hip", "modern" setting comprised of a "pulsing", "swanky lounge", a more "soothing dining" room and "über-cool outdoor seating"; though "great for sharing", the "portions are disappointingly modest" for the price – "free parking", on the other hand, is "nirvana."

NEW Rodizio   ▽ 22 | 18 | 22 | $43
Brazilian Steakhouse *Brazilian*

Somerville | 129 Broadway (bet. Michigan & Wisconsin Aves.) | 617-776-1129

Hard-core carnivores "won't leave hungry" from this Somerville newcomer specializing in "succulent, moist" Brazilian barbecue served tableside and an all-you-can-eat buffet of "tasty" sides; the yellow-walled, brightly lit room is a bit utilitarian, while the prices veer toward the expensive.

	FOOD	DECOR	SERVICE	COST

RooBar Ⓜ *American* — 21 | 20 | 21 | $37

Plymouth | Cordage Park | 10 Cordage Park Circle (Court St.) | 508-746-4300 | www.theroobar.com
See review in Cape Cod Directory.

Rosebud Diner *Diner* — 16 | 18 | 18 | $16

Somerville | 381 Summer St. (bet. Cutter Ave. & Grove St.) | 617-666-6015
"Have your eggs" with a side of "sass" at this "tiny" Davis Square diner housed in a "real-deal" dining car from 1941, where "wise-cracking waitresses" dish out "jet fuel coffee" and "filling", "bad-for-you food served just right" and for cheap; in short, it makes for a "fun and funky" experience that "remains true to its beginnings."

Royal East *Chinese* — 20 | 14 | 21 | $24

Central Square | 782-792 Main St. (Windsor St.) | Cambridge | 617-661-1660 | www.royaleast.com
"Low prices do not mean low quality" at this Central Square "banquet restaurant" where "meals can soar" – just "let the owner guide you" to the "fresh" Cantonese seafood and other "authentic" specialties; how-ever, if you fail to "ignore the Americanized" options, you'll join in the chorus of critics who bemoan it "never truly distinguishes" itself.

Rubin's *Deli* — 19 | 9 | 14 | $22

Brookline | 500 Harvard St. (Kenwood St.) | 617-731-8787 | www.rubinskosher.com
An "endearingly gruff appeal" draws Brookliners to this "popular ko-sher establishment" where "dependable" deli fare and "Jewish soul food" made with "care and attention to authenticity" are served up in "reasonably sized and -priced portions" by occasionally "surly" staffers; while the kitchen is making strides to somewhat "modern-ize the menu", "nostalgics" urge it to "stick to corned beef."

NEW Rudi's Resto-Café & Bar *American* — – | – | – | ∇

Roxbury | Hampton Inn Crosstown Ctr. | 811 Massachusetts Ave. (Melnea Cass Blvd.) | 617-345-5432 | www.rudisrestocafe.com
With a sleek industrial look and tall glass walls that overlook the Hampton Inn's courtyard, this affordable New American serves as a cosmopolitan beacon in Roxbury's gritty Newmarket Square area on the cusp of the South End; it's a two-for-one venue with a lounge for night owls and a dining room for business and pleasure.

Rustic Kitchen *Italian* — 20 | 20 | 20 | $38

Park Square | Radisson Hotel Boston | 210 Stuart St. (bet. Church St. & Park Pl.) | 617-423-5700
Hingham | Derby Street Shoppes | 94 Derby St. (Cushing St.) | 781-749-2700
www.rustickitchen.biz
"Fresh, comforting" menus of "basic Italian with a little flair" plus "cool", "modern" atmospheres make for "great scenes" at these "casual" Hingham and Park Square sibs that up their ante with "knowledgeable waiters" and "bartenders that rock"; but the fare's more pleasing "to the eye than to the palate" judge gourmands who "expect more for the price."

	FOOD	DECOR	SERVICE	COST

☑ Ruth's Chris Steak House *Steak* | 24 | 23 | 23 | $64 |

Downtown Crossing | Old City Hall | 45 School St. (Province St.) | 617-742-8401 | www.ruthschris.com

"Nothing beats a steak sizzling in butter" at this New Orleans–based chain where the "melt-in-your-mouth" chops are "cooked to perfection" and delivered on "hot plates" by "attentive" servers; "nestled in Old City Hall" near Downtown Crossing, the "fantastic setting" makes it a "must for special occasions", and while some find it "too expensive", the "off-the-charts" prices are manageable "so long as your boss doesn't care how much you spend."

Sabur *Mediterranean* | ▽ 22 | 21 | 22 | $35 |

Somerville | 212 Holland St. (bet. Claremon & Moore Sts.) | 617-776-7890 | www.saburrestaurant.com

Many who've "stumbled onto" this "cozy" "neighborhood place" with "copper-topped tables" and an open hearth in Somerville's Teele Square have become "addicted" to its "unusual, delicious" fare encompassing "many regions" of the Eastern Mediterranean, the Balkans, Greece and North Africa among them; "knowledgeable and friendly" staffers help to navigate the menu, helping to make for a wholly "memorable" experience; P.S. you've "never seen such original brunch food!"

Sage *Italian* | 24 | 20 | 21 | $52 |

South End | 1395 Washington St. (bet. Pelham & Union Park Sts.) | 617-248-8814 | www.sageboston.com

"Take some sage advice": you "need to experience [chef-owner] Anthony Susi's brilliance and creativity" – and now that his somewhat "pricey" contemporary Italian has moved from "tiny North End" digs to "larger", "modern-Euro" South End environs, more people "can get into" it; presiding over the "spectacular" menu and "strong wine list" are "genuine" servers who "attend to your needs without hovering", both in the full-dining area or the enoteca side, which proffers its own "smart" bar fare.

Sagra *Italian* | 16 | 16 | 15 | $31 |

Somerville | 400 Highland Ave. (Clarendon St.) | 617-625-4200 | www.sagrarestaurant.com

"You get a lot for the price" at this "pretty standard Italian" eatery in Davis Square – and while a few folks admit their "delight" at the dishes, just as many cop to feeling "underwhelmed"; reports of service "slow" and "attitude"-filled crop up more often than not, leaving some Somervilleans wondering if the space, which has changed hands "a number of times over the years", is "cursed."

Sakurabana ☒ *Japanese* | 25 | 12 | 19 | $31 |

Financial District | 57 Broad St. (Milk St.) | 617-542-4311 | www.sakurabanaonline.com

"A must for lunchers in the Financial District", this Japanese "staple" is "always jammed" ("get there early to snag a table") with "suits" digging into an "extensive selection" of "fresh sushi" served in "abundant amounts" and at "reasonable prices"; fare

this "fabulous" "needs a more upscale facility", but "fast service" gets everyone in, out and back to work right quick; P.S. dinner's not as "crazy."

Salts ☒ Ⓜ *American/French* 26 | 22 | 26 | $61

Central Square | 798 Main St. (bet. Cherry & Windsor Sts.) | Cambridge | 617-876-8444 | www.saltsrestaurant.com

Although "not an informal" experience, the "friendly" yet "refined" staff at this "quaint" Central Square spot done up in "elegant burgundy, black" and tan decor "makes you feel right at home" as they ferry "impeccably crafted" French–New American fare filled with "creative" yet "accessible" "twists" that render it "simultaneously gourmet and comforting"; indeed, it's "exactly what fine dining should be", right up to the "pricey" ("but worth it") tabs.

Salvatore's ◑ *Italian* 20 | 18 | 17 | $33

Seaport District | 225 Northern Ave. (D St.) | 617-737-5454 | www.salvatoresboston.com

"Big portions" of "well-prepared" classic Italian fare come for "wonderful prices" at this fairly recent addition to the Seaport dining scene; the "bright", modern decor leaves a few tradition-seekers "cold" (the patio's "nice"), and some of the "friendly" staffers can't mask their "inexperience", but optimists encourage "with a little work", it's "potentially a great spot."

Sanctuary ☒ Ⓜ *Eclectic* ▽ 19 | 20 | 18 | $26

Financial District | 189 State St. (Atlantic Ave.) | 617-573-9333 | www.sanctuaryboston.com

Large Buddhas and "clean lines" create the "cool atmosphere" at this tri-level Financial District club, which plies after-workers with "great martinis" and "tasty", "quality" Eclectic "morsels" priced to allow for all-night noshing.

Sandrine's *French* 24 | 22 | 23 | $48

Harvard Square | 8 Holyoke St. (bet. Mass. Ave. & Mt. Auburn St.) | Cambridge | 617-497-5300 | www.sandrines.com

Both "traditional and innovative Alsatian" fare ("combining the best of French and German" cuisines) fill the "astounding" *carte* at this "tasteful" Harvard Square bistro boasting "old-world elegance" in its "comfortable, inviting" setting; though generally "unobtrusive", the "serious, professional" servers can "match entrees" to selections from the "first-class wine and beer list", helping to make the entire "delectable experience" "worth the price."

S&S *Deli* 18 | 13 | 16 | $21

Inman Square | 1334 Cambridge St. (bet. Hampshire & Prospect Sts.) | Cambridge | 617-354-0777 | www.sandsrestaurant.com

A "no-frills, solid performer" since 1919, this Inman Square "staple" attracts "endless lines" for its "massive" weekend brunches, though it's "huge menu" of "homey", "real deli" fare gets doled out by the "surly", "efficient" staff every other day of the week too; a contingency of foes fume it's too "pricey" for being "consistently mediocre", but let's face it, it must be "doing something right."

Santarpio's Pizza ●🖘 *Pizza* | 25 | 8 | 13 | $17 |

East Boston | 111 Chelsea St. (bet. Paris Pl. & Porter St.) | 617-567-9871 |
www.santarpiospizza.com

"Pizza aficionados" "brave the lines" and the "sketchy" "dump" setting of this East Boston "landmark" where "surly", "crusty" servers "yell at nonregulars" as they dole out "superb thin-crust" pies as well as "inexpensive", "succulent homemade sausages and tasty lamb kebabs"; yes, with the exception of the fare, the experience has "many flaws", but "everyone needs to go" "at least once" – it's "a rite of passage."

Saporito's Ⓜ *Italian* | ▽ 26 | 15 | 24 | $50 |

Hull | 11 Rockland Circle (George Washington Blvd.) | 781-925-3023 |
www.saporitoscafe.com

Urbanites aplenty "schlep" to this "old cottage" in a "remote neighborhood" in Hull where "passionate", "gracious owners" offer up a "beautiful bounty" of "fresh, unique" Northern Italian fare; the dining room is "intimate but not stunning" (the wooden booths in particular are "uncomfortable"), and the prices are a smidge "high", but obviously none of that matters, as it's "always packed."

Sapporo *Japanese/Korean* | ▽ 21 | 15 | 20 | $33 |

Newton | 81 Union St., downstairs (Beacon St.) | 617-964-8044

"Locals love" this family-owned neighborhood spot in Newton Centre where the Japanese-Korean cooking is the "real thing" and the staff is "friendly"; the "small" subterranean setting includes a nine-seat sushi bar and is also renowned for some mighty "great box lunches."

Saraceno *Italian* | ▽ 23 | 21 | 22 | $39 |

North End | 286 Hanover St. (bet. Parmenter & Prince Sts.) | 617-227-5353 |
www.saracenos.com

"Step back in time" at this "classic Italian" in the North End where a "red-gravy" menu straight out of the "Sinatra era" has stayed "consistent" for the last 25 years; the triple-decker layout lures tourists to the ground floor and "regulars upstairs", while the over-the-top, "fresco"-festooned basement is an "excellent date spot"; no matter where you wind up, service is "attentive" and the mood "old school."

Sasso ● *Italian* | 21 | 23 | 22 | $53 |

Back Bay | 116 Huntington Ave. (Garrison St.) | 617-247-2400 |
www.sassoboston.com

With soaring "high ceilings" and a "sophisticated" air, this "lovely" Back Bay Italian (the "sister restaurant" to the North End's Lucca) proffers "upscale" fare in an "impressive" formal dining room or a "quiet mezzanine"; though it inhabits a "cursed" location (ex Ambrosia, ex Blackfin), admirers find it "super all the way" – so long as you bring someone "paying with euros" to settle the "expensive" bill.

NEW Scampo *Italian* | 22 | 24 | 22 | $55 |

Beacon Hill | Liberty Hotel | 215 Charles St. (Cambridge St.) |
617-536-2100 | www.scampoboston.com

The "old Charles Street Jail", now the "hot" Liberty Hotel, is home to this "excellent new addition" to Beacon Hill, where star chef Lydia

Shire showcases a "truly interesting" Italian menu ("prison food it's not") in "Boston's latest place to be seen"; the "cosmopolitan", brick-walled setting is comprised of "various seating areas" – bar, counters, tables, an alfresco patio – but no matter where you sit, you'll find "polished service", "rapacious pricing" and a noise level somewhere between "vibrant" and "deafening."

Scarlet Oak Tavern *Steak* | 20 | 24 | 20 | $45 |

Hingham | 1217 Main St. (Whiting St.) | 781-749-8200 | www.scarletoaktavern.com

This "old inn turned restaurant" in Hingham gives the "quiet South Shore" a jolt with "spacious", "beautifully redone" digs oozing "farmhouse chic" as well as a "vibrant bar" area with a fireplace; the "well-prepared" steaks and American comfort items are debatable, however: "better than average" vs. "doesn't knock your socks off."

Scollay Square *American* | 19 | 19 | 20 | $37 |

Beacon Hill | 21 Beacon St. (Bowdoin St.) | 617-742-4900 | www.scollaysquare.com

A "solid" choice for Beacon Hill "power-lunching" and eavesdropping on local "politicos and wannabes", this retro-minded American manages to "channel the spirit of the old red-light district of the same name" in a "lofty-ceilinged" space decorated with "photos of Boston in earlier eras" (or alfresco on an outdoor patio); look for a "midrange" menu of classic comfort "standards", "friendly" staffers and an overall "fun vibe."

Scoozi *Italian* | 18 | 14 | 15 | $26 |

Back Bay | 235 Newbury St. (Fairfield St.) | 617-247-8847 | www.scooziboston.com

Maybe the staff's "clueless", but the "location's plum" at this "hip" Back Bay Italian where the "fun Euro atmosphere" ("bring your cigarettes and biggest sunglasses") and "amazing patio" outshine the merely "standard Italian" grub; still, the pizzas are "yummy" and the prices "cheap", though many say "what you're really paying for is an outdoor seat on Newbury Street."

Scutra 🅑 *Eclectic* | 23 | 20 | 22 | $45 |

Arlington | 92 Summer St. (Mill St.) | 781-316-1816 | www.scutra.com

"Unexpected" for Arlington, this "out-of-the-way" "suburban sleeper" run by a husband-and-wife team offers "beautifully prepared" Eclectic dishes for "reasonable" dough; though nitpickers say it "tries too hard to be interesting", most find it "memorable", with special kudos for its "cozy", recently "expanded" setting and "pleasant", "professional" service.

Seiyo *Japanese* | ▽ 25 | 24 | 22 | $35 |

South End | 1721C Washington St. (Mass. Ave.) | 617-447-2183 | www.seiyoboston.com

This "great little" South End sushi bar renowned for its "extensive" menu of "high-quality" fish satisfies both "novices and more adventurous" types; "fast" service and "simple", "chic" decor add to its al-

lure, and even though it's "no longer BYO", there's an attached "wine store" with a "good selection" of labels.

☑ Sel de la Terre *French*   `23` `21` `22` `$46`

NEW **Back Bay** | Mandarin Oriental | 774 Boylston St. (Fairfield St.) | 617-266-8800
Waterfront | 255 State St. (Atlantic Ave.) | 617-720-1300
Natick | Natick Collection | 1245 Worcester St. (Rte. 9W) | 508-650-1800
www.seldelaterre.com

Originally opened on the Waterfront, with recent spin-offs in the Natick Collection and the Back Bay, this "notable" French chainlet (itself a more casual spin-off of L'Espalier) offers "high-quality" Provençal cuisine in "stylish" but "rustic" settings; the "skilled" cooking is paired with a "wine list to suit all pocketbooks" served by a "quick", "down-to-earth" team, while "phenomenal" breads from on-site bakeries ice the cake; the only quibble: there's "nothing country about the prices."

NEW Sensing *French*   `-` `-` `-` `E`

Waterfront | Fairmont Battery Wharf | 3 Battery Wharf (Commercial St.) | 617-994-9000 | www.sensingrestaurant.com

Chef Guy Martin has exported his upscale Paris restaurant of the same name to the Waterfront's Fairmount Battery Wharf where he's serving an internationally influenced contemporary French menu that makes use of local ingredients; a chef's table made with tiger-eye marble overlooks the open kitchen, adding a sexy counterpoint to the silk curtains and sycamore tabletops.

Seoul Food *Korean*   ▽ `22` `8` `17` `$19`

Porter Square | 1759 Massachusetts Ave. (bet. Forest & Prentiss Sts.) | Cambridge | 617-864-6299

"Really authentic Korean home cooking" ("like eating at a street food stall in Asia") is yours at this "tiny" Porter Square "hole-in-the-wall" where the "mom-and-pop" owners are so hands-on they'll "tell you off if you don't stir your bibimbop properly"; penny-pinchers praise the "cheap" tabs, but given its "nothing-to-look-at" looks, it "does mostly take-out business."

Serafina Ristorante *Italian*   ▽ `20` `19` `19` `$48`

Concord | 195 Sudbury Rd. (Thoreau St.) | 978-371-9050 | www.serafinaristorante.com

"Slightly different preparations of common dishes" are the calling cards of this Concord Northern Italian "staple" boasting an encyclopedic menu that offers "plenty of choices for even the fussiest of diners"; frequented by "authors" (yoo-hoo, "Doris Kearns Goodwin"), "not-so-famous locals" and random "mature" types, it also enjoys quite the "lively" bar scene.

75 Chestnut *American*   `21` `21` `21` `$38`

Beacon Hill | 75 Chestnut St. (bet. Brimmer & River Sts.) | 617-227-2175 | www.75chestnut.com

"Like putting on a comfy cardigan", this "charming" American feels "welcoming" to all "even though it's in posh Beacon Hill"; many regu-

lars "flock to the bar" for "free cheese and crackers" and the "fantastic wines and drinks", while families are "never let down" by the "solid" "comfort food" (at "price points to match all budgets") and "congenial" service in the "cozy" dining room, especially on "wintry nights."

Shabu-Zen *Japanese*   22 | 16 | 17 | $25
Allston | 80 Brighton Ave. | 617-782-8888
Chinatown | 16 Tyler St. (bet. Beach & Kneeland Sts.) | 617-292-8828
www.shabuzen.com
"Really get to know your friends" as you "dip your food in the same broth" at these "interactive" shabu-shabu specialists in Allston and Chinatown, where "cook-it-yourself" types have "fun" making their own Japanese hot pot meals; first-timers applaud the "novelty" aspect of these "unique experiences", and even though there's "not much service" by definition, they're "affordable" and "perfect first date spots."

Shanghai Gate *Chinese*   ▽ 24 | 16 | 15 | $21
Allston | 204 Harvard Ave. (Commonwealth Ave.) | 617-566-7344
"In case you thought all Chinese food tastes the same", this "refreshingly original" Allston storefront whips up "truly authentic" Shanghainese dishes with "strong flavors" that just might "knock your socks off"; the "off-the-beaten-path" address, "sketchy" decor and "lousy" service are all forgotten when the "great-deal" bill appears.

Shangri-La Ⓜ *Taiwanese*   23 | 9 | 15 | $18
Belmont | 149 Belmont St. (School St.) | 617-489-1488
"Weekend dim sum" brings "long queues" to this "small" Belmont Chinese offering "unusual", "authentic Taiwanese" cooking for an "affordable" price; despite "sparse decor" and "rude" servers more "interested in turning tables" than waiting on you, diehards insist the "excellent" chow keeps them "coming back."

Shanti: Taste of India *Indian/Pan-Asian*   - | - | - | M
Dorchester | 1111 Dorchester Ave. (Savin Hill Ave.) | 617-929-3900 |
www.shantiboston.com
An "undiscovered gem" in Dorchester, this "solid" Indian purveys an "authentic", "carefully seasoned" menu that also throws regional dishes from Bangladesh and Pakistan into the mix; "attentive" service, "good-deal" lunch buffets and a "comfortable" interior (including surprisingly "lush bathrooms") are all part of the package.

Shawarma King Ⓜ *Lebanese*   22 | 7 | 15 | $13
Brookline | 1383 Beacon St. (Harvard St.) | 617-731-6035 |
www.thebestshawarmaking.com
For a taste of "Lebanon in Brookline", check out this "tiny", "crowded" spot offering the namesake dish and other standards rendered with a "delicious tang"; "large servings", "inexpensive" tabs and "late-night" hours trump the "noisy" acoustics, "oblivious" staffers and the inevitable "garlic breath", but insiders agree "takeout is the thing" what with the "not-elegant" setting.

	FOOD	DECOR	SERVICE	COST

Sherborn Inn, The *New England* `19` `20` `18` `$38`

Sherborn | The Sherborn Inn | 33 N. Main St./Rte. 16 (Rte. 27) | 508-655-9521 | www.sherborninn.com

Set in a "Colonial-era" inn, this "charming" Sherborn eatery offers New England "comfort food at a comfort price" either in a "fireplace"-equipped tavern or a more-formal dining room; although "nothing to write home about" generally, it's "good for the 'burbs", and regulars are hopeful that it's "found its groove" now that there's a "new chef" and a rejiggered menu.

Shogun Ⓜ *Japanese* ▽ `23` `16` `21` `$30`

Newton | 1385 Washington St. (Elm St.) | 617-965-6699 | www.shogunwestnewton.com

They're "always happy to see you" at this West Newton "local favorite" that "changed hands recently", though the "sushi chef for the last 20 years" remains on board; regulars relish the "inexpensive" pricing and "small", homey environs, and though the Japanese dishes lean toward the "predictable", ultimately it's a "good neighborhood restaurant" that "doesn't feel overdone."

Sibling Rivalry *American* `24` `22` `23` `$54`

South End | 525 Tremont St. (Berkeley St.) | 617-338-5338 | www.siblingrivalryboston.com

At this "hip" South End "gimmick that works", diners choose from two "inventive" New American menus conceived by "dueling brothers" Bob and David Kinkead "using the same main ingredients"; the "interesting theme" continues in the dining rooms (one "reasonably elegant", the other "fun and lighthearted"), which along with the "cool patio", get "crazy" "noisy"; as for the battles of value and service, they're still being waged, with "overpriced" leading "worth it" and "solicitous" ahead of "disinterested."

Sichuan Garden *Chinese* `22` `15` `17` `$25`

Brookline | 295 Washington St. (Harvard St.) | 617-734-1870
Woburn | 2 Alfred St. (Rte. 95) | 781-935-8488
www.sichuangarden2.com

There's "no need to go to Chinatown" for "spicy" chow thanks to these "wow"-inducing Brookline/Woburn alternatives that "don't turn down the heat for the New England palate"; insiders stick to the "authentic Sichuan" offerings (the "generic Chinese food is just ok"), but no matter what you order, prices are "decent" and communication with the staff "difficult."

Ⓩ Sichuan Gourmet *Chinese* `27` `16` `21` `$24`

Framingham | 271 Worcester Rd./Rte. 9 (bet. Ordway & Pierce Sts.) | 508-626-0248 | www.laosichuan.com

"When they say spicy, they mean it" at this "find in Framingham", where the "outstanding" Sichuan cooking can "make your eyeballs sweat" and leave you "breathing fire" (though "wimps" report that it can "tone down the heat if requested"); given all the fireworks on the plate, the atmosphere is "irrelevant", though some manage to remember the "cheap" pricing, "busy" pace and "somewhat harried" service.

Sidney's Grille *American* ▽ 21 | 19 | 20 | $33

Central Square | Le Meridien Hotel | 20 Sidney St. (Green St.) | Cambridge | 617-577-0200 | www.sidneysgrille.com

A "refuge from the bustle of Cambridge", this "quiet" Central Square New American in the Le Meridien offers just "what you'd expect from a hotel restaurant", including a "great weekend brunch"; an "excellent location", spacious layout and "reasonable price-to-quality" ratio make up for the fact that there's "no ambiance."

Silvertone Bar & Grill ⓩ *American* 21 | 16 | 19 | $25

Downtown Crossing | 69 Bromfield St. (Tremont St.) | 617-338-7887 | www.silvertonedowntown.com

"Rock-solid" American comfort food and "potent cocktails" collide at this "hidden" Downtown Crossing underground lair that lures "young professionals" seeking "after-work" thrills in a "retro", "speakeasy"-esque setting; sure, it can be "too damn noisy" and "crowded", but that's to be expected given the "honest" pricing, "sassy service" and that "to-die-for mac 'n' cheese."

Siros *Italian* ▽ 19 | 20 | 20 | $42

North Quincy | Marina Bay | 307 Victory Rd. (Marina Dr.) | 617-472-4500 | www.sirosrestaurants.com

It's "all about being outside" at this longtime Italian overlooking Quincy's Marina Bay, where the "cool" waterfront location (and boat-docking facilities) trumps the "decent" albeit "solid" Italian grub; service is "good" and the ambiance "pleasant", but economists figure it's "a bit expensive" for the area.

NEW 606 Congress *American* 21 | 23 | 22 | $42

Seaport District | Renaissance Boston Waterfront Hotel | 606 Congress St. (D St.) | 617-476-5606 | www.renaissancebostonwaterfront.com

Appealing "American-style tapas" offered in portions more "generous" than the norm – not to mention "yummy" cocktails – have admirers congregating at this "big, open, sleek" Seaport District hotel eatery; as with any small-plates place, it can be "a tad pricey", but it's generally "worth it", especially factoring in the "smooth service."

Sixty2 on Wharf Ⓜ *Italian* ▽ 24 | 21 | 21 | $44

Salem | 62 Wharf St. (Derby St.) | 978-744-0062 | www.sixty2onwharf.com

Bringing a "breath of fresh air" to Salem's Pickering Wharf district, this "upscale" Italian offers a "modern", "carefully prepared" menu via an "ambitious young chef", along with a well-parsed wine list; "uneven service" (sometimes "friendly", sometimes "over-rehearsed") seems to be its only shortcoming.

Skipjack's *Seafood* 20 | 17 | 19 | $37

Back Bay | 199 Clarendon St. (bet. Boylston St. & St. James Ave.) | 617-536-3500

Newton | 55 Needham St. (Rte. 128) | 617-964-4244

NEW Foxboro | Patriots Place | 226 Patriot Pl. (Washington St.) | 508-543-2200

(continued)

Skipjack's

Natick | 1400 Worcester Rd./Rte. 9 (Speen St.) | 508-628-9900
www.skipjacks.com

Afishionados assert this "'other' Boston seafood chain" holds its own with "excellent value and freshness"; critics counter it "doesn't hold a candle" to its rival, specifying "mediocre" quality and an "unimaginative" menu, but an "eager-to-please staff" and "relaxed, comfortable" setting help make it, at the least, a "good alternative."

Sky *American*

19 | 19 | 19 | $38

Norwood | 1369 Providence Hwy. (Sumner St.) | 781-255-8888
Sudbury | 120 Boston Post Rd./Rte. 20 (Old Country Rd.) | 978-440-8855
www.sky-restaurant.com

"Popular" with "large groups" and "young families", these Norwood and Sudbury New Americans serve "solid", "interesting" fare in a "comfortable" setting decked out in "funky decor"; while naysayers feel "no urge to return" to the "noisy and crowded" environs for dishes they consider "too pricey" and "average at best", partyers "go for the bar scene."

Smith & Wollensky *Steak*

23 | 23 | 22 | $63

Back Bay | The Castle at Park Sq. | 101 Arlington St. (Columbus Ave.) | 617-423-1112 | www.smithandwollensky.com

The Back Bay's "lovely" old Armory ("unique" in its "faux-medieval" architecture) is the "treasured setting" of this homage to dry-aged prime, in which "energetic", "knowledgeable" staffers serve a "testosterone"-filled clientele "big steaks, big drinks and big bills"; it doesn't stray too far from its "chain formula", leading originality-seekers to opine "you won't leave disappointed, but you won't remember it either."

NEW Sofra Bakery & Café *Mideastern*

26 | 19 | 17 | $14

Huron Village | 1 Belmont St. (Mt. Auburn St.) | Cambridge | 617-661-3161 | www.sofrabakery.com

"It hasn't ironed out the wrinkles yet", but the "early read is promising" on this "quaint and different" Middle Easterner near Huron Village, a "wonderful addition" that "feeds cravings" for chef Ana Sortun's "Oleana without the reservations or cost"; "out-of-this-world pastries" and savories win raves, though it's "a bit cramped" amid the kilim rugs and could use "more seating."

Sol Azteca *Mexican*

20 | 19 | 19 | $28

Brookline | 914A Beacon St. (bet. Park Dr. & St. Mary's St.) | 617-262-0909
Newton | 75 Union St. (Beacon St.) | 617-964-0920
www.solaztecarestaurants.com

Fans of the "reliable", "authentic Mexican" fare served by these separately owned Brookline and Newton cantinas proclaim "the *sol* shines bright here", citing "reasonable prices" and "pleasant" "outdoor seating" that's "perfect" for enjoying "amazing sangria" and "potent margaritas"; inside, the "friendly and helpful" servers navigate a "somewhat cramped", "cozy" setup featuring tiled tabletops.

	FOOD	DECOR	SERVICE	COST

Solea Restaurant & Tapas Bar ● *Spanish*   23 | 21 | 21 | $36

Waltham | 388 Moody St. (Cushing St.) | 781-894-1805 |
www.solearestaurant.com

"Dalí's less self-conscious, easier-to-get-into younger sibling" provides Waltham diners with a "festive" "Spanish atmosphere" that's
"perfect" for a midpriced "romantic dinner" or just nibbling on a
"great selection of tapas"; diners have a choice between a "fun and
social" bar that's "crowded after work with young professionals"
and a "quieter", recently "expanded" dining area, both of which are
patrolled by "helpful" servers.

Soma ⊠ *American*   ▽ 22 | 21 | 18 | $43

Beverly | 256 Cabot St. (bet. Dane & Hale Sts.) | 978-524-0033 |
www.somabeverly.com

A "great place before the North Shore Music Theater", this Beverly
hipster attracts with an "extraordinary martini bar" and "wonderful
cocktails" served in a modern yet "warm atmosphere" featuring exotic
woods; while "fun", the Mediterranean-influenced New American fare
is "inconsistent", plus ticket-holders often have to "wait for it."

Something Savory ⊠ *Eclectic*   ▽ 22 | 12 | 20 | $23

Arlington | 1312 Massachusetts Ave. (Park Ave.) | 781-648-0333 |
www.somethingsavory.com

Locals laud this "sweet" "neighborhood joint" and its "limited but interesting" Eclectic roster of "creative" "Caribbean-style food" that
makes patrons "glad to live in Arlington"; the "small storefront" space
lacking "ambiance" is really "more of a take-out place" and caterer, but
that doesn't stop the "love" for the "spicy" vittles and "good-value"
tabs; P.S. "it's even better now that it serves beer, wine and sangria."

Sonsie ● *Eclectic*   20 | 21 | 18 | $40

Back Bay | 327 Newbury St. (bet. Hereford St. & Mass. Ave.) |
617-351-2500 | www.sonsieboston.com

"Still the place to see and be seen", this Back Bay Eclectic draws "a
trendy, sexy crowd" and is "great for celebrity sightings" at its mahogany bar, "intimate" "downstairs wine room" and "front cafe tables" providing "views of the Newbury Street scene"; while fans
cheer the "interesting" midpriced menu, "hangover-curing brunch"
and "pizza to die for", foes snipe it's "average with big attitude."

Sophia's Grotto *Mediterranean*   23 | 22 | 24 | $32

Roslindale | 22R Birch St. (bet. Belgrade Ave. & Corinth St.) |
617-323-4595 | www.sophiasgrotto.com

Lots of "surprises" await at this "cute nook" in Roslindale that serves a
"varied and well-executed menu" of Mediterranean fare including
"wood-fired pizza" in a "lovely, cozy, festive" space with a "wonderful
patio"; "friendly service" and "reasonable prices" further enchant.

Sorella's ⊅ *American*   ▽ 26 | 18 | 21 | $27

Jamaica Plain | 386-388 Centre St. (Sheridan St.) | 617-524-2016

A Jamaica Plain "tradition", this "real neighborhood joint" serves
"astoundingly varied" American breakfasts starring "more omelets

and waffles than you can shake a stick at" that are "so darn good, they might be illegal"; "a down-home atmosphere" permeates the "funky surroundings", and a "friendly staff" strives to accommodate "brutally" "long lines on weekends."

Sorelle *Coffeehouse* ▽ 23 | 19 | 21 | $14
Charlestown | 1 Monument Ave. (Main St.) | 617-242-2125 ⊟
Charlestown | 100 City Sq. (Chelsea St.) | 617-242-5980
www.sorellecafe.com

This duo of Charlestown coffeehouses-cum-cafes provides locals with a "bright, cheerful" spot in which to "read, work or study" while enjoying "addictive coffee", "fresh, high-quality" "bakery items" and "top-notch sandwiches"; the "roomy, contemporary" City Square location "has WiFi" and a wine bar, while the "tiny but nicely located" Monument Avenue location is "more intimate."

☑ Sorellina *Italian* 27 | 28 | 26 | $65
Back Bay | 1 Huntington Ave. (Dartmouth St.) | 617-412-4600 |
www.sorellinaboston.com

"Luxurious", "modern", "perfectly lit" black-and-white decor makes for a "visually stunning" setting at this "awesome experience" in the Back Bay, while just as "wow"-worthy is Jamie Mammano's Italian fare filled with "contemporary" "twists" and "sumptuous combinations of fresh ingredients"; "caring, professional service" helps to create a "terrific ambiance" overall that leaves admirers "wishing" they "could afford to go more often."

Sorento's *Italian/Persian* 18 | 13 | 17 | $29
Marlborough | 128 Main St. (bet. Court & Florence Sts.) | 508-486-0090 |
www.sorentos.com

"Quick, basic Italian" fare of the "pasta, pizza and salad" variety is served (slightly incongruously) alongside a menu of Persian specialties at this "dependable", "easy and familiar" Marlborough haunt; true, the offerings are "average", but they're "big enough to share" and "affordable."

Sorriso ☒ *Italian* 20 | 19 | 19 | $35
Leather District | 107 South St. (bet. Beach & Essex Sts.) | 617-259-1560 |
www.sorrisoboston.com

Serving "reasonably priced rustic Italian dishes" and "great pizzas", this Leather District trattoria "draws a professional crowd" for "value" lunches, while at night it's a "quieter, cozier scene"; service is "efficient and quick", and there's a "mellow, romantic feel" in the "deceptively big", "high-ceilinged" space that's also a "nice place for a drink after work."

Soul Fire *BBQ* 21 | 17 | 19 | $20
Allston | 182 Harvard Ave. (Commonwealth Ave.) | 617-787-3003 |
www.soulfirebbq.com

Some aficionados "swear by" the "tremendous barbecue" dished out at this "often overlooked" "neighborhood gem" "in the middle of Allston" – while others call it "nothing special"; but the "well-organized" space with its "cool ambiance" and "soul music in the

background", plus a "friendly" staff and "great prices", have fans hailing the package as "perfect in so many ways"; N.B. table service was added post-Survey.

Sound Bites *American/Mideastern* | 22 | 14 | 16 | $15 |

Somerville | 704 Broadway (Boston Ave.) | 617-623-8338

Sound Bites BBQ & Grill *American/Mideastern*

Somerville | Ball Sq. | 711 Broadway (bet. Josephine & Willow Aves.) | 617-623-9464

www.soundbitesrestaurant.com

Since relocating to "larger quarters", "the inevitable lines" for this Somerville American's "unbelievable breakfasts" "now move quicker" and "service isn't as rushed"; so while the "wait is shorter", there still is one, but it's "worth it" for such "huge portions for your buck"; Mideastern plates join the menu lineup at lunch and dinner and at the sibling BBQ & Grill.

South End Buttery *Coffeehouse/Sandwiches* | 21 | 18 | 19 | $18 |

South End | 314 Shawmut Ave. (Union Park St.) | 617-482-1015 | www.southendbuttery.com

Fans of this "charming" bakery – a "favorite breakfast/brunch spot" "in a gorgeous part of the South End" – are "so glad it expanded" to include an "adorable" "new bistro" (which the scores may not reflect) serving "innovative" New American fare to add to the "fantastic cupcakes"; detractors call it "overrated", but pets-lovers like that "a portion of the proceeds are donated" to local animal rescue causes – and you can "bring your dog if sitting outside."

South Street Diner ● *Diner* | 16 | 12 | 16 | $17 |

Leather District | 178 Kneeland St. (South St.) | 617-350-0028 | www.southstreetdiner.com

In a "city that shuts down early", this "always packed" Leather District "institution" is "one of only" a handful of places "open all night", meaning you can "get your grease on" "in the wee hours of the morning" via budget-boosting "old-time diner" fare; while the whole experience may be "ok" at best, with the help of the "friendly, quirky staff", it "serves its purpose."

Spice Thai Cuisine *Thai* | ∇ 21 | 15 | 14 | $20 |

Harvard Square | 24 Holyoke St. (Mt. Auburn St.) | Cambridge | 617-868-9560 | www.spicethaicuisine.com

With its "convenient Harvard Square location", this "small" eatery where "the prices are right" is a "regular haunt" for lovers of "reliable", "tasty Thai food"; while "service is generally efficient and fast", customers "disappointed by the no-alcohol" policy can opt for takeout; P.S. "'spicy' means it", but "you can ask for a milder version."

NEW Sportello Ⓢ *Italian* | - | - | - | M |

Seaport District | 348 Congress St. (Farnsworth St.) | 617-737-1234 | www.sportelloboston.com

Homemade pastas, soups and salads take center stage at this upscale take on a funky, affordable Italian trattoria courtesy of

chef Barbara Lynch (No. 9 Park); done up in brushed chrome and white-and-brown tones, its coffee shop–like setting includes wraparound counter seating and a take-out area serving sweet and savory snacks.

☒ Square Café *American*

26 | 26 | 23 | $45

Hingham | 150 North St. (bet. Central & Main Sts.) | 781-740-4060 | www.thesquarecafe.com

"Obviously popular" with a "local crowd", this "South Shore trea-sure" "in the heart of Hingham" serves a "small but interesting menu" of "consistently high-quality" New American comfort food; devotees appreciate "friendly service" and "cozy" environs, "stun-ningly decorated and lively with people", while bestowing extra ku-dos on the "well-priced and smartly chosen wine list."

St. Alphonzo's Kitchen ☒ *American*

▽ 22 | 12 | 23 | $22

South Boston | 87 A St. (W. 3rd St.) | 617-269-2233

Though its fans feel like they're "the only ones who know about it", they're enthusiastically spreading the word about this "hidden" Southie "gem", a "tiny" "gourmet diner" whipping up New American cooking that "makes both bellies and wallets happy."

Stanhope Grille *American*

▽ 23 | 20 | 23 | $43

Back Bay | Jurys Boston Hotel | 350 Stuart St. (Berkeley St.) | 617-532-3827 | www.jurysdoyle.com

Discoverers of this "modern restaurant" decorated in earth tones and "hidden" inside the "vibrant" Jurys Boston Hotel in the Back Bay judge it a "gem" for an "outstanding" New American menu that offers "something for everyone"; "impeccable service" extends to the sunken "outdoor patio", "a wonderful place to dine during warm weather."

Stars on Hingham Harbor *Diner*

16 | 12 | 15 | $24

Hingham | 3 Otis St./Rte. 3A (North St.) | 781-749-3200 | www.eatwellinc.com

"A cut above a diner", this "popular spot" is a "fun place for the fam-ily" to command a booth and chow down on "wonderful breakfasts" and well-priced "classic" American "staples" (including "burgers to kill for") in a "relaxed" – and "quite noisy" – setting "across from Hingham Harbor"; "spotty service" irks, but it's nothing that can't be washed away by "amazing beers", plus "sports on plasma TVs", at the bar.

Stella ◑ *Italian*

24 | 22 | 21 | $44

South End | 1525 Washington St. (W. Brookline St.) | 617-247-7747 | www.bostonstella.com

There's "always a buzz" at this "hip and chic" Italian South Ender "out of South Beach"; "trendy" crowds brave the "noisy" setting be-cause "it's the place" "to see and be seen" "along bustling Washington Street", and though some cry "overhyped", the con-verted contend "service is just right" and the menu's "takes on pasta and pizza" are "inventive."

	FOOD	DECOR	SERVICE	COST
	22	18	21	$40

talian

Water....n | 47 Main St./Rte. 20 (Rte. 16) | 617-924-9475 |
www.stellinarestaurant.com

This "longtimer" in Watertown Square provides "a treat that won't break the bank" with its "solid" "seasonal Italian fare from different regions"; the setting includes an interior trattoria that exudes "cozy" "warmth", a "beautiful patio" "with a fountain" that "transports you to another world" and a bar where chatty Cathys enjoy "dining and schmoozing."

Stephanie's on Newbury _American_ | 20 | 19 | 18 | $37 |

Back Bay | 190 Newbury St. (Exeter St.) | 617-236-0990 |
www.stephaniesonnewbury.com

A "Back Bay staple" for its "prime" "sidewalk patio" that's "a people-watching haven", this midpriced New American's "stylish home cooking" "hits the spot" for those "craving comfort food"; "service can be spotty" in the "warm" clubby space, though the biggest complaint is that it can be "noisy" and is "so popular, you typically have to wait."

Steve's Greek Restaurant _Greek_ | 20 | 10 | 17 | $20 |

Back Bay | 316 Newbury St. (Hereford St.) | 617-267-1817
Faneuil Hall | Faneuil Hall Mktpl. | 1 Faneuil Hall Sq. (Congress St.) |
617-263-1166

This "reliable neighborhood institution" – "an informal haven among Newbury Street's countless upscale restaurants" – offers "straightforward", "quick and tasty", "classic Greek" fare; with "inexpensive" prices, a "small", plain dining area and "fast service", it's the "closest thing to a diner in the Back Bay"; N.B. the Faneuil Hall food-court take-out stall offers a similar menu and value.

STIX Restaurant & Lounge ●☒ _Eclectic_ | 17 | 17 | 18 | $36 |

Back Bay | 35 Stanhope St. (bet. Berkeley & Clarendon Sts.) |
617-456-7849 | www.stixboston.com

For a meal with an "interesting twist", diners detour to this "hip" Back Bay sibling of 33 Restaurant for its "innovative" "food on skewers" with "tremendous dipping sauces"; the "funky decor" ("the bar lights up in colors"), "friendly staff" and "innovative" drinks make for a "fun atmosphere", though some snap it "can get expensive" for "meat lollipops" that are "better in concept than practice."

Stockyard _Steak_ | 15 | 13 | 16 | $33 |

Brighton | 135 Market St. (N. Beacon St.) | 617-782-4700 |
www.stockyardrestaurant.com

"A neighborhood standby for decades", this "huge" Brighton steakhouse's "many rooms" are packed with "families and locals" chowing down on "substantial fare without the frills"; the "decor and staff are pretty old-school" (there's "lots of dark wood"), and while herds herald the "solid" fare as a "good value", crossed carnivores beef it's "lost its mojo."

	FOOD	DECOR	SERVICE	COST

Stone Soup Cafe ✍ *Eclectic* ▽ 25 | 17 | 21 | $37

Ipswich | 0 Central St. (Market St.) | 978-356-4222

Fans of this "satisfying stop" in quiet Ipswich praise its "fresh", sometimes "unusual" Eclectic fare focusing on soup "ingredients available for the season", "monster sandwiches" and Thursday–Sunday–only dinners; it's "not a big place" (with "no pretense about decor"), but with such "low" prices, "the wait is worth it", especially for the "top-notch brunch."

Strega Restaurant & Lounge Ⓜ *Italian* ▽ 21 | 19 | 18 | $38

Salem | 94 Lafayette St. (Peabody St.) | 978-741-0004 | www.stregasalem.com

"Glitzophiles" and lovers of "authentic Italian" fare "wait in line" for seats at this Salem trattoria's "lovely" dining area; detractors who determine the "service could be better" and the moderately priced food is "spotty" suggest "sticking to" the "big, inviting bar" for some "great atmosphere."

Strega Ristorante *Italian* 21 | 18 | 19 | $45

North End | 379 Hanover St. (bet. Clark & Fleet Sts.) | 617-523-8481 | www.stregaristorante.com

Cheerleaders of this "noisy" North End Italian with "mobster movies playing" on "a bank of TVs" and "service that's a little in your face" contend that the "super-modern" decor and "fun atmosphere" – plus a "pretty good chance of running into a celeb" – enhance "authentic" dishes that "you can tell a lot of love goes into"; "disappointed" dons differ, calling it a "Hollywood caricature" with "way more hype than it's worth."

Strip-T's Ⓧ *American* ▽ 22 | 12 | 18 | $19

Watertown | 93 School St. (Arsenal St.) | 617-923-4330 | www.stripts.com

"Long live this little neighborhood" "gem" that's "worth the trip" to "the backstreets of Watertown" root supporters of the "funky", "family-run" venue's "offbeat menu" of "healthy, fresh and yummy" "comfort food" (e.g. "amazing" "homemade soups"); the "homey" "quarters are a little cramped", so some say it's "mostly a take-out spot", but the "friendly" service, "hearty portions" and "bargain" prices can "soothe the soul."

Sugar & Spice *Thai* 20 | 16 | 17 | $19

Porter Square | 1933 Massachusetts Ave. (Davenport St.) | Cambridge | 617-868-4200 | www.sugarspices.com

A "friendly", "quick" staff serves "delicious and affordable" Thai fare in a "pleasant, modern room" with "eclectic, funky" decor at this Porter Square spot; while it "won't make you think you're in Bangkok", the "fresh ingredients" and "decent-sized portions" should at least "hold you over until your next trip."

Suishaya ● *Japanese/Korean* ▽ 21 | 14 | 14 | $30

Chinatown | 2 Tyler St. (Beach St.) | 617-423-3848

This small Chinatown Korean also serves an assortment of Japanese fare and stays open until 2 AM nightly, attracting night owls with its

affordable prices and "ginormous Japanese beer cans"; but sushi lovers are forewarned – you could wind up "waiting forever" due to uneven service.

Sultan's Kitchen ☒ *Turkish* 24 | 8 | 13 | $17

Financial District | 116 State St. (Broad St.) | 617-570-9009 | www.sultans-kitchen.com

"Long lines" of Financial District workers ignore the "gruff service" and lack of atmosphere at this "crazy popular change from the usual sandwich place" and focus on the "fresh, flavorful" doner kebab and other Turkish fare that's "inexpensive" and "prepared to order"; the interior is "not much to look at" and the "tables are cramped", so most admirers simply "get takeout."

Summer Winter ☒ *American* 24 | 22 | 20 | $54

Burlington | Boston Marriott Burlington | 1 Mall Rd. (I-95, exit 33B) | 781-221-6643 | www.markandclarkrestaurants.com

"Fans of Arrows" in Ogunquit, Maine, are "not disappointed" by this "fantastic" venue from owners Mark Gaier and Clark Frasier in the Burlington Marriott, an "incredible" "suburban" "surprise" that offers "beautifully presented" New American fare spotlighting local ingredients including "produce from an on-premises greenhouse"; the "casual yet refined" atmosphere gets kudos, so occasionally "below-par" service has diners concluding "once the kinks are worked out" it should be across-the-board "excellent."

Sunset Cafe *American/Portuguese* ▽ 19 | 14 | 15 | $23

Inman Square | 851 Cambridge St. (bet. Hunting & Willow Sts.) | Cambridge | 617-547-2938 | www.thesunsetcafe.net

Despite a "convenient location" in Inman Square and "good" "Portuguese dishes at low prices", the big attraction of this American-Iberian is live "fado music on the weekends"; while some sit on their hands for "neglectful service", admirers applaud the "wine selection" while deeming it a wholly "underappreciated gem."

Sunset Cantina ❶ *Pub Food* 20 | 17 | 19 | $22

Boston University | 916 Commonwealth Ave. (bet. Pleasant & St. Paul Sts.) | 617-731-8646

Sunset Grill & Tap ❶ *Pub Food*

Allston | 130 Brighton Ave. (Harvard Ave.) | 617-254-1331 | www.allstonsfinest.com

"Beer connoisseurs" "always have a good time" pouring over the "enormous global beer list" ("over 100 on tap", seemingly "countless by the bottle") at this "designed-for-fun" B.U. grill, which augments its "stars" with a "huge menu" featuring "every type" of American pub fare "imaginable"; the Allston cantina concentrates on an "extensive tequila selection" (with a more Southwestern focus on the grub), while both are "loud, crowded" and "well priced."

Super Fusion Cuisine *Asian Fusion* ▽ 27 | 8 | 20 | $28

Brookline | 690A Washington St. (Beacon St.) | 617-277-8221

A "secret for outstanding sushi", this "unique" Washington Square "hole-in-the-wall" is a "real find" with "value" prices on "wonder-

fully fresh" rolls and Japanese fusion fare boasting "striking taste combinations"; "what it lacks in space and decor" (the "cramped quarters" have "limited seating"), "it easily makes up for in taste, price and innovation", plus "takeout is always an option."

Sweet Basil Ⓜ⇄ *Italian*   25 | 16 | 22 | $33

Needham | 942 Great Plain Ave. (Highland Ave.) | 781-444-9600 | www.sweetbasilneedham.com

"Thank goodness" it has "doubled in size" cheer Needhamites who shower a "chorus of kudos" upon this "crazy busy" "bargain" and its "ridiculously big portions" of "loaded-with-garlic", "delicious traditional Italian dishes"; though "it's still very tight and noisy, who cares", shrug fans, when there's also BYO and "friendly service" – now "if they only took reservations and credit cards."

Taberna de Haro Ⓢ *Spanish*   23 | 18 | 20 | $37

Brookline | 999 Beacon St. (St. Mary's St.) | 617-277-8272 | www.tabernaboston.com

A "fantastic wine list" complements the "authentic and uncompromising" selection of "wonderfully savory" tapas that flows from this Brookline Spaniard's "open kitchen" to the "charming", "cozy" dining room where "happy people eating well" sit "elbow to elbow"; though it can be "a little pricey" and "slow", the "delicious" fare and "neighborhood feel" leave most shouting "*olé!*"

Tacos El Charro *Mexican*   ▽ 23 | 10 | 19 | $19

Jamaica Plain | 349 Centre St. (Hyde Sq.) | 617-522-2578

"Tucked away" in a corner of Jamaica Plain, this "true Mexican" "hole-in-the-wall" may "look a bit rough around the edges", but its amigos applaud the "authentic", "outstanding tacos and enchiladas"; "good prices" and "sweet employees" make it all the more "worth finding;" P.S. only beer and wine are served, so there's sangria, but "no margaritas."

Tacos Lupita *Mexican/Salvadoran*   25 | 6 | 14 | $11

Revere | 107 Shirley Ave. (Walnut Ave.) | 781-284-2430 Ⓜ⇄
Somerville | 13 Elm St. (Porter St.) | 617-666-0677 ⇄
Lynn | 129 Munroe St. (Washington St.) | 781-593-6437
Lawrence | 505 Broadway (Manchester St.) | 978-681-4517 Ⓜ⇄

This quartet's lack of decor may "make you wince", but its Mexican-Salvadoran fare "will make you swoon", from the "mouthwatering pork" and "mean burritos" to "perfect guacamole" and "homemade tortillas"; since it's staffed by "unhurried ladies whose respect you gotta earn", the service is "hit-or-miss", but economical "eat-and-runners" agree it delivers plenty of "bang for your buck."

Taiwan Cafe ◑⇄ *Taiwanese*   23 | 8 | 15 | $19

Chinatown | 34 Oxford St. (Beach St.) | 617-426-8181

Adventurers seeking "lunch specials" and "late-night" fixes "jam pack" this "no-frills" "storefront" in Chinatown that serves up "amazing" Taiwanese fare; cognoscenti coax "don't be scared" off by "authentic" dishes that spotlight the likes of "intestines" and

"fermented tofu", as there are also offerings "for the faint of heart" – all delivered "fresh", "cheap" and "fast."

Tamarind Bay Bistro & Bar *Indian*   24 | 15 | 18 | $30

Harvard Square | 75 Winthrop St. (JFK St.) | Cambridge | 617-491-4552

Tamarind Bay Coastal Indian Kitchen *Indian*

NEW **Brookline** | 1665 Beacon St. (Winthrop Rd.) | 617-277-1752

www.tamarind-bay.com

This "cheerful", "unconventional Indian" in Harvard Square (with a new seafood-centric Brookline sib) features "subtle" "sauces made from scratch" in "refined" and "innovative" dishes that "trump the minimalist service and decor"; though some grouse it's "expensive" for having "subterranean" digs, optimists opine it's "a welcome change."

Z Tangierino ● *Moroccan*   24 | 26 | 21 | $45

Charlestown | 83 Main St. (Pleasant St.) | 617-242-6009 |
www.tangierino.com

With its "delicious" French-inspired Moroccan menu, "belly dancers" and a hookah lounge "draped with silk and velvet", this "swank, sexy" and "seductive spot" in Charlestown offers an "exotic" experience that's "almost as good" as being in Tangiers; despite the "unpolished" service and "cramped" seating, most say a night here is "as cool as it gets" and "easily worth the inflated prices"; N.B. a new subterranean lounge, Koullshi, opened post-Survey.

Tango *Argentinean/Steak*   21 | 20 | 22 | $31

Arlington | 464 Massachusetts Ave. (Swan Pl.) | 781-443-9000 |
www.tangoarlington.com

"Carnivores cry no more over the price of steak" since this Arlington Argentinean offers "meat, meat and more meat" – plus "tasty side dishes" – at a "great value"; while some beef that it's merely "trying hard and getting close" to true authenticity, they're stampeded by cheerers of the "scrumptious" selection and staff that "treats you like family", plus it "really classes up" the neighborhood.

Tanjore *Indian*   22 | 14 | 17 | $24

Harvard Square | 18 Eliot St. (Bennett St.) | Cambridge | 617-868-1900 |
www.tanjoreharvardsq.com

When habitués of Harvard Square "have a hankering", they head to this "small and friendly" Indian for "interesting regional dishes" that are "well made" and employ "just the right spice"; the "comprehensive menu" features dishes that "other places don't", and the "good value" is a bonus for diners "on a budget."

Tantric *Indian*   20 | 18 | 20 | $29

Theater District | 123 Stuart St. (Tremont St.) | 617-367-8742 |
www.tantricgrill.com

This "hip" Theater District spot features a "lovely" yet "funky setting" for dining on "delicately spiced", "upscale" Indian that "won't break the budget"; though purists pout it has "more style than substance", fans say the "presentation", "creative" "specialty drinks", summer "sidewalk scene" and staff that "understands curtain times while making you feel welcome" all add up to a "reliable go-to."

Tapéo *Spanish*

22 | 20 | 19 | $37

Back Bay | 266 Newbury St. (bet. Fairfield & Gloucester Sts.) | 617-267-4799 | www.tapeo.com

Tapas lovers congregate at this "cozy" "charmer" in the Back Bay, but the "rich, exotic fare" also includes Spanish entrees; foes suspect some servers "couldn't care less" while lamenting prices that get you "a little for a lot", but "after all, it is Newbury Street" – thankfully, there's a sidewalk patio to take the "great people-watching" scene in.

Taqueria Mexico *Mexican*

22 | 10 | 19 | $16

Waltham | 24 Charles St. (bet. Moody & Prospect Sts.) | 781-647-0166

"As close as you can come to the real thing" in Waltham, this taqueria doles out "killer" "homestyle Mexican cooking" priced for "solid values"; the setting, festooned with "slightly dingy" "hats and blankets", "lacks", while the "service is sometimes painfully slow" (although certainly "friendly").

☒ Taranta *Italian/Peruvian*

27 | 21 | 23 | $44

North End | 210 Hanover St. (Cross St.) | 617-720-0052 | www.tarantarist.com

A "breath of fresh air" blows through the North End courtesy of chef-owner José Duarte's "creative" "fusion" of Peruvian and Southern Italian cuisines (gourmands report that the "surprising mix of flavors works incredibly well") at this "charming" spot with three "lovely", "traditional" levels and a "lively", "knowledgeable" staff; it's "a little expensive, but worth it", especially to environmentalists who award it bonus points for having "gone completely green."

Tartufo *Italian*

22 | 17 | 20 | $43

Newton | 22 Union St. (bet. Beacon St. & Langley Rd.) | 617-244-8833 | www.tartuforestaurant.com

"Reasonably varied and well-executed Italian" fare "appropriate for a neighborhood restaurant" is what's on offer at this "tasteful" Newtonian; when it fills, the "noise level can be monstrous" because with "wood floors and tables [so] close together", there's "no place for the sound to go", but the staff is so "nice", it's "a pleasure eating there anyway."

Tasca *Spanish*

23 | 20 | 22 | $28

Brighton | 1612 Commonwealth Ave. (Washington St.) | 617-730-8002 | www.tascarestaurant.com

"Bring your friends and bring your appetite" to this "quaint", "festive" Brighton Spaniard, because not only is there a "great variety" of "wonderfully crafted", "tasty tapas", but it's "reasonably priced", meaning everyone can "try a lot of different dishes"; "frequent special events include musical performances", "flamenco dancers" and "multicourse dinners" paired with wine or "sublime sangria", while "friendly" service is a constant; P.S. "sign up for e-mails" for "generous" "special deals and offers."

Tavern in the Square *American* 17 | 16 | 15 | $24

Central Square | 730 Massachusetts Ave. (bet. Inman & Prospect Sts.) | Cambridge | 617-868-8800
Porter Square | Porter Exchange Bldg. | 1815 Massachusetts Ave. (Somerville Ave.) | Cambridge | 617-354-7766
www.taverninthesquare.com

"College crowds" frequent these "deafening" sports pubs in Central and Porter squares to "cheer" the goings-on on the "tons" of "great big TVs" "visible from every table"; the "simple" American grub that's "slowly" served to them may not get as much applause, but most say it's sufficiently "solid" – "affordable"-tab seekers, on the other hand, admit to "usually eating here out of necessity rather than choice."

Tavern on the Water *American* 13 | 16 | 14 | $26

Charlestown | Charlestown Navy Yard | 1 Pier 6 (bet. 1st Ave. & 8th St.) | 617-242-8040 | www.tavernonthewater.com

Since all you're getting is "marginal" American pub grub and merely "ok service", "you don't want to be stuck inside" this "kind of dumpy" "dive" tavern in the Charlestown Navy Yard; you do, however, need to check out the "divine view of the city skyline" from its "fantastic waterfront" patio, best enjoyed "post-work" with "a bottle of beer."

NEW Tavolo *Italian* - | - | - | I

Dorchester | The Carruth | 1918 Dorchester Ave. (Ashmont St.) | 617-822-1918 | www.tavolopizza.com

The "kid brother" of chef-owner Chris Douglass' "Ashmont Grill up the street" and Icarus in Boston's South End, this "small" new Dorchester Italian displays colorful decor (aqua floors, artful designs on a chalkboard wall) that feels funky and upscale, "homey and urban all at once"; while a few early samplers report it's "still working out the kinks", its "simple", pizza-centric menu sure "packs a punch", and for puny tabs no less.

Teatro Ⓜ *Italian* 24 | 21 | 21 | $44

Theater District | 177 Tremont St. (bet. Avery & West Sts.) | 617-542-6418 | www.teatroboston.com

A Theater District "hit", this renovated synagogue-cum-"urban trattoria" presents a "scrumptious", "fresh approach to Italian food with a wonderfully light touch" (and "the price is right" too); "crowded tables", "a narrow room" and "unique arched" ceilings instigate "impossible noise levels" (it's "too loud to converse"), but if you "go after" curtain time, you may discover the more "comfortable setting" the "subdued" lighting and "courteous", "attentive" staff intended.

Temple Bar ◑ *American* 20 | 21 | 18 | $33

Porter Square | 1688 Massachusetts Ave. (Sacramento St.) | Cambridge | 617-547-5055 | www.templebarcambridge.com

"Dark, sultry" and "trendy", this Porter Square resto-lounge draws an "attractive crowd" for "creative drinks" tempered by a "wide selection" of "dependable" New American fare with "often interesting twists" and "decent prices"; if the "energetic scene" gets "too noisy", just sink into an "enormous round booth" or snag a spot on

the "nice" patio (a must for a "fantastic brunch") and enjoy the "great people-watching."

Tempo ☒ *American*　　　　　　　21 | 20 | 22 | $38

Waltham | 474 Moody St. (Maple St.) | 781-891-9000 | www.tempobistro.com

"Newbury Street meets Waltham" at this "lively", "trendy" New American whose "cool atmosphere" and decor is of the "type one would find in Boston" – "just more reasonably priced"; the "extensive menu includes everything" ("comfort", "innovation", "great wines"), and the "friendly" staffers can point you away from what's "unexceptional" and toward what's "great."

☒ Ten Tables *American/European*　　　27 | 20 | 25 | $43

Jamaica Plain | 597 Centre St. (Pond St.) | 617-524-8810

☒ Ten Tables Cambridge *American/European*

NEW **Harvard Square** | 5 Craigie St. (Berkeley St.) | Cambridge | 617-576-5444

www.tentables.net

"Locals are lucky" to have this "homey" spot in Jamaica Plain, as its European–New American fare is "prepared with love", served with "gusto" by a "knowledgeable" staff and loaded with "spectacular", "surprising tastes and textures"; those "loathe to give it a good review" because, "true" to its name, there are just 10 tables – and it's "10 times as good as" many more expensive competitors – now send their friends to Harvard Square where an offshoot opened post-Survey.

Terramia Ristorante *Italian*　　　　26 | 19 | 24 | $48

North End | 98 Salem St. (Parmenter St.) | 617-523-3112 | www.terramiaristorante.com

"In the North End's highly competitive Italian" scene, this "brilliant" "gem" "wins hearts" with a "heavenly" selection of "upscale", "creatively interpreted" fare that's "beautifully presented and equally delicious" (and includes "no chicken Parmesan or cheese ravioli"); "there's no room to move" in the "tiny" environs and "no coffee or dessert means it's not a place to linger", even though the "efficient", "personable" servers may make you want to.

Thai Basil *Thai*　　　　　　　　　23 | 16 | 17 | $25

Back Bay | 132 Newbury St. (bet. Clarendon & Dartmouth Sts.) | 617-578-0089

To "revive yourself after a day of shopping on Newbury Street", this "casual", "unpretentious" Back Bay Thai – "a little hard to spot" due to its "lower-level" setting – provides "tasty" "staples" that "fulfill every craving"; you don't need a lot of cash, but "patience" is required, especially at lunchtime when the "service could be more attentive."

NEW **Thaitation** *Thai*　　　　　　　– | – | – | I

Fenway | 129 Jersey St. (bet. Park Dr. & Queensberry St.) | 617-585-9909 | www.thaitation.com

The Fenway branch of Brown Sugar Cafe may have closed, but locals can still Thai one on in the same space thanks to this newcomer, a cozy, inexpensive cafe serving lunch, dinner and cocktails; dressed

up with a fresh coat of yellow paint, the tile-floored interior boasts hanging artwork and outdoor seating for warmer months.

1369 Coffee House ⊅ *Coffeehouse* | 20 | 17 | 19 | $9 |

Central Square | 757 Massachusetts Ave. (Pleasant St.) | Cambridge | 617-576-4600

Inman Square | 1369 Cambridge St. (Springfield St.) | Cambridge | 617-576-1369

www.1369coffeehouse.com

A steady stream of "quirky" "characters" files into these "indie coffee shops" for "fantastic" java, teas and "tasty treats" ("sweets, soups, salads, sandwiches") whose "inexpensive" tabs earn Boston's No. 1 Bang for the Buck rating; the "friendly" "hipster" staff facilitates a "community vibe", making them "nice places to read a book" and "relax" – "if you can find a seat" (beware "squatters with laptops"); P.S. "Central Square features outdoor seating in summer", while Inman Square's got a stack of games, "nice perks" both.

33 Restaurant & Lounge 图M *American* | 20 | 22 | 19 | $46 |

Back Bay | 33 Stanhope St. (bet. Berkeley & Clarendon Sts.) | 617-572-3311 | www.33restaurant.com

"Stylish, sleek" and "Euro-chic", this "vibrant" Back Bay venue's "techno" decor (a bar with a "funky" "light show", exposed-brick walls) attracts a "best-dressed crowd" for "pricey" New American meals that, while offering "no fireworks", "never disappoint" either; "it morphs into a nightclub after hours" when everyone "moseys downstairs for dancing" and "amazing wines" – of course, if you're looking for a "relaxing experience", it could all prove to be "a little too much."

Tomasso Trattoria & Enoteca 图 *Italian* | 24 | 20 | 22 | $48 |

Southborough | 154 Turnpike Rd./Rte. 9 (Breakneck Hill Rd.) | 508-481-8484 | www.tomassotrattoria.com

"A little bit of Italy in, believe it or not, Southborough", this venue offers "well-thought-out" large and "tapas-style" plates imbued with "unexpected twists" in an "elegant" yet "casual" setting where an "open kitchen adds to the excitement"; "in spite of criticism of its prices" (and there's lots of it), there are values found in the "thoughtful wine" program, about which the "friendly" staff offers "excellent advice."

Tom Shea's *New England/Seafood* | ▽ 20 | 15 | 19 | $38 |

Essex | 122 Main St./Rte. 133 (Rte. 22) | 978-768-6931 | www.tomsheas.com

This "quiet" seafooder is known more for its "fabulous views" of the Essex River ("go early to get an outside table") and "graceful" staff than for its "fatigued" interior or "standard" (but "pleasant enough") fare; however, "new owners" have gone to work, starting with a major post-Survey renovation that most likely outdates the Decor score.

☑ Top of the Hub ◐ *American* - | 20 | 26 | 21 | $56 |

Back Bay | Prudential Ctr. | 800 Boylston St., 52nd fl. (Ring Rd.) | 617-536-1775 | www.topofthehub.net

"If you want to impress a date, clients" or "out-of-towners", "natives" "recommend" this "glam" New American atop the Prudential

Center, which boasts "amazing" "360-degree views" "you will never forget"; if the fare "can't match" the setting, it is "better" than many "expect", while the "winning wine list", nightly live jazz and mostly "professional" staff serve to sweeten the "expensive" deal.

☑ Toro *Spanish*
26 | 21 | 20 | $43

South End | 1704 Washington St. (Springfield St.) | 617-536-4300 | www.toro-restaurant.com

"Bullfight-level noise" emanates from this "rustic", "tiny" South End Spaniard, giving the "droves of people clamoring for a cramped table" an accurate idea of the "wild" time "famed chef Ken Oringer" has in store for them via his "mouthwateringly delicious" tapas, which "range from authentic to trendy" ("you have to try" the "decadent" grilled corn specialty); "no reservations" mean "excruciating" lines, and "all those small plates" lead to "big bills", but is it "worth it? – absolutely."

Tosca Ⓜ *Italian*
25 | 24 | 23 | $52

Hingham | 14 North St. (Mill St.) | 781-740-0080 | www.toscahingham.com

"Capturing the essence of each season", the Northern Italian cuisine whipped up at this "vibrant" venture "impresses" Hingham diners with "not fussy, just terrific" preparations – especially "awesome wood-fired grill" items – "time after time"; it's "expensive but worth it" when one factors in the "attentive servers" and forgives that the "brick, wood" and other "hard surfaces" make the room often "quite noisy."

NEW Townsend's ● *American*
▽ 19 | 23 | 21 | $34

Hyde Park | 81 Fairmount Ave. (Truman Pkwy.) | 617-333-0306

Hyde Park "couples and families" applaud this "terrific addition" to the area because its "quite tasty", "upscale" New American gastro-pub fare is offered for "down-to-earth prices"; additionally, the "service is terrific", the "wine list is extensive" and the space is filled with "charm and warmth" despite being somewhat "cavernous"; a few "inconsistencies" have been detected, but fans are sticking around while it "gets the kinks out", as it "fills a real need."

NEW Trata Pizza *Pizza*
- | - | - | I

Harvard Square | 49 Mt. Auburn St. (Plympton St.) | Cambridge | 617-349-1650

Thin-crust pizza and late hours are the draws at this airy Harvard Square arrival opened by the Irish brothers who own Daedalus two doors down; hardwood floors, warmly colored walls hung with original artwork and seating alongside windows (which open onto the street in summer) bring a refreshing, slightly upscale feel to the space.

☑ Trattoria di Monica *Italian*
26 | 20 | 22 | $45

North End | 67 Prince St. (Salem St.) | 617-720-5472 | www.trattoriadimonica.com

☑ Vinoteca di Monica *Italian*
North End | 143 Richmond St. (bet. Hanover & North Sts.) | 617-227-0311 | www.monicasonline.com

"Out-of-this-world pastas" with "inventive sauces" "entice" North Enders to this "cozy" trattoria ("one of the smallest restaurants ever")

whose "sleek" yet "warm" vinoteca sibling "enhances" an already "outstanding" Italian menu with "amazing specials"; but "caveat emptor": many of said specials are "shockingly priced" compared to their "counterparts", and the otherwise "professional" staffers "don't tell you" the costs when they "recite the long list" – so "make sure to ask!"

Trattoria Il Panino *Italian* | 23 | 16 | 20 | $34 |

North End | 11 Parmenter St. (Hanover St.) | 617-720-1336 | www.trattoriailpanino.com

"Old-world pasta" preparations and other "high-quality" Italian "home cooking" make for "special" meals at this "low-key", moderately priced North End trattoria where "cheerful servers" maneuver among tightly "packed wooden tables" in a "tiny" interior with "windows on one side, a minute open kitchen on the other"; in lovely weather, "sit outside on the patio" for an even more "beautiful evening."

Trattoria Pulcinella *Italian* | ▽ 20 | 18 | 19 | $45 |

Huron Village | 147 Huron Ave. (Concord Ave.) | Cambridge | 617-491-6336 | www.trattoriapulcinella.net

Huron Village's "unpretentious" yet "fine neighborhood trattoria" offers a "varied menu" of "simple Italian fare done well"; the "homey atmosphere" is "enhanced by personal service", making it feel like dining in a sometimes "crowded", sometimes "quiet" "friend's home" – until the "top-shelf" tabs are delivered, that is.

Z Trattoria Toscana Ⓢ *Italian* | 26 | 20 | 27 | $35 |

Fenway | 130 Jersey St. (Park Dr.) | 617-247-9508

"A corner of Tuscany" "hidden away" "on a quiet side street off the Fenway", this "quaint", "lovely place" "delights" its fans with "charismatic", "funny" servers and "delicious", "memorable" Italian preparations "priced reasonably"; but it "frustrates" them too with a "no-reservations" policy that sometimes leads to "long waits" – which are, ultimately, "well worth it."

Tremont 647/Sister Sorel *American* | 21 | 18 | 21 | $38 |

South End | 647 Tremont St. (W. Brookline St.) | 617-266-4600 | www.tremont647.com

"There's always a party" at this "funky", "hip South End eatery" where chef-owner Andy Husbands' New American comfort food exhibits a "surprising" amount of "inventive", "tasty" "twists" for being so "reasonably priced"; the revelry spills over to next door's "exotic-drinks" retreat Sister Sorel and extends to the "great patio", especially during "fabulous", "fun" weekend brunch service when the "warm" "servers dress in their PJs."

Tresca *Italian* | 23 | 22 | 21 | $51 |

North End | 233 Hanover St. (Cross St.) | 617-742-8240 | www.trescanorthend.com

Italophiles aver this North Ender's "fine cuisine" with "some interesting twists" "gets it right", as does the "great wine list" and "Tuscan Villa ambiance", comprised of a "loud, busy" upstairs dining room and a "happening downstairs bar" with large windows that

provide "an interesting perspective of the Hanover Street bustle"; as for the tabs, they're "a little pricey", but warranted.

Trident Booksellers & Cafe ● *Eclectic* | 19 | 15 | 16 | $18 |

Back Bay | 338 Newbury St. (Mass. Ave.) | 617-267-8688 |
www.tridentbookscafe.com

If the idea of "eating a homestyle breakfast in a bookstore" is "cool" to you, then this Back Bay "brainiac" bastion "is your place" – and the "granola"-noshing atmosphere is also available for "lunch/coffee/snack/whatever", as the Eclectic eats (think "quick bites, smoothies") are served until midnight daily; it's "probably more expensive than it's worth" (often "slow service" doesn't help), but the "WiFi is free."

☒ Troquet ☒Ⓜ *American/French* | 27 | 22 | 25 | $63 |

Theater District | 140 Boylston St. (bet. Charles & Tremont Sts.) |
617-695-9463 | www.troquetboston.com

"Amazing by-the-glass pairings" in either "2- or 4-oz. servings" from a "deep wine list" that's "priced to enjoy" make this "classy" Theater District haunt "an oenophile's delight" – and the French–New American cuisine, featuring "incredible cheeses", "rises to the occasion" with "fantastic, creative" preparations (this is where the "expense" comes in); while the second-floor space gets "noisy" "when full", "great views of the Common" appeal to "romantics", as do staffers who "anticipate every need without being obtrusive."

Tryst *American* | 22 | 22 | 22 | $42 |

Arlington | 689 Massachusetts Ave. (Rte. 60) | 781-641-2227 |
www.trystrestaurant.com

With its "lovely", "modern decor", "warm, informative staff" and "accessible menu" of "finely crafted" New American fare running the gamut from "reasonably priced to expensive", this Arlington eatery is a true "oasis" in the 'burbs; "families are welcome" at the "excellent" Sunday jazz brunch, while trysters deem the bar a "classy place to meet" for "amazing" cocktails, "delicious wines" and "great nibbles."

Turner Fisheries ☒ *Seafood* | 21 | 20 | 20 | $49 |

Back Bay | Westin Copley Pl. | 10 Huntington Ave. (Dartmouth St.) |
617-424-7425 | www.turnersboston.com

Back Bay guests expecting a "typical" hotel restaurant are "pleasantly surprised" by this "big fish house" with "high-end" (if "generic") decor in the Westin Copley Place, because though its "seafood is not imaginative", it is "fresh and well made" (the "rich" clam chowder is a "superb" standout); however, a contingency "disappointed" by "inconsistent quality" in both the fare and service says, in the long run, it's "not worth the price."

Tuscan Grill *Italian* | 24 | 18 | 20 | $45 |

Waltham | 361 Moody St. (bet. Spruce & Walnut Sts.) | 781-891-5486 |
www.tuscangrillwaltham.com

Waltham's "old reliable" Tuscan "chugs along" in fine form, as the "wood-grilled meats, homemade pastas" and "classics with a little

extra flair" continue to be "delicious" and "well worth the price"; the "cozy setting" – a "convincing version of an Italian country inn" with only "slightly cheesy murals" – still gets "crowded" and "noisy", but thankfully, the service is as "warm and friendly" as it ever was.

Tu Y Yo *Mexican*   24 | 16 | 21 | $29

Somerville | 858 Broadway (Powderhouse Circle) | 617-623-5411

"Adventurers" "looking to expand their repertoire" find plenty that's "different" at this "truly remarkable" Somerville Mexican prized for its "real-deal" dishes ("no tacos or burritos") made using "recipes handed down from generation to generation"; the fare (which the "friendly" servers "know very well") is just as "colorful and exotic" as the decor – and a "shade pricey", truth be told.

28 Degrees ●Ⓜ *American*   20 | 25 | 20 | $42

South End | 1 Appleton St. (Tremont St.) | 617-728-0728 | www.28degrees-boston.com

The "NYC" "party vibe" at this "trendy" South End lounge attracts "glam" "under-40s" seeking the *Sex and the City* experience" of "swanky sofas", "trippy projections", "cool bathrooms" and sometimes "chilly" receptions from the "hot help"; "dynamite martinis" at "tony" prices are the drinks of choice, while an "interesting menu" of "delicious" New American "little dishes" provides sustenance; P.S. if "loud DJs" irk you, try the "fantastic" patio.

21st Amendment *Pub Food*   17 | 16 | 18 | $22

Beacon Hill | 150 Bowdoin St. (bet. Beacon & Mt. Vernon Sts.) | 617-227-7100 | www.21stboston.com

"Mingle with lobbyists", "politicos" and "State House staffers" at this "old-school" "after-work hangout" in Beacon Hill offering a "dark" yet "cheerful atmosphere" and "dependable" pub fare ("outstanding sliders", "great nachos") that soaks up the booze at "an appropriate price"; "familiar songs" and "unpretentious" service also make it a spot for "easy, casual" dinners and "satisfying" "lunches on a cold day."

29 Newbury *American*   20 | 18 | 19 | $39

Back Bay | 29 Newbury St. (bet. Arlington & Berkeley Sts.) | 617-536-0290 | www.29newbury.com

"Typically hopping with alfresco diners", this "cozy", "sophisticated" Newbury Street New American is a "still-trendy" "staple" for "super people-watching" over generally "tasty" fare and "strong drinks"; though most Back Bay shoppers give it props for "reasonable prices" and "accommodating" service, dissenters dis it's "too expensive for what you get": "small portions" and "attitude."

T.W. Food *American/French*   26 | 20 | 25 | $64

Huron Village | 377 Walden St. (Concord Ave.) | Cambridge | 617-864-4745 | www.twfoodrestaurant.com

This "lovely, sedate spot tucked away" in Huron Village "features fabulous farm-to-table" New American–New French cuisine in a "creative menu" that "changes depending on what is fresh"; the "in-

timate" quarters and "friendly yet professional service" keep the focus on the "thoughtful" fare – however, though it "tries hard", some find it a bit "precious" and "expensive."

224 Boston Street *American*   22 | 20 | 21 | $36

Dorchester | 224 Boston St. (Mass. Ave.) | 617-265-1217 |
www.224bostonstreet.com

With a "trendy", "snug" interior, a "funky bar" and a "classy garden", this New American "oasis" in an "offbeat" Dorchester location is "right for every season" and occasion; indeed, the "reasonably priced" "comfort food taken up a couple notches" and "friendly, fun staff" have pleased an "eclectic clientele" "for decades", while leaving newcomers "delightfully surprised."

UBurger *Burgers*   23 | 12 | 16 | $11

Kenmore Square | 636 Beacon St. (Kenmore St.) | 617-536-0448
NEW **Boston University** | 1022 Commonwealth Ave. | 617-487-4855
www.uburgerboston.com

"An exemplary tribute to ground cow", this "Kenmore Square burger 'n' shake shack" flips "seriously delicious", "juicy patties" that are "reasonably priced to start" – that is, before you start "customizing" them with a "most creative mixture of things" and pairing them with "fries hand-cut right in front of you" and "to-die-for frappes"; the "aluminum-", TV- and "student-laden" digs are "a little strange", but "you're not going for the decor, are you?"; N.B. the Boston University branch opened post-Survey.

UFood Grill *Health Food*   18 | 11 | 17 | $12

Downtown Crossing | 530 Washington St. (DeLafayette Ave.) |
617-451-0043
Fenway | LandMark Ctr. | 201 Brookline Ave. (Park Dr.) | 857-254-0082
Watertown | 222 Arsenal St. (bet. Beechwood Ave. & Louise St.) |
617-923-7676
Bedford | 347 Great Rd. (Shawsheen Ave.) | 781-271-1100
www.ufoodgrill.com

"The old 'Knowfat' has changed its name but not its concept": this rebranded chain still serves "fairly nutritious" fast food ("bison burgers", "fries baked rather than fried") at "inexpensive prices" in "cafeterialike" settings; "you feel good about yourself afterwards" because it's "healthier" than the competition – but that's not enough to entice piners of the "real thing", who think the fare here "tastes a little off."

Umbria ⓩ *Italian/Steak*   23 | 21 | 21 | $45

Financial District | 295 Franklin St. (Broad St.) | 617-338-1000 |
www.umbriaristorante.com

For a "romantic" meal in a neighborhood not know for it – the Financial District – this "super-cute" Italian delivers with "dim lighting", exposed brick and "intimate" seating; "delicious, fresh pastas are made simply" alongside more "innovative" fare, and while it's "a little expensive", the "friendly staff" can offer "advice" about "great values" on the "exceptional wine list"; N.B. the multilevel venue also includes a bar, lounge, nightclub and party space.

	FOOD	DECOR	SERVICE	COST

Uncle Pete's Hickory Ribs *BBQ*   25 | 11 | 19 | $23

Revere | 72 Squire Rd. (bet. Graves Rd. & Patriot Pkwy.) | 781-289-7427 |
www.unclepetes.com

"Unexpectedly yummy" influences dot the menu of this "first-rate ribbery" – located "in Revere of all places" – where "mouthwatering", "brontosaurus-sized" BBQ with "meat falling off the bones" share the table with the likes of "unique Asian slaw" and "Thai-sauced chicken"; there's "no atmosphere", but when "warm and friendly Uncle Pete" himself comes by to "inform you of the various" offerings, the feeling is "downright homey."

Union Bar & Grille *American*   24 | 23 | 24 | $47

South End | 1357 Washington St. (bet. Union Park & Waltham Sts.) |
617-423-0555 | www.unionrestaurant.com

"Serving many functions" – from "a dusky date" to dinner with a "group of people that can't agree on anything" to "a post-hangover Sunday brunch" – this "gorgeous" "pillar of the South End scene" plies "carefully executed", "interesting" New American fare that's "not inexpensive", but "more affordable than others of a similar caliber"; "a quiet night is not the norm here", what with the "conducive-to-conversation" "round leather booths" and "vibrant" service.

⚡ Union Oyster House *New England/Seafood*   20 | 19 | 18 | $39

Faneuil Hall | 41 Union St. (bet. Hanover & North Sts.) | 617-227-2750 |
www.unionoysterhouse.com

"An experience not to be missed", this "historic landmark" near Faneuil Hall – dating back to 1826, it's "the oldest restaurant in continuous service in the entire United States" (or "so they claim") – "deserves its great reputation for oysters, clams" and other "reliable New England" seafood "classics" prepared by "fun" and "friendly shuckers"; with a location on the Freedom Trail, its "atmospheric" "warren of nooks" unsurprisingly "caters to tourists", but it's a "destination for locals" too – "at least once."

Upper Crust *Pizza*   23 | 11 | 16 | $16

Back Bay | 222 Newbury St. (Fairfield St.) | 617-262-0090
Beacon Hill | 20 Charles St. (Beacon St.) | 617-723-9600
South End | 683 Tremont St. (W. Newton St.) | 617-927-0090
NEW **Harvard Square** | 49 Brattle St. (Church St.) | Cambridge |
617-497-4111
Brookline | 286 Harvard St. (Beacon St.) | 617-734-4900
Lexington | 41 Waltham St. (Mass. Ave.) | 781-274-0089
Waltham | 435 Moody St. (Chestnut St.) | 781-736-0044
Salem | 118 Washington St. (bet. Essex & Front Sts.) | 978-741-2787
NEW **Newburyport** | 44 State St. (Essex St.) | 978-463-3313
NEW **Plymouth** | 15 Court St. (bet. Brewster & North Sts.) |
508-747-6000
www.theuppercrustpizzeria.com
Additional locations throughout the Boston area

When devotees "debate the defining Boston pie", this local chain places in the upper ranks for "slices the size of your head" and whole pizzas with "chewy"/"crispy" thin crusts available with

"myriad fresh toppings" and "awesome whole-wheat" dough; "some locations are obviously better than others" – both decor- and servicewise – and a contingency of crusty connoisseurs calls the 'za "vastly overrated" and "overpriced", but since a new store seemingly "pops up every few months", it's clearly "doing something right."

☑ UpStairs on the Square *American*   24 | 24 | 22 | $49

Harvard Square | 91 Winthrop St. (JFK St.) | Cambridge | 617-864-1933 | www.upstairsonthesquare.com

"Really two restaurants in one", this "zany" yet "fine" New American "overlooking a bustling park" in Harvard Square offers a "less-expensive" dining area, dubbed the Monday Club Bar, that's "like stepping into a page" of "*Through the Looking-Glass*", while the upstairs Soirée Room provides "the full upscale treatment" amid "gold chairs, playful sconces and jewel-toned walls" (mostly in shades of pink); "rivaling" the "quirky" decor are "lovingly pre-pared", "professionally served" victuals that are just as "bright", "fun", "innovative" and "fantastic."

Veggie Planet ☞ *Pizza/Vegetarian*   23 | 10 | 13 | $14

Harvard Square | Club Passim | 47 Palmer St. (Church St.) | Cambridge | 617-661-1513 | www.veggieplanet.net

"Carnivores" "dragged kicking and screaming" to this "inspired", "inexpensive" Harvard Square vegetarian soon exclaim "who knew meatless could be painless?" – indeed, foodstuffs like "stellar piz-zas", "awesome" salads and "amazing vegan" options "wow" them while nourishing their "social conscience"; the "pierced and tat-tooed" make it an evening by catching an act at "renowned folk" venue Club Passim, which is attached, but people persnickety about "cavelike" "basement locations" and "surly service" only come when they can "muster the patience."

vela Ⓜ *Italian*   ▽ 21 | 17 | 22 | $39

Wellesley | 312 Washington St. (Maugus Ave.) | 781-235-4449 | www.velawellesley.com

"An unexpected delight" awaits in this Wellesley "basement" whose "sparse decor" belies Italian cuisine "prepared with obvi-ous love" – or so say admirers who further expound on "serious pricing" that's "a comparative bargain" for "this kind of quality"; on the other hand are "disappointed" diners who deem them "way too expensive" for "mediocrity."

Via Lago Ⓢ *American*   ▽ 20 | 13 | 18 | $23

Lexington | 1845 Massachusetts Ave. (Bedford St./Rte. 225) | 781-861-6174 | www.vialagocatering.com

"If you're in Lexington", this "friendly" "storefront" works for "easy take-out" breakfasts and lunches – and quite well, in fact, as the American fare is "fresh, creative and affordable"; in the evening, it "turns into" a "table-service" supper spot, with "home cooking" that's of equally "remarkable quality" for being so "reasonably priced."

	FOOD	DECOR	SERVICE	COST

~~Via Matta~~ ●🅈 *Italian* — 25 | 23 | 22 | $55

Park Square | 79 Park Plaza (Arlington St.) | 617-422-0008 |
www.viamattarestaurant.com

Another "heavenly" "Michael Schlow production", this "spiffy, modern
trattoria" in Park Square" is known for its "sophisticated power-scene
vibe" ("celebrity sightings are the norm"), but the real "star" is "precisely crafted", "high-end Italian" fare that's "traditional" and "creative at the same time", "seasonal" and served alongside "some killer
staples"; the "professionally run" environs include a "cool bar" and
a "lovely" patio that proves to be a "romantic" respite in the summer.

Vicki Lee's Ⓜ *Bakery* — ▽ 25 | 18 | 19 | $14

Belmont | 105 Trapelo Rd. (Common St.) | 617-489-5007 |
www.vickilees.com

From its "sunny" corner perch in Belmont's Cushing Square, this
"bright, cheery" breakfast and lunch spot provides an "interesting,
gourmet menu" of sandwiches and soups followed by "otherworldly pastries"; the "friendly, helpful" staff sways folks who can't
help grousing that it's "wickedly overpriced", even as they lament
that it's "not open for dinner."

Victoria's Diner *Diner* — ▽ 20 | 13 | 18 | $21

Roxbury | 1024 Massachusetts Ave. (New Market Sq.) | 617-442-5965

At this "comfortable" and "cute little diner" in Roxbury, "new
ownership is taking chances" with "lots of new additions" to its
"large", "not-expensive" menu – and it's still "a big hit with the after-
church crowd" as well as "midnight-breakfast" cravers (it's open 24
hours Thursday–Saturday); the staff is "nice" and "you'll always
see someone you know" – two more reasons why, to some, it
feels like "home."

Village Fish *Italian/Seafood* — 20 | 14 | 17 | $34

Needham | 970 Great Plain Ave. (bet. Chapel St. & Highland Ave.) |
781-449-0544 | www.thevillagefish.com

Brookline Village's loss is Needham's gain, as this relocated spot's
"plentiful portions" of "solid, dependable", "fresh fish" "with an
Italian slant" (often "served in the pan") make it "a great addition"
to its new neighborhood; both the "simple setting" and the
"service could use some sprucing up", but "reasonable prices"
help to keep it "packed every single night without fail" – and
subsequently "very noisy."

Village Smokehouse *BBQ* — 19 | 16 | 18 | $27

Brookline | 1 Harvard St. (Washington St.) | 617-566-3782 |
www.villagesmokehouse.com

"Get your hands dirty" plowing through "mountains of saucy, perfectly cooked meat" at this "Texas BBQ" pit in Brookline Village that
blessedly "puts rolls of paper towels on every table" – and if the kids
start "fighting and screaming", don't worry about reproach from the
staffers, they "don't bat an eye at anything"; yup, it's "noisy", "festive" and you'll "leave smelling smoky" – but you'll "smack your lips
all the way home."

Village Sushi & Grill *Japanese/Korean*
▽ 23 | 18 | 22 | $33

Roslindale | 14 Corinth St. (Birch St.) | 617-363-7874 |
www.villagesushiandgrill.com

Sushi mavens find it "hard to believe everyone doesn't know about"
this "hidden gem in Roslindale Village", a "wonderful" midpriced joint
that serves "incredibly fresh" fin fare in addition to a varied Japanese
and Korean menu; whether seated in the "comfortable" modern dining
room or "cute outdoor courtyard in the summer", those satisfying
"cravings" appreciate "quick service" from an "enthusiastic staff."

Vinalia 🅢 *American*
17 | 18 | 17 | $35

Downtown Crossing | Summer Exchange Bldg. | 101 Arch St. (Summer St.) |
617-737-1777 | www.vinaliaboston.com

"One of the more popular business-lunch destinations in the city",
this Downtown Crossing New American also draws "strong crowds
after work" thanks to its "fantastic wine list" ("definitely go for the
pairings"), "rowdy bar" and "relaxing", "upscale dining room"; alas,
the midpriced menu "disappoints" detractors who dub it "ordinary",
while also grousing about "inattentive" service.

Vin & Eddie's Ⓜ *Italian*
▽ 17 | 16 | 20 | $43

Abington | 1400 Bedford St./Rte. 18 (bet. Rtes. 58 & 139) | 781-871-1469 |
www.vin-eddies.com

In quiet Abington, this "down-home" haunt pleases with its "great
wine list" and menu that has "more variety and sophistication than the
usual Italian"; "attentive, helpful" servers navigate the "busy" room
where a wall-sized mural depicting a courtyard scene has served as the
backdrop for many first-dates and family dinners over the years.

Vinny's at Night 🅢 *Italian*
23 | 13 | 19 | $29

Somerville | 76 Broadway (Hathorn St.) | 617-628-1921

"It's definitely an experience" at this "quirky" yet "fascinating" Italian
"tucked away" in back of a "tiny" "convenience store" that dishes out
"phenomenal" "red sauce" and "generous servings" of "outrageously
delicious" "homemade pasta, sausage" and other moderately priced
Sicilian fare; yes, there's "no atmosphere" in the "packed" dining room,
but fans swear "dealing with the crowds and noise" "is half the fun."

NEW Vintage *American/Italian*
- | - | - | M

West Roxbury | 1430 VFW Pkwy. (Spring St.) | 617-469-2600 |
www.vintagewestroxbury.com

New owners have converted this former West Roxbury steakhouse
into a dinner-only outpost of Alfredo's in Quincy, serving a similar
American-Italian menu of midpriced pizza, pasta and parmigiana
classics; what hasn't changed is the predecessor's large and swanky
interior, filled with booths, alcoves and fireplaces.

Vlora ◑ *Mediterranean*
22 | 21 | 20 | $40

Back Bay | 545 Boylston St. (bet. Clarendon & Dartmouth Sts.) |
617-638-9699 | www.vloraboston.com

"Quite literally" a "hidden gem", this sophomore situated "on the
basement level" of its Back Bay building may be "hard to find", but

it's "worth" the "challenge" for "interesting", midpriced "Pan-Mediterranean cuisine" that gets "a breath of fresh air" from "Albanian touches"; though the "odd location", "unpredictable bar crowd" and "service kinks" "can make the experience less appealing", enamored eaters find the "clean, modern decor" "satisfying."

Volle Nolle 🗷🚭 Sandwiches — ∇ 26 | 18 | 25 | $13

North End | 351 Hanover St. (Fleet St.) | 617-523-0003

Devotees of this casual North End sandwich shop done up in tin ceilings and lipstick-red chairs declare that its takes on the subject are "creative", as are the "great" sides; the "personable staff" makes up for the "small dining area", but it really is "better for takeout."

Vox Populi ● American — 16 | 17 | 16 | $35

Back Bay | 755 Boylston St. (bet. Exeter & Fairfield Sts.) | 617-424-8300 | www.voxboston.com

"Trendy and fun", this Back Bay "nightspot" is often "full of pretty" "young professionals" tossing back "wonderful cocktails" (e.g. "fabulous martinis") while soaking up the "sexy" "singles scene" and "cool decor"; "sidewalk tables" enable "great people-watching", but "disappointed" diners find the New American menu "quite pricey for what it is", so many just stick to "finger food."

Wagamama Noodle Shop — 18 | 15 | 17 | $20

Faneuil Hall | Faneuil Hall Mktpl. | Quincy Mkt. (Congress St.) | 617-742-9242

Harvard Square | 57 JFK St. (Winthrop St.) | Cambridge | 617-499-0930 | www.wagamama.us

"Finally across the Pond", this "wildly popular" "British import" ladles "noodles galore" at its "fun and hip" twinset in Faneuil Hall and Harvard Square; the "tremendous selection" of "fresh and creative" ramen, soups and stir-fries is "good, cheap and satisfying", and the "cafeterialike atmosphere" can be "comfortable if you don't mind" "shared seating" at "long communal tables"; while some slurpers "feel rushed", clock-watchers appreciate the "quick service."

Walden Grille American — 15 | 13 | 14 | $36

Concord | 24 Walden St. (Main St.) | 978-371-2233 | www.waldengrille.com

Set in a former fire station, this "narrow" "little spot just off the main square" "in adorable, historic Concord" serves a "comprehensive menu" of New American fare that locals recommend "for lunch while shopping"; since it's "not too exciting for dinner", some suggest it's "best to eat at the bar" where the "upbeat atmosphere" trumps the "mediocre food" and "spotty service."

Warren Tavern American — 16 | 20 | 16 | $24

Charlestown | 2 Pleasant St. (Main St.) | 617-241-8142 | www.warrentavern.com

This "authentic tavern from Colonial times" (circa 1780) offers visitors a "nice bit of history" – "with the low ceilings to prove it" – as a backdrop for "solid" American pub grub and "a pint", "just the way our forefathers liked it"; though "lively" groups of "locals" leave some

claiming it's "too crowded", while others gripe service "needs improving", it's "cool" to "have a burger" "where Paul Revere hung out."

Washington Square Tavern   *American* | 22 | 19 | 19 | $32 |

Brookline | 714 Washington St. (Beacon St.) | 617-232-8989 | www.washingtonsquaretavern.com

"Word has gotten out", but Brookliners brave "long waits" "again and again" at this "cozy" "neighborhood hangout" offering "heartwarming" American gastropub fare "kicked up many notches" along with "a great beer selection" and a "reasonably priced" "wonder" of a wine list; some say the "intimate", "publike" setting is "a bit noisy", and service varies from "attentive" to "dismal", but "regulars" insist it's "a real treat."

West on Centre   *American* | 18 | 18 | 19 | $33 |

West Roxbury | 1732 Centre St. (Belgrade Ave.) | 617-323-4199 | www.westoncentreboston.com

"Families and first dates" mix in the "cozy" and "romantic" environs of this "casual", "reasonably priced" "neighborhood place" in West Roxbury serving "middle-of-the-road" American fare with "interesting twists"; though it's sometimes "noisy" when a "big bar crowd" is on hand "to watch a game", most locals still find it something to "boast about."

West Side Lounge   *American* | 22 | 19 | 21 | $33 |

Porter Square | 1680 Massachusetts Ave. (bet. Shepard & Wendell Sts.) | Cambridge | 617-441-5566 | www.westsidelounge.com

"Dark lighting" doesn't dim the "friendly vibe" of this "hip but laidback" lounge in Porter Square, where "classy" American bar food at "a fair price" complements "creative drinks" (e.g. "over-the-top martinis"), making an ideal perch "for a casual dinner-date" or just "lingering"; a "helpful staff" adds to the lure for loyal "locals" and "Harvard law kids."

NEW Wheeler's Café & Ice Cream Bar   *Vegan* | - | - | - | I |

Back Bay | 334 Massachusetts Ave. (Huntington Ave.) | 617-247-0047 | www.wheelersboston.com

Though it used to serve only sorbets and ice creams made with soy, cashew or almond milks, this counter-serve cafe near Symphony Hall now offers salads, sandwiches and other all-day vegan fare, as well as loose-leaf teas and Fair Trade coffees; the simple setting gets a boost from local artwork, free WiFi and a couch for loungers.

Wine Cellar   Ⓜ *Continental/Fondue* | 20 | 18 | 18 | $44 |

Back Bay | 30 Massachusetts Ave. (bet. Beacon & Marlborough Sts.) | 617-236-0080 | www.bostoncellar.com

An "encyclopedic" wine list "lives up to the name" of this "cozy" "little place" in the Back Bay that's "hard to find" but "worth checking out" for its fondue-focused Continental menu and "romantic" surroundings; the "not-so-fond" warn that it's "pricey" and has occasional lapses in service, but big dippers say if you want "the real thing" beyond just "cheese and chocolate", "go here."

	FOOD	DECOR	SERVICE	COST

Wonder Spice Cafe *Cambodian/Thai* | 21 | 14 | 19 | $22

Jamaica Plain | 697 Centre St. (Burroughs St.) | 617-522-0200
With so much variety of "fresh" Cambodian and Thai fare, "you can go again and again" to this Jamaica Plain "hot spot" and find new "delights" every time; a "simple setting", patio and "nice staff" all help to make it a "pleasant" place for "affordable" meals.

Woodman's *New England/Seafood* | 23 | 10 | 13 | $28

Essex | 121 Main St./Rte. 133 (Rte. 128) | 978-768-6057 | www.woodmans.com
"Allegedly the place where fried clams were invented", this "authentic seafood dive" in Essex has become an "ultimate tourist destination" and a "quintessential" New England "summer ritual" that involves "huge portions" of "crunchy, fresh" battered seafood plus "long waits" at a "self-service" counter; foes rue the "inflated" prices, saying this "tourist trap" is "more flash than substance", while friends call it "absolutely worth the trip."

Woody's Grill & Tap *American* | 22 | 16 | 20 | $21

Fenway | 58 Hemenway St. (Westland Ave.) | 617-375-9663
Both a "student hot spot" and a "casual" "neighborhood place", this "cozy" Fenway "find" where "friendly service reigns" has "come a long way" with its "wood-fired pizza pies" and affordable American standards; a "surprisingly good selection of craft beers" fuels the "informal" atmosphere that's a "comfortable" spot to "meet" for a meal or "to watch sports."

Wu Chon House *Japanese/Korean* | 22 | 14 | 18 | $23

Somerville | 290 Somerville Ave. (Union Sq.) | 617-623-3313 | www.wuchonhouse.com
Somervilleans in search of "adventure" seek out this Union Square eatery's "good portions" of "delicious", budget-friendly Korean cuisine featuring a "fabulous selection of side dishes", plus some Japanese fare; the decor may be a bit "bland" and the service just "average", but "plenty of choices" help make it a "solid" choice.

Xinh Xinh *Chinese/Vietnamese* | ▽ 25 | 9 | 22 | $15

Chinatown | 7 Beach St. (Washington St.) | 617-422-0501
You can "smell the lemongrass down the street" from this Chinatown "standout" featuring an "expansive menu" of "fresh" Chinese and Vietnamese fare that includes "exceptional grilled dishes" and "tasty" fruit shakes; the "hole-in-the-wall" "decor leaves something to be desired", but the "helpful" service and "inexpensive" tabs help make it a "find."

Yama *Japanese* | 22 | 15 | 18 | $33

Andover | 63 Park St. (bet. Florence & Whittier Sts.) | 978-749-9777 | www.yamaandover.com
Wellesley | 245 Washington St. (Rte. 9) | 781-431-8886 | www.yamawellesley.com
"Good suburban sushi" and other "fresh", "standard" Japanese fare take the spotlight at these midpriced sibs in Andover and Wellesley,

FOOD | DECOR | SERVICE | COST

where "minimal" decor and "variable" service are overlooked because "it's really all about" the "fun", varied menu; "wonderful portions" and lack of "pretense" make it "great for families" or a "casual night out", but "be sure to bring your own sake" to the Washington Street location, which is liquor-free.

Yangtze River Chinese
17 | 13 | 16 | $23

Lexington | 21-25 Depot Sq. (Mass. Ave.) | 781-861-6030 | www.yangtzelexington.com

"Popular with students" and "families", this Lexington "stalwart" is known for Mandarin specialties and a buffet that's "a great deal all around"; service can be "mediocre" and the selection seems "sparse" to some, but it's "dependable" for "more than reasonable prices."

Za Pizza
25 | 19 | 23 | $22

Arlington | 138 Massachusetts Ave. (Milton St.) | 781-316-2334 | www.zarestaurant.com

"Truly inventive pizzas" and "terrific salads" with "delicious twists on old favorites" all feature "fresh, local ingredients" at this "barebones" yet "comfortable" Arlington joint that's "run by the same folks who do EVOO so well"; "capable", "attitude"-free service makes for a "kid-friendly" atmosphere too.

Zabaglione Italian
▽ 22 | 17 | 20 | $42

Ipswich | 10 Central St. (Market St.) | 978-356-5466

Café Zabaglione Italian

Ipswich | 1 Market St. (Central St.) | 978-356-6484
www.zabaglioneristorante.com

For a "quiet dinner" of "traditional Italian cuisine", this Ipswich eatery fits the bill with "intimate" digs, "pleasant" service and "well-prepared" fare paired with "decent wines" and followed by "special-treat" desserts; penny-pinchers who find the tabs "generally pretty pricey" for the area head to "the more informal cafe" around the corner, where lunch is also offered.

Zaftigs Delicatessen Deli
21 | 16 | 18 | $22

Brookline | 335 Harvard St. (bet. Babcock & Stedman Sts.) | 617-975-0075 | www.zaftigs.com

Brookline's "nonkosher Jewish"-style "staple" is often "mobbed" by hearty eaters drawn to its "heaping amounts of brunch food" (including "to-die-for banana-stuffed French toast"), "otherworldly" "overstuffed" sandwiches and other "traditional deli favorites" that leave patrons "pleasantly plump"; sticklers snipe that despite the "fun factor" and the "friendly" staff's "cute T-shirts", such "ho-hum" fare "wouldn't last a week in NYC."

Zebra's Bistro & Wine Bar American
24 | 24 | 24 | $46

Medfield | 21 North St. (Rte. 109) | 508-359-4100 | www.zebrasbistro.com

Medford's "oasis in the suburbs" is "a favorite for date night" with its "cozy lounge" and "romantic" dining room perfect for a "leisurely dinner" of "inventive", "memorable" fare from an "ever-changing" New American menu that includes "quality sushi"; "constantly im-

proving" service is "great", but skeptics say the experience is "not quite close enough" to the city's to "justify Boston prices."

Zen *Japanese* ▽ 24 | 18 | 21 | $30

Beacon Hill | 21A Beacon St. (bet. Park & Tremont Sts.) | 617-371-1230 | www.zensushibar.com

Sushi savorers decree the "fresh, tasty" and "inventive rolls" at this Japanese "jewel" on Beacon Hill "will lead you to enlightenment"; a fittingly "quiet" upstairs dining room is a "peaceful" setting for meditating on "flavorful" dishes and "a decent sake selection"; add in moderate prices that "can't be beat", and a coterie of locals admits it's "hard to go elsewhere."

Zócalo Cocina Mexicana *Mexican* 22 | 19 | 21 | $26

Brighton | 1414 Commonwealth Ave. (Kelton St.) | 617-277-5700 | www.zocalobrighton.com

Arlington | 203A Broadway (bet. Adams & Foster Sts.) | 781-643-2299 | www.zocaloarlington.com 🗷

With its "colorful", "festive interior", it "feels as if you're actually in Mexico" at this Arlington and Brighton duo where the "quality" south-of-the-border fare includes "ceviche made fresh", guacamole prepared "tableside", "out-of-this-world chiles rellenos" and "imaginative sangrias"; despite "cramped" surroundings and occasional "waits", "reasonable prices" and "service with a smile" make it "welcoming."

Zoe's *Chinese* 19 | 12 | 17 | $20

Somerville | 296 Beacon St. (Eustis St.) | 617-864-6265

"Strongly flavored", "truly authentic" Sichuan is the specialty of this Somerville "hole-in-the-wall" where menu offerings that go "above and beyond the usual choices" are "so-so on some nights" but mostly "good" – and "for the price", it's worth "taking a chance"; raters note the surroundings could use "an update", but its post-Survey move across the street may result in improvement.

Zon's *American* 24 | 22 | 22 | $30

Jamaica Plain | 2 Perkins St. (Centre St.) | 617-524-9667 | www.zonsjp.com

Patrons of this Jamaica Plain American declare it "has a lot to offer", from its menu of "hearty comfort food with flair" that has "something for everyone" (e.g. "superb burgers", "mac 'n' cheese to die for") to a "cozy, funky atmosphere" and "friendly" service; the "sexy red interior" makes it especially "perfect for a date or a wine-soaked dinner with friends."

ZuZu! *Eclectic/Mideastern* 20 | 17 | 17 | $27

Central Square | The Middle East | 474 Massachusetts Ave. (Brookline St.) | Cambridge | 617-864-3278 | www.mideastclub.com

"Funky" red, gold and bronze decor, a "young, loud, indie" clientele and a "generally indifferent" staff give this "hip" Central Square spot that shares space with The Middle East a particularly "Cambridge-quirky" vibe; the Eclectic fare is "quite tasty", making it a "unique" meal option in a place that "doesn't take itself too seriously"; P.S. there's a DJ or "live music" after dinner nightly.

Cape Cod

	FOOD	DECOR	SERVICE	COST

TOP FOOD

27 Inaho | *Japanese*
Front St. | *Continental/Italian*
Pisces | *Med./Seafood*
Red Pheasant | *Amer./French*
Bramble Inn | *Amer.*

TOP DECOR

29 28 Atlantic | *American*
26 Chatham Bars Inn | *American*
Belfry Inne | *American*
Chillingsworth | *French*
Red Inn | *New England*

Z Abba *Mediterranean/Thai* | 27 | 21 | 24 | $54 |

Orleans | 89 Old Colony Way (bet. Old Tote & West Rds.) | 508-255-8144 |
www.abbarestaurant.com

For "scrumptious" flavors you "won't come across anywhere else",
hit this "old house" in Orleans where chef Erez Pinhas creates an
"imaginative culinary fusion" of Med and Thai cuisines, which is
"beautifully presented" (along with a "superb wine list") by "knowledgeable" servers; insiders warn that "long waits, even with reservations", and "high prices" are unavoidable, but the "cramped"
interior can be skipped for the "quieter, more spacious" deck.

Academy Ocean Grille M *Eclectic/Seafood* | 22 | 19 | 20 | $45 |

Orleans | 2 Academy Pl. (Orleans Rd.) | 508-240-1585 |
www.academyoceangrille.com

"New owners" have "updated the decor" and "enlarged the bar" at this
"small", "relaxed" Eclectic seafooder in Orleans, but it remains a
"charming spot for an intimate dinner" (the patio is especially "great
in summer", while a fireplace keeps it "cozy" in winter); better still,
the "competently served", "fresh" fare comes at "a decent price."

Adrian's *American/Italian* | ▽ 16 | 13 | 17 | $34 |

North Truro | Outer Reach Resort | 535 Rte. 6 (near Pilgrim Heights) |
508-487-4360 | www.adriansrestaurant.com

"Great views" of the bay are the real draw at this "casual", "family-
friendly" North Truro eatery doling out American breakfasts and
Italian dinners – which may be "ordinary" at best ("please update the
menu"), but at least feature "fine pizzas"; the interior "lacks charm",
but the deck is "nice" (at "sunset" in particular) "if it's not too buggy."

Alberto's Ristorante *Italian* | 20 | 19 | 20 | $41 |

Hyannis | 360 Main St. (Barnstable Rd.) | 508-778-1770 | www.albertos.net

Tourists and locals alike "count on" – and get – "satisfaction" from
everything they order off the "wide-ranging menu" at this longtime
Hyannis Northern Italian boasting a "romantic", "elegant" interior
and sidewalk cafe; whippersnappers protest it "needs a youth move-
ment", but "early birds" are too busy digging into their "bargain"
"sunset dinners" to pay them any mind.

Amari Bar & Ristorante *Italian* | 22 | 21 | 21 | $34 |

East Sandwich | 674 Rte. 6A (Jones Ln.) | 508-375-0011 |
www.amarirestaurant.com

"Generous portions" of "hearty red-sauce Italian" "like grammie
used to make" (at prices she would love) "draw quite a crowd" to

this "rustic" East Sandwich eatery, "even during the long winter"; fans forgive that the "huge", fireplace-blessed setting can get "way too noisy", instead letting themselves be soothed by live music Friday and Saturday; P.S. "you don't want to forget that reservation."

Anthony's Cummaquid Inn Ⓜ *Continental* | 18 | 18 | 18 | $41 |

Yarmouth Port | 2 Main St./Rte. 6A (Willow St.) | 508-362-4501 | www.pier4.com

The location makes this "large" Yarmouth Port Continental a "tourist haven", as the "views of the bay" are "second to none", especially if you "get there before sunset"; though many find everything "enjoyable", old-timers who "remember what the name used to mean" deem it a "shame" that the decor's so "dated" and the fare "mediocre."

Aqua Grille *American/Seafood* | 19 | 19 | 20 | $36 |

Sandwich | 14 Gallo Rd. (Town Neck Rd.) | 508-888-8889 | www.aquagrille.com

A "favorite" for "sunny lunches", this Sandwich "standby" proffers "reliable, tasty", midpriced New American seafood in "nonstressful" surroundings featuring a "great bar" and "interesting views of the Cape Cod Canal"; dinners are also "pleasant", especially with the increased likelihood that the "friendly service" won't be "slow."

Ardeo *Mediterranean* | 20 | 17 | 20 | $28 |

South Yarmouth | Union Plaza | 23 Whites Path (Station Ave.) | 508-760-1500

Ardeo Grille at Kings Way *Mediterranean*

Yarmouth Port | 81 Kings Circuit (Oak Glen) | 508-362-7730

Ardeo on Main *Mediterranean*

Hyannis | 644 Main St. (Sea St.) | 508-790-1115

Ardeo Tuscan Tavern *Mediterranean*

Brewster | 280 Underpass Rd. (Independence Way) | 508-896-4200 www.ardeocapecod.com

"Reasonable prices" for "well-flavored" Mediterranean dishes with "Middle Eastern accents" – "innovative pizzas" being the highlight – keep this "unpretentious" Cape mini-chain "busy" with "families and large groups"; "efficient", "friendly staffs" help to make everyone feel "welcome" when they arrive and "delighted" when they leave.

Arnold's Lobster & Clam Bar 🐝 *Seafood* | 23 | 14 | 14 | $28 |

Eastham | 3580 Rte. 6 (Nauset Rd.) | 508-255-2575 | www.arnoldsrestaurant.com

"Be prepared to wait in line" for the "ultimate fried seafood experience" at this "no-frills", cash-only "clam shack" in Eastham, also known for a "super-fresh raw bar" and "awesome hot lobster rolls"; with ice cream, alcohol and miniature golf also on-site, it's easy to see how the annual "must-do" "family" "tradition" can get so "expensive."

Barley Neck Inn Dining Room *American* | 20 | 20 | 18 | $40 |

East Orleans | Barley Neck Inn | 5 Beach Rd. (bet. Barley Neck Rd. & Main St.) | 508-255-0212 | www.barleyneck.com

Housed in a former sea captain's manor, this "reliable" New American offers a "fresh"-seafood-focused menu in several "elegant",

"romantic" rooms, one of which includes a fireplace for winter dining; adjoining is Joe's Beach Road Bar & Grille, a more "casual" "place for a quick bite to eat", drinks and weekend live music.

Baxter's Boathouse *New England/Seafood*   18 | 16 | 15 | $28

Hyannis | 177 Pleasant St. (South St.) | 508-775-4490 | www.baxterscapecod.com

"You can't beat the views" at this seasonal "old-school" New England "boaters' hangout" on Hyannis Harbor, the site of "tourists" "rubbing elbows with salty" locals inside (home of a Thursday–Saturday night piano bar) or on the deck, where plates of "greasy"-"great" fried seafood must often be shielded from "pesky gulls"; though dollar-watchers calculate it's "overpriced" for what it is, even they make the "annual visit."

Bayside Betsy's *American*   15 | 15 | 17 | $31

Provincetown | 177 Commercial St. (Winthrop St.) | 508-487-6566 | www.baysidebetsys.com

"Lovely" harbor views are "the best part" of this "campy, cute" "P-town fixture" offering a "scene-y bar" and "good enough" all-day New American fare at "reasonable prices"; "it's jammed in the summer with tourists", so the "wait for a table can be long" and "Greenland might melt before you're served", but "Betsy herself is charming", and a little of that goes a long way.

Bee-Hive Tavern *American*   19 | 20 | 20 | $30

East Sandwich | 406 Rte. 6A (bet. Atkins Rd. & Jacobs Meadow) | 508-833-1184

Valued by visitors as a convenient "stop for lunch when driving home from the Cape" and by locals as an "efficient" "alternative" year-round, this "bee-themed" American cottage in East Sandwich emits "country charm" thanks in part to a "friendly staff"; the "relaxed" mood is bolstered by fare that, while vacillating between "average" and "very good", does the trick for reasonably priced "comfort."

Belfry Inne & Bistro Ⓜ *American*   25 | 26 | 22 | $50

Sandwich | Belfry Inne | 8 Jarves St. (bet. Main St. & Rte. 6A) | 508-888-8550 | www.belfryinn.com

Adorned with stained-glass windows and other "elegant" "remnants" from its past as a church, this "enchanting" Sandwich bistro is a "real find" for "clever, tasty" and wholly "divine" New American dishes; "saintly service" and live weekend jazz piano are two more blessings – just be prepared to dig deep when the basket is passed; N.B. a more casual lunch is available in the adjoining Painted Lady cafe.

Betsy's Diner *Diner*   18 | 19 | 18 | $19

Falmouth | 457 Main St. (bet. King St. & Lantern Ln.) | 508-540-0060

"If you're nostalgic for the '50s", this Falmouth diner is "the place to go" for American comfort food served by a "chatty staff" in "authentic" retro environs; "tourists line up for the dynamite breakfast", but lunch and dinner are equally "fun" – albeit possibly "not so good for the arteries" ("the 'eat heavy' sign outside says it all").

Bistro at Crowne Pointe *American*   22 | 21 | 22 | $50

Provincetown | Crowne Pointe Historic Inn & Spa | 82 Bradford St. (Prince St.) | 508-487-6767 | www.crownepointe.com

"Quiet, romantic" dinners are the stock in trade of this "intimate" Provincetown bistro boasting "charming" High Victorian decor and "amazing views", not to mention "inventive, attractively presented" New American fare; "polite, skillful service" and an "impressive wine list" complete the "memorable" (and somewhat pricey) picture; N.B. lunch available for guests of the Crowne Pointe Historic Inn & Spa only.

🆕 Blackfish Ⓜ *American*   24 | 23 | 21 | $49

Truro | 17 Truro Center Rd. (Castle Rd.) | 508-349-3399

"Bravo" to this "classy" Truro addition proffering a "creative" "combination of rich, gourmet" New American fare and "knockout" "fresh" seafood in the former Blacksmith Shop restaurant decked out with brick walls, copper-top tables and a concrete bar; while many feel the service "could be more attentive" for such "upscale" pricing, that doesn't stop it from being "packed with tourists" (those in-the-know say "go on a weeknight" for less "noise").

Bleu *French*   25 | 21 | 21 | $43

Mashpee | Mashpee Commons | 10 Market St. (North St.) | 508-539-7907 | www.bleurestaurant.com

Though "set in a Mashpee Commons storefront", Francophiles deem dining at this "lively" "change of pace for Cape Cod" is "almost like being in France", as it offers "authentic bistro" fare (alongside some "novel" yet equally "satisfying" "seasonal" preparations) and "a bit of attitude"; the "cozy" setting – swathed in multiple shades of blue – has an "urbane" feel that matches the slightly "pricey" dinner tabs (lunch is a relative "bargain").

Blue Moon Bistro ◗ *Mediterranean*   24 | 20 | 22 | $40

Dennis | 605 Main St./6A (New Boston Rd.) | 508-385-7100 | www.bluemoonbistro.net

Despite its "small, simple" setting, this "real gem" in historic Dennis shines with "superb" Mediterranean meals that are only "a little expensive"; the "nice people" who operate it make "whole families" feel welcome, and they in turn "love it year-round", especially before performances at the nearby Cape Cod Center for the Arts.

Bookstore & Restaurant *Seafood*   19 | 15 | 16 | $34

Wellfleet | 50 Kendrick Ave. (Commercial St.) | 508-349-3154 | www.wellfleetoyster.com

"Talk about fresh and sweet!" – the oysters are just-harvested at this "reliable standby" for "value" seafood in Wellfleet (the menu's broad, but your best bet is to "stick to the basics"); if "long waits", "old-time-everything" decor and service that can seem "uncaring" rankle, hit the patio or second-floor deck and get lost in the "wonderful" harbor views or a volume from the attached tome-seller.

	FOOD	DECOR	SERVICE	COST

☑ Bramble Inn Ⓜ *American* | 27 | 25 | 27 | $65

Brewster | Bramble Inn | 2019 Main St./Rte. 6A (bet. Breakwater Rd. & Crocker Ln.) | 508-896-7644 | www.brambleinn.com

"An amazing experience" awaits in this "charming" 1861 Brewster farmhouse where "absolutely fabulous, innovative but not precious" New American "works of art" are ferried by "outstanding" servers in four "quaint, elegant" Victorian dining rooms "enhanced" by a "beautiful new bar"; "superb wines" can turn "pricey" tabs into "wallet-busters", but they're "worth it" for such a "special night out."

Brazilian Grill *Brazilian* | 21 | 16 | 19 | $37

Hyannis | 680 Main St. (bet. Sea & Stevens Sts.) | 508-771-0109

"Vegans beware!" – though there's a "fine salad bar" at this "upbeat", reasonably priced Brazilian rodizio in Hyannis, it's hard to escape "solicitous" staffers who are so "efficient in their singular task: bringing you piles and piles" of "succulent" grilled meats in many "fantastic choices"; indeed, you'll have to "beg them to stop" – and "you'll be so disappointed" when they do (for best results, "don't eat for a week" beforehand).

☑ Brewster Fish House *Seafood* | 26 | 18 | 23 | $47

Brewster | 2208 Main St./Rte. 6A (Stonehenge Dr.) | 508-896-7867

An "annoying no-reservations policy" that leads to nearly "intolerable waits" makes getting into this "tiny" Brewster venue a "pain in the neck", but "it's all worth it in the end" for "perfectly prepared" seafood sprinkled with "mouthwatering" "nouvelle twists" and complemented by a "strong wine list"; it may "look like nothing" from the outside, but "unfailingly polite" staffers (not to mention "somewhat pricey" checks) help give it that fine-dining air.

Bubala's by the Bay *Eclectic/Seafood* | 16 | 14 | 16 | $32

Provincetown | 183-85 Commercial St. (bet. Court & Winthrop Sts.) | 508-487-0773 | www.bubalas.com

Watching the "parade of beautiful men and their dogs down Commercial Street" from the "see-and-be-seen patio" is "the main event" at this P-town "standby" that also exhibits "great views of the bay" from the "air-conditioned interior"; indeed, the "vast", seafood-heavy Eclectic menu seems "marginal" (and often "a bit pricey") to the "busy" scene, which also trumps "uninspired" decor and servers who swing from "humorous" to "torturous."

Buca's Tuscan Roadhouse *Italian* | 23 | 21 | 22 | $47

Harwich | 4 Depot Rd. (Rte. 28) | 508-432-6900 | www.bucasroadhouse.com

You're in Harwich, but you "might as well be in Tuscany" when you sup at this "charming" "gem" serving Northern Italian cuisine that's sometimes "traditional", sometimes "innovative" and always "superb"; the "romantic" setting – marked by beamed ceilings, red-and-white-checked tablecloths and a fireplace – feels even warmer thanks to a "gracious", "knowledgeable" staff, and while it's a tad expensive, the "excellent wine list" displays "fair prices."

	FOOD	DECOR	SERVICE	COST

Cafe Edwige/Edwige at Night *American*   26 | 17 | 21 | $48

Provincetown | 333 Commercial St. (bet. Freeman & Standish Sts.) | 508-487-2008 | www.edwigeatnight.com

"Wonderful breakfasts", "amazing brunches" and "creative", "carefully constructed" dinners complemented by "imaginative drinks" command somewhat elevated prices at this "bustling" second-floor Provincetown New American employing an "accommodating" staff; the "snug", "funky" setting offers "no ocean view or special atmosphere", but the wooden "booths by the window are great for people-watching – if not a little hard on the backside."

Cape Sea Grille *American*   26 | 24 | 23 | $50

Harwich Port | 31 Sea St. (Rte. 28) | 508-432-4745 | www.capeseagrille.com

At this "elegant" Harwich Port seasider, the "superb attention to detail" extends from the "sophisticated" New American cuisine (starring "refreshing takes on Cape Cod favorites", "perfectly paired" with a "superb wine list") to the "idyllic setting" in an "old sea captain's house" and the "winning", "well-paced" service; for the "perfect special occasion", insiders say "ask for the porch" – and bring a mass of moolah.

Captain Frosty's *New England/Seafood*   21 | 10 | 16 | $18

Dennis | 219 Main St./Rte. 6A (S. Yarmouth Rd.) | 508-385-8548 | www.captainfrosty.com

"A Cape Cod vacation isn't complete without a drive" to this Dennis "throwback" clam shack where fried New England seafood "cravings" (there are also "great lobster rolls", burgers, etc.) are sated with "overflowing" portions and for "reasonable prices"; it's what "memories are made of", especially if you "save room" for "soft-swirl ice cream."

Captain Kidd, The *Pub Food*   18 | 20 | 20 | $28

Woods Hole | 77 Water St. (Luscombe Ave.) | 508-548-8563 | www.thecaptainkidd.com

"Beautiful views of quaint Eel Pond", "friendly service" and moderate prices make this nautically themed Woods Hole "charmer" a "nice" choice "while waiting for the ferry to Martha's Vineyard"; the pub food is "tasty" enough, if "nothing fancy", while the deck's "great in summer", the interior's "cozy in winter" and the whole enterprise is "fun for kids" always.

Captain Linnell House Ⓜ *American*   22 | 25 | 23 | $53

Orleans | 137 Skaket Beach Rd. (West Rd.) | 508-255-3400 | www.linnell.com

"Dress up" without feeling "out of place" at this "elegant" "old sea captain's" "mansion" in Orleans, where "experienced servers" present a "varied menu" of Traditional American fare "with flair" in "classy" French neo-classic dining rooms that overlook sprawling lawns; since this is the kind of "costly" "evening you save for", "romance"-seekers urge you come "without the kids" – "please!"

	FOOD	DECOR	SERVICE	COST

Captain Parker's Pub *New England* | 18 | 14 | 18 | $26 |

West Yarmouth | 668 Rte. 28 (W. Yarmouth Rd.) | 508-771-4266 |
www.captainparkers.com

Connoisseurs "put up with" often long "waits" for the "exceptional",
"thick and creamy" clam chowder for which this "homey", "rustic"
(and possibly "long in the tooth") West Yarmouth "destination" is
"famous"; many feel the rest of the New England fare is purely
"passable", though on the upside, it's "moderately priced."

Casino Wharf *Italian/Seafood* ∇ 20 | 21 | 21 | $48 |

Falmouth | 286 Grand Ave. (bet. Dartmouth Ct. & Falmouth Heights Rd.) |
508-540-6160 | www.casinowharffx.com

"Spectacular views of Vineyard Sound", especially "on the deck overlooking the beach", create a "lovely" backdrop at this Falmouth
Heights venture offering "solid" Northern Italian seafood and pasta; it
can get "noisy" with chatter and live entertainment (nightly in-season,
Friday and Saturday off), but the "elegant" environs abet romance.

Catch of the Day *Seafood* | 25 | 13 | 22 | $29 |

Wellfleet | 975 Rte. 6 (Marconi Beach Rd.) | 508-349-9090 |
www.wellfleetcatch.com

Wellfleet day-trippers expecting "standard clam-shack" fare at this
"unpretentious" market discover "quite a find" in seafood that's not
only "fresh, fresh, fresh" but "perfectly prepared" and "value" priced;
a "pleasant staff", wine and beer make it "great for a nice lunch" on
premises, but "don't overlook takeout" for a picnic at a nearby beach.

Chapoquoit Grill *American* | 22 | 15 | 20 | $34 |

West Falmouth | 410 W. Falmouth Hwy./Rte. 28A (Brick Kiln Rd.) |
508-540-7794 | www.chapoquoitgrill.com

"Don't be fooled" by the "ordinary" setting of this West Falmouth
"mainstay" – the wood-fired brick-oven pizzas are "spectacular"
and the rest of the "creative" New American dinners are what "you
would expect at a more upscale restaurant" (and an "excellent
value" too); "throngs of people, especially in summer", keep it per-
petually "lively" – and make waits for tables often "lengthy."

Chart Room *New England/Seafood* | 20 | 18 | 18 | $36 |

Cataumet | 1 Shipyard Ln. (Shore Rd.) | 508-563-5350

Many Cataumet summerers make this "old-timer" a "weekly" "ritual", creating "a mob scene" where the waits for tables and for the
"predictable" but "tasty" New England seafood take "forever"; no
matter, they just cool their heels with "deadly but delicious mud-
slides" while listening to the "lively entertainment" and taking in the
"beautiful sunset" and "magical" harbor views; P.S. the "to-die-for
lobster sandwich" is "not on the menu", but "everyone orders it."

Chatham Bars Inn *American* | 22 | 26 | 23 | $55 |

Chatham | Chatham Bars Inn | 297 Shore Rd. (bet. Chatham Bars Ave. &
Seaview St.) | 508-945-0096 | www.chathambarsinn.com

You half "expect to bump into Gatsby" at this "absolutely elegant"
oceanside Chatham "luxury hotel" with "several great" eateries,

FOOD | DECOR | SERVICE | COST

starting with an "airy" main room filled with "old-world charm" and a "dressy crowd" supping on "imaginative" New American fare "well prepared and presented" by "attentive" servers; "less fancy" but still generally "splendid" are the tavern and the beach grill, the latter boasting "amazing views"; all venues, meanwhile, command "premium prices."

Chatham Squire *Eclectic*

| 18 | 14 | 18 | $29 |

Chatham | 487 Main St. (bet. Chatham Bars Ave. & Seaview St.) | 508-945-0945 | www.thesquire.com

"Townies and tourists" "mingle easily" at this "informal" "Chatham institution" with a "family-friendly" "restaurant side" doling out "basic pub fare" and Eclectic entrees "at decent prices" and a "terrific" "tavern side" "bustling" with "overwhelming crowds" (expect "huge waits" in season); the setting – festooned with a "colorful" collection of license plates – is "outdated on purpose", but thankfully, "cool and shady in the summer and warm and cozy in the winter."

☑ Chillingsworth Ⓜ *French*

| 27 | 26 | 26 | $73 |

Brewster | 2449 Main St./Rte. 6A (Foster Rd.) | 508-896-3640 | www.chillingsworth.com

For "grand events", Brewster bigwigs choose this "formal" "heaven" set on a "charming" 300-year-old estate where the "sensational" chef-owner "injects New England flair" into "glorious" New French prix fixes, which are then conveyed by "graceful" servers in "romantic rooms"; though said splurgers say it's "worth every penny", the hoi polloi would rather hit the "more laid-back" adjacent bistro for the same "excellence" offered à la carte at "a fraction of the price."

Circadia Bistro *American*

| ▽ 23 | 18 | 19 | $49 |

Harwich Port | 86 Sisson Rd. (Gilbert Ln.) | 508-432-2769 | www.circadiabistro.com

"Outstanding" New American cuisine "prepared with the skills associated with good French cooking" and "friendly service" shine at this Harwich Port venue, a "lovely" 1830s Cape Cod country house whose "formal" dining room seems "more Colonial inn" to some (and just plain "dated" to others); "for lower-priced", "lighter" fare, try the "cozy" tavern side whose fireplace provides an especially "warm welcome during the bleak winter."

Ciro & Sal's *Italian*

| 20 | 18 | 16 | $41 |

Provincetown | 4 Kiley Ct. (Commercial St.) | 508-487-6444 | www.ciroandsals.com

"Part of the fabric of the Cape" for more than 50 years, this "P-town perennial" still delivers "reliable", "no-nonsense" Northern Italian fare in a "cutesy" yet "cramped" "below-street-level" dining room with hanging Chianti bottles; it can be "romantic" ("if there aren't too many loud parties"), "especially next to the fireplace in winter", but during the high season, when service becomes "erratic", many locals would just as soon leave the "dark dungeon" to the "tourists."

	FOOD	DECOR	SERVICE	COST

Clancy's of Dennisport *American*
| | 22 | 18 | 21 | $30 |

Dennisport | 8 Upper County Rd. (bet. Rtes. 134 & 28) | 508-394-6661 |
www.clancysrestaurant.com

Clancy's Fish 'n Chips & Beach Bar *American*
Dennisport | 228 Lower County Rd. (Shad Hole Rd.) | 508-394-6900 |
www.clancysfishnchips.com

"Be prepared to wait" for "hours" "during the summer" for this
Dennisport duo "popular" with "locals" and "knowledgeable tourists" requiring a "typical Cape Cod menu" with "value" (the
American "burgers, sandwiches and seafood" are sold in "portions
big enough to share"); there's a "great view of the river" at the
Upper County Road locale, but both offer "screened-in" "outdoor
dining", not to mention "friendly" staffers.

Cobie's Clam Shack ⊄ *Seafood*
| | 19 | 7 | 12 | $18 |

Brewster | 3260 Main St. (Linnell Landing Rd.) | 508-896-7021 |
www.cobies.com

Folks with a "hankering for seafood" wax "nostalgic" when they
pedal up to this "self-serve" stand "on the bike trail near Nickerson
State Park" in Brewster, a "summer stop" since 1948 for fried clams,
lobster rolls, chowder, ice cream and more, all served in "good portion sizes for the money"; it may be "no better or worse than similar
joints", but for an "in-the-rough" experience, it "hits the spot."

Cooke's Seafood *Seafood*
| | - | - | - | I |

Orleans | 1 S. Orleans Rd. (Rte. 28) (Rte. 6A) | 508-255-5518
Hyannis | 1120 Iyannough Rd. (Rte. 132) (Bearses Way) | 508-775-0450
Mashpee | 7 Ryans Way (Great Neck Rd.) | 508-477-9595
www.cookesseafood.com

For more than 30 years, this Orleans landmark – which has spun off lo-
cales in Hyannis and Mashpee – has stood as an inexpensive yellow
beacon to seafoodies craving whole-belly fried clams, lobster rolls and
other fish fixes; after getting their fare from the counter, guests either
settle into the dining room, which is festooned with Cape-themed
paintings, eat under an awning on the patio or take it to the beach.

Coonamessett Inn *American*
| | 18 | 20 | 20 | $37 |

Falmouth | Coonamessett Inn | 311 Gifford St. (Jones Rd.) | 508-548-2300 |
www.capecodrestaurants.org

"An older crowd tends" to spend "nicer occasions" at this "charming" Falmouth "institution" offering "old-school" American fare
that, while "not very inspiring", is "well prepared" and conveyed by
an "attentive, experienced staff" (Sunday brunch in particular is
"great"); their grandkids, though, regard it as a bit of a "stuffy"
"function farm", marveling "it's not 1959 anymore, but you'd never
know it" were it not "for the prices."

Dan'l Webster Inn *American*
| | 20 | 22 | 21 | $44 |

Sandwich | Dan'l Webster Inn | 149 Main St. (Rte. 130) | 508-888-3622 |
www.danlwebsterinn.com

Whether in the "expensive, elegant" main room, the "less-
expensive", "warm and cozy tavern" or the "light and airy" botanical

conservatory, patrons enjoy the "old Colonial charm" of this Sandwich "institution" – serving "modestly ambitious, well-executed" New American fare – just as they have for "over 30 years"; but since it's almost "exactly the same" as it ever was, modish types would rather "leave it to the blue hairs."

Devon's *American/French* | 24 | 20 | 22 | $50 |

Provincetown | 401½ Commercial St. (Washington Ave.) | 508-487-4773 | www.devons.org

"Organic and seasonal" ingredients pepper the "inventive", "refined" New American–French menu proffered at this "charming" all-day "Cape Cod beach cottage" in Provincetown, where "Devon himself" ensures that the service stays "warm" and "attentive"; "prices are high", but they're "worth every penny" assure admirers who also appreciate that the "wine list complements the food so well."

Dolphin *Seafood* | 21 | 17 | 21 | $46 |

Barnstable | 3250 Main St./Rte. 6A (Hyannis Rd.) | 508-362-6610 | www.thedolphinrestaurant.com

This Barnstable "townie bar" adequately sates "families", "judges and lawyers" who desire "nothing fancy" in their "fresh seafood" and Traditional American dishes, but do require "reliability" and "friendly" service; the decor may be somewhat "tired", but sitting "by the fire on a chilly night" is as "cozy as can be."

Dunbar Tea Room *British/Tearoom* | 22 | 22 | 20 | $26 |

Sandwich | Dunbar Tea Shop | 1 Water St. (Main St.) | 508-833-2485 | www.dunbarteashop.com

"You swear you're in the English countryside" when you come upon this "wonderful" carriage house in old Sandwich Village vending "high-tea lunch choices" ("satisfying" sandwiches, "baked goods to die for") amid "elegant", "pristine" and, natch, "feminine decor"; just "come at an off-hour if you don't want a long wait" and "slow" service.

Enzo *French* | ▽ 24 | 20 | 23 | $53 |

Provincetown | Enzo Guest House | 186 Commercial St. (Court St.) | 508-487-7555 | www.enzolives.com

Formerly serving Italian, this "charming" Victorian guest-house restaurant in P-town has recently revised its menu to feature "varied, interesting" and ultimately "fabulous" French Provençal dishes, about which the "friendly", "knowledgeable" servers advise; what hasn't changed are the "lovely, intimate" rooms and the "street-level terrace", offering "great" views of the "flamboyant traffic passing by."

Fairway Restaurant & Pizzeria *American* | 18 | 14 | 19 | $26 |

North Eastham | 4295 State Hwy./Rte. 6 (Brackett Rd.) | 508-255-3893 | www.fairwaycapecod.com

In the morning, "great breakfasts" are served alongside "the best gossip" in town to "North Eastham's finest" at this "friendly, family-run" "coffee shop"; in the evenings, its bar is a "fun place" to "watch the Sox", while the booths host groups chowing down on American grub – it may be "so-so", but there's "loads of it", providing "top value for your buck"; N.B. no lunch.

Fanizzi's by the Sea *American/Italian*

20 | 21 | 21 | $32

Provincetown | 539 Commercial St. (Kendall Ln.) | 508-487-1964 |
www.fanizzisrestaurant.com

Like "being in a houseboat at high tide" with "water lapping at the
window", this "casual" Provincetown East Ender that "juts out into
the bay" is "popular with locals" who find its "reasonable"
American-Italian seafood "dependably good" ("just not distinctive") and the staff "always nice"; "one of the few places" "open
year-round", it's even more appreciated as a "cozy" "off-season re-
source."

Fazio's Trattoria *Italian*

20 | 15 | 15 | $36

Hyannis | 294 Main St. (Center St.) | 508-775-9400 | www.fazio.net
Fans feel this "cozy", "basic" Hyannis Italian "doesn't get the attention it deserves" for its "homemade pastas", "fantastic pizzas" and
"great breads", all of which are "not too expensive"; but perhaps
that's because some customers only "used to recommend it" –
currently, they can't stop "fuming" over the "indifferent service" and
"terrible acoustics."

Finely JP's *American*

21 | 18 | 20 | $40

Wellfleet | 554 Rte. 6 (Castanga Dr.) | 508-349-7500
Whether they find the New American cuisine created at this
Wellfleet year-rounder "super" or "marginal", or the service "personable" or "not worth mentioning", "customers always seem
happy" that "the price is right"; thankfully, the "modern, open
room", "relaxing deck" and "ample parking" bear "no hassles."

Firefly Woodfire Grill & Bar ❶ *Eclectic*

20 | 17 | 16 | $36

Falmouth | 271 Main St. (Shore St.) | 508-548-7953 |
www.fireflywoodfiregrill.com

Large, "nice crowds" fill this Falmouth "fun spot" for "good people-
watching" from the "cute tables on the sidewalk" and the "chic bar"
scene; as for sustenance, some just come for "pizza and drinks" because the rest of the "extensive variety" of "adequate" Eclectic fare
may be "too expensive for what you get"; peace-seekers, meanwhile, "avoid it" altogether due to the "excessive noise."

Fishmonger's Cafe *American/Seafood*

18 | 19 | 18 | $35

Woods Hole | 56 Water St. (Luscombe Ave.) | 508-540-5376
"Its days as a hippie enclave are a distant memory" applaud supporters of this all-day New American in "quaint Woods Hole", where
new owners have made "creative" "improvements" to the menu
(more seafood and Mediterranean accents, "less sprouts"); unfortunately, foes are "disappointed" that the "unexciting" fare doesn't
fully complement the "friendly service" and "terrific water views."

Five Bays Bistro *American*

25 | 20 | 22 | $50

Osterville | 825 Main St. (Wianno Ave.) | 508-420-5559 |
www.fivebaysbistro.com

"Stylish", "upscale" Ostervilleans "meet and greet" at the "active
bar" of this "dynamite" New American with a "warm, contemporary

setting" and "friendly" service; if the dining area is on your agenda ("reservations are necessary"), be prepared to "yell across the table to converse" – or just "wear earplugs", focus your attention on the "plate-licking good" victuals and be proud that you can "afford it."

Friendly Fisherman's *Seafood* ▽ 24 | 12 | 16 | $21

North Eastham | 4580 Rte. 6 (Oak Rd.) | 508-255-6770

"Be careful" or "you'll drive by this little fish market" in North Eastham, a mecca for "large", "wonderful lobster rolls" and "ultrafresh" fried seafood, also doled out in "huge portions"; so what if there's "no atmosphere"? – it's "convenient" for "trips to the National Seashore", "less touristy than others" and quite a BYO "deal."

☑ Front Street *Continental/Italian* 27 | 20 | 24 | $49

Provincetown | 230 Commercial St. (Masonic Pl.) | 508-487-9715 | www.frontstreetrestaurant.com

"You can't go wrong" with anything off the "delicious, gourmet" Continental *carte*, the "extensive" Italian menu (starring "expertly made favorites") or the "awesome wine list" at this "expensive" Provincetown two-for-one with "faultless service" and a "cave-like" yet "romantic" "windowless" setting in a Victorian house; "be sure to make advance reservations", because space is tight and it's "always packed."

Gina's by the Sea Ⓜ *Italian* 21 | 16 | 21 | $39

Dennis | 134 Taunton Ave. (Chapin Beach Rd.) | 508-385-3213 | www.ginasbythesea.com

Dennis locals think "tourists are usually unable to find this" "fun, funky" "hole-in-the-wall Italian" – but it's "worth trying", if not for a "taste of Old Cape Cod" ("average" though it may be), then at least "for its character and for the characters who work there"; just "get there early, as it's already jammed by 6 PM."

Gracie's Table Ⓜ *Spanish* 23 | 19 | 23 | $42

Dennis | 800 Main St./Rte. 6A (Scargo Hill Rd.) | 508-385-5600 | www.graciestablecapecod.com

"Tired of fish?" – "excite your taste buds" with the "many wonderful flavors" found in the Spanish (particularly Basque) tapas "nicely presented" at this "solid establishment" near Dennis' Cape Playhouse; the colorfully decorated, bi-level space can sometimes feel "cramped" with parties letting the "interesting cocktails" flow freely while "ordering several things to share" ("hence driving the price up").

HannaH's Fusion Bar & Bistro *Asian Fusion* 24 | 20 | 22 | $41

Hyannis | 615 Main St. (Sea St.) | 508-778-5565 | www.hannahsbistro.com

"Different from most things on the Cape", this "solid player" in Hyannis has "highly skilled hands" fashioning a "wide variety" of "inventive", "delicious" and "beautifully presented" Asian fusion fare; "urban-trendy" design features (clean lines, low lighting), a happening bar with a "nice wine list" and "fancy" pricing add to the "city" feeling.

	FOOD	DECOR	SERVICE	COST

Heather *American*
| - | - | - | E |

Mashpee | South Cape Village | 20 Joy St. (bet. Charles St. & Donna's Ln.) | 508-539-0025 | www.restaurantheather.com

Surprise, surprise – hidden inside the South Cape Village shopping center in Mashpee is this bustling dinner-only New American that honors the seasons with a menu featuring local seafood and innovative dishes; the venue is separated into a candlelit dining room with tablecloths, mesquite floors and walls adorned with local artists' paintings and a patio for summertime alfresco dining.

Hemisphere *New England*
| ∇ 17 | 19 | 19 | $33 |

Sandwich | 98 Town Neck Rd. (Freeman Ave.) | 508-888-6166 | www.hemispherecapecod.com

"Awe-inspiring views" of "Cape Cod Bay and the canal" create returnees to this beach-themed Sandwich New Englander, especially since they feel just as "comfortable dressing up [to dine] inside" as they do "sitting on the deck in shorts sipping a cocktail"; indeed, the atmosphere "more than makes up for" times when the "standard fish house fare" dips from "solid" to "unfortunate."

Impudent Oyster *Seafood*
| 23 | 18 | 21 | $42 |

Chatham | 15 Chatham Bars Ave. (Main St.) | 508-945-3545

Whether you opt for the "sunny upstairs room" or the "noisy", "cozy bar" with "mussels and a glass of wine" at this "fun", "friendly" "fixture" in "charming Chatham", you're guaranteed "high-quality" seafood in "fantastic combinations"; dinner prices are geared to the "affluent", while "lunch is a better deal", and it's especially "great off season, since you have to make a reservation well in advance to get in during the summer."

⊠ Inaho ⊠ *Japanese*
| 27 | 20 | 20 | $42 |

Yarmouth Port | 157 Main St./Rte. 6A (Summers St.) | 508-362-5522 | www.inahocapecod.com

"Right on target" cheer maki mavens of this Yarmouth Port Japanese and its "perfectly prepared", "totally terrific" sushi and "innovative, delicious specials", all of which easily "surpass the decor", as there's "a tight fit between tables" that necessitates "pulling in every time" a staffer passes (some of them are "slow" and "sullen"); meals here can be "expensive", but they're "worth it" – and "cheaper than flying to Tokyo."

Island Merchant ● *American/Caribbean*
| - | - | - | M |

Hyannis | 302 Main St. (bet. Barnstable Rd. & Center St.) | 508-771-1337 | www.theislandmerchant.com

Have a "fun" island experience right in Hyannis at this "tiny place" displaying an "interesting", moderately priced Caribbean-flecked New American menu, fake palm trees and bright colors; "music lovers" dig the live acts on most evenings, cinephiles on a budget come for $2-burger movie nights in the winter, while everyone raises their glasses to the "great rum punch and other drinks" served at all times.

	FOOD	DECOR	SERVICE	COST

JT's Seafood *Seafood*
17 | 13 | 15 | $29

Brewster | 2689 Main St./Rte. 6A (Winslow Landing Rd.) | 508-896-3355 | www.jt-seafood.com

The promise of "right-off-the-boat" seafood followed by ice cream incites "huge lines" of "families" at "all times of the day" at this "cafeteria-style" clam shack in Brewster; the window workers do their best to be "quick and efficient", and while some numbers-crunchers calculate it's a "good value for the money", others deem it too "expensive" for such "ordinary" eats.

Karoo Kafe *S African*
▽ 24 | 18 | 19 | $18

Provincetown | 338 Commercial St. (Center St.) | 508-487-6630 | www.karookafe.com

Ready to try "wild boar sausage, ostrich burgers or snail rangoon"? – then slide into this eatery where the "different-for-the-area" South African fare is "well prepared" and "inexpensive", the latter another "rarity in P-town"; adventurers say the "small indoor/outdoor" digs' bold colors and art lend it an exotic feel, and the "friendly" staff helps to render it "always a good choice", particularly for "quick", "casual lunches."

Kate's Seafood 🗷Ⓜ *Seafood*
▽ 20 | 9 | 16 | $19

Brewster | 285 Paines Creek Rd. (bet. Lower Rd. & Main St./Rte. 6A) | 508-896-9517

"The sign saying 'fried seafood, ice cream' tells all you need to know" about this inexpensive "roadside clam shack" in Brewster, which dispenses its "great" 'n' "greasy" goods (featuring "iconic on-ion blossoms") via "window service" to "families" at "picnic tables"; some sweet-toothed surveyors "only go" for the "many flavors" of cold cones, which they take "to the beach at Paine's Creek to watch the sunset."

La Cucina Sul Mare *Italian*
25 | 18 | 22 | $40

Falmouth | 237 Main St. (Walker St.) | 508-548-5600 | www.lacucinasulmare.com

"Roll up your sleeves" before digging into the "huge portions" of "traditional Italian" fare "beautifully prepared" at this Falmouth "jewel" where a "husband-and-wife team (he's in the kitchen)" directs a "strong staff"; the "small" interior and "great patio" get quite "crowded", leading to "long waits on summer weekends", but if you can "be patient", perhaps with "a drink at the bar", "you won't be let down."

L'Alouette *French*
26 | 20 | 25 | $49

Harwich Port | 787 Main St./Rte. 28 (Julien Rd.) | 508-430-0405 | www.lalouettebistro.com

"Don't expect to diet" at this Harwich Port "gem", as its "superb French" fare is classically "rich – but worth the calorie splurge" (and the "Cape prices"); excitement-seekers are "put off" by the "standard white-tablecloth" decor ("designed for an older crowd" *peut-être?*), but even they appreciate that the "tables are not on top of each other", not to mention the "lovely service" and "top-notch wine list."

Landfall *Seafood*
18 | 21 | 19 | $36

Woods Hole | 2 Luscombe Ave. (Water St.) | 508-548-1758 | www.woodshole.com/landfall

"Watching the Martha's Vineyard ferries coming and going" while dining on "simply grilled" (some say "predictable") seafood has been a "family tradition" since 1946 at this "lively" Woods Hole seafood "standby" with a somewhat "kitschy" "nautical"-themed dining room and a deck "overlooking the harbor"; but tipplers who only come to "relax with a beer" think it's now "better known for its bar scene."

Laura & Tony's Kitchen *American*
-｜-｜-｜ I

North Eastham | Blue Dolphin Inn | 5950 Rte. 6 (Nauset Rd.) | 508-240-6096 | www.lauraandtonyskitchen.com

North Easthamers "really can't beat" the "all-you-can-eat" breakfasts laid out at this funky, "relaxing" American, "especially at the price": under $10; the "gracious owners" also operate a catering service.

Laureen's *Eclectic*
▽ 23 | 19 | 19 | $29

Falmouth | 170 Main St. (Townhall Sq.) | 508-540-9104 | www.laureensrestaurant.com

"Falmouth's version of a chick flick" could be filmed at this "charming, bistro-style" cafe with an airy, arty atmosphere and an "interesting" Eclectic menu that stars "wonderful" pastries for breakfast, "gourmet sandwiches" for lunch and "creative Middle Eastern" and Mediterranean fare for dinner; "friendly service" lets diners relax in the "quaint" room or "people-watch" from the "cute outdoor tables."

Liam's at Nauset Beach *Seafood*
20 | 9 | 13 | $19

East Orleans | 239 Beach Rd. (Surf Path) | 508-255-3474

"Onion ring heaven" ("possibly the best" ever) can be found at this "ramshackle shed" on an East Orleans sand dune, also serving "fried fish and ice cream" that can be taken to "funky" "picnic tables" or back to your blanket; critics carp about paying relatively "costly" tabs and "waiting in long lines for ordinary takeout", but "when you're at Nauset Beach, there's no better place – in fact, there's no other place."

Lobster Pot *Eclectic/Seafood*
22 | 17 | 20 | $38

Provincetown | 321 Commercial St. (Standish St.) | 508-487-0842 | www.ptownlobsterpot.com

The "slightly downtrodden exterior" (look for the "neon sign") "belies" the "delicious lobsters" that "just come so easily out of their shells", plus Eclectic "takes on traditional seafood dishes" (all only "slightly above market prices") at this P-town "tourist landmark"; the bi-level space is a real "madhouse in summer", so "prepare to wait", hope to "get a window" for "amazing views" and "pray for nice people to be seated around you", as "they will be really close."

Lorraine's *Mexican*
▽ 20 | 16 | 15 | $38

Provincetown | 133 Commercial St. (Pleasant St.) | 508-487-6074 | www.lorrainesrestaurant.vpweb.com

Everyone agrees this "small, dark, no-frills" Provincetown Mexican set in a teak-and-mahogany edifice boasts an "amazing tequila se-

lection", from which "margaritas that don't skimp" are made; while surveyors split on the suppers ("superb" vs. "lacking distinct flavors") and service ("friendly" vs. "dreadful"), they concur once more about the question of reservations: make them or risk an "interminable wait."

Mac's Seafood Market & Grill *Seafood* | 24 | 15 | 17 | $30 |
Wellfleet | 265 Commercial St. (Kendrick Ave.) | 508-349-0404

Mac's Shack *Seafood*
Wellfleet | 91 Commercial St. (Railroad Ave.) | 508-349-6333
www.macsseafood.com

Proof that "you can't judge a book by it's cover", these "plain" Wellfleet fisheries "expertly prepare" "just-out-of-the-ocean" seafood ("not all fried!") and "generous ice cream scoops", plus "unusual selections" like "wonderful sushi" and burritos; at the beachside grill, "you stand in line, order, they call your number and you eat at picnic tables in the sand" (ideally during an "astounding sunset"), while the roadside-shack sibling offers interior dining as well as a patio.

Marshside, The *Seafood* | 15 | 25 | 17 | $33 |
Dennis | 28 Bridge St. (Sesuit Neck Rd.) | 508-385-4010 | www.themarshside.com

"Bright, cheerful", "spacious" and "spectacular" are some of the accolades raining down on this longtime seafood purveyor's "great new building", which still boasts "gorgeous views" of the East Dennis marsh; now, patrons suggest, "rebuild the menu" of "nondescript" fare (it's "rather pricey" too), train the "inexperienced" members of the staff and "take reservations" (as it stands, you can "expect long waits at the bar or on the porch outside").

Mews *American* | 27 | 25 | 25 | $54 |
Provincetown | 429 Commercial St. (Lovetts Ct.) | 508-487-1500 | www.mews.com

"Life doesn't get any better" than at this year-rounder in P-town's East End, where "upbeat", "refined" staffers make "right-on recommendations" about the "divine" New American fare (the "chef does wonderful things with fresh, local ingredients"); the "more elegant", "romantic" downstairs dining room boasts "million-dollar views" of the bay, while the "lively" upstairs cafe is a place to enjoy "cheaper choices" and an "out-of-this-world vodka selection" with "a group of friends"; P.S. "make reservations way in advance."

Misaki *Japanese* | ▽ 24 | 14 | 16 | $31 |
Hyannis | 379 W. Main St. (Pitchers Way) | 508-771-3771 | www.misakisushi.com

"While it doesn't look like much on the outside" (or inside for that matter), this Japanese joint in Hyannis employs "skilled sushi chefs" whose "top-notch" creations exhibit pure "artistry", and at "reasonable prices" no less; though complaints about "off-putting" staffers abound, there are early reports that new owners have introduced "friendlier", more "efficient" service.

Moby Dick's *New England/Seafood*   23 | 14 | 17 | $27
Wellfleet | 3225 Rte. 6 (Gull Pond Rd.) | 508-349-9795 |
www.mobydicksrestaurant.com
It "looks like a tourist trap", but this "high-quality", "-nautical"-themed
Wellfleet "institution" turns out "gigantic portions" of "all the usual"
seafood suspects at "moderate prices" (BYO makes it even "easier
on the wallet"); the lines that lead to its "odd but effective hybrid" of
counter and (picnic) table service are "beyond ridiculous", but it's
"worth every minute" – and "you'll think about it all winter."

Naked Oyster Bistro & Raw Bar *Seafood*   25 | 19 | 22 | $47
Hyannis | 20 Independence Dr. (Rte. 132) | 508-778-6500 |
www.nakedoyster.com
"If you're looking for 'typical Cape', go someplace else", since this
"upscale" "gem" "tucked away" in a Hyannis strip mall maintains a
"happening", "modern setting" (mahogany accents, handcrafted,
shell-shaped light fixtures) to present its "sophisticated menu" of
"exquisite" seafood, which is "served up by a courteous staff";
"don't expect bargains", but do count on "a wait in season" if you
didn't "call for reservations" first.

Napi's *Eclectic*   19 | 20 | 18 | $38
Provincetown | 7 Freeman St. (Bradford St.) | 508-487-1145 |
www.napis-restaurant.com
This "funky institution on a backstreet in Provincetown" is "where
locals go off-season" to get a little bit of "everything, from Greek to
Italian to Brazilian" ("great vegetarian choices" and "Portuguese
specialties" too); "matching" the Eclectic menu is the "quirky", art-
strewn decor – it may be "over the top", but it's got real "character";
P.S. there's "free parking", "no small benefit" in these parts.

Nauset Beach Club *Italian*   25 | 21 | 22 | $52
East Orleans | 222 Main St. (Beach Rd.) | 508-255-8547 |
www.nausetbeachclub.com
A "temple to Northern Italian cooking", this "high-end" East Orleans
venture offers an "exciting menu" "prepared with imagination and
flair", complemented by an "extensive wine list" and presented by
"sincere, gracious" staffers; though its evokes its name with "earth
tones" and wicker (it's "not a beach club"), some feel the setting's
"marred by being noisy", "dark" and "cramped" – but they're in the
minority, as most attest to "top-notch experiences" all around.

☒ Not Your Average Joe's *American*   18 | 16 | 18 | $26
Hyannis | Cape Cod Mall | 793 Iyannough Rd. (Airport Rd.) |
508-778-1424 | www.notyouraveragejoes.com
See review in Boston Directory.

Ocean House ☒ *American*   25 | 25 | 24 | $48
Dennisport | 425 Old Wharf Rd. (Depot St.) | 508-394-0700 |
www.oceanhouserestaurant.com
"Artfully prepared" New American cuisine with a "heavy Pan-Asian
influence" served by a "professional, friendly" staff "always

matches and usually exceeds" the "picture-perfect postcard view" of Nantucket Sound at this Dennisport "gem"; "even if you only go for appetizers" and "fantastic drinks" at the "happening bar", "it's worth the visit" – just try to arrive before sunset, "bring someone you want to impress" (and plenty of cash) and "program the GPS so you don't get lost."

Optimist Café, The *American/British*   ▽ 21 | 21 | 22 | $22
Yarmouth Port | 134 Rte. 6A (Clark Rd.) | 508-362-1024 | www.optimistcafe.com

"What a delightful spot!" – this inexpensive American-British cafe set in an 1849 captain's residence in Yarmouth Port "lives up to its name" with gingerbread trim outside, "funky"/cheery interiors featuring works by local artists and "fun service"; "tasty" lunches and high teas offer a "nice break from typical Cape fare", while "little girls" swoon over "wonderful breakfast" fare like heart-shaped waffles.

Orleans Inn *American*   17 | 17 | 19 | $38
Orleans | Orleans Inn | 21 Rte. 6A (Orleans Rotary) | 508-255-2222 | www.orleansinn.com

When dining at this renovated Victorian-cum-American inn eatery, the "porch in summer", with its "nice view of Orleans Town Cove", is "the place to be" (the interior's a bit "fuddy-duddy"); the eats are "pedestrian", but they're not too highly priced, so one "can see why families like it."

Osteria La Civetta *Italian*   - | - | - | M
Falmouth | 133 Main St. (Post Office Rd.) | 508-540-1616 | www.osterialacivetta.com

From the "pleasant", "rustic" setting to the "woman from Bologna" who owns and runs it to the "handmade pastas" and other "simple, exquisite" Northern Italian dishes, this "intimate" Falmouth storefront "feels and tastes authentic"; the portions are "not big" and prices run at a "slight premium", but it's "worth visiting" – and bringing home some imported meats and cheeses from the retail section too.

Oyster Company Raw Bar & Grill *Seafood*   23 | 17 | 21 | $35
Dennisport | 202 Depot St. (Rte. 28) | 508-398-4600 | www.theoystercompany.com

"As one would expect from the name", the "raw bar is exceptional" at this "Cape Cod–casual" Dennisport "gem" ("the owners farm their own Quivet Neck oysters"), while the rest of the seafood menu is "creatively prepared" and "scrumptious", as are other items "for the burgers-and-beer crowd"; it's a "tourist favorite", but factor in "neighborly" service and "reasonable prices", and it's "clear" to see why "locals like it too."

Paddock *New England/Seafood*   20 | 19 | 20 | $40
Hyannis | West End Rotary | 20 Scudder Ave. (Main St.) | 508-775-7677 | www.paddockcapecod.com

"Pleasant" and "reliable", this "family-run" Hyannis haunt serves "tasty", slightly "pricey" New England seafood in "several different"

"old-world" "fine dining" rooms (young 'uns peg them as "time warps"); its convenient location next to the Melody Tent makes it a "great stop before or after a concert", and while service might be a little "slow" at peak times, the "experienced" staff works to make "you feel like a VIP at all times."

☑ Pisces *Mediterranean/Seafood*

27 | 19 | 23 | $51

Chatham | 2653 Main St. (Forest Beach Rd.) | 508-432-4600 | www.piscesofchatham.com

"Just-caught seafood" with "imaginative", "flavorful" Mediterranean preparations is ferried by "friendly, knowledgeable" servers at this "charming" Chatham "diamond"; the "intimate" "beach-chic", artwork-festooned setting gets "loud" and "crowded" (it "definitely requires reservations") and "prices are high", but for diehards, "weekends on the Cape aren't great" without an evening here.

Port, The *American/Seafood*

23 | 23 | 21 | $40

Harwich Port | 541 Main St./Rte. 28 (Sea St.) | 508-430-5410 | www.theportrestaurant.com

Things just "keep getting better" at this "modern, trendy restaurant in traditional Harwich Port", what with the addition of a "first-class" raw bar and "increased offerings" on the "creative", "sparkling" New American seafood menu; "a younger crowd" is as attracted to the "buzzy", "big-city" scene as it is to the "attractive", "efficient" staffers, even when some toss "a bit of 'tude."

Post Office Café ❶ *American*

16 | 12 | 14 | $27

Provincetown | 303 Commercial St. (Standish St.) | 508-487-3892

The "ordinary" American "diner fare" at this "bland" box is "priced at the lower end" for P-town, but it's "nothing to write home about"; "all dishes" are delivered "with a side of staff attitude" (sometimes it's flat-out "disdainful"), but that and the "crowded, loud" and "chaotic" atmosphere is "just part of the experience."

Red Inn *New England*

24 | 26 | 23 | $60

Provincetown | Red Inn | 15 Commercial St. (Province Lands Rd.) | 508-487-7334 | www.theredinn.com

"Enter through a delightful garden", start off with a "huge, delicious cocktail" "on the deck" while "looking out at the bay at sunset" ("breathtaking"), then settle in for "expertly prepared" (and "expensive") New England fare featuring "wonderful" local fish at this "class act" in an "incredible old hotel" nearly "on the tip of Provincetown"; "knowledgeable", "hospitable" service furthers its deserved reputation as a "sublime", "romantic getaway."

☑ Red Pheasant *American/French*

27 | 24 | 25 | $53

Dennis | 905 Main St./Rte. 6A (Elm St.) | 508-385-2133 | www.redpheasantinn.com

Whether in summer when the "luscious gardens" "bloom" or "in the dead of winter" "when the big fireplace is roaring", this "lovely antique" barn in Dennis provides a "special", "formal" setting for

"gourmet" New American cuisine that "emphasizes seasonal" ingredients ("high-end seafood", "exceptionally prepared game") and "complex" French twists; "pleasant, efficient" staffers and an "incredible wine list" are two more reasons why enthusiasts save up their dough to "go back over and over again."

Regatta of Cotuit at the Crocker House *American*

25 | 23 | 24 | $57

Cotuit | 4631 Falmouth Rd./Rte. 28 (Rte. 130) | 508-428-5715 | www.regattaofcotuit.com

"Anyone who considers themselves a foodie will have an enjoyable evening" at this historic Federal mansion in Cotuit, as the New American fare is "interesting" and wholly "memorable" (those who query some of the more "oddball combinations" depend on the "impeccable" servers – they really "know the menu"); "special-occasion" celebrators and "couples" laud it too, especially the seven "serene", "cozy" dining rooms – it's just "not a family place", least of all because of the "expense."

Roadhouse Cafe *Seafood/Steak*

20 | 19 | 19 | $43

Hyannis | 488 South St. (Sea St.) | 508-775-2386 | www.roadhousecafe.com

"Escape" from "busy Hyannis" to this "convivial" hangout offering "lots of choices in terms of both" environments – which include "somewhat upscale" dining rooms, a "lighter-fare" bistro and a bar, all featuring wood paneling and nautical antiques – and "terrific" seafood and steaks served in "nice portions"; jazz on Mondays, a pianist on weekends and valet parking are "added bonuses."

RooBar *American*

21 | 20 | 21 | $37

Falmouth | 285 Main St. (Cahoon Ct.) | 508-548-8600
Chatham | 907 Main St. (bet. Heritage & Snow Lns.) | 508-945-9988
www.theroobar.com

"Trendy comes to Cape Cod" in the form of these "terribly chic, hopelessly noisy" "crowd-pleasers" with New American menus that offer "something to tickle anyone's taste" – and with everything from "$12 pizzas to $25 entrees", every budget to boot; expect "hopping bars" at both the Falmouth locale and the Chatham iteration, which boasts the bonus of a "covered patio"; N.B. the Plymouth location exhibits a slightly more upscale feel.

Ross' Grill *American*

22 | 22 | 21 | $44

Provincetown | 237 Commercial St. (bet. Gosnold St. & Masonic Pl.) | 508-487-8878 | www.rossgrillptown.com

"Comfortably chic" environs with "gorgeous views" of Provincetown Harbor create a "memorable" setting for "smart", "reliable" New American fare paired with "terrific" *vins* at this only "slightly higher priced" eatery/wine bar; repeat customers cheer the mostly "friendly" service and the fact that it "now takes reservations" – "a major plus for a place with an inevitable line and so few tables."

	FOOD	DECOR	SERVICE	COST

Scargo Café *American*
20 | 18 | 21 | $35

Dennis | 799 Main St./Rte. 6A (bet. Corporation Rd. & Hope Ln.) | 508-385-8200 | www.scargocafe.com

"Catch dinner before the theater" or yuck it up with the "locals" over "a nightcap afterward" at this year-rounder "across from the Cape Playhouse" in Dennis serving "solid", "reasonably priced" ("albeit not particularly inventive") New American vittles; the "comfortable", woody space (dating from 1865) is "well-run" by two brothers who ensure the staff provides a "friendly" greeting upon arrival, "a kind thank you when leaving" and "attentive" service in between.

Siena *Italian*
21 | 20 | 19 | $38

Mashpee | Mashpee Commons | 38 Nathan Ellis Hwy. (Rte. 28) | 508-477-5929 | www.siena.us

Sating both the "spaghetti-and-meatballs crowd" and osso buco-cravers is never easy, but this "big, noisy" Mashpee Commons Italian with "nice outdoor seating" "deserves an A for effort": "if you want something, it's somewhere on the menu", and brought in "huge portions" for moderate prices to boot; indeed, "just about everyone" leaves "satisfied" – unless they're trying to catch a movie next door and they're stuck with a "spotty" server.

Sir Cricket's Fish & Chips ⊅ *Seafood*
24 | 8 | 19 | $18

Orleans | 38 Rt. 6A (Orleans Rd.) | 508-255-4453

There's "nothing fancy" at this "busy" Orleans spot – just "fabulous" "English-style fish 'n' chips" and other inexpensive, "excellent seafood from the store next door"; there's also "not much in terms of seating" (what there is resembles a "high-school cafeteria"), so get it to go.

Stir Crazy Ⓜ *Cambodian*
23 | 16 | 20 | $28

Pocasset | 570 MacArthur Blvd., Rte. 28 (Portside Dr.) | 508-564-6464 | www.stircrazyrestaurant.com

"Gifted" chef-owner Bopha Samms serves up a "welcome change" – namely "delectable", "affordable" Cambodian cuisine with "fresh ingredients" and a "local twist" – just as she has for the past 20 years at her place in Pocasset; "generous but not overwhelming portions" are brought by "friendly" staffers in the pleasant digs, which feature authentic artwork and a bar.

Terra Luna *American*
24 | 18 | 20 | $46

North Truro | 104 Shore Rd. (Windigo Ln.) | 508-487-1019

This "noteworthy" North Truro New American "feels like a neighborhood" "standard" thanks to a "casual", "rustic", "low-key setting" (the former site of a stagecoach stop) and an "interesting" "combo of seasonal specials and reliable" classics; it's "quite popular", but "small", so be sure to ask the "friendly" staffers for "a table with elbow room."

Trevi Café & Wine Bar *Mediterranean*
- | - | - | M

Mashpee | Mashpee Commons | 25 Market St. (Fountain St.) | 508-477-0055 | www.trevicafe.com

From the fountain at the front entrance to the awning-topped patio, this Mashpee venue exhibits European flair that extends to

its midpriced Mediterranean menu of tapas, pastas, panini and more; with hardwood floors and candlelight, the casual dining room is a romantic escape, while the granite bar is a place to get lost in television.

Z Twenty-Eight Atlantic *American*　　26 | 29 | 25 | $65

Chatham | Wequassett Inn | 2173 Orleans Rd./Rte. 28 (Pleasant Bay Rd.) | 508-430-3000 | www.wequassett.com

You "must see" the "beautiful" decor and "phenomenal" view of Pleasant Bay at this all-day dining room in a "fancy" Chatham resort, but you also have to sample the New American cuisine, which often travels "beyond creative and delicious", all the way to "rapturous"; with "top-notch service" added to the mix, it's unsurprisingly "over-the-top expensive", but if you come "knowing what you're getting into", you'll "leave feeling elated."

Vining's Bistro *Eclectic*　　∇ 24 | 17 | 24 | $44

Chatham | Gallery Bldg. | 595 Main St. (Seaview St.) | 508-945-5033

"Leave your children home" before seeking out this "hard-to-find" second-floor bistro "overlooking Main Street" in Chatham, where the "casual" setting's as "understated" as the "sophisticated" Eclectic "menu offering a wealth of perfectly [wood-] grilled meats and seafood" is "adventurous"; the "friendly" staff also has an "excellent wine selection" on hand, adding to experiences that "never disappoint."

Whitman House　　∇ 21 | 23 | 21 | $36
Restaurant, The *American*

Truro | 7 Great Hollow Rd. | 508-487-1740 | www.whitmanhouse.com

"Take your favorite aunt" for a "fantastic" meal at this "classy", "cozy" American set in an 1894 inn on four acres of landscaped grounds in Truro; run by the same family for more than four decades, the delightfully "old-fashioned" setting includes four Early American dining rooms as well as the more casual Bass Tavern.

Wicked Oyster *American/Seafood*　　24 | 19 | 22 | $43

Wellfleet | 50 Main St. (off Rte. 6) | 508-349-3455

"If it swims around the Cape, it's likely on the menu" (and "typically caught that day") at this "lively" New American in a "charming" early-1700s Wellfleet home providing "pleasant, prompt service" and "dazzlingly prepared", "deliciously wonderful" seafood-centric breakfasts, lunches and dinners (they're "great bangs for the buck" too); the "casual", "charming" room is "large", but so popular, "reservations are absolutely necessary in season."

Wild Goose Tavern *American*　　∇ 21 | 21 | 21 | $35

Chatham | Chatham Wayside Inn | 512 Main St. (bet. Chatham Bars Ave. & Library Ln.) | 508-945-5590 | www.wildgoosetavern.com

A "great menu variety", featuring plenty of "pub-style" American fare, and "chipper service" draw "families" to this Chatham tavern,

which pleasantly surprises moms and dads "expecting a hard hit to the wallet" with moderate prices; the "spacious" dining room "can be noisy" (good for when you want to "talk without being over-heard"), while the bar is a "fun place" "to meet locals."

Winslow's Tavern *American*

20	21	18	$38

Wellfleet | 316 Main St. (bet. Bank St. & Holbrook Ave.) | 508-349-6450 | www.winslowstavern.com

Wellfleet families find the "wonderful" New American fare, "afford-able prices" and mostly "friendly service" "more than enough to warrant a return trip" to this "great old building", while oenophiles toast the "unique wine list", which they explore over "more casual meals" at the "upstairs bar"; "tables by the window overlooking the patio" are prized in the "white-all-over" main room, but "eating out-side" may be best, since the "noise level" inside is "unbelievable."

Martha's Vineyard

TOP FOOD

27 Détente | *American*
   Larsen's Fish Mkt. | *Seafood*
26 Bite | *Seafood*
   L'Étoile | *French*
25 Atria | *American*

TOP DECOR

26 Outermost Inn | *American*
   Lambert's Cove | *American*
   L'Étoile | *French*
   Beach Plum | *American*
25 Atria | *American*

Alchemy *American* | 22 | 23 | 20 | $49 |

Edgartown | 71 Main St. (bet. School & Summer Sts.) | 508-627-9999
"Cosmopolitan ambiance" materializes at this "expensive" New American where "trendy pretty people" come "to be seen" in the "handsome" lounge upstairs (the milieu of "value bar snacks") and "lively bistro" downstairs, which features outdoor seating "overlooking the always interesting Edgartown streetscape"; the "solid, tasty" dishes and "great wines" keep it a "perennial favorite" for locals, except in January, when it's closed.

Art Cliff Diner *Diner* | 24 | 17 | 21 | $18 |

Vineyard Haven | 39 Beach Rd. (Five Corners) | 508-693-1224
Some "island secret" – "impossibly long waits" prove the "dreamy crêpes", waffles and omelets are all-too-common knowledge at this "kitschy" "longtime tradition"; so drag yourself to Vineyard Haven "at the crack of dawn" and "bring the paper" and a "bottle of champagne for mimosas", because "a trip to the Vineyard is not complete without breakfast" here; P.S. lunches are equally "fabulous" – and popular.

NEW Atlantic *Seafood* | - | - | - | M |

Edgartown | 2 Main St. (Water St.) | 508-627-7001 | www.atlanticmv.com
"Young" cooks "turn out some fine fare" at this casual Edgartown seafooder with a midpriced menu focusing on fresh ingredients; owned by the same folks as the exclusive Boathouse club upstairs, the space feels like an upscale watering hole with white wainscoting and a marble bar, while exhibiting TV sports and harbor views.

Atria *American* | 25 | 25 | 24 | $60 |

Edgartown | 137 Main St. (bet. Green & Pine Sts.) | 508-627-5850 | www.atriamv.com
"Clever combinations result in truly delicious dishes" at this "refreshingly different" Edgartown New American committed to "local, organic" ingredients, "impeccable service" and "expensive" tabs; a "Hollywood crowd" likes to be seen in the "exquisite", "sophisticated dining room", "romantic" types choose the "elegant", "candle-filled garden", while a nightcap in the "chic yet casual" cellar lounge is "highly recommended" to all.

Balance 🅢🅜 *American* ▽ | 23 | 17 | 19 | $57 |

Oak Bluffs | 9 Oak Bluffs Ave. | 508-696-3000 | www.balancerestaurant.com
Critiques of this Oak Bluffs New American's cavernous "new space" are, unfortunately, not stellar: though it's "intended to be hip", it

comes off as a "cheap cafeteria", with "loud, loud, loud" acoustics to match; regardless, the "generous" portions of "creative", somewhat pricey fare, which is ferried by "upbeat" staffers, keep many "coming back."

Beach Plum Inn *American* | 25 | 26 | 26 | $61 |

Menemsha | Beach Plum Inn | 50 Beach Plum Ln. (North Rd.) | 508-645-9454 | www.beachpluminn.com

"Timed right, you'll see a beautiful sunset while eating expertly prepared", "inspired" New American cuisine plated like "mini architectural wonders" at this "secluded, serene" and "romantic retreat" with "gorgeous views" of Menemsha Harbor; "impeccable service" bolsters the feeling that you've been "invited to an elite dinner party" – although this one ends with a "pricey" bill (it's "worth it"); N.B. BYOB.

Bite, The ⊯ *Seafood* | 26 | 11 | 17 | $20 |

Menemsha | 29 Basin Rd. (North Rd.) | 508-645-9239 | www.thebitemenemsha.com

"It's fried seafood nirvana" at this cash-only take-out "shack with picnic tables crammed by the roadside" in Menemsha; though the "prices clearly reflect its status as a landmark", that doesn't stop clam-diggers from joining the "long lines" ("nothing to be intimidated by"), then taking the short walk to the beach for a "beautiful" "sunset picnic."

⚡ Black Dog Tavern *American* | 19 | 18 | 18 | $33 |

Vineyard Haven | 20 Beach St. Ext. (Water St.) | 508-693-9223 | www.theblackdog.com

"Crowds still line up" for "great breakfasts" and "worthy lunches" at this "casual" American "icon" "overlooking the gorgeous harbor" in Vineyard Haven; some say that "dinner is good too", just as many counter it's "unexciting", but either way, it's "not overly expensive", "fine for kids" and "you can advertise that you've eaten here" with "all manner of clothing and accessories with its ubiquitous" logo; N.B. BYOB.

Chesca's *Eclectic/Italian* | 23 | 22 | 23 | $52 |

Edgartown | 38 N. Water St. (Winter St.) | 508-627-1234
Edgartonians find it "hard to choose" from the selection of "well-prepared", "delicious" Italian-inspired Eclectic fare proffered at this "noisy" yet "fun night out", and though it's pricey, they deem it "reasonable for the quality and location"; "no reservations" for parties under six mean there's "always a wait", but it's easily dealt with by "sitting on the porch" with an "inventive cocktail" and "watching the crowds go by."

David Ryan's *American* | 15 | 16 | 16 | $36 |

Edgartown | 11 N. Water St. (Main St.) | 508-627-4100 | www.davidryans.com

"Edgartown singles" advise "stick to the cocktails" and microbrews at this bi-level "prototypical tourist trap", because it's "much better for nightlife" than dining; that said, when you're "walking around town and in need of a comfortable" meal, the location is "conve-

nient", while the American fare is "acceptable" (if "too salty") and moderately priced.

☒ Détente *American*   27 | 22 | 24 | $69

Edgartown | 3 Nevin Sq. | Winter St. (Water St.) | 508-627-8810 | www.detentemv.com

It may just be wishful thinking when some surveyors opine that "not everyone knows about" this "terrific", "tucked away" Edgartonian, since you need to "make a reservation early" if you want to experience chef Kevin Crowell's "adventurous", "awesome" New American creations and his wife Suzanna's "charming" hostessing skills; "service is helpful without being obsequious", so whether you eat in the "pleasant" if "cramped" interior or the "small", "beautiful garden", you can expect a "lovely meal" – and a "pricey" check.

Home Port *New England/Seafood*   20 | 17 | 18 | $47

Menemsha | 512 North Rd. (Basin Rd.) | 508-645-2679 | www.homeportmv.com

"Thank God" this nearly 80-year-old BYO seafood "legend" in Menemsha "has been spared" from closing and the new owners who bought it in early 2009 plan to keep it "chugging along" with the same "simply prepared", "fresh seafood" (it costs "a lot of money", "but at least the portions are large"); there's a "cramped, loud" dining room, but there's also "fabulous takeout" to "eat on picnic tables" or, better still, bring to the beach for a "beautiful sunset" meal.

Jimmy Seas Pan Pasta *Italian*   23 | 13 | 19 | $34

Oak Bluffs | 38 Kennebec Ave. (off Post Office Sq.) | 508-696-8550

"They roast garlic like nobody's business" at this Oak Bluffs Italian, so "follow your nose" and "bring a hearty appetite" for "hot, steamy pans" of "fantastic pasta" and "fabulous seafood" served in portions "mammoth" "enough to feed a small army" (expect a surcharge if you "plan to split"); just "get there early" or be prepared for an "awful wait" to be "scrunched" into the "tiny", "noisy" space.

Lambert's Cove Inn *American*   25 | 26 | 25 | $60

West Tisbury | Lambert's Cove Inn & Restaurant | 90 Manaquayak Rd. (Lambert's Cove Rd.) | 508-693-2298 | www.lambertscoveinn.com

Check into this "lovely", "British-y" dining room in a "charming country inn" "nestled" in West Tisbury, a "romantic" place where "you can have a private conversation" while savoring views of a "slice-of-heaven" garden and "superb" American cuisine made with "excellent ingredients" and "presented in delicate, unique ways"; "impeccable" servers add to the "terrific evening", which is expectedly "expensive", even though you have to "bring your own alcohol."

Larsen's Fish Market *Seafood*   27 | 10 | 20 | $23

Menemsha | 56 Basin Rd. (North Rd.) | 508-645-2680

"Basically a take-out place within a fish market", this Menemsha counter doles out "cardboard plates of oysters, shucked in front of your eyes", "luscious lobster rolls", "freshly steamed steamers" and other "amazingly fresh", "simple" seafood "right off the boat"; it's

"all to be eaten outside" on "wooden crates" or at "the beach watching the sunset" – an "unforgettable meal", and a "reasonable" one at that.

Lattanzi's *Italian* | 21 | 17 | 20 | $48 |

Edgartown | Old Post Office Sq. (bet. Main & Winter Sts.) | 508-627-8854 | www.lattanzis.com

Go for the "cozy, elegant" "fine-dining option" or the casual "pizza division" with a "nice patio" at this "delightful" Edgartown *duetto* where "innovative" Tuscan touches abound in "great" thin-crust, brick-oven pies, pastas and other "Italian comfort foods", all "solid values" "for the island"; whichever side you choose, the "friendly" staff "cares to have you as a guest."

Le Grenier *French* | 23 | 16 | 23 | $51 |

Vineyard Haven | 92 Main St. (bet. Church St. & Colonial Ln.) | 508-693-4906 | www.legrenierrestaurant.com

"As old as the money that makes it successful", this Vineyard Haven BYO with an "awkward" location "up a long flight of stairs" and a rustic setting with exposed beams "perfectly executes" "classical French cuisine", which is brought to table by "positively delightful" staffers; the "stagnant menu" "may run against the tide of modernity", but the "core group of stalwarts" that frequents it declares "it's awfully nice to have the choice available."

L'Étoile *French* | 26 | 26 | 23 | $73 |

Edgartown | 22 N. Water St. (Winter St.) | 508-627-5187 | www.letoile.net

"Save up for a special occasion" (like "popping the question"), then make a reservation for this New French "delight" in Edgartown delivering "wonderful everything": "exceptional" cuisine, wines and surroundings, which include a "relaxing bar" with a "lighter menu"; in addition, already "efficient" servers "go the extra mile for you", ensuring a wholly "lovely evening."

Lola's ◐ *Cajun/Creole* | 22 | 22 | 20 | $41 |

Oak Bluffs | 15 Island Inn Rd. (Beach Rd.) | 508-693-5007 | www.lolassouthernseafood.com

"Nothing else comes close to what you find" at this "spirited, inviting" Oak Bluffs venue where "large groups of families and friends" come for "fantastic", "reasonably priced" Cajun-Creole dishes, "many with fresh local seafood", served alongside "exciting live music"; later in the evening, "younger" folks "party on" with "dancing and drinks" brought by staffers that stay "enthusiastic" even while "clearly overextended"; P.S. the "hearty" Sunday jazz brunch is also "fabulous."

Lure *American* | ▽ 21 | 21 | 22 | $68 |

Edgartown | Winnetu Oceanside Resort | 31 Dunes Rd. (Katama Rd.) | 508-627-3663 | www.luremv.com

"If weather permits", take the "delightful" complimentary water taxi from Edgartown to this "cavernous" New American at the Winnetu Oceanside Resort for a "grown-up" New American meal in the "civilized dining room" or on the patio; "if you can't find a sitter", you'll be relegated to a separate space, the milieu of toys and "chicken fin-

gers" but "pleasant" nonetheless – just come "before dark", because it's "priced more for the scenery than for the food."

Net Result *Seafood*   25 | 12 | 19 | $21

Vineyard Haven | Tisbury Marketplace | 79 Beach Rd. (Lagoon Pond Rd.) | 508-693-6071 | www.mvseafood.com

"For a true taste of the sea", join the line for this "often-crowded" "dockside seafood store with a carry-out kitchen" in Vineyard Haven, where "incredibly fresh" fish and "wonderfully prepared sushi" are "cheerfully provided" "at affordable prices"; there are "a few picnic tables available" outside, but they fill up quickly, so you're probably better off heading to the "nearby beach."

Newes from America *Pub Food*   18 | 20 | 19 | $28

Edgartown | Kelley House | 23 Kelley St. (N. Water St.) | 508-627-4397 | www.kelley-house.com

It "feels like a whaling-ship captain may walk in at any moment" to this "cozy", "welcoming" "Colonial-era building" that's "everything a New England pub should be": a "laid-back" haunt for "generous servings" of "quality", "reasonably priced" sandwiches, burgers and snacks to soak up "excellent beers"; no wonder "locals congregate year-round" to "catch a ballgame" on TV while chatting with the "nice folks" on staff.

Offshore Ale Co. *American*   20 | 20 | 19 | $27

Oak Bluffs | 30 Kennebec Ave. (Healey Way) | 508-693-2626 | www.offshoreale.com

"Kids of all ages love the free baskets of peanuts (or perhaps they just love throwing the shells on the floor)" at this Oak Bluffs brewpub, but there's more to adore than that, namely "nonpretentious" American grub ("phenomenal pizzas", "great burgers", etc.) and "incredible homemade beers", all "affordable"; the "occasional live band" keeps it "absolutely fun", even in winter when there's a "fire going."

☒ Outermost Inn ☒ *American*   25 | 26 | 23 | $85

Aquinnah | Outermost Inn | 81 Lighthouse Rd. (State Rd.) | 508-645-3511 | www.outermostinn.com

For the ultimate "romantic getaway", "leave the kids with a sitter" (they're not allowed if they're under 12) and head to this "spectacular" New American in a "lovely" ocean-view Aquinnah inn for an "imaginative, well-prepared" and "extremely pricey" prix fixe; a "terrific" staff buoys the "elegant but casual" vibe, which is even more of a "special treat" if you get to "see the sunset"; P.S. the BYO policy "has gone by the wayside."

Park Corner Bistro *American*   ▽ 22 | 20 | 20 | $47

Oak Bluffs | 20H Kennebec Ave. (off Circuit Ave.) | 508-696-9922 | www.parkcornerbistro.com

While it's "on a busy corner in Oak Bluffs", this "tiny" spot with an equally "intimate bar" "never feels rushed or noisy" while its "sweet and attentive" staff ferries "interesting" American bistro fare with French influences and "great cocktails"; after some recent changes in focus, tough customers feel it still "has to decide what it is", but even they can't resist the "terrific brunch."

🆕 Salt Water 🚫 *Eclectic* — — — M

Vineyard Haven | Tisbury Marketplace | 79 Beach Rd. (off Beach St. & Water St.) | 508-338-4666 | www.saltwaterrestaurant.com

Early admirers call this Eclectic BYO a "great addition to Vineyard Haven", especially since there's plenty of room in the "sparse" yet "pleasant" dining room (with vaulted ceilings, many windows and sweeping view of a lagoon) to sample its "enjoyable" all-day wares; there are a few reports of sketchy service, but "maybe it needs time" to find its sea legs.

Sharky's Cantina ☾ *Mexican* 21 20 20 $20

🆕 **Edgartown** | 266 Upper Main St. (Chase Rd.) | 508-627-6565
Oak Bluffs | 31 Circuit Ave. (Narragansett Ave.) | 508-693-7501 | www.sharkyscantina.com

"Don't expect miracles" and you'll have "fun" at these "kitschy" Edgartown and Oak Bluffs Mexican "joints" that are always "loaded with locals and tourists" digging into "big stuffed burritos" and other "standard fare"; "reasonable prices" make it an option "for the whole family", while a heady selection of tequilas and "great margaritas" abet "special times out for grown-ups."

🆕 Sidecar Café & Bar *New England* — — — I

Oak Bluffs | 16 Kennebec Ave. (Lake Ave.) | 508-693-6261 | www.sidecarcafeandbar.com

At this Oak Bluffs newcomer, the New England fare exhibits some "memorable" Italian flair and "beautiful execution" that "speaks of a chef and owner who care about what they are doing", even as they keep prices low; the light, intimate space displays local art, the bar is a "great" place to "meet for drinks" and the sidewalk tables prove to be an entertaining vantage point for "people-watching."

Slice of Life *American* — — — M

Oak Bluffs | 50 Circuit Ave. (bet. Lake & Samoset Aves.) | 508-693-3838 | www.sliceoflifemv.com

This quaint, all-day, year-round cafe just a stone's throw from the ocean in Oak Bluffs may not have water views or outdoor seating, but it has cultivated a loyal following that starts its day at the espresso bar with a pastry, picks up a specialty sandwich for lunch and then returns for moderately priced New American dinners; a post-Survey change of ownership was expected, but not any changes.

Sweet Life Café *American* 25 22 23 $62

Oak Bluffs | 63 Circuit Ave. (bet. Narragansett & Pequot Aves.) | 508-696-0200 | www.sweetlifemv.com

Lovers of this "jewel of a find in Oak Bluffs" keep "searching for an excuse" to go back for its "just wonderful" New American–New French "gourmet home cooking"; the restored Victorian setting is "beautiful indoors or out" ("if you can, eat in the garden") and an especially "lovely spot for date night", made even more attractive by "friendly, attentive" staffers (if not the "prices you're paying").

	FOOD	DECOR	SERVICE	COST

Theo's *American*   ▽ 24 | 25 | 24 | $50

Chilmark | Inn at Blueberry Hill | 74 North Rd. (bet. Old Farm Rd. & Tea Ln.) | 508-645-3322 | www.blueberryinn.com

Set inside the Inn at Blueberry Hill on "beautiful" former farmlands in Chilmark, this New American maintains a "perfectly nice, long" "enclosed porch" on which to serve "consistently good" fare (pricey, but the "Sunday rustic suppers are a bargain"); besides the "heavenly" setting, "wonderfully relaxed" meals are achieved via staffers who are "so focused" on their customers, who in turn breathe easy having remembered to bring their own alcohol.

NEW Waterside Market *American*   - | - | - | M

Vineyard Haven | 76 Main St. (Union St.) | 508-693-8899 | www.watersidemarket.com

Not far from the ferry terminal in Vineyard Haven, this homey, moderately priced newcomer is a cafe, coffee bar, specialty-foods market and generally "easy stop" for a "wide selection" of American breakfasts and lunches made with "fresh ingredients" by an "enthusiastic staff."

NEW Water St. *Eclectic*   - | - | - | E

Edgartown | Harbor View Hotel & Resort | 131 N. Water St. (Cottage St.) | 508-627-7000 | www.harbor-view.com

Newly opened and already "living up to" its "spectacular" setting in the Harborview Hotel & Resort, this "beautiful room" pairs panoramas of Edgartown Harbor with "delightful", "creative" Eclectic cuisine utilizing seasonal ingredients and "cooked to perfection"; "excellent" service is another aspect that elicits a sincere "wow."

Zapotec *Southwestern*   19 | 16 | 21 | $29

Oak Bluffs | 14 Kennebec Ave. (Lake Ave.) | 508-693-6800 | www.zapotecrestaurant.com

Southwestern fare may seem "incongruous on the Vineyard", however, it is what's for dinner at this "old" Oak Bluffs "cottage"; the tabs are "inexpensive", but "you have to put up with" bright, "cheesy decorations" and a "small, overcrowded space" to get them; "be prepared to wait" when its "busy", perhaps at the bar, since the fare's "better" after "a pretty good margarita" or two.

Zephrus *American*   20 | 19 | 20 | $38

Vineyard Haven | Mansion House | 9 Main St. (State Rd.) | 508-693-3416 | www.zephrus.com

This Vineyard Haven hotel BYO blows hot and cold – the "enjoyable" "screened-in porch" trumps the "uninspired" interior, and the New American fare is "somewhat uneven" (the "standards" are "solid", while the "innovations" "could use some attention"), just as the menu "varies wildly in price" (thankfully, it's mostly "reasonable"); one fact, however, is indisputable: the "convenient location" is "hard to beat."

Nantucket

TOP FOOD

28] Company/Cauldron | *American*
27] Topper's | *American*
26] Le Languedoc | *French*
     Black-Eyed Susan's | *Amer.*
25] Straight Wharf | *Seafood*

TOP DECOR

27] Galley Beach | *Eclectic*
     Topper's | *American*
25] Chanticleer | *French*
     Straight Wharf | *Seafood*
     Pearl | *Asian Fusion/French*

Alice's Restaurant *American/Thai*

▽ 18 | 12 | 18 | $30

Nantucket | Nantucket Airport | 14 Airport Rd. (Old South Rd.) | 508-228-6005

Fans aver the all-day American-Thai fare at this "dependable", moderately priced Nantucket airport eatery is "worth flying in for" – critics of "strange menus", on the other hand, would order "only if stranded"; one thing's for sure, "you can't beat the view if you like planes."

American Seasons *American*

25 | 23 | 22 | $67

Nantucket | 80 Centre St. (W. Chester St.) | 508-228-7111 | www.americanseasons.com

"Each visit is a voyage of discovery" at this folksy, "candlelit" Nantucket "foodies' paradise" where "genius" chef Michael LaScola turns "cutting-edge ingredients" into "knock-your-socks-off" New American regional riffs under the headings Down South, New England and Pacific Coast; some object to "spending a lot" for sometimes "haughty" (though "knowledgeable") service, but they're drowned out by groupies clinking glasses of "stellar all-American wines."

Arno's *American*

16 | 15 | 16 | $36

Nantucket | 41 Main St. (bet. Federal & Orange Sts.) | 508-228-7001 | www.arnos.net

"Breakfast is the best bet" at this "cozy" bi-level "original", while, "depending on the day", the American comfort-food lunches and dinners swing between "so-so" and "great"; nevertheless, it's a "standby" for families since it's "reasonably priced" ("hard to find" on Nantucket).

Black-Eyed Susan's ⊄ *American*

26 | 15 | 21 | $36

Nantucket | 10 India St. (Centre St.) | 508-325-0308 | www.black-eyedsusans.com

"Everyone raves" about the "fantastic" American breakfasts at this "funky", "dinerlike" "Nantucket classic", but "dinners are also amazing"; even though BYO "keeps prices down", the cash-only policy is an "unpleasant surprise" for some – as are the "ridiculously long waits" and often "loud, hot" digs; escaping the "cramped" tables by "sitting at the counter and watching the short-order show", meanwhile, often generates happy revelations.

Boarding House *American*

21 | 19 | 20 | $62

Nantucket | 12 Federal St. (India St.) | 508-228-9622 | www.boardinghouse-pearl.com

"Earthy", "inventive" New American fare made with "quality" market-driven ingredients ("expensive relative to off-island" but "not the

highest on Nantucket") is what's for dinner at this more "humble" sibling to "flashy" Pearl next door; most opt for the "unparalleled social scene" and "great people-watching" on the patio ("worth the wait" for), but there are also admirers of the "crowded, noisy" bar and "romantically lit" cellar, even though it's "still a basement."

Brant Point Grill *American*   21 | 24 | 21 | $64
Nantucket | White Elephant Hotel | 50 Easton St. (Harbor View Way) | 508-228-2500 | www.whiteelephanthotel.com
"Killer views" of Nantucket Harbor and "convenience" draw guests of the White Elephant Hotel to its all-day eatery for "well-prepared" New American dishes and drinks at the "friendly bar"; locals, on the other hand, peg it as "just a tiny bit boring" for being so "pricey."

Brotherhood of Thieves *American*   18 | 20 | 18 | $33
Nantucket | 23 Broad St. (bet. Centre & Federal Sts.) | 508-228-2551 | www.brotherhoodofthieves.com
Dispelling the notion that "everyone on Nantucket wears Ralph Lauren", this "unpretentious" "tradition" gives "local" "families" "a lot of bang for the buck" with "hearty" pub-leaning American grub ("don't leave the island without sampling the curly fries" and "awesome burgers"); the "modern" upstairs "isn't as cozy" as the "rustic" brick-and-beam "watering-hole"-like space downstairs, but the "best seats in the house" may in fact be outside.

Cambridge Street 🗷 Ⓜ *Eclectic*   - | - | - | M
Nantucket | 12 Cambridge St. (New South Rd.) | 508-228-7109
The local artwork on the walls and "young people" at the bar are "worth watching" at this "funky little bistro", just as the "fun", "inventive" Eclectic eats – starring "great burgers", thin-crust pizzas and barbecue – merit noshing; despite the hip scene up front, a children's menu and "reasonable prices" mean it's family-friendly at the tables.

Centre Street Bistro *American*   ▽ 16 | 11 | 12 | $34
Nantucket | Meeting House | 29 Centre St. (bet. Chestnut & India Sts.) | 508-228-8470 | www.nantucketbistro.com
If you're a Nantucket local, you'll end up at this New American Meeting House eatery with "limited atmosphere" in the off-season because, even though it's a crapshoot whether you'll "leave hungry" or "satisfied", it's "cheap"; likewise, if you're a summer tourist, you'll be "caught" here "when you run out of money – and you will."

Chanticleer Ⓜ *French*   25 | 25 | 24 | $76
Siasconset | 9 New St. (Milestone Rd.) | 508-257-6231 | www.thechanticleer.net
There are "no rivals in Siasconset" fawn fans of this "Nantucket classic" where "languorous lunches" and "romantic dinners" star "excellent wines" and "spectacular" French cuisine created with "local seafood and produce"; dining outside "beneath a canopy of roses" and among "beautiful hydrangeas" is "lovely", while the "elegant" interior rooms "do justice to the historic" cottage – but all that's not

enough to impress numbers-crunchers who calculate it's "not worth the exalted prices."

Cinco *Nuevo Latino* ▽ 26 | 24 | 25 | $69

Nantucket | 5 Amelia Dr. (Old South Rd.) | 508-325-5151 | www.cinco5.com

"Islanders would rather you didn't know about" this "comfortable" Nantucket "gem" where "enthusiastic", "helpful servers guide" you in choosing from the "intriguing" variety of "creative" Nuevo Latino tapas and "super" Spanish wines; the "romantic", "candlelit", modern-art-bedecked spot is "a touch out of the way", which means they can keep "dancing on the patio" among themselves – at least for the time being.

Cioppino's *American* 19 | 17 | 20 | $47

Nantucket | 20 Broad St. (bet. Centre & Federal Sts.) | 508-228-4622 | www.cioppinos.com

"You won't go wrong" if you order the namesake seafood-and-pasta dish at this "stalwart" in an old, cozy clapboard home, and although some culinary critics judge it "doesn't always get" all of its New American cuisine "right", the "great variety" and "large portions" equal "values"; the "charismatic" staff adds to a vibe that's "friendly in all respects", and relaxing too, especially on the "excellent patio."

Club Car *Continental* 20 | 19 | 21 | $64

Nantucket | 1 Main St. (Easy St.) | 508-228-1101 | www.theclubcar.com

Traditionalists get "old-style" Continental "classics" from "fabulous" staffers at this "simple, white-tablecloth" "charmer" "in the heart of town", and afterwards, they join other "rich weekenders and singles over 40" in the "crowded, fun bar" – a "high-style" annex set in a 19th-century railway club car – for "live piano" and "creative drinks"; only modernists can't jump onboard, dissing "so-so", "sauce-on-everything" preparations and "inflated prices."

Z Company of the Cauldron *American* 28 | 24 | 25 | $71

Nantucket | 5 India St. (bet. Centre & Federal Sts.) | 508-228-4016 | www.companyofthecauldron.com

"Ethereal" meals are conjured nightly at this "cozy", "friendly" "romantic" offering an "ever-changing, ever-inspired" New American prix fixe in "a dinner-party-like environment" with harp music (three nights a week) and candlelight; the set menu can be a "deal breaker for picky eaters" (especially considering it's so costly), but for "true gourmands", it's the "most innovative and rewarding experience" Nantucket has to offer.

DeMarco *Italian* 22 | 18 | 20 | $67

Nantucket | 9 India St. (bet. Centre & Federal Sts.) | 508-228-1836 | www.demarcorestaurant.com

"Thirty years in the same location" and it's "still got it" applaud acolytes of this venture proffering an "upscale" Northern Italian menu ("somewhat limited" but often "amazing") in a "charming" 19th-century townhouse; it's often packed, so "if you can't get a table" in

.the "bit-cramped upstairs" dining room, ask the "welcoming, atten-tive" staff to find you a spot at the "lively, attractive bar."

Even Keel Cafe *American*   19 | 14 | 16 | $31

Nantucket | 40 Main St. (Federal St.) | 508-228-1979 |
www.evenkeelcafe.com

From sunup to well after sundown, it's "smooth sailing" at this "un-assuming little place" with a "beautiful, serene" patio – at least as far as the "bountiful", "reliable", "reasonably priced" New American fare is concerned; when it comes to service, well, when it's "busy", "you might keel over before you even get" a "cup of coffee."

Fifty-Six Union *Eclectic*   22 | 21 | 23 | $63

Nantucket | 56 Union St. (E. Dover St.) | 508-228-6135 |
www.fiftysixunion.com

"Nobody's worried about who's who" at this "year-round gem" "on the edge of town" – what draws "mingling natives" is the "at-tentive service" and "creative" Eclectic fare ("not an expansive menu, but each item is choice"); yes, this is "serious food", but "you can take the kids", especially if you choose the more "bistro"-like of the two interior rooms (bedecked with local art and sculptures) or the patio.

Fog Island Cafe *American*   21 | 15 | 19 | $21

Nantucket | 7 S. Water St. (India St.) | 508-228-1818 |
www.fogisland.com

Not only is this "cozy", basic cafe a "great spot" for "delicious, hearty, healthy", "quick breakfasts" ("especially for families", be-cause it's cheap), but it also "gets the juices flowing" with New American lunches and in-season dinners; "weather permitting", ask the "friendly", "attentive" servers to find you a spot "out back" to "enjoy the ocean air."

☒ Galley Beach *Eclectic*   24 | 27 | 23 | $78

Nantucket | 54 Jefferson Ave. (off N. Beach St.) | 508-228-9641
If "spectacular sunsets", a "beautiful beach" setting with "waves crashing in the background" and "fantastic food" are "what you pine for", book this "famously romantic" sand-side spot whose "phe-nomenal" outdoor "real estate" and "out-of-this-world" Eclectic cui-sine are "worth" "paying through the nose for"; also on deck is a "professional staff" trained to anticipate "every need" of its patrons, on whom "blue blazers, stripes and khakis" abound.

Jetties, The *Italian/New England*   ▽ 14 | 18 | 11 | $25

Nantucket | 4 Bathing Beach Rd. (Hulbert Ave.) | 508-228-2279 |
www.thejettiesnantucket.com

"For family fun, you can't beat" this "very casual" Italian–New Englander, as the "kids can play on the beach while you have an adult conversation" on the deck or a drink while listening to the oc-casional "nice live music" at the bar; just make sure you're well into vacation mode, because the "lackluster food" is "lackadaisically served" (it's cheap at least).

	FOOD	DECOR	SERVICE	COST

Le Languedoc Bistro *French*

26	22	25	$63

Nantucket | Le Languedoc Inn | 24 Broad St. (bet. Centre & Federal Sts.) | 508-228-2552 | www.lelanguedoc.com

"All the classics" plus "enough inventiveness to keep you coming back" "year after year" – not to mention "an appealing wine list" – is the "tantalizing" formula at this "lovely" French "gem" with a patio, a more formal dining room and a "cozy" bistro/bar below ("cheaper than upstairs" but still "*très* delicious"); the staff's simultaneous "professional" and "laid-back" tone adds to an experience enthusiasts cheer is "wonderful in every way."

Lo La 41° ⚫ *Eclectic*

21	22	20	$55

Nantucket | 15 S. Beach St. (Sea St.) | 508-325-4001 | www.lola41.net

"High-octane" to the nth degree, this "chicly decorated", "intimate spot" is known more for a "wildly hopping" "bar scene", but its "black Armani"–sporting habitués say the Eclectic victuals (there's a "great sushi" menu as well as a bistro *carte*) are "fantastic" too; however, holdouts warn the "small portions" are "way too expensive, even for Nantucket", and the "noise level is impossible" (next time, they might try the "divine patio").

Nantucket Lobster Trap *Seafood*

19	15	18	$46

Nantucket | 23 Washington St. (Coffin St.) | 508-228-4200 | www.nantucketlobstertrap.com

"If you've got a hankering for no-frills lobster", this "institution of shirt-staining" is "the place to go" for "more than ample portions" of "decent seafood" at "low prices" ("for the island"); the servers do their best to be "nice and accommodating" while getting "high volumes" of "tourists" fed and out of the "bland", "noisy" environs, but there's "always a line" of more waiting to get in.

Òran Mór *Eclectic*

24	23	24	$75

Nantucket | 2 S. Beach St. (Whalers Ln.) | 508-228-8655 | www.oranmorbistro.com

An "awe-inspiring" "use of seasonal ingredients" is the forte of this "enchanting" Eclectic, as "unforgettable" for its "remarkable" fare as it is for an "elegant", "quaint" setting up a flight of "copper stairs" ("perfect for a romantic rendezvous"); in accord with the "veritable symphony" of tastes are an "excellent wine list" and an "attentive staff", and while it's "not cheap", "if anyplace on this expensive island is worth it", it's this one.

Pearl *Asian Fusion/French*

24	25	22	$69

Nantucket | 12 Federal St. (India St.) | 508-228-9701 | www.boardinghouse-pearl.com

"Hip and stylish" folks who "want it all" find it at this Asian fusion-New French "party" that entices with a "tremendous bar", "delicious libations", "friendly, helpful servers" and "cool", "unexpected decor" that reminds them of weekends spent in "New York"/"LA"/"Miami"/"Monte Carlo"; the "innovative" fare is "fabulous" too, although belt-tighteners blanch "it's hard to enjoy the fresh fish when you're gagging on the prices."

	FOOD	DECOR	SERVICE	COST

Pi Pizzeria *Pizza* ▽ 23 | 12 | 20 | $32

Nantucket | 11 W. Creek Rd. (bet. Orange & Pleasant Sts.) | 508-228-1130 | www.pipizzeria.com

"Escape the buzz of Downtown" Nantucket and get "your pizza fix" all in one fell swoop at this parlor baking wood-fired, thin-crust Neapolitan "lusciousness" and additional moderately priced Italian dishes of "solid quality"; there's "always a line" for a table, but take-out is an option, as is the bar.

Queequeg's *Eclectic* 25 | 20 | 24 | $48

Nantucket | 6 Oak St. (Fedral St.) | 508-325-0992 | www.queequegsnantucket.com

"What a treat!" cheer boosters of this "casual" "little jewel" "in the heart of N'tucket town", where the "nice variety" of Eclectic eats is "delightful and delicious all-around", not to mention "reasonably priced" (in island terms); bonus points are earned because "you can usually get a table" in the "snug", "lovely", whale-art-sporting interior, if not on the "adorable" deck.

Ropewalk, The *Seafood* - | - | - | M

Nantucket | 1 Straight Wharf (Easy St.) | 508-228-8886 | www.theropewalk.com

Taking its name from its past as a building where ropes for ships were made, this waterside seafooder boasts a patio, three dining rooms, two drinks bars, a raw bar and views of Nantucket Harbor; it's quite a hip scene, but moderate prices make it smart for families too.

Sconset Café ♉ *American* 21 | 16 | 19 | $48

Siasconset | 8 Main St. (Post Office Sq.) | 508-257-4008 | www.sconsetcafe.com

"Run by 'Sconseters for 'Sconseters", this "charming", "cash-only" New American provides "homemade muffins" for breakfast, "great sandwiches after a bike ride" in the afternoon and "fresh, lively" dinners amid candlelight and "ever-changing exhibits of local artists"; service can be "slow" when "crowded", but you're on "island time", so just "relax" and pour another glass from the stash you picked up at the wine-and-books store next door.

SeaGrille *Seafood* 22 | 17 | 21 | $49

Nantucket | 45 Sparks Ave. (bet. Pleasant St. & Sanford Rd.) | 508-325-5700 | www.theseagrille.com

Sure, this "Nantucket tradition" "provides the seafood staples", but it "can also cut loose" with "marvelous" "daily specials"; the digs may be slightly "dated", but as long as it remains "open year-round", "makes everyone feel welcome" (especially "families" with "kids") and delivers "value", "locals" will keep recommending it as a "solid performer."

Sfoglia ⊠ *Italian* 24 | 18 | 21 | $62

Nantucket | 130 Pleasant St. (bet. Chins Way & W. Creek Rd.) | 508-325-4500 | www.sfogliarestaurant.com

"High-quality fresh ingredients" are evident in the "creative" fare proffered at this Italian, which employs "friendly, attentive" staffers

to "help guide" diners through the "limited, quirky menu" ("pricey", but "worth it for the bread" alone); both private and "communal tables" fill the "just-redesigned", "shabby-chic" setting, which some aesthetes "don't really dig."

Ships Inn *Californian/French*

24	22	22	$68

Nantucket | Ships Inn | 13 Fair St. (Lucretia Mott Ln.) | 508-228-0040 | www.shipsinnnantucket.com

Only "knowledgeable Nantucketers dine" at this "seasonal" "gem" serving "superb", "creative" Californian-French fare, since it's virtually "hidden" in the "basement" of an 18th-century whaling captain's mansion; it's "on the edge of town", so couples can take "a romantic walk" at the end of their "lovely evening" – but the "friendly staff" and "inviting", "cozy bar" make many "want to linger."

Slip 14 *American*

18	17	19	$48

Nantucket | 14 Old South Wharf (New Whale St.) | 508-228-2033 | www.slip14.com

"Finish up your Nantucket jaunt" at this "casual" New American "family" "respite" near the ferries, which offers "wonderful outdoor seating" on a "fun wharf" (inside's a little "dark"); dollar-watchers who deem the vittles "overpriced" for being only "ok" stick to "sweet specialty cocktails" at the "nice bar", which hops with a "twentysomething crowd later in the evening."

Straight Wharf *Seafood*

25	25	24	$73

Nantucket | 6 Harbor Sq. (Straight Wharf) | 508-228-4499 | www.straightwharfrestaurant.com

"On a warm summer night", there may not be a more "gorgeous" or "romantic" setting than the dining porch "overlooking the harbor" at this "standout", but the "absolutely beautiful" interior is an equally "tantalizing" "Nantucket habitat" in which to enjoy "inspiring" "high-end seafood" that "utilizes local ingredients effectively"; a "split personality" emerges later in the evening when "jocks" and their quarry create a "loud", "lively bar scene", which is "thankfully, separated from the main room."

Summer House *American*

20	23	19	$71

Siasconset | Summer House | 17 Ocean Ave. (Magnolia Ave.) | 508-257-9976 | www.thesummerhouse.com

A "pianist plays delightful music to accompany" New American meals in this "very expensive" Siasconset inn's "simple but elegant" main room (off of which sits a "great old porch"), while ocean breezes cool at its "beachside bistro"; yes, its location on the coast is undeniably "beautiful", but with "hit-or-miss" dishes and occasional "attitude" from the staff, some suspect it "coasts on the location."

Sushi by Yoshi *Japanese*

25	13	19	$37

Nantucket | 2 E. Chestnut St. (Water St.) | 508-228-1801 | www.sushibyyoshi.com

Nantucketers feel "lucky to have a sushi place" that's as "inventive", "super-fresh" and "affordable" as this "jewel"; some say it's "worth the wait" to eat in the "small" "mob scene" ("BYOB,

baby!"), but many feel it's "better to do takeout" – the rolls and sashimi "travel well."

Z Topper's *American*   27 | 27 | 26 | $95

Nantucket | Wauwinet Inn | 120 Wauwinet Rd. (2 mi. north of Polpis Rd.) | 508-228-8768 | www.wauwinet.com

"Stuff your wallet" with "big bucks", take the "romantic" "water shuttle" "across the harbor from town" and get to this "special-occasion spot" at the Wauwinet Inn "in time to see the sunset"; next up is the "divine culinary experience" of chef David Daniels' "handsomely plated", "exquisite" New American cuisine, which is presented by "impeccable" servers alongside a "deftly crafted wine list" in a "beautiful" dining room and "lovely", less-formal patio – just "don't expect large portions" and "you won't be disappointed"; P.S. lunch and brunch are just as "memorable."

29 Fair Street **M** *Continental*   22 | 23 | 19 | $63

Nantucket | 29 Fair St. (Martins Ln.) | 508-228-7800 | www.29fair.com

The owners of the "famed Summer House" have turned the old Woodbox restaurant, set in a 300-year-old building, into this Continental "hideaway" where diners "venture back in time" via three candlelit rooms sporting original brick fireplaces, exposed beams and antique sconces; boosters find the pricey offerings "great", while a minority pronounces them merely fair, citing a "limited menu" filled with dishes that are "not unique" enough.

Z 21 Federal *American*   24 | 23 | 23 | $68

Nantucket | 21 Federal St. (bet. Chestnut & Oak Sts.) | 508-228-2121 | www.21federal.com

"After all these years", this "quintessential" Nantucket New American in a "handsome", "romantic" Greek Revival edifice complete with a "charming patio" still "pampers" via "delectable creations" made with "local provender" that virtually "dances on the plate"; though a few critics carp that it's "way too expensive" (and perhaps "pretentious"), Federalists affirm it "should never change."

BOSTON/
CAPE COD & THE ISLANDS
INDEXES

LOCATION MAPS

All places are in Boston area unless otherwise noted (CC=Cape Cod; MV=Martha's Vineyard; Nan=Nantucket).

Cuisines

Includes restaurant names, locations and Food ratings.

AFGHAN

☑ Helmand | **E Cambridge**	26

AMERICAN (NEW)

Alchemist | **Jamaica Plain**	17
Alchemy | **MV**	22
Alice's | **Nan**	18
American Seasons | **Nan**	25
Aqua Grille | **CC**	19
Ariadne | **Newton**	21
NEW Asana | **Back Bay**	-
Atria | **MV**	25
Aura | **Seaport Dist**	22
Avenue One | **D'town Cross**	18
Azure | **Back Bay**	22
Baker's Best | **Newton**	22
Balance | **MV**	23
Bambara | **E Cambridge**	20
Barley Neck Inn | **CC**	20
Bayside Betsy's | **CC**	15
Beach Plum | **MV**	25
Beehive | **S End**	18
Belfry Inne | **CC**	25
Bistro/Crowne Pointe | **CC**	22
Black-Eyed Susan's | **Nan**	26
NEW Blackfish | **CC**	24
Blarney Stone | **Dorchester**	16
blu | **Theater Dist**	21
Blue on Highland | **Needham**	17
Boarding Hse. | **Nan**	21
☑ Bramble Inn | **CC**	27
Brant Point | **Nan**	21
Bravo | **MFA**	21
Brenden Crocker's | **Beverly**	25
☑ Bristol | **Back Bay**	24
Brownstone | **Back Bay**	15
Burtons | **Fenway**	21
Cafe Edwige/at Night | **CC**	26
Café Fleuri | **Financial Dist**	22
Cape Sea Grille | **CC**	26
☑ Catch | **Winchester**	27
Central Kitchen | **Central Sq**	24
Centre St. Bistro | **Nan**	16
Chapoquoit Grill | **CC**	22
Chatham Bars Inn | **CC**	22
Church | **Fenway**	20
Cioppino's | **Nan**	19
Circadia Bistro | **CC**	23
Clink | **Beacon Hill**	19
Club Cafe | **S End**	18
☑ Company/Cauldron | **Nan**	28
Daedalus | **Harv Sq**	17
NEW Daily Grill | **Back Bay**	19
Dalia's Bistro | **Brookline**	19
Dalya's | **Bedford**	23
Dan'l Webster | **CC**	20
☑ Détente | **MV**	27
Devlin's | **Brighton**	20
Devon's | **CC**	24
District | **Leather Dist**	17
NEW Drink | **Seaport Dist**	-
☑ Duckworth's | **Gloucester**	29
NEW Ecco | **E Boston**	-
Even Keel | **Nan**	19
Fava | **Needham**	25
51 Lincoln | **Newton**	23
Finely JP's | **CC**	21
Fishmonger's | **CC**	18
Five Bays Bistro | **CC**	25
Flat Iron | **W End**	22
flora | **Arlington**	24
Fog Island | **Nan**	21
Franklin | **multi.**	26
Full Moon | **Huron Vill**	20
Garden at Cellar | **Harv Sq**	25
Gardner Museum | **MFA**	20
Gargoyles | **Somerville**	24
NEW G Bar | **Swampscott**	21
Geoffrey's | **Roslindale**	19
Glory | **Andover**	21
Grafton St. Pub | **Harv Sq**	17
Grapevine | **Salem**	25
Harvest | **Harv Sq**	25
Heather | **CC**	-
Highland Kitchen | **Somerville**	23

NEW Hungry Mother | **Kendall Sq**	27
Icarus | **S End**	25
Independent | **Somerville**	18
Isabella | **Dedham**	24
Island Merchant | **CC**	-
Jacob Wirth | **Theater Dist**	17
Jer-Ne | **Theater Dist**	20
J's Nashoba | **Bolton**	26
Laurel | **Back Bay**	20
Left Bank | **Tyngsboro**	21
Lexx | **Lexington**	17
LiNEaGe | **Brookline**	23
Living Room | **Waterfront**	15
NEW Local, The | **W Newton**	-
Locke-Ober | **D'town Cross**	24
Lure | **MV**	21
Lyceum B&G | **Salem**	23
NEW Market | **Financial Dist**	16
Masona Grill | **W Roxbury**	25
Meritage | **Waterfront**	27
Met B&G | **Natick**	21
Metropolitan | **Chestnut Hill**	21
Mews | **CC**	27
Navy Yard | **Charlestown**	23
North St. Grille | **N End**	23
Novel | **Back Bay**	-
Ocean House | **CC**	25
OM Rest. | **Harv Sq**	19
Outermost Inn | **MV**	25
Park Corner | **MV**	22
Persephone | **Seaport Dist**	25
Pops | **S End**	22
Port | **CC**	23
Prose | **Arlington**	24
Redline | **Harv Sq**	17
Red Pheasant | **CC**	27
Red Rock Bistro | **Swampscott**	20
Red Sky | **Faneuil Hall**	18
Regatta of Cotuit | **CC**	25
RooBar | **multi.**	21
Ross' Grill | **CC**	22
NEW Rudi's | **Roxbury**	-
Salts | **Central Sq**	26
Scargo Café | **CC**	20
Sconset Café | **Nan**	21
Sibling Rivalry | **S End**	24
Sidney's | **Central Sq**	21
NEW 606 Congress | **Seaport Dist**	21
Sky | **multi.**	19
Slice of Life | **MV**	-
Slip 14 | **Nan**	18
Soma | **Beverly**	22
South End Buttery | **S End**	21
Square Café | **Hingham**	26
St. Alphonzo's | **S Boston**	22
Stanhope Grille | **Back Bay**	23
Stephanie's | **Back Bay**	20
Summer House | **Nan**	20
Sweet Life | **MV**	25
Temple Bar | **Porter Sq**	20
Tempo | **Waltham**	21
Ten Tables | **multi.**	27
Terra Luna | **CC**	24
Theo's | **MV**	24
33 Rest. | **Back Bay**	20
Top of Hub | **Back Bay**	20
Topper's | **Nan**	27
NEW Townsend's | **Hyde Park**	19
Tremont 647 | **S End**	21
Troquet | **Theater Dist**	27
Tryst | **Arlington**	22
Turner Fish | **Back Bay**	21
28 Atlantic | **CC**	26
28 Degrees | **S End**	20
29 Newbury | **Back Bay**	20
21 Federal | **Nan**	24
T.W. Food | **Huron Vill**	26
224 Boston St. | **Dorchester**	22
Union B&G | **S End**	24
UpStairs on Sq. | **Harv Sq**	24
Vinalia | **D'town Cross**	17
Vox Populi | **Back Bay**	16
Walden Grille | **Concord**	15
West Side Lounge | **Porter Sq**	22
Wicked Oyster | **CC**	24
Winslow's Tavern | **CC**	20
Zebra's Bistro | **Medfield**	24
Zephrus | **MV**	20
Zon's | **Jamaica Plain**	24

BOSTON/CAPE COD

CUISINES

AMERICAN (TRADITIONAL)

Adrian's	CC	16
Amrheins	S Boston	18
Art Cliff Diner	MV	24
Ashmont Grill	Dorchester	22
Audubon Circle	Kenmore Sq	21
Barker Tavern	Scituate	23
Beacon St. Tavern	Brookline	20
Bee-Hive Tavern	CC	19
Betsy's Diner	CC	18
Biltmore B&G	Newton	18
Birch St. Bistro	Roslindale	19
Black Cow	multi.	19
☑ Black Dog Tavern	MV	19
Black Sheep	Kendall Sq	21
Blue22	Quincy	19
Boston/Salem Beer	multi.	18
Brotherhood/Thieves	Nan	18
Cambridge Common	Harv Sq	17
Capt. Kidd	CC	18
Capt. Linnell	CC	22
Capt. Parker's	CC	18
Charley's	multi.	18
Charlie's Kitchen	Harv Sq	17
Charlie's Sandwich	S End	23
Cheers	multi.	14
☑ Cheesecake	multi.	18
Cioppino's	Nan	19
Clancy's	CC	22
Coda	S End	22
NEW Comfort	Watertown	-
Coolidge Corner	Brookline	17
Coonamessett Inn	CC	18
Cygnet	Beverly	21
David Ryan's	MV	15
Dillon's	Back Bay	16
NEW DJ's/Garden	W End	-
Dog Bar	Gloucester	23
Dolphin	CC	21
☑ Eastern Stand.	Kenmore Sq	22
Fairway	CC	18
Fanizzi's	CC	20
Flash's	Park Sq	18
Good Life	D'town Cross	17
Greg's	Watertown	19

Haley House	Roxbury	24
Halfway Cafe	multi.	17
Harry's	Westborough	20
Harvard Gardens	Beacon Hill	17
NEW High St. Grill	North Andover	-
Houston's	Faneuil Hall	22
James's Gate	Jamaica Plain	16
Joe's American	multi.	16
John Harvard's	multi.	16
Johnny D's	Somerville	19
Johnny's Lunch.	Newton	18
NEW Jury Room	Quincy	19
Lambert's Cove	MV	25
Landing	multi.	16
Laura & Tony's	CC	-
Lucky's Lounge	Seaport Dist	18
Marshside	CC	15
NEW Max/Dylan	multi.	-
Mike's	S End	20
Miracle of Science	Central Sq	19
Mission B&G	MFA	19
M.J. O'Connor's	Park Sq	-
Mr. Bartley's	Harv Sq	24
NewBridge	Chelsea	24
Newes/America	MV	18
☑ Not Average Joe's	multi.	18
☑ Oak Room	Back Bay	25
Oceana	Waterfront	24
Offshore Ale	MV	20
Optimist Café	CC	21
Orleans	Somerville	17
Orleans Inn	CC	17
Paramount	Beacon Hill	23
Pie Bakery	Newton	18
Pleasant Cafe	Roslindale	18
Post Office	CC	16
Scollay Sq.	Beacon Hill	19
75 Chestnut	Beacon Hill	21
Silvertone B&G	D'town Cross	21
Sorella's	Jamaica Plain	26
Sound Bites	Somerville	22
South St. Diner	Leather Dist	16
Stars on Hingham	Hingham	16
Strip-T's	Watertown	22

Summer Winter | **Burlington**	24
Sunset Cafe | **Inman Sq**	19
Sunset Grill/Cantina | **multi.**	20
Tavern in Sq. | **multi.**	17
Tavern on Water | **Charlestown**	13
21st Amendment | **Beacon Hill**	17
Via Lago | **Lexington**	20
Victoria's Diner | **Roxbury**	20
NEW Vintage | **W Roxbury**	-
Warren Tavern | **Charlestown**	16
Washington Sq. | **Brookline**	22
NEW Waterside Mkt. | **MV**	-
West on Centre | **W Roxbury**	18
Whitman House | **CC**	21
Wild Goose | **CC**	21
Woody's Grill | **Fenway**	22

ARGENTINEAN

Tango | **Arlington**	21

ARMENIAN

Karoun | **Newton**	22

ASIAN

NEW Asana | **Back Bay**	-

ASIAN FUSION

Z Blue Ginger | **Wellesley**	26
HannaH's Fusion | **CC**	24
Z Maxwell's 148 | **Natick**	26
Pearl | **Nan**	24
Ponzu | **Waltham**	23
Super Fusion | **Brookline**	27

BAKERIES

Athan's Café | **multi.**	23
Baker's Best | **Newton**	22
flour bakery | **multi.**	26
Haley House | **Roxbury**	24
Hi-Rise | **multi.**	24
Neighborhood Rest. | **Somerville**	23
Panificio | **Beacon Hill**	19
South End Buttery | **S End**	21
Vicki Lee's | **Belmont**	25

BARBECUE

Bison County BBQ | **Waltham**	18
Blue Ribbon BBQ | **multi.**	25

Z East Coast | **Inman Sq**	25
Firefly's | **multi.**	20
NEW High St. Grill | **North Andover**	-
Jake's Dixie | **Waltham**	17
NewBridge | **Chelsea**	24
Redbones BBQ | **Somerville**	22
Roadhouse Craft Beer & BBQ | **Brookline**	-
Soul Fire | **Allston**	21
Uncle Pete's Ribs | **Revere**	25
Village Smokehse. | **Brookline**	19

BELGIAN

Publick House | **Brookline**	21

BRAZILIAN

Brazilian Grill | **CC**	21
Café Belô | **multi.**	20
Café Brazil | **Allston**	23
Don Ricardo's | **S End**	23
Midwest | **Inman Sq**	20
Muqueca | **Inman Sq**	24
NEW Rodizio | **Somerville**	22

BRITISH

Cornwall's | **Kenmore Sq**	15
Dunbar Tea | **CC**	22
Optimist Café | **CC**	21

BURGERS

Audubon Circle | **Kenmore Sq**	21
b. good | **multi.**	19
Brotherhood/Thieves | **Nan**	18
Cambridge Common | **Harv Sq**	17
Charlie's Kitchen | **Harv Sq**	17
Christopher's | **Porter Sq**	17
NEW Franky/Boys | **Brookline**	-
Miracle of Science | **Central Sq**	19
Mr. Bartley's | **Harv Sq**	24
UBurger | **multi.**	23

CAJUN

Border Cafe | **multi.**	19
Lola's | **MV**	22

CALIFORNIAN

Caliterra | **Financial Dist**	16
Cottage | **Wellesley**	19

Picante | **Central Sq**	19
Ships Inn | **Nan**	24

CAMBODIAN
☑ Elephant Walk | **multi.**	23
Floating Rock | **Revere**	-
Stir Crazy | **CC**	23
Wonder Spice | **Jamaica Plain**	21

CAPE VERDEAN
Rest. Cesaria | **Dorchester**	-

CARIBBEAN
Island Merchant | **CC**	-

CHILEAN
Chacarero | **D'town Cross**	-

CHINESE
(* dim sum specialist)
Bernard's | **Chestnut Hill**	24
Billy Tse | **multi.**	20
Changsho | **Porter Sq**	20
Chau Chow* | **Chinatown**	21
Chef Chang's | **Brookline**	20
Chef Chow's | **Brookline**	20
China Pearl* | **multi.**	21
China Sky | **Wellesley**	19
CK Shanghai | **Wellesley**	22
East Ocean | **Chinatown**	24
Emperor's Gdn.* | **Chinatown**	21
Golden Temple | **Brookline**	21
NEW Grand Chinatown | **N Quincy**	-
Imperial Seafood* | **Chinatown**	24
Jumbo | **multi.**	23
Little Q | **Quincy**	25
Lotus Blossom | **Sudbury**	22
Mary Chung | **Central Sq**	21
Mifune | **Arlington**	20
New Shanghai | **Chinatown**	16
Peach Farm | **Chinatown**	25
Peking Cuisine | **Newton**	21
P.F. Chang's | **multi.**	19
Qingdao Gdn.* | **Porter Sq**	24
Royal East | **Central Sq**	20
Shanghai Gate | **Allston**	24

Sichuan Garden | **multi.**	22
☑ Sichuan Gourmet | **Framingham**	27
Xinh Xinh | **Chinatown**	25
Yangtze River* | **Lexington**	17
Zoe's | **Somerville**	19

COFFEEHOUSES
Café Algiers | **Harv Sq**	18
Caffe Paradiso | **N End**	17
Darwin's | **Harv Sq**	24
Mr. Crepe | **Somerville**	18
Sorelle | **Charlestown**	23
South End Buttery | **S End**	21
1369 Coffee Hse. | **multi.**	20
Trident | **Back Bay**	19

COFFEE SHOPS/ DINERS
Art Cliff Diner | **MV**	24
Betsy's Diner | **CC**	18
Charlie's Kitchen | **Harv Sq**	17
Charlie's Sandwich | **S End**	23
Deluxe Town | **Watertown**	22
Harry's | **Westborough**	20
Johnny's Lunch. | **Newton**	18
Mike's | **S End**	20
Rosebud | **Somerville**	16
South St. Diner | **Leather Dist**	16
Stars on Hingham | **Hingham**	16
Victoria's Diner | **Roxbury**	20

COLOMBIAN
Rincon Limeno | **E Boston**	-

CONTINENTAL
Anthony Cummaquid | **CC**	18
Cafe Escadrille | **Burlington**	19
Café Fleuri | **Financial Dist**	22
Club Car | **Nan**	20
☑ Front St. | **CC**	27
Locke-Ober | **D'town Cross**	24
NEW Marliave | **D'town Cross**	22
29 Fair St. | **Nan**	22
Wine Cellar | **Back Bay**	20

CREOLE
Lola's | **MV**	22

CUBAN

Chez Henri | **Harv Sq**	24
El Oriental/Cuba | **Jamaica Plain**	24

DELIS

Bottega | **Brookline**	24
Darwin's | **Harv Sq**	24
Hot Tomatoes | **N End**	22
Rubin's | **Brookline**	19
S&S | **Inman Sq**	18
Zaftigs | **Brookline**	21

DESSERT

Z Bristol | **Back Bay**	24
Café Fleuri | **Financial Dist**	22
Caffe Paradiso | **N End**	17
Finale | **multi.**	23
flour bakery | **multi.**	26
Hi-Rise | **multi.**	24
Picco | **S End**	22
Pie Bakery | **Newton**	18

DOMINICAN

Merengue | **Roxbury**	-

ECLECTIC

Academy Ocean | **CC**	22
Z Banq | **S End**	21
Blue Room | **Kendall Sq**	25
Boloco | **multi.**	18
NEW Bond | **Financial Dist**	-
Bravo | **MFA**	21
Bubala's | **CC**	16
Bullfinch's | **Sudbury**	21
Café at Taj | **Back Bay**	20
Cambridge St. | **Nan**	-
Centre St. Café | **Jamaica Plain**	25
Chatham Squire | **CC**	18
Chesca's | **MV**	23
Christopher's | **Porter Sq**	17
Columbus Café | **S End**	19
Z Cuchi Cuchi | **Central Sq**	22
Deep Ellum | **Allston**	18
Delux Cafe | **S End**	21
Equator | **S End**	18
Z EVOO | **Somerville**	27
Exchange St. Bistro | **Malden**	20

Fifty-Six Union | **Nan**	22
Fire & Ice | **multi.**	16
Firefly Woodfire | **CC**	20
Z Galley Beach | **Nan**	24
Glenn's | **Newburyport**	23
Johnnie's on Side | **W End**	17
Laureen's | **CC**	23
Lobster Pot | **CC**	22
Lo La 41° | **Nan**	21
LTK | **Seaport Dist**	20
Metropolis Cafe | **S End**	23
Middlesex | **Central Sq**	17
Mount Blue | **Norwell**	18
Napi's | **CC**	19
Òran Mór | **Nan**	24
Purple Cactus | **Jamaica Plain**	21
Queequeg's | **Nan**	25
Red House | **Harv Sq**	20
NEW Salt Water | **MV**	-
Sanctuary | **Financial Dist**	19
Scutra | **Arlington**	23
Something Savory | **Arlington**	22
Sonsie | **Back Bay**	20
STIX | **Back Bay**	17
Stone Soup | **Ipswich**	25
Trident | **Back Bay**	19
Vining's Bistro | **CC**	24
NEW Water St. | **MV**	-
ZuZu! | **Central Sq**	20

ERITREAN

Asmara | **Central Sq**	21

ETHIOPIAN

Addis Red Sea | **multi.**	22
Asmara | **Central Sq**	21

EUROPEAN

Z Eastern Stand. | **Kenmore Sq**	22
Z Ten Tables | **multi.**	27

FONDUE

NEW Melting Pot | **multi.**	20
Wine Cellar | **Back Bay**	20

FRENCH

Z Aujourd'hui | **Back Bay**	28
Bleu | **CC**	25

BOSTON/CAPE COD

CUISINES

Bon Savor | **Jamaica Plain**	20
Butcher Shop | **S End**	25
Chanticleer | **Nan**	25
Ⓩ Chillingsworth | **CC**	27
Ⓩ Clio/Uni | **Back Bay**	27
Devon's | **CC**	24
Ⓩ Elephant Walk | **multi.**	23
Enzo | **CC**	24
Hungry i | **Beacon Hill**	24
Jasmine | **Brighton**	24
Le Grenier | **MV**	23
Le Languedoc | **Nan**	26
Le Lyonnais | **Acton**	23
Ⓩ L'Espalier | **Back Bay**	28
L'Étoile | **MV**	26
Ⓩ Lumière | **Newton**	27
Mantra | **D'town Cross**	18
Ⓩ Mistral | **S End**	27
Mr. Crepe | **Somerville**	18
Ⓩ No. 9 Park | **Beacon Hill**	28
Paris Creperie | **Brookline**	22
Pearl | **Nan**	24
Ⓩ Petit Robert | **Needham**	24
Ⓩ Radius | **Financial Dist**	26
Ⓩ Red Pheasant | **CC**	27
Salts | **Central Sq**	26
Sandrine's | **Harv Sq**	24
Ⓩ Sel de Terre | **Back Bay**	23
NEW Sensing | **Waterfront**	-
Ships Inn | **Nan**	24
Sweet Life | **MV**	25
T.W. Food | **Huron Vill**	26

FRENCH (BISTRO)

Ⓩ Aquitaine | **S End**	23
Aquitaine Bis | **Chestnut Hill**	23
Beacon Hill Bistro | **Beacon Hill**	22
bia bistro | **Cohasset**	24
Bistro 712 | **Norwood**	24
Cassis | **Andover**	26
Chez Henri | **Harv Sq**	24
Ⓩ Coriander Bistro | **Sharon**	27
Ⓩ Craigie on Main | **Central Sq**	27
Ⓩ Hamersley's Bistro | **S End**	27
Kingston Station | **D'town Cross**	20
L'Alouette | **CC**	26

Les Zygomates | **Leather Dist**	22
Ⓩ Petit Robert | **multi.**	24
Pierrot Bistrot | **Beacon Hill**	24
Pigalle | **Theater Dist**	26
Ⓩ Sel de Terre | **multi.**	23
Ⓩ Troquet | **Theater Dist**	27

FRENCH (BRASSERIE)

Bouchée | **Back Bay**	21
Brasserie Jo | **Back Bay**	20
Gaslight Brasserie | **S End**	21
La Voile | **Back Bay**	23
Miel | **Waterfront**	21

GERMAN

Jacob Wirth | **Theater Dist**	17

GREEK

Aegean | **multi.**	21
Demos | **multi.**	21
Ⓩ Ithaki Med. | **Ipswich**	26
Kouzina | **Newton**	23
Steve's Greek | **multi.**	20

HEALTH FOOD

(See also Vegetarian)

b. good | **multi.**	19

HUNGARIAN

Jasmine | **Brighton**	24

INDIAN

Bhindi Bazaar | **Back Bay**	22
Bombay Club | **multi.**	20
Bukhara | **Jamaica Plain**	23
Cafe of India | **Harv Sq**	22
Diva Indian | **Somerville**	22
NEW Ghazal | **Jamaica Plain**	-
Grain & Salt | **Allston**	-
Haveli | **Inman Sq**	-
Himalayan Bistro | **W Roxbury**	24
India Pavilion | **Central Sq**	20
India Quality | **Kenmore Sq**	24
India Quality/Punjab | **Allston**	24
Kashmir | **Back Bay**	23
Kebab Factory | **Somerville**	24
Mantra | **D'town Cross**	18

Masala Art	**Needham**	23
Mela	**S End**	24
Namaskar	**Somerville**	23
New Mother India	**Waltham**	22
Passage to India	**multi.**	20
Punjab	**Arlington**	25
Punjabi Dhaba	**Inman Sq**	24
Rani	**Brookline**	20
Shanti India	**Dorchester**	-
Tamarind Bay	**multi.**	24
Tanjore	**Harv Sq**	22
Tantric	**Theater Dist**	20

IRISH

Burren	**Somerville**	14
Doyle's	**Jamaica Plain**	15
Green Briar	**Brighton**	17
James's Gate	**Jamaica Plain**	16
Matt Murphy's	**Brookline**	22

ISRAELI

| NEW Jerusalem Pita | **Brookline** | - |

ITALIAN

(N=Northern; S=Southern)
Abbondanza	**Everett**	23
Adrian's	**CC**	16
Alberto's	N	**CC**	20
Al Dente	**N End**	22
Alta Strada	**Wellesley**	21
Amari	**CC**	22
Amelia's Kitchen	**Somerville**	22
Amelia's Trattoria	**Kendall Sq**	22
Anchovies	**S End**	20
Angelo's	**Stoneham**	26
Antico Forno	S	**N End**	23
Antonio's Cucina	**Beacon Hill**	22
Appetito	**Newton**	19
Artichokes	**Malden**	21
Artú	**multi.**	21
Assaggio	**N End**	24
Bacco	**N End**	21
Basta Pasta	**Central Sq**	24
Bella's	**Rockland**	19
Bertucci's	**multi.**	17
bia bistro	**Cohasset**	24
NEW Bina Osteria	**D'town Cross**	-

Bin 26	**Beacon Hill**	21
Z Bistro 5	N	**W Medford**	27
Bon Caldo	**Norwood**	22
Bottega	N	**Brookline**	24
Bricco	**N End**	25
Bridgeman's	N	**Hull**	26
Buca's Tuscan	N	**CC**	23
Butcher Shop	**S End**	25
Caffe Tosca	**Hingham**	24
Caliterra	**Financial Dist**	16
Canestaro	**Fenway**	19
Cantina Italiana	S	**N End**	22
Carlo's Cucina	**Allston**	25
Z Carmen	**N End**	26
Casino Wharf	N	**CC**	20
Chesca's	**MV**	23
Ciao Bella	**Back Bay**	19
Ciro & Sal's	N	**CC**	20
NEW Croma	**Plymouth**	19
Daily Catch	**multi.**	24
dante	**E Cambridge**	24
Davide Rist.	N	**N End**	24
Da Vinci	**Park Sq**	22
Z Davio's	N	**multi.**	25
Z Delfino	**Roslindale**	27
DeMarco	N	**Nan**	22
Donatello	**Saugus**	24
Eclano	**N End**	18
NEW Erbaluce	**Park Sq**	-
Euno	S	**N End**	24
Fanizzi's	**CC**	20
Fazio's	**CC**	20
Figs	**multi.**	23
Filippo	**N End**	21
Five North Sq.	**N End**	22
Florentine Cafe	**N End**	21
Z Front St.	**CC**	27
Z Galleria Umberto	**N End**	26
Z Giacomo's	**multi.**	25
Gina's	**CC**	21
Grapevine	**Salem**	25
Greg's	**Watertown**	19
Grotto	N	**Beacon Hill**	25
Z Il Capriccio	N	**Waltham**	27
Il Panino	**N End**	23
Incontro	**Franklin**	22

Ivy Rest. | **D'town Cross**	20
Jetties | **Nan**	14
Jimmy Seas | **MV**	23
Joe Tecce's | S | **N End**	19
Z La Campania | **Waltham**	28
La Cantina | **Framingham**	20
La Cucina/Mare | **CC**	25
La Fam. Giorgio | **N End**	23
La Galleria 33 | **N End**	26
La Morra | N | **Brookline**	24
L'Andana | N | **Burlington**	25
La Summa | S | **N End**	22
Lattanzi's | N | **MV**	21
Lil Vinny's | S | **Somerville**	20
Limoncello | **N End**	22
L'Osteria | **N End**	23
Lucca | N | **N End**	25
Maggiano's | **Park Sq**	19
Mamma Maria | N | **N End**	25
Marco Romana | **N End**	26
Mare | **N End**	26
NEW Marliave | **D'town Cross**	22
Massimino's Cucina | **N End**	23
Maurizio's | **N End**	25
Z Maxwell's 148 | **Natick**	26
Mother Anna's | **N End**	21
Nauset Beach | N | **CC**	25
Nebo | **N End**	21
Z No. 9 Park | **Beacon Hill**	28
NEW Olivadi | **Norwood**	–
Orleans | **Somerville**	17
NEW Orta | **Hanover**	–
Osteria La Civetta | N | **CC**	–
Out of the Blue | **Somerville**	22
Pagliuca's | S | **N End**	22
Panificio | **Beacon Hill**	19
Paolo's Trattoria | **Charlestown**	21
Papa Razzi | **multi.**	18
Pellino's | N | **Marblehead**	–
Piattini | **Back Bay**	23
Piccola Venezia | **N End**	22
Piccolo Nido | **N End**	24
Pi Pizzeria | S | **Nan**	23
Pizzeria Regina | **Medford**	24
Polcari's | **multi.**	17
Pomodoro | **multi.**	24

Z Prezza | **N End**	27
Z Rialto | **Harv Sq**	26
NEW Rist. Damiano | **N End**	–
Rist. Fiore | **N End**	21
Rist. Lucia | S | **multi.**	21
Rist. Marcellino | S | **Waltham**	16
Rist. Toscano | N | **Beacon Hill**	24
Rist. Villa Francesca | **N End**	19
Riva | **Scituate**	26
Rocca | **S End**	24
Rustic Kitchen | **multi.**	20
Sage | **S End**	24
Sagra | **Somerville**	16
Salvatore's | **Seaport Dist**	20
Saporito's | N | **Hull**	26
Saraceno | **N End**	23
Sasso | **Back Bay**	21
NEW Scampo | **Beacon Hill**	22
Scoozi | **Back Bay**	18
Serafina | N | **Concord**	20
Sfoglia | **Nan**	24
Siena | **CC**	21
Siros | **N Quincy**	19
62 on Wharf | **Salem**	24
Z Sorellina | **Back Bay**	27
Sorento's | N | **Marlborough**	18
Sorriso | **Leather Dist**	20
NEW Sportello | **Seaport Dist**	–
Stella | **S End**	24
Stellina | **Watertown**	22
Strega Rest. | **Salem**	21
Strega Rist. | **N End**	21
Sweet Basil | **Needham**	25
Z Taranta | S | **N End**	27
Tartufo | S | **Newton**	22
NEW Tavolo | **Dorchester**	–
Teatro | **Theater Dist**	24
Terramia | **N End**	26
Tomasso | **Southborough**	24
Tosca | N | **Hingham**	25
NEW Trata Pizza | **Harv Sq**	–
Tratt. Il Panino | **N End**	23
Z Tratt. di Monica/Vinoteca | **N End**	26
Z Tratt. Toscana | N | **Fenway**	26
Tratt. Pulcinella | **Huron Vill**	20

Tresca	**N End**	23
Tuscan Grill	N	**Waltham**	24
Umbria	**Financial Dist**	23
vela	**Wellesley**	21
Via Matta	**Park Sq**	25
Village Fish	**Needham**	20
Vin & Eddie's	N	**Abington**	17
Vinny's at Night	S	**Somerville**	23
NEW Vintage	**W Roxbury**	-
Zabaglione	**Ipswich**	22

JAPANESE

(* sushi specialist)

Apollo Grill*	**Chinatown**	17
Billy Tse*	**N End**	20
Blue Fin*	**multi.**	22
Cafe Sushi*	**Harv Sq**	17
China Sky*	**Wellesley**	19
Douzo*	**Back Bay**	24
Z FuGaKyu*	**multi.**	25
Ginza*	**multi.**	23
Haru*	**Back Bay**	20
Z Inaho*	**CC**	27
JP Seafood*	**Jamaica Plain**	23
Kayuga	**multi.**	24
Kaze	**Chinatown**	23
Koreana*	**Central Sq**	21
Lotus Blossom*	**Sudbury**	22
Mifune*	**Arlington**	20
Misaki*	**CC**	24
Montien*	**Theater Dist**	23
Mr. Sushi*	**multi.**	21
Net Result*	**MV**	25
New Ginza*	**Watertown**	24
Oga's*	**Natick**	26
Z Oishii*	**multi.**	27
Osushi*	**Back Bay**	23
Z o ya*	**Leather Dist**	28
Sakurabana*	**Financial Dist**	25
Sapporo*	**Newton**	21
Seiyo*	**S End**	25
Shabu-Zen	**Chinatown**	22
Shogun*	**Newton**	23
Suishaya*	**Chinatown**	21
Sushi by Yoshi*	**Nan**	25
Village Sushi*	**Roslindale**	23
Wagamama	**multi.**	18

Wu Chon	**Somerville**	22
Yama*	**multi.**	22
Zen*	**Beacon Hill**	24

JEWISH

Zaftigs	**Brookline**	21

KOREAN

(* barbecue specialist)

Apollo Grill*	**Chinatown**	17
JP Seafood	**Jamaica Plain**	23
Kayuga	**multi.**	24
Koreana*	**Central Sq**	21
New Jang Su*	**Burlington**	23
Sapporo	**Newton**	21
Seoul Food	**Porter Sq**	22
Suishaya	**Chinatown**	21
Village Sushi	**Roslindale**	23
Wu Chon	**Somerville**	22

KOSHER

Rami's	**Brookline**	23
Rubin's	**Brookline**	19

LEBANESE

Byblos	**Norwood**	24
Cafe Barada	**Porter Sq**	23
Phoenicia	**Beacon Hill**	21
Shawarma King	**Brookline**	22

MALAYSIAN

Penang	**Chinatown**	22

MEDITERRANEAN

Z Abba	**CC**	27
Ardeo	**CC**	20
Athan's Café	**multi.**	23
Avila	**Theater Dist**	24
Bar 10	**Back Bay**	17
Blue Moon Bistro	**CC**	24
Café Mangal	**Wellesley**	25
Cafeteria	**Back Bay**	17
Z Caffe Bella	**Randolph**	26
Casablanca	**Harv Sq**	22
Chiara	**Westwood**	26
Z Ithaki Med.	**Ipswich**	26
Kouzina	**Newton**	23
La Voile	**Back Bay**	23
Les Zygomates	**Leather Dist**	22
Z Mistral	**S End**	27

Z Oleana | **Inman Sq**	28
Z Olives | **Charlestown**	25
Z Pisces | **CC**	27
Porcini's | **Watertown**	22
Rendezvous | **Central Sq**	26
Sabur | **Somerville**	22
Sophia's | **Roslindale**	23
Trevi Café | **CC**	-
Vlora | **Back Bay**	22

MEXICAN

Baja Betty's | **Brookline**	20
Cantina la Mexicana | **Somerville**	24
Casa Romero | **Back Bay**	23
Cilantro | **Salem**	18
El Sarape | **Braintree**	25
Forest Cafe | **Porter Sq**	20
José's | **Huron Vill**	19
La Paloma | **Quincy**	21
La Verdad | **Fenway**	22
Lorraine's | **CC**	20
Olecito/Olé | **Inman Sq**	24
Picante | **Central Sq**	19
Purple Cactus | **Jamaica Plain**	21
Sharky's | **MV**	21
Sol Azteca | **multi.**	20
Tacos El Charro | **Jamaica Plain**	23
Tacos Lupita | **multi.**	25
Taqueria Mexico | **Waltham**	22
Tu Y Yo | **Somerville**	24
Zócalo Cocina | **multi.**	22

MIDDLE EASTERN

Café Algiers | **Harv Sq**	18
Cafe Jaffa | **Back Bay**	22
Middle East | **Central Sq**	17
Rami's | **Brookline**	23
Red Fez | **S End**	18
NEW Sofra Bakery | **Huron Vill**	26
Sound Bites | **Somerville**	22
ZuZu! | **Central Sq**	20

MONGOLIAN

Little Q | **Quincy**	25

MOROCCAN

Z Tangierino | **Charlestown**	24

NEPALESE

Himalayan Bistro | **W Roxbury**	24
Kathmandu Spice | **Arlington**	22

NEW ENGLAND

Arno's | **Nan**	16
Baxter's | **CC**	18
Capt. Frosty's | **CC**	21
Capt. Parker's | **CC**	18
Chart Room | **CC**	20
Durgin-Park | **Faneuil Hall**	17
Fireplace | **Brookline**	21
Z Gibbet Hill | **Groton**	24
Green St. | **Central Sq**	24
Hemisphere | **CC**	17
Henrietta's | **Harv Sq**	23
Home Port | **MV**	20
Jasper White's | **multi.**	21
Jetties | **Nan**	14
Landfall | **CC**	18
Longfellow's | **Sudbury**	18
Maddie's Sail | **Marblehead**	18
Merchants Row | **Concord**	-
Moby Dick's | **CC**	23
No Name | **Seaport Dist**	19
Out of the Blue | **Somerville**	22
Paddock | **CC**	20
Parker's | **D'town Cross**	22
Red Inn | **CC**	24
Sherborn Inn | **Sherborn**	19
NEW Sidecar Café | **MV**	-
Tom Shea's | **Essex**	20
Z Union Oyster | **Faneuil Hall**	20
Woodman's | **Essex**	23

NOODLE SHOPS

Dong Khanh | **Chinatown**	22
Noodle St. | **Boston U**	19
No. 1 Noodle | **Newton**	18
Wagamama | **multi.**	18

NORTH AFRICAN

Baraka Cafe | **Central Sq**	26

NUEVO LATINO

Betty's Wok | **MFA**	19
Cinco | **Nan**	26
Naked Fish | **multi.**	19

PAKISTANI

NEW Ghazal	**Jamaica Plain**	–
Grain & Salt	**Allston**	–

PAN-ASIAN

Betty's Wok	**MFA**	19
Billy Tse	**multi.**	20
Blue22	**Quincy**	19
Grasshopper	**Allston**	20
Island Hopper	**Back Bay**	19
Jae's	**multi.**	20
Kowloon	**Saugus**	17
NEW Lavender Asian	**Sudbury**	–
Ma Soba	**Beacon Hill**	20
Myers + Chang	**S End**	23
Noodle St.	**Boston U**	19
No. 1 Noodle	**Newton**	18
Pho République	**S End**	21
Shanti India	**Dorchester**	–

PERSIAN

Lala Rokh	**Beacon Hill**	23
Sorento's	**Marlborough**	18

PERUVIAN

Don Ricardo's	**S End**	23
Machu Picchu	**Somerville**	19
Masona Grill	**W Roxbury**	25
Rincon Limeno	**E Boston**	–
Z Taranta	**N End**	27

PIZZA

Antico Forno	**N End**	23
Bertucci's	**multi.**	17
Bluestone Bistro	**Brighton**	17
Cambridge, 1.	**multi.**	22
Emma's Pizza	**Kendall Sq**	24
Fairway	**CC**	18
Figs	**multi.**	23
Z Galleria Umberto	**N End**	26
Hot Tomatoes	**N End**	22
Lattanzi's	**MV**	21
Nebo	**N End**	21
Picco	**S End**	22
Pi Pizzeria	**Nan**	23
Pizzeria Regina	**multi.**	24
Pleasant Cafe	**Roslindale**	18

Polcari's	**multi.**	17
Santarpio's Pizza	**E Boston**	25
Scoozi	**Back Bay**	18
Sophia's	**Roslindale**	23
NEW Tavolo	**Dorchester**	–
NEW Trata Pizza	**Harv Sq**	–
Upper Crust	**multi.**	23
Veggie Planet	**Harv Sq**	23
Woody's Grill	**Fenway**	22
Za	**Arlington**	25

POLISH

Café Polonia	**S Boston**	24

POLYNESIAN

Kowloon	**Saugus**	17

PORTUGUESE

Atasca	**Kendall Sq**	23
Casa Portugal	**Inman Sq**	21
Neighborhood Rest.	**Somerville**	23
Sunset Cafe	**Inman Sq**	19

PUB FOOD

Audubon Circle	**Kenmore Sq**	21
Black Cow	**multi.**	19
Blarney Stone	**Dorchester**	16
Boston/Salem Beer	**multi.**	18
NEW Brighton Beer	**Brighton**	–
Bukowski Tav.	**multi.**	17
Burren	**Somerville**	14
Cambridge Common	**Harv Sq**	17
Capt. Kidd	**CC**	18
Cheers	**multi.**	14
Coolidge Corner	**Brookline**	17
Cornwall's	**Kenmore Sq**	15
Doyle's	**Jamaica Plain**	15
Green Briar	**Brighton**	17
Halfway Cafe	**multi.**	17
John Harvard's	**multi.**	16
Johnny D's	**Somerville**	19
Joshua Tree	**multi.**	15
NEW Littlest	**Financial Dist**	–
Matt Murphy's	**Brookline**	22
Mission B&G	**MFA**	19
M.J. O'Connor's	**Seaport Dist**	–
Newes/America	**MV**	18

Publick House	**Brookline**	21
Sunset Grill/Cantina	**multi.**	20
21st Amendment	**Beacon Hill**	17
Warren Tavern	**Charlestown**	16

RUSSIAN

Café St. Petersburg	**Newton**	19

SALVADORAN

Tacos Lupita	**multi.**	25

SANDWICHES

All Star	**Inman Sq**	23
Angelo's	**Stoneham**	26
Boloco	**multi.**	18
Cafe Podima	**Beacon Hill**	19
flour bakery	**multi.**	26
Haley House	**Roxbury**	24
Hi-Rise	**multi.**	24
Other Side	**Back Bay**	19
Oxford Spa	**Porter Sq**	21
Parish Cafe	**Back Bay**	22
Sorelle	**Charlestown**	23
South End Buttery	**S End**	21
Stone Soup	**Ipswich**	25
Strip-T's	**Watertown**	22
Vicki Lee's	**Belmont**	25
Volle Nolle	**N End**	26

SEAFOOD

Academy Ocean	**CC**	22
Anthony's	**Seaport Dist**	18
Aqua Grille	**CC**	19
Arnold's Lobster	**CC**	23
NEW Atlantic	**MV**	-
Atlantica	**Cohasset**	15
Atlantic Fish	**Back Bay**	23
Azure	**Back Bay**	22
Back Eddy	**Westport**	22
Z B&G Oysters	**S End**	26
Barking Crab	**Seaport Dist**	16
Barley Neck Inn	**CC**	20
Baxter's	**CC**	18
Bite	**MV**	26
Bookstore & Rest.	**CC**	19
Boston Sail	**Waterfront**	15
Z Brewster Fish	**CC**	26

Bubala's	**CC**	16
Capt. Frosty's	**CC**	21
Captain's Table	**Wellesley**	-
Casino Wharf	**CC**	20
Z Catch	**Winchester**	27
Catch of the Day	**CC**	25
Chart House	**Waterfront**	21
Chart Room	**CC**	20
Z Clam Box	**Ipswich**	26
Cobie's Clam	**CC**	19
Cooke's	**CC**	-
Court House	**E Cambridge**	22
Daily Catch	**multi.**	24
Dolphin	**CC**	21
Dolphin Seafood	**multi.**	18
Z East Coast	**Inman Sq**	25
East Ocean	**Chinatown**	24
Fanizzi's	**CC**	20
Finz	**multi.**	20
Fishmonger's	**CC**	18
Friendly Fisherman	**CC**	24
Z Giacomo's	**multi.**	25
Great Bay	**Kenmore Sq**	23
Home Port	**MV**	20
Imperial Seafood	**Chinatown**	24
Impudent Oyster	**CC**	23
JT's Seafood	**CC**	17
Jumbo	**multi.**	23
Kate's Seafood	**CC**	20
KingFish Hall	**Faneuil Hall**	22
Landfall	**CC**	18
Larsen's Fish	**MV**	27
Z Legal Sea	**multi.**	22
Liam's	**CC**	20
Lobster Pot	**CC**	22
Mac's	**CC**	24
Maddie's Sail	**Marblehead**	18
Marshside	**CC**	15
McCormick/Schmick	**multi.**	21
Metro 9 Steak	**Framingham**	19
Moby Dick's	**CC**	23
Morse Fish	**S End**	21
Naked Fish	**multi.**	19
Naked Oyster	**CC**	25
Nantucket Lobster	**Nan**	19
Z Neptune Oyster	**N End**	27

Net Result	**MV**	25
No Name	**Seaport Dist**	19
Oceana	**Waterfront**	24
Oceanaire	**Financial Dist**	24
Out of the Blue	**Somerville**	22
Oyster Co.	**CC**	23
Paddock	**CC**	20
Peach Farm	**Chinatown**	25
☑ Pisces	**CC**	27
Port	**CC**	23
Roadhouse	**CC**	20
Ropewalk	**Nan**	-
SeaGrille	**Nan**	22
Sir Cricket's	**CC**	24
Skipjack's	**multi.**	20
Smith/Wollensky	**Back Bay**	23
Straight Wharf	**Nan**	25
Tamarind Bay	**Brookline**	24
Tom Shea's	**Essex**	20
Turner Fish	**Back Bay**	21
☑ Union Oyster	**Faneuil Hall**	20
Village Fish	**Needham**	20
Wicked Oyster	**CC**	24
Woodman's	**Essex**	23

SMALL PLATES

(See also Spanish tapas specialist)

Bar 10	Med.	**Back Bay**	17
NEW Bond	Eclectic	**Financial Dist**	-
Clink	Amer.	**Beacon Hill**	19
☑ Cuchi Cuchi	Eclectic	**Central Sq**	22
District	Amer.	**Leather Dist**	17
NEW Drink	Amer.	**Seaport Dist**	-
Flat Iron	Amer.	**W End**	22
Ivy Rest.	Italian	**D'town Cross**	20
La Morra	Italian	**Brookline**	24
Masa	SW	**S End**	23
☑ Meritage	Amer.	**Waterfront**	27
Middlesex	Eclectic	**Central Sq**	17
Persephone	Amer.	**Seaport Dist**	25
Piattini	Italian	**Back Bay**	23
NEW Rist. Damiano	Italian	**N End**	-
Sanctuary	Eclectic	**Financial Dist**	19
NEW 606 Congress	Amer.	**Seaport Dist**	21

Sophia's	Med.	**Roslindale**	23
Trevi Café	Med.	**CC**	-

SOUL FOOD

Chef Lee's	**Dorchester**	-

SOUTH AFRICAN

Karoo Kafe	**CC**	24

SOUTH AMERICAN

Bon Savor	**Jamaica Plain**	20
Rattlesnake	**Back Bay**	12

SOUTHERN

Chef Lee's	**Dorchester**	-
☑**NEW** Hungry Mother	**Kendall Sq**	27

SOUTHWESTERN

Cottonwood	**Back Bay**	18
Masa	**multi.**	23
Rattlesnake	**Back Bay**	12
Zapotec	**MV**	19

SPANISH

(* tapas specialist)

BarLola*	**Back Bay**	18
Cinco*	**Nan**	26
Dalí*	**Somerville**	25
NEW Estragon*	**S End**	-
Gracie's Table*	**CC**	23
Solea*	**Waltham**	23
Taberna de Haro*	**Brookline**	23
Tapéo*	**Back Bay**	22
Tasca*	**Brighton**	23
☑ Toro*	**S End**	26

STEAKHOUSES

☑ Abe & Louie's	**Back Bay**	26
NEW Bokx	**Newton Lower Falls**	23
Bonfire	**Park Sq**	21
☑ Capital Grille	**multi.**	26
☑ Davio's	**multi.**	25
Fleming's Prime	**Park Sq**	24
Frank's Steak	**Porter Sq**	18
☑ Gibbet Hill	**Groton**	24
☑ Grill 23	**Back Bay**	25
Hilltop Steak	**Saugus**	16
Jimmy's Steer	**multi.**	20

KO Prime | **D'town Cross**	24
Max Stein's | **Lexington**	18
Met B&G | **Natick**	21
Metro 9 Steak | **Framingham**	19
Metropolitan | **Chestnut Hill**	21
Midwest | **Inman Sq**	20
Mooo... | **Beacon Hill**	24
☑ Morton's | **multi.**	25
☑ Oak Room | **Back Bay**	25
Palm | **Back Bay**	23
Pellana | **Peabody**	26
Plaza III | **Faneuil Hall**	21
Roadhouse | **CC**	20
☑ Ruth's Chris | **D'town Cross**	24
Scarlet Oak | **Hingham**	20
Smith/Wollensky | **Back Bay**	23
Stockyard | **Brighton**	15
Tango | **Arlington**	21
Umbria | **Financial Dist**	23

TAIWANESE

MuLan Taiwanese | **Kendall Sq**	23
Shangri-La | **Belmont**	23
Taiwan Cafe | **Chinatown**	23

TEAROOMS

Dunbar Tea | **CC**	22
Optimist Café | **CC**	21

TEX-MEX

☑ Anna's | **multi.**	22
Boca Grande | **multi.**	19
Boloco | **multi.**	18
Border Cafe | **multi.**	19
Cactus Club | **Back Bay**	16
Fajitas/'Ritas | **D'town Cross**	16

THAI

☑ Abba | **CC**	27
Alice's | **Nan**	18
Amarin Thailand | **multi.**	22
Bamboo | **Brighton**	23
Bangkok Bistro | **Brighton**	22
Bangkok Blue | **Back Bay**	21
Bangkok City | **Back Bay**	20
Brown Sugar/Similans | **multi.**	25
Chilli Duck | **Back Bay**	21

Dok Bua | **Brookline**	24
Equator | **S End**	18
Erawan of Siam | **Waltham**	22
Green Papaya | **Waltham**	20
House of Siam | **S End**	24
Jamjuli | **Newton**	19
Khao Sarn Cuisine | **Brookline**	24
King & I | **Beacon Hill**	22
Lam's | **Newtonville**	21
Montien | **multi.**	23
9 Tastes | **Harv Sq**	20
NEW Pho n' Rice | **Somerville**	-
Spice Thai | **Harv Sq**	21
Sugar & Spice | **Porter Sq**	20
Thai Basil | **Back Bay**	23
NEW Thaitation | **Fenway**	-
Wonder Spice | **Jamaica Plain**	21

TIBETAN

House of Tibet | **Somerville**	-
Martsa's on Elm | **Somerville**	21

TURKISH

Brookline Family | **Brookline**	21
Café Mangal | **Wellesley**	25
Sultan's Kitchen | **Financial Dist**	24

VEGETARIAN

(* vegan)

Grasshopper* | **Allston**	20
Grezzo* | **N End**	23
UFood | **multi.**	18
Veggie Planet | **Harv Sq**	23
NEW Wheeler's* | **Back Bay**	-

VENEZUELAN

La Casa/Pedro | **Watertown**	21
Orinoco | **multi.**	25

VIETNAMESE

Dong Khanh | **Chinatown**	22
Lam's | **Newtonville**	21
Le's | **multi.**	21
Pho Hoa | **multi.**	22
Pho Lemongrass | **Brookline**	20
NEW Pho n' Rice | **Somerville**	-
Pho Pasteur | **Chinatown**	23
Xinh Xinh | **Chinatown**	25

Locations

Includes restaurant names, cuisines, Food ratings and, for locations that are mapped, top list and map coordinates.

Boston

ALLSTON/ BOSTON U./ BRIGHTON

Athan's Café	*Med./Bakery*	23
Bamboo	*Thai*	23
Bangkok Bistro	*Thai*	22
Bluestone Bistro	*Pizza*	17
Boloco	*Eclectic*	18
NEW Brighton Beer	*Pub*	-
Brown Sugar/Similans	*Thai*	25
Café Brazil	*Brazilian*	23
Carlo's Cucina	*Italian*	25
Deep Ellum	*Eclectic*	18
Devlin's	*Amer.*	20
Grain & Salt	*Indian/Pakistani*	-
Grasshopper	*Pan-Asian/Vegan*	20
Green Briar	*Pub*	17
India Quality/Punjab	*Indian*	24
Jasmine	*French/Hungarian*	24
Joshua Tree	*Pub*	15
Le's	*Viet.*	21
Noodle St.	*Pan-Asian*	19
Shabu-Zen	*Japanese*	22
Shanghai Gate	*Chinese*	24
Soul Fire	*BBQ*	21
Stockyard	*Steak*	15
Sunset Grill/Cantina	*Pub*	20
Tasca	*Spanish*	23
UBurger	*Burgers*	23
Zócalo Cocina	*Mex.*	22

BACK BAY
(See map on page 242)

TOP FOOD

L'Espalier	*French*	**D3**	28
Aujourd'hui	*French*	**C8**	28
Clio/Uni	*French*	**D1**	27
Sorellina	*Italian*	**D5**	27
Capital Grille	*Steak*	**E1**	26

LISTING

☑ Abe & Louie's	*Steak*	**D4**	26
NEW Asana	*Amer./Asian*	**E4**	-
Atlantic Fish	*Seafood*	**D4**	23
☑ Aujourd'hui	*French*	**C8**	28
Azure	*Amer.*	**D5**	22
Bangkok Blue	*Thai*	**D5**	21
Bangkok City	*Thai*	**F2**	20
BarLola	*Spanish*	**C5**	18
Bar 10	*Med.*	**E5**	17
Bertucci's	*Italian*	**E6**	17
b. good	*Health*	**D3**	**E6**	19
Bhindi Bazaar	*Indian*	**E1**	22
Boloco	*Eclectic*	**D3**	**E1**	18
Bottega	*Italian*	**D3**	24
Bouchée	*French*	**D5**	21
Brasserie Jo	*French*	**F4**	20
☑ Bristol	*Amer.*	**C9**	24
Brownstone	*Amer.*	**F6**	15
Bukowski Tav.	*Pub*	**E2**	17
Cactus Club	*Tex-Mex*	**E2**	16
Café at Taj	*Eclectic*	**C7**	20
Cafe Jaffa	*Mideast.*	**E3**	22
Cafeteria	*Med.*	**D3**	17
☑ Capital Grille	*Steak*	**E1**	26
Casa Romero	*Mex.*	**D3**	23
Charley's	*Amer.*	**D3**	18
☑ Cheesecake	*Amer.*	**F4**	18
Chilli Duck	*Thai*	**E3**	21
Ciao Bella	*Italian*	**D4**	19
☑ Clio/Uni	*French*	**D1**	27
Cottonwood	*SW*	**C6**	18
NEW Daily Grill	*Amer.*		19
Dillon's	*Amer.*	**E2**	16
Douzo	*Japanese*	**F6**	24
Fire & Ice	*Eclectic*	**D7**	16
☑ Grill 23	*Steak*	**D7**	25
Haru	*Japanese*	**E5**	20
Island Hopper	*Pan-Asian*	**E1**	19
Jasper White's	*New Eng.*	**E2**	21
Joe's American	*Amer.*	**D5**	16
Kashmir	*Indian*	**D3**	23
Laurel	*Amer.*	**E7**	20
La Voile	*French/Med.*	**C6**	23
☑ Legal Sea	*Seafood*	**E4**	22

Rincon Limeno | *Colombian/Peruvian* — ⌐

Santarpio's Pizza | *Pizza* 25⌐

Tacos Lupita | *Mex./Salvadoran* 25⌐

Uncle Pete's Ribs | *BBQ* 25⌐

CHINATOWN/ LEATHER DIST.

(See map on page 240)

TOP FOOD

o ya | *Japanese* | **H9** 28⌐

Pizzeria Regina | *Pizza* | **H10** 24⌐

Kaze | *Japanese* | **G7** 23⌐

Taiwan Cafe | *Taiwanese* | **H7** 23⌐

Jumbo | *Chinese/Seafood* | **H8** 23⌐

LISTING

Apollo Grill | *Japanese/Korean* | **H7** 17⌐

Chau Chow | *Chinese* | **G7** 21⌐

China Pearl | *Chinese* | **H7** 21⌐

District | *Amer.* | **H8** 17⌐

Dong Khanh | *Viet.* | **H7** 22⌐

East Ocean | *Chinese/Seafood* | **H6** 24⌐

Emperor's Gdn. | *Chinese* | **H6** 21⌐

Ginza | *Japanese* | **I7** 23⌐

Imperial Seafood | *Chinese/Seafood* | **H8** 24⌐

Jumbo | *Chinese/Seafood* | **H8** 23⌐

Kaze | *Japanese* | **G7** 23⌐

Les Zygomates | *French/Med.* | **H9** 22⌐

New Shanghai | *Chinese* | **I7** 16⌐

Z o ya | *Japanese* | **H9** 28⌐

Peach Farm | *Chinese/Seafood* | **H7** 25⌐

Penang | *Malaysian* | **H6** 22⌐

Pho Hoa | *Viet.* | **H6** 22⌐

Pho Pasteur | *Viet.* | **H6** 23⌐

Pizzeria Regina | *Pizza* | **H10** 24⌐

Shabu-Zen | *Japanese* | **H7** 22⌐

Sorriso | *Italian* | **I8** 20⌐

South St. Diner | *Diner* | **I9** 16⌐

Suishaya | *Japanese/Korean* | **H7** 21⌐

Taiwan Cafe | *Taiwanese* | **H7** 23⌐

Xinh Xinh | *Chinese/Viet.* | **H6** 25⌐

DORCHESTER/ MATTAPAN/ ROXBURY/ WEST ROXBURY

Ashmont Grill | *Amer.* 22⌐

Blarney Stone | *Pub* 16⌐

Chef Lee's | *Southern* — ⌐

Haley House | *Amer.* 24⌐

Himalayan Bistro | *Indian/Nepalese* 24⌐

Masona Grill | *Amer./Peruvian* 25⌐

Merengue | *Dominican* — ⌐

Pho Hoa | *Viet.* 22⌐

Rest. Cesaria | *Cape Verd.* — ⌐

NEW Rudi's | *Amer.* — ⌐

Shanti India | *Indian/Pan-Asian* — ⌐

NEW Tavolo | *Italian* — ⌐

224 Boston St. | *Amer.* 22⌐

Victoria's Diner | *Diner* 20⌐

NEW Vintage | *Amer./Italian* — ⌐

West on Centre | *Amer.* 18⌐

DOWNTOWN CROSSING

(See map on page 240)

TOP FOOD

Ruth's Chris | *Steak* | **C8** 24⌐

Locke-Ober | *Amer./Continental* | **E7** 24⌐

KO Prime | *Steak* | **D7** 24⌐

Parker's | *New Eng.* | **C8** 22⌐

Silvertone B&G | *Amer.* | **D7** 21⌐

LISTING

Avenue One | *Amer.* | **F6** 18⌐

NEW Bina Osteria | *Italian* | **F6** — ⌐

Chacarero | *Chilean* | **D7** | **E8** — ⌐

Fajitas/'Ritas | *Tex-Mex* | **F6** 16⌐

Good Life | *Amer.* | **F8** 17⌐

Hot Tomatoes | *Pizza* | **G8** 22⌐

Ivy Rest. | *Italian* | **E6** 20⌐

Kingston Station | *French* | **F8** 20⌐

KO Prime | *Steak* | **D7** 24⌐

Locke-Ober | *Amer./Continental* | **E7** 24⌐

Mantra | *French/Indian* | **E6** 18⌐

NEW Marliave | *Continental/Italian* | **D7** 22⌐

NEW Max/Dylan | *Amer.* | **F6** — ⌐

Parker's | *New Eng.* | **C8** 22⌐

Z Ruth's Chris | *Steak* | **C8** 24⌐

Silvertone B&G | *Amer.* | **D7** 21⌐

UFood | *Health* | **F6** 18⌐

Vinalia | *Amer.* | **E8** 17⌐

FANEUIL HALL

(See map on page 238)

TOP FOOD

Pizzeria Regina	Pizza	**F6**	24
Houston's	Amer.	**G5**	22
KingFish Hall	Seafood	**G6**	22
McCormick/Schmick	Seafood	**F6**	21
Plaza III	Steak	**F6**	21

LISTING

Bertucci's	Italian	**G5**	17
Bombay Club	Indian	**G6**	20
Cheers	Pub	**F6**	14
Durgin-Park	New Eng.	**F6**	17
Houston's	Amer.	**G5**	22
KingFish Hall	Seafood	**G6**	22
McCormick/Schmick	Seafood	**F6**	21
Pizzeria Regina	Pizza	**F6**	24
Plaza III	Steak	**F6**	21
Red Sky	Amer.	**F5**	18
Steve's Greek	Greek	**G5**	20
☑ Union Oyster	New Eng./Seafood	**E5**	20
Wagamama	Noodles	**G6**	18

FENWAY/ KENMORE SQUARE/ MFA

(See map on page 244)

TOP FOOD

Tratt. Toscana	Italian	**E6**	26
India Quality	Indian	**B7**	24
Petit Robert	French	**B7**	24
Great Bay	Seafood	**B7**	23
Elephant Walk	Cambodian/French	**C2**	23

LISTING

Audubon Circle	Pub	**C3**	21
Bertucci's	Italian	**B6**	17
Betty's Wok	Nuevo Latino/ Pan-Asian	**F11**	19
Boca Grande	Tex-Mex	**B6**	19
Boloco	Eclectic	**G9**	**H2**	18
Boston/Salem Beer	Pub	**C5**	18
Bravo	Eclectic	**H7**	21
Burtons	Amer.	**E4**	21

Cambridge, 1.	Pizza	**E4**	22
Canestaro	Italian	**E6**	19
Church	Amer.	**E5**	20
Cornwall's	Pub	**B5**	15
☑ Eastern Stand.	Amer./Euro.	**B6**	22
☑ Elephant Walk	Cambodian/French	**C2**	23
Gardner Museum	Amer.	**G5**	20
Great Bay	Seafood	**B7**	23
India Quality	Indian	**B7**	24
La Verdad	Mex.	**C7**	22
Mission B&G	Pub	**J2**	19
☑ Petit Robert	French	**B7**	24
NEW Thaitation	Thai	-
☑ Tratt. Toscana	Italian	**E6**	26
UBurger	Burgers	**A7**	23
UFood	Health	**E4**	18
Woody's Grill	Amer.	**D9**	22

FINANCIAL DISTRICT

(See map on page 238)

TOP FOOD

Radius	French	**K5**	26
Sakurabana	Japanese	**H6**	25
Sultan's Kitchen	Turkish	**G6**	24
Oceanaire	Seafood	**G3**	24
Umbria	Italian/Steak	**I7**	23

LISTING

Boloco	Eclectic	**H5**	**J5**	**J6**	18
NEW Bond	Eclectic	**I6**	-
Café Fleuri	Amer./Continental	**I6**	22
Caliterra	Calif./Italian	**H7**	16
NEW Littlest	Pub	**I7**	-
NEW Market	Amer.	**G6**	16
Oceanaire	Seafood	**G3**	24
☑ Radius	French	**K5**	26
Sakurabana	Japanese	**H6**	25
Sanctuary	Eclectic	**G7**	19
Sultan's Kitchen	Turkish	**G6**	24
Umbria	Italian/Steak	**I7**	23

JAMAICA PLAIN

Alchemist	Amer.	17
Bon Savor	French/South Amer.	20
Bukhara	Indian	23

Centre St. Café | *Eclectic*	25
Doyle's | *Pub*	15
El Oriental/Cuba | *Cuban*	24
NEW Ghazal | *Indian*	-
James's Gate | *Amer./Irish*	16
JP Seafood | *Japanese/Korean*	23
Purple Cactus | *Eclectic/Mex.*	21
Sorella's | *Amer.*	26
Tacos El Charro | *Mex.*	23
Z Ten Tables | *Amer./Euro.*	27
Wonder Spice | *Cambodian/Thai*	21
Zon's | *Amer.*	24

NORTH END
(See map on page 238)

TOP FOOD

Neptune Oyster | *Seafood* | **D5**	27
Taranta | *Italian/Peruvian* | **D5**	27
Prezza | *Italian* | **C7**	27
Carmen | *Italian* | **D6**	26
Tratt. di Monica/Vinoteca | *Italian* | **D6**	26

LISTING

Al Dente | *Italian* | **C5**	22
Antico Forno | *Italian* | **D5**	23
Artú | *Italian* | **C6**	21
Assaggio | *Italian* | **C6**	24
Bacco | *Italian* | **C5**	21
Billy Tse | *Pan-Asian* | **D8**	20
Bricco | *Italian* | **D6**	25
Caffe Paradiso | *Coffee* | **D6**	17
Cantina Italiana | *Italian* | **C6**	22
Z Carmen | *Italian* | **D6**	26
Daily Catch | *Italian/Seafood* | **C6**	24
Davide Rist. | *Italian* | **C8**	24
Eclano | *Italian* | **D5**	18
Euno | *Italian* | **C5**	24
Filippo | *Italian* | **A4**	21
Five North Sq. | *Italian* | **D7**	22
Florentine Cafe | *Italian* | **C6**	21
Z Galleria Umberto | *Italian* | **D6**	26
Z Giacomo's | *Italian* | **C6**	25
Grezzo | *Vegan* | **C6**	23
Hot Tomatoes | *Pizza* | **D7**	22
Il Panino | *Italian* | **D6**	23
Joe's American | *Amer.* | **E8**	16

Joe Tecce's | *Italian* | **C4**	19
La Fam. Giorgio | *Italian* | **C5**	23
La Galleria 33 | *Italian* | **C5**	26
La Summa | *Italian* | **C7**	22
Limoncello | *Italian* | **D6**	22
L'Osteria | *Italian* | **C5**	23
Lucca | *Italian* | **D6**	25
Mamma Maria | *Italian* | **D7**	25
Marco Romana | *Italian* | **D6**	26
Mare | *Italian* | **D6**	26
Massimino's Cucina | *Italian* | **B4**	23
Maurizio's | *Italian* | **C7**	25
Mother Anna's | *Italian* | **D5**	21
Nebo | *Pizza* | **C4**	21
Z Neptune Oyster | *Seafood* | **D5**	27
North St. Grille | *Amer.* | **D7**	23
Pagliuca's | *Italian* | **D6**	22
Piccola Venezia | *Italian* | **D6**	22
Piccolo Nido | *Italian* | **D7**	24
Pizzeria Regina | *Pizza* | **C5**	24
Pomodoro | *Italian* | **C6**	24
Z Prezza | *Italian* | **C7**	27
NEW Rist. Damiano | *Italian* | **D6**	-
Rist. Fiore | *Italian* | **D6**	21
Rist. Lucia | *Italian* | **B7**	21
Rist. Villa Francesca | *Italian* | **D6**	19
Saraceno | *Italian* | **D6**	23
Strega Rist. | *Italian* | **C7**	21
Z Taranta | *Italian/Peruvian* | **D5**	27
Terramia | *Italian* | **C5**	26
Tratt. Il Panino | *Italian* | **D6**	23
Z Tratt. di Monica/Vinoteca | *Italian* | **C6** | **D6**	26
Tresca | *Italian* | **D6**	23
Volle Nolle | *Sandwiches* | **C6**	26

PARK SQUARE
(See map on page 242)

TOP FOOD

Via Matta | *Italian* | **C8**	25
Davio's | *Italian/Steak* | **D8**	25
Fleming's Prime | *Steak* | **D8**	24
Finale | *Dessert* | **C8**	23
Da Vinci | *Italian* | **D7**	22

LISTING

Bonfire | *Steak* | **C8**	21
Da Vinci | *Italian* | **D7**	22

Z Davio's | *Italian/Steak* | **D8**	25
NEW Erbaluce | *Italian* | **D8**	-
Finale | *Dessert* | **C8**	23
Flash's | *Amer.* | **D7**	18
Fleming's Prime | *Steak* | **D8**	24
Z Legal Sea | *Seafood* | **C8**	22
Maggiano's | *Italian* | **C8**	19
McCormick/Schmick | *Seafood* | **C8**	21
NEW Melting Pot | *Fondue* | **D7**	20
M.J. O'Connor's | *Pub* | **K10**	-
Rustic Kitchen | *Italian* | **D8**	20
Via Matta | *Italian* | **C8**	25

SEAPORT DISTRICT

Anthony's | *Seafood*	18
Aura | *Amer.*	22
Barking Crab | *Seafood*	16
Daily Catch | *Italian/Seafood*	24
NEW Drink | *Amer.*	-
flour bakery | *Bakery*	26
LTK | *Eclectic*	20
Lucky's Lounge | *Amer.*	18
M.J. O'Connor's | *Pub*	-
Z Morton's | *Steak*	25
No Name | *New Eng./Seafood*	19
Persephone | *Amer.*	25
Salvatore's | *Italian*	20
NEW 606 Congress | *Amer.*	21
NEW Sportello | *Italian*	-

SOUTH BOSTON

Amrheins | *Amer.*	18
Café Polonia | *Polish*	24
Franklin | *Amer.*	26
St. Alphonzo's | *Amer.*	22

SOUTH END

(See map on page 242)

TOP FOOD

Oishii | *Japanese* | **G9**	27
Hamersley's Bistro | *French* | **G7**	27
Mistral | *French/Med.* | **E7**	27
Toro | *Spanish* | **J6**	26
flour bakery | *Bakery* | **I6**	26

LISTING

Addis Red Sea | *Ethiopian* | **G7**	22
Anchovies | *Italian* | **G5**	20

Z Aquitaine | *French* | **G7**	23
Z B&G Oysters | *Seafood* | **G7**	26
Z Banq | *Eclectic* | **H8**	21
Beehive | *Amer.* | **G7**	18
Butcher Shop | *French/Italian* | **G7**	25
Charlie's Sandwich | *Diner* | **G5**	23
Club Cafe | *Amer.* | **E7**	18
Coda | *Amer.* | **F6**	22
Columbus Café | *Eclectic* | **H4**	19
Delux Cafe | *Eclectic* | **F6**	21
Don Ricardo's | *Brazilian/Peruvian* | **H7**	23
Equator | *Eclectic/Thai* | **J5**	18
NEW Estragon | *Spanish*	-
flour bakery | *Bakery* | **I6**	26
Franklin | *Amer.* | **G8**	26
Gaslight Brasserie | *French* | **H8**	21
Z Giacomo's | *Italian* | **G5**	25
Z Hamersley's Bistro | *French* | **G7**	27
House of Siam | *Thai* | **H4**	24
Z Icarus | *Amer.* | **F8**	25
Jae's | *Pan-Asian* | **H4**	20
Masa | *SW* | **F8**	23
Mela | *Indian* | **G7**	24
Metropolis Cafe | *Eclectic* | **G7**	23
Mike's | *Diner* | **J5**	20
Z Mistral | *French/Med.* | **E7**	27
Morse Fish | *Seafood* | **H7**	21
Myers + Chang | *Pan-Asian* | **G9**	23
Z Oishii | *Japanese* | **G9**	27
Orinoco | *Venez.* | **I6**	25
Z Petit Robert | *French* | **G5**	24
Pho République | *Pan-Asian* | **H7**	21
Picco | *Dessert/Pizza* | **F8**	22
Pops | *Amer.* | **G7**	22
Red Fez | *Mideast.* | **G9**	18
Rocca | *Italian* | **H9**	24
Sage | *Italian* | **H8**	24
Seiyo | *Japanese* | **J5**	25
Sibling Rivalry | *Amer.* | **F7**	24
South End Buttery | *Coffee/Sandwiches* | **H7**	21
Stella | *Italian* | **I7**	24
Z Toro | *Spanish* | **J6**	26
Tremont 647 | *Amer.* | **H6**	21
28 Degrees | *Amer.* | **F8**	20

| Union B&G | *Amer.* | **H8** | 24 |
| Upper Crust | *Pizza* | 23 |

| Flat Iron | *Amer.* | 22 |
| Johnnie's on Side | *Eclectic* | 17 |

THEATER DISTRICT

(See map on page 240)

TOP FOOD

Troquet	*Amer./French*	**G4**	27
Pigalle	*French*	**H4**	26
Avila	*Med.*	**G4**	24
Teatro	*Italian*	**G5**	24
Montien	*Thai*	**H5**	23

LISTING

Avila	*Med.*	**G4**	24
blu	*Amer.*	**G6**	21
Jacob Wirth	*Amer./German*	**H6**	17
Jer-Ne	*Amer.*	**G6**	20
Montien	*Thai*	**H5**	23
P.F. Chang's †	*Chinese*	**G4**	19
Pigalle	*French*	**H4**	26
Tantric	*Indian*	**H5**	20
Teatro	*Italian*	**G5**	24
☑ Troquet	*Amer./French*	**G4**	27

WATERFRONT

(See map on page 238)

TOP FOOD

Meritage	*Amer.*	**I8**	27
Oceana	*Amer./Seafood*	**G8**	24
Sel de Terre	*French*	**G8**	23
Legal Sea	*Seafood*	**G8**	22
Miel	*French*	**K7**	21

LISTING

Boston Sail	*Seafood*	**E8**	15
Chart House	*Seafood*	**F9**	21
☑ Legal Sea	*Seafood*	**G8**	22
Living Room	*Amer.*	**E8**	15
☑ Meritage	*Amer.*	**I8**	27
Miel	*French*	**K7**	21
Oceana	*Amer./Seafood*	**G8**	24
☑ Sel de Terre	*French*	**G8**	23
NEW Sensing	*French*	**B7**	–

WEST END

| Boston/Salem Beer | *Pub* | 18 |
| NEW DJ's/Garden | *Amer.* | – |

Cambridge

CAMBRIDGEPORT/ EAST CAMBRIDGE

☑ Anna's	*Tex-Mex*	22
Bambara	*Amer.*	20
Boca Grande	*Tex-Mex*	19
☑ Cheesecake	*Amer.*	18
Court House	*Seafood*	22
dante	*Italian*	24
☑ Helmand	*Afghan*	26
Brown Sugar/Similans	*Thai*	25

CENTRAL SQUARE

(See map on page 246)

TOP FOOD

Craigie on Main	*French*	**B1**	27
Baraka Cafe	*African*	**H8**	26
Salts	*Amer./French*	**H10**	26
Rendezvous	*Med.*	**H8**	26
Central Kitchen	*Amer.*	**H9**	24

LISTING

Asmara	*Eritrean/Ethiopian*	**G7**	21
Baraka Cafe	*African*	**H8**	26
Basta Pasta	*Italian*	**G5**	24
Bertucci's	*Italian*	**H10**	17
Central Kitchen	*Amer.*	**H9**	24
☑ Craigie on Main	*French*	**B1**	27
☑ Cuchi Cuchi	*Eclectic*	**H10**	22
Green St.	*New Eng.*	**G8**	24
India Pavilion	*Indian*	**G7**	20
Koreana	*Japanese/Korean*	**F8**	21
Mary Chung	*Chinese*	**H8**	21
Middle East	*Mideast.*	**H8**	17
Middlesex	*Eclectic*	**H9**	17
Miracle of Science	*Pub*	**H9**	19
Picante	*Calif./Mex.*	**G7**	19
Rendezvous	*Med.*	**H8**	26
Royal East	*Chinese*	**H10**	20
Salts	*Amer./French*	**H10**	26
Sidney's	*Amer.*	**H9**	21
Tavern in Sq.	*Amer.*	**H9**	17
1369 Coffee Hse.	*Coffee*	**G7**	20
ZuZu!	*Eclectic/Mideast.*	**H8**	20

HARVARD SQUARE

(See map on page 246)

TOP FOOD

Ten Tables	*Amer./Euro.*	**B2**	27
Rialto	*Italian*	**E3**	26
Garden at Cellar	*Amer.*	**F6**	25
Harvest	*Amer.*	**D3**	25
Darwin's	*Coffee/Deli*	**D2**	24

LISTING

Bertucci's	*Italian*	**D3**	17
b. good	*Health*	**D4**	19
Boloco	*Eclectic*	**E4**	18
Bombay Club	*Indian*	**D4**	20
Border Cafe	*Cajun/Tex-Mex*	**D3**	19
Café Algiers	*Mideast.*	**D3**	18
Cafe of India	*Indian*	**D3**	22
Cafe Sushi	*Japanese*	**E5**	17
Cambridge Common	*Pub*	**A3**	17
Cambridge, 1.	*Pizza*	**D3**	22
Casablanca	*Med.*	**D3**	22
Charlie's Kitchen	*Diner*	**E3**	17
Chez Henri	*Cuban/French*	**A3**	24
Daedalus	*Amer.*	**E4**	17
Darwin's	*Coffee/Deli*	**D2**	**D6**	24
Dolphin Seafood	*Seafood*	**E5**	18
Finale	*Dessert*	**E4**	23
Fire & Ice	*Eclectic*	**D3**	16
Garden at Cellar	*Amer.*	**F6**	25
Grafton St. Pub	*Amer.*	**E4**	17
Harvest	*Amer.*	**D3**	25
Henrietta's	*New Eng.*	**E3**	23
Hi-Rise	*Bakery/Sandwiches*	**D3**	24
John Harvard's	*Pub*	**E4**	16
✓ Legal Sea	*Seafood*	**D2**	22
Le's	*Viet.*	**E4**	21
Mr. Bartley's	*Burgers*	**E4**	24
9 Tastes	*Thai*	**D4**	20
OM Rest.	*Amer.*	**E3**	19
Red House	*Eclectic*	**E3**	20
Redline	*Amer.*	**D4**	17
✓ Rialto	*Italian*	**E3**	26
Sandrine's	*French*	**E4**	24
Spice Thai	*Thai*	**E4**	21
Tamarind Bay	*Indian*	**E3**	24
Tanjore	*Indian*	**E3**	22

✓ Ten Tables	*Amer./Euro.*	**B2**	27
NEW Trata Pizza	*Pizza*	**E4**	–
Upper Crust	*Pizza*		23
✓ UpStairs on Sq.	*Amer.*	**E3**	24
Veggie Planet	*Pizza/Veg.*	**D3**	23
Wagamama	*Noodles*	**D4**	18

HURON VILLAGE

Full Moon	*Amer.*	20
Hi-Rise	*Bakery/Sandwiches*	24
Jasper White's	*New Eng.*	21
José's	*Mex.*	19
NEW Sofra Bakery	*Mideast.*	26
Tratt. Pulcinella	*Italian*	20
T.W. Food	*Amer./French*	26

INMAN SQUARE

(See map on page 246)

TOP FOOD

Oleana	*Med.*	**E10**	28
East Coast	*BBQ/Seafood*	**D9**	25
Muqueca	*Brazilian*	**D10**	24
Olecito/Olé	*Mex.*	**D9**	24

LISTING

All Star	*Sandwiches*	**D9**	23
Bukowski Tav.	*Pub*	**D9**	17
Casa Portugal	*Portug.*	**D9**	21
✓ East Coast	*BBQ/Seafood*	**D9**	25
Haveli	*Indian*	**D9**	–
Midwest	*Brazilian/Steak*	**D10**	20
Montien	*Thai*	**D9**	23
Muqueca	*Brazilian*	**D10**	24
✓ Oleana	*Med.*	**E10**	28
Olecito/Olé	*Mex.*	**D9**	24
Punjabi Dhaba	*Indian*	**D9**	24
S&S	*Deli*	**D9**	18
Sunset Cafe	*Amer./Portug.*	**E11**	19
1369 Coffee Hse.	*Coffee*	**D9**	20

KENDALL SQUARE

Amelia's Trattoria	*Italian*	22
Atasca	*Portug.*	23
Black Sheep	*Amer.*	21
Blue Room	*Eclectic*	25
Emma's Pizza	*Pizza*	24
✓ NEW Hungry Mother	*Amer.*	27

Menus, photos, voting and more – free at ZAGAT.com

Z Legal Sea	*Seafood*	22
MuLan Taiwanese	*Taiwanese*	23

PORTER SQUARE

Addis Red Sea	*Ethiopian*	22
Z Anna's	*Tex-Mex*	22
Blue Fin	*Japanese*	22
Boca Grande	*Tex-Mex*	19
Cafe Barada	*Mideast.*	23
Changsho	*Chinese*	20
Christopher's	*Eclectic*	17
Z Elephant Walk	*Cambodian/French*	23
Forest Cafe	*Mex.*	20
Frank's Steak	*Steak*	18
Oxford Spa	*Sandwiches*	21
Passage to India	*Indian*	20
Qingdao Gdn.	*Chinese*	24
Seoul Food	*Korean*	22
Sugar & Spice	*Thai*	20
Tavern in Sq.	*Amer.*	17
Temple Bar	*Amer.*	20
West Side Lounge	*Amer.*	22

Nearby Suburbs

ARLINGTON/ BELMONT/ WINCHESTER

Blue Ribbon BBQ	*BBQ*	25
Z Catch	*Amer./Seafood*	27
flora	*Amer.*	24
Jimmy's Steer	*Steak*	20
Kathmandu Spice	*Nepalese*	22
Kayuga	*Japanese/Korean*	24
Mifune	*Chinese/Japanese*	20
Mr. Sushi	*Japanese*	21
Z Not Average Joe's	*Amer.*	18
Prose	*Amer.*	24
Punjab	*Indian*	25
Rist. Lucia	*Italian*	21
Scutra	*Eclectic*	23
Shangri-La	*Taiwanese*	23
Something Savory	*Eclectic*	22
Tango	*Argent./Steak*	21
Tryst	*Amer.*	22
Vicki Lee's	*Bakery*	25

Za	*Pizza*	25
Zócalo Cocina	*Mex.*	22

BRAINTREE/QUINCY

Bertucci's	*Italian*	17
Blue22	*Amer./Pan-Asian*	19
Z Cheesecake	*Amer.*	18
China Pearl	*Chinese*	21
El Sarape	*Mex.*	25
Firefly's	*BBQ*	20
NEW Grand Chinatown	*Chinese*	-
Joe's American	*Amer.*	16
NEW Jury Room	*Amer.*	19
La Paloma	*Mex.*	21
Z Legal Sea	*Seafood*	22
Little Q	*Mongolian*	25
Pho Hoa	*Viet.*	22
Pizzeria Regina	*Pizza*	24
Siros	*Italian*	19

BROOKLINE

Z Anna's	*Tex-Mex*	22
Athan's Café	*Med./Bakery*	23
Baja Betty's	*Mex.*	20
Beacon St. Tavern	*Amer.*	20
Bertucci's	*Italian*	17
b. good	*Health*	19
Boca Grande	*Tex-Mex*	19
Bottega	*Italian*	24
Brookline Family	*Turkish*	21
Chef Chang's	*Chinese*	20
Chef Chow's	*Chinese*	20
Coolidge Corner	*Pub*	17
Dalia's Bistro	*Amer.*	19
Dok Bua	*Thai*	24
Finale	*Dessert*	23
Fireplace	*New Eng.*	21
NEW Franky/Boys	*Burgers*	-
Z FuGaKyu	*Japanese*	25
Ginza	*Japanese*	23
Golden Temple	*Chinese*	21
Jae's	*Pan-Asian*	20
NEW Jerusalem Pita	*Israeli*	-
Kayuga	*Japanese/Korean*	24
Khao Sarn Cuisine	*Thai*	24
La Morra	*Italian*	24
LiNEaGe	*Amer.*	23

Matt Murphy's | *Pub*	22
Mr. Sushi | *Japanese*	21
Orinoco | *Venezuelan*	25
Paris Creperie | *French*	22
Pho Lemongrass | *Viet.*	20
Pomodoro | *Italian*	24
Publick House | *Pub*	21
Rami's | *Mideast.*	23
Rani | *Indian*	20
Roadhouse Craft Beer & BBQ	-
Rubin's | *Deli*	19
Shawarma King | *Lebanese*	22
Sichuan Garden | *Chinese*	22
Sol Azteca | *Mex.*	20
Super Fusion | *Asian Fusion*	27
Taberna de Haro | *Spanish*	23
Tamarind Bay | *Indian*	24
Upper Crust | *Pizza*	23
Village Smokehse. | *BBQ*	19
Washington Sq. | *Amer.*	22
Zaftigs | *Deli*	21

CHESTNUT HILL

Aquitaine Bis | *French*	23
Bernard's | *Chinese*	24
Bertucci's | *Italian*	17
Z Capital Grille | *Steak*	26
Charley's | *Amer.*	18
Z Cheesecake | *Amer.*	18
Z Legal Sea | *Seafood*	22
Le's | *Viet.*	21
Metropolitan | *Steak*	21
Z Oishii | *Japanese*	27
Papa Razzi | *Italian*	18

DEDHAM/
HYDE PARK/
ROSLINDALE

Birch St. Bistro | *Amer.*	19
Z Delfino | *Italian*	27
Finz | *Seafood*	20
Geoffrey's | *Amer.*	19
Halfway Cafe | *Pub*	17
Isabella | *Amer.*	24
Joe's American | *Amer.*	16
Pleasant Cafe | *Amer.*	18
Sophia's | *Med.*	23

NEW Townsend's | *Amer.*	19
Village Sushi | *Japanese/Korean*	23

LEXINGTON

Lexx | *Amer.*	17
Max Stein's | *Steak*	18
Z Not Average Joe's | *Amer.*	18
Upper Crust | *Pizza*	23
Via Lago | *Amer.*	20
Yangtze River | *Chinese*	17

MEDFORD/
SOMERVILLE

Amelia's Kitchen | *Italian*	22
Z Anna's | *Tex-Mex*	22
Bertucci's | *Italian*	17
Z Bistro 5 | *Italian*	27
Boloco | *Eclectic*	18
Burren | *Pub*	14
Café Belô | *Brazilian*	20
Cantina la Mexicana | *Mex.*	24
Dalí | *Spanish*	25
Diva Indian | *Indian*	22
Z EVOO | *Eclectic*	27
Gargoyles | *Amer.*	24
Highland Kitchen | *Amer.*	23
House of Tibet | *Tibetan*	-
Independent | *Amer.*	18
Johnny D's | *Amer.*	19
Joshua Tree | *Pub*	15
Kebab Factory | *Indian*	24
Lil Vinny's | *Italian*	20
Machu Picchu | *Peruvian*	19
Martsa's on Elm | *Tibetan*	21
Mr. Crepe | *French*	18
Namaskar | *Indian*	23
Neighborhood Rest. | *Portug.*	23
Orleans | *Amer./Italian*	17
Out of the Blue | *Seafood*	22
NEW Pho n' Rice | *Thai/Vietnamese*	-
Pizzeria Regina | *Pizza*	24
Redbones BBQ | *BBQ*	22
NEW Rodizio | *Brazilian*	22
Rosebud | *Diner*	16
Sabur | *Med.*	22
Sagra | *Italian*	16

Menus, photos, voting and more – free at ZAGAT.com

Sound Bites	*Amer./Mideast.*	22
Tacos Lupita	*Mex./Salvadoran*	25
Tu Y Yo	*Mex.*	24
Vinny's at Night	*Italian*	23
Wu Chon	*Japanese/Korean*	22
Zoe's	*Chinese*	19

NEEDHAM/NEWTON/WABAN

Amarin Thailand	*Thai*	22
Appetito	*Italian*	19
Ariadne	*Amer.*	21
Baker's Best	*Amer.*	22
Bertucci's	*Italian*	17
Biltmore B&G	*Amer.*	18
Blue on Highland	*Amer.*	17
Blue Ribbon BBQ	*BBQ*	25
NEW Bokx	*Steak*	23
Café St. Petersburg	*Russian*	19
Fava	*Amer.*	25
51 Lincoln	*Amer.*	23
Jamjuli	*Thai*	19
Johnny's Lunch.	*Diner*	18
Jumbo	*Chinese/Seafood*	23
Karoun	*Armenian/Mideast.*	22
Kouzina	*Greek/Med.*	23
Lam's	*Thai/Viet.*	21
NEW Local, The	*Amer.*	-
Z Lumière	*French*	27
Masala Art	*Indian*	23
No. 1 Noodle	*Pan-Asian*	18
Z Not Average Joe's	*Amer.*	18
Peking Cuisine	*Chinese*	21
Z Petit Robert	*French*	24
Pie Bakery	*Amer./Dessert*	18
Sapporo	*Japanese/Korean*	21
Shogun	*Japanese*	23
Skipjack's	*Seafood*	20
Sol Azteca	*Mex.*	20
Sweet Basil	*Italian*	25
Tartufo	*Italian*	22
Village Fish	*Italian/Seafood*	20

WALTHAM/WATERTOWN

Aegean	*Greek*	21
Bison County BBQ	*BBQ*	18

NEW Comfort	*Amer.*	-
Deluxe Town	*Diner*	22
Demos	*Greek*	21
Z Elephant Walk	*Cambodian/French*	23
Erawan of Siam	*Thai*	22
Green Papaya	*Thai*	20
Greg's	*Amer./Italian*	19
Halfway Cafe	*Pub*	17
Z Il Capriccio	*Italian*	27
Jake's Dixie	*BBQ*	17
Z La Campania	*Italian*	28
La Casa/Pedro	*Venez.*	21
Naked Fish	*Nuevo Latino/Seafood*	19
New Ginza	*Japanese*	24
New Mother India	*Indian*	22
Z Not Average Joe's	*Amer.*	18
Ponzu	*Asian Fusion*	23
Porcini's	*Med.*	22
Rist. Marcellino	*Italian*	16
Solea	*Spanish*	23
Stellina	*Italian*	22
Strip-T's	*Amer.*	22
Taqueria Mexico	*Mex.*	22
Tempo	*Amer.*	21
Tuscan Grill	*Italian*	24
UFood	*Health*	18
Upper Crust	*Pizza*	23

Outlying Suburbs

NORTH OF BOSTON

Abbondanza	*Italian*	23
Angelo's	*Italian*	26
Artichokes	*Italian*	21
Black Cow	*Pub*	19
Blue Fin	*Japanese*	22
Border Cafe	*Cajun/Tex-Mex*	19
Brenden Crocker's	*Amer.*	25
Burtons Grill	*Amer.*	21
Cassis	*French*	26
Z Cheesecake	*Amer.*	18
China Pearl	*Chinese*	21
Cilantro	*Mex.*	18
Z Clam Box	*Seafood*	26
Cygnet	*Amer.*	21
Dog Bar	*Amer.*	23

Donatello | *Italian*	24
🅩 Duckworth's | *Amer.*	29
Exchange St. Bistro | *Eclectic*	20
Finz | *Seafood*	20
Franklin | *Amer.*	26
NEW G Bar | *Amer.*	21
Glenn's | *Eclectic*	23
Glory | *Amer.*	21
Grapevine | *Amer./Italian*	25
NEW High St. Grill | *Amer./BBQ*	–
Hilltop Steak | *Steak*	16
🅩 Ithaki Med. | *Med.*	26
Jimmy's Steer | *Steak*	20
Joe's American | *Amer.*	16
Kowloon | *Pan-Asian*	17
Landing | *Amer.*	16
🅩 Legal Sea | *Seafood*	22
Lyceum B&G | *Amer.*	23
Maddie's Sail | *New Eng./Seafood*	18
Masa | *SW*	23
Naked Fish | *Nuevo Latino/Seafood*	19
🅩 Not Average Joe's | *Amer.*	18
Passage to India | *Indian*	20
Pellana | *Steak*	26
Pellino's | *Italian*	–
P.F. Chang's | *Chinese*	19
Polcari's | *Italian*	17
Red Rock Bistro | *Amer.*	20
Boston/Salem Beer | *Pub*	18
Sichuan Garden | *Chinese*	22
62 on Wharf | *Italian*	24
Soma | *Amer.*	22
Stone Soup | *Eclectic*	25
Strega Rest. | *Italian*	21
Tacos Lupita | *Mex./Salvadoran*	25
Tom Shea's | *New Eng./Seafood*	20
Upper Crust | *Pizza*	23
Woodman's | *New Eng./Seafood*	23
Yama | *Japanese*	22
Zabaglione | *Italian*	22

SOUTH OF BOSTON

Atlantica | *Seafood*	15
Back Eddy | *Seafood*	22
Barker Tavern | *Amer.*	23
Bella's | *Italian*	19

bia bistro | *French/Italian*	24
Bistro 712 | *French*	24
Bon Caldo | *Italian*	22
Bridgeman's | *Italian*	26
Burtons Grill | *Amer.*	21
Byblos | *Lebanese*	24
🅩 Caffe Bella | *Med.*	26
Caffe Tosca | *Italian*	24
Chiara | *Med.*	26
🅩 Coriander Bistro | *French*	27
NEW Croma | *Italian*	19
🅩 Davio's | *Italian/Steak*	25
Halfway Cafe | *Pub*	17
Incontro | *Italian*	22
Joe's American | *Amer.*	16
Mount Blue | *Eclectic*	18
🅩 Not Average Joe's | *Amer.*	18
NEW Olivadi | *Italian*	–
NEW Orta | *Italian*	–
Papa Razzi | *Italian*	18
Pizzeria Regina | *Pizza*	24
Riva | *Italian*	26
RooBar | *Amer.*	21
Rustic Kitchen | *Italian*	20
Saporito's | *Italian*	26
Scarlet Oak | *Steak*	20
Skipjack's | *Seafood*	20
Sky | *Amer.*	19
🅩 Square Café | *Amer.*	26
Stars on Hingham | *Diner*	16
Tosca | *Italian*	25
Upper Crust | *Pizza*	23
Vin & Eddie's | *Italian*	17

WEST OF BOSTON

Aegean | *Greek*	21
Alta Strada | *Italian*	21
Amarin Thailand | *Thai*	22
🅩 Blue Ginger | *Asian Fusion*	26
Border Cafe | *Cajun/Tex-Mex*	19
Bullfinch's | *Eclectic*	21
Café Belô | *Brazilian*	20
Cafe Escadrille | *Continental*	19
Café Mangal | *Med.*	25
🅩 Capital Grille | *Steak*	26
Captain's Table | *Seafood*	–

☑ Cheesecake | *Amer.*	18
China Sky | *Chinese/Japanese*	19
CK Shanghai | *Chinese*	22
Cottage | *Calif.*	19
Dalya's | *Amer.*	23
Dolphin Seafood | *Seafood*	18
Firefly's | *BBQ*	20
☑ FuGaKyu | *Japanese*	25
☑ Gibbet Hill | *New Eng./Steak*	24
Halfway Cafe | *Pub*	17
Harry's | *Diner*	20
Joe's American | *Amer.*	16
John Harvard's | *Pub*	16
☑ J's Nashoba | *Amer.*	26
La Cantina | *Italian*	20
L'Andana | *Italian*	25
NEW Lavender Asian | *Asian*	-
Left Bank | *Amer.*	21
☑ Legal Sea | *Seafood*	22
Le Lyonnais | *French*	23
Longfellow's | *New Eng.*	18
Lotus Blossom | *Chinese/Japanese*	22
☑ Maxwell's 148 | *Asian Fusion/Italian*	26
NEW Melting Pot | *Fondue*	20
Merchants Row | *New Eng.*	-
Met B&G | *Amer./Steak*	21
Metro 9 Steak | *Seafood/Steak*	19
Naked Fish | *Nuevo Latino/Seafood*	19
New Jang Su | *Korean*	23
Oga's | *Japanese*	26
☑ Oishii | *Japanese*	27
Papa Razzi | *Italian*	18
P.F. Chang's | *Chinese*	19
Pizzeria Regina | *Pizza*	24
☑ Sel de Terre | *French*	23
Serafina | *Italian*	20
Sherborn Inn | *New Eng.*	19
☑ Sichuan Gourmet | *Chinese*	27
Skipjack's | *Seafood*	20
Sky | *Amer.*	19
Sorento's | *Italian/Persian*	18
Summer Winter | *Amer.*	24
Tomasso | *Italian*	24
UFood | *Health*	18
vela | *Italian*	21

Walden Grille | *Amer.*	15
Yama | *Japanese*	22
Zebra's Bistro | *Amer.*	24

Far Outlying Areas

CAPE COD

☑ Abba | *Med./Thai*	27
Academy Ocean | *Eclectic/Seafood*	22
Adrian's | *Amer./Italian*	16
Alberto's | *Italian*	20
Amari | *Italian*	22
Anthony Cummaquid | *Continental*	18
Aqua Grille | *Amer./Seafood*	19
Ardeo | *Med.*	20
Arnold's Lobster | *Seafood*	23
Barley Neck Inn | *Amer.*	20
Baxter's | *New Eng./Seafood*	18
Bayside Betsy's | *Amer.*	15
Bee-Hive Tavern | *Amer.*	19
Belfry Inne | *Amer.*	25
Betsy's Diner | *Diner*	18
Bistro/Crowne Pointe | *Amer.*	22
NEW Blackfish | *Amer.*	24
Bleu | *French*	25
Blue Moon Bistro | *Med.*	24
Bookstore & Rest. | *Seafood*	19
☑ Bramble Inn | *Amer.*	27
Brazilian Grill | *Brazilian*	21
☑ Brewster Fish | *Seafood*	26
Bubala's | *Eclectic/Seafood*	16
Buca's Tuscan | *Italian*	23
Cafe Edwige/at Night | *Amer.*	26
Cape Sea Grille | *Amer.*	26
Capt. Frosty's | *New Eng./Seafood*	21
Capt. Kidd | *Pub*	18
Capt. Linnell | *Amer.*	22
Capt. Parker's | *New Eng.*	18
Casino Wharf | *Italian/Seafood*	20
Catch of the Day | *Seafood*	25
Chapoquoit Grill | *Amer.*	22
Chart Room | *New Eng./Seafood*	20
Chatham Bars Inn | *Amer.*	22
Chatham Squire | *Eclectic*	18
☑ Chillingsworth | *French*	27
Circadia Bistro | *Amer.*	23
Ciro & Sal's | *Italian*	20

Clancy's	*Amer.*	22	Ocean House	*Amer.*	25
Cobie's Clam	*Seafood*	19	Optimist Café	*Amer./British*	21
Cooke's	*Seafood*	-	Orleans Inn	*Amer.*	17
Coonamessett Inn	*Amer.*	18	Osteria La Civetta	*Italian*	-
Dan'l Webster	*Amer.*	20	Oyster Co.	*Seafood*	23
Devon's	*Amer./French*	24	Paddock	*New Eng./Seafood*	20
Dolphin	*Seafood*	21	**Z** Pisces	*Med./Seafood*	27
Dunbar Tea	*British/Tearoom*	22	Port	*Amer./Seafood*	23
Enzo	*French*	24	Post Office	*Amer.*	16
Fairway	*Amer.*	18	Red Inn	*New Eng.*	24
Fanizzi's	*Amer./Italian*	20	**Z** Red Pheasant	*Amer./French*	27
Fazio's	*Italian*	20	Regatta of Cotuit	*Amer.*	25
Finely JP's	*Amer.*	21	Roadhouse	*Seafood/Steak*	20
Firefly Woodfire	*Eclectic*	20	RooBar	*Amer.*	21
Fishmonger's	*Amer./Seafood*	18	Ross' Grill	*Amer.*	22
Five Bays Bistro	*Amer.*	25	Scargo Café	*Amer.*	20
Friendly Fisherman	*Seafood*	24	Siena	*Italian*	21
Z Front St.	*Continental/Italian*	27	Sir Cricket's	*Seafood*	24
Gina's	*Italian*	21	Stir Crazy	*Cambodian*	23
Gracie's Table	*Spanish*	23	Terra Luna	*Amer.*	24
HannaH's Fusion	*Asian Fusion*	24	Trevi Café	*Med.*	-
Heather	*Amer.*	-	**Z** 28 Atlantic	*Amer.*	26
Hemisphere	*New Eng.*	17	Vining's Bistro	*Eclectic*	24
Impudent Oyster	*Seafood*	23	Whitman House	*Amer.*	21
Z Inaho	*Japanese*	27	Wicked Oyster	*Amer./Seafood*	24
Island Merchant	*Amer./Carib.*	-	Wild Goose	*Amer.*	21
JT's Seafood	*Seafood*	17	Winslow's Tavern	*Amer.*	20
Karoo Kafe	*S African*	24		
Kate's Seafood	*Seafood*	20		

MARTHA'S VINEYARD

La Cucina/Mare	*Italian*	25	Alchemy	*Amer.*	22
L'Alouette	*French*	26	Art Cliff Diner	*Diner*	24
Landfall	*Seafood*	18	**NEW** Atlantic	*Seafood*	-
Laura & Tony's	*Amer.*	-	Atria	*Amer.*	25
Laureen's	*Eclectic*	23	Balance	*Amer.*	23
Liam's	*Seafood*	20	Beach Plum	*Amer.*	25
Lobster Pot	*Eclectic/Seafood*	22	Bite	*Seafood*	26
Lorraine's	*Mex.*	20	**Z** Black Dog Tavern	*Amer.*	19
Mac's	*Seafood*	24	Chesca's	*Eclectic/Italian*	23
Marshside	*Seafood*	15	David Ryan's	*Amer.*	15
Mews	*Amer.*	27	**Z** Détente	*Amer.*	27
Misaki	*Japanese*	24	Home Port	*New Eng./Seafood*	20
Moby Dick's	*New Eng./Seafood*	23	Jimmy Seas	*Italian*	23
Naked Oyster	*Seafood*	25	Lambert's Cove	*Amer.*	25
Napi's	*Eclectic*	19	Larsen's Fish	*Seafood*	27
Nauset Beach	*Italian*	25	Lattanzi's	*Italian*	21
Z Not Average Joe's	*Amer.*	18		

Le Grenier | *French*	23
L'Étoile | *French*	26
Lola's | *Cajun/Creole*	22
Lure | *Amer.*	21
Net Result | *Seafood*	25
Newes/America | *Pub*	18
Offshore Ale | *Amer.*	20
☑ Outermost Inn | *Amer.*	25
Park Corner | *Amer.*	22
NEW Salt Water | *Eclectic*	-
Sharky's | *Mex.*	21
NEW Sidecar Café | *New Eng.*	-
Slice of Life | *Amer.*	-
Sweet Life | *Amer.*	25
Theo's | *Amer.*	24
NEW Waterside Mkt. | *Amer.*	-
NEW Water St. | *Eclectic*	-
Zapotec | *SW*	19
Zephrus | *Amer.*	20

NANTUCKET

Alice's | *Amer./Thai*	18
American Seasons | *Amer.*	25
Arno's | *Amer.*	16
Black-Eyed Susan's | *Amer.*	26
Boarding Hse. | *Amer.*	21
Brant Point | *Amer.*	21
Brotherhood/Thieves | *Amer.*	18
Cambridge St. | *Eclectic*	-
Centre St. Bistro | *Amer.*	16

Chanticleer | *French*	25
Cinco | *Nuevo Latino*	26
Cioppino's | *Amer.*	19
Club Car | *Continental*	20
☑ Company/Cauldron | *Amer.*	28
DeMarco | *Italian*	22
Even Keel | *Amer.*	19
Fifty-Six Union | *Eclectic*	22
Fog Island | *Amer.*	21
☑ Galley Beach | *Eclectic*	24
Jetties | *Italian/New Eng.*	14
Le Languedoc | *French*	26
Lo La 41° | *Eclectic*	21
Nantucket Lobster | *Seafood*	19
Òran Mór | *Eclectic*	24
Pearl | *Asian Fusion/French*	24
Pi Pizzeria | *Pizza*	23
Queequeg's | *Eclectic*	25
Ropewalk | *Seafood*	-
Sconset Café | *Amer.*	21
SeaGrille | *Seafood*	22
Sfoglia | *Italian*	24
Ships Inn | *Calif./French*	24
Slip 14 | *Amer.*	18
Straight Wharf | *Seafood*	25
Summer House | *Amer.*	20
Sushi by Yoshi | *Japanese*	25
☑ Topper's | *Amer.*	27
29 Fair St. | *Continental*	22
☑ 21 Federal | *Amer.*	24

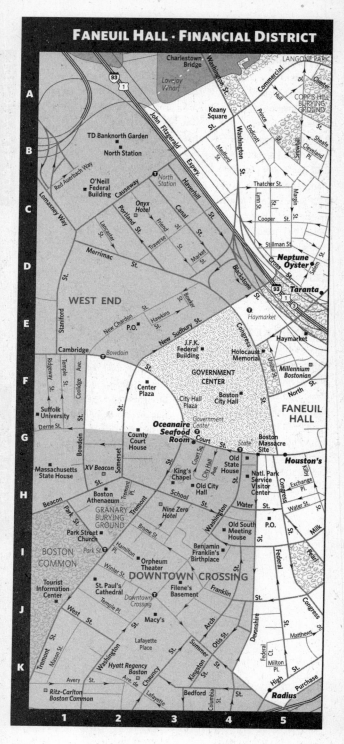

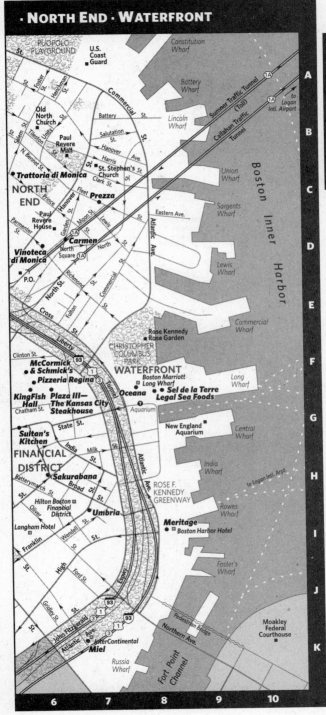

PUOPOLO PLAYGROUND

U.S. Coast Guard

Constitution Wharf

Battery Wharf

Sumner Traffic Tunnel (Toll)

to Logan Intl. Airport

Commercial St.

Lincoln Wharf

Callahan Traffic Tunnel

Old North Church

Battery St.

Paul Revere Mall

Salutation St.

Hanover Ave.

Harris St.

Union Wharf

Trattoria di Monica

St. Stephen's Church

Clark St.

NORTH END

Prezza

Eastern Ave.

Sargents Wharf

Paul Revere House

Atlantic Ave.

Carmen

North Square

Lewis Wharf

Vinoteca di Monica

P.O.

Richmond St.

Commercial Wharf

North St.

Fulton St.

Boston Inner Harbor

Cross St.

Liberty

Clinton St.

Rose Kennedy Rose Garden

CHRISTOPHER COLUMBUS PARK

McCormick & Schmick's

WATERFRONT

Pizzeria Regina

Boston Marriott Long Wharf

Long Wharf

KingFish Hall

Plaza III— The Kansas City Steakhouse

Oceana

Sel de la Terre

Legal Sea Foods

Chatham St.

Aquarium

State St.

Sultan's Kitchen

New England Aquarium

Central Wharf

FINANCIAL DISTRICT

India St.

Milk St.

to Logan Intl. Arpt.

Sakurabana

Broad St.

India Wharf

Batterymarch St.

ROSE F. KENNEDY GREENWAY

Hilton Boston Financial District

Oliver St.

Umbria

Rowes Wharf

Langham Hotel

Franklin St.

Wendell St.

Meritage

Boston Harbor Hotel

High St.

Ford St.

Foster's Wharf

Gridley St.

Moakley Federal Courthouse

John Fitzgerald

Pedestrian Bridge

Northern Ave.

InterContinental

Miel

Atlantic Ave.

Russia Wharf

Fort Point Channel

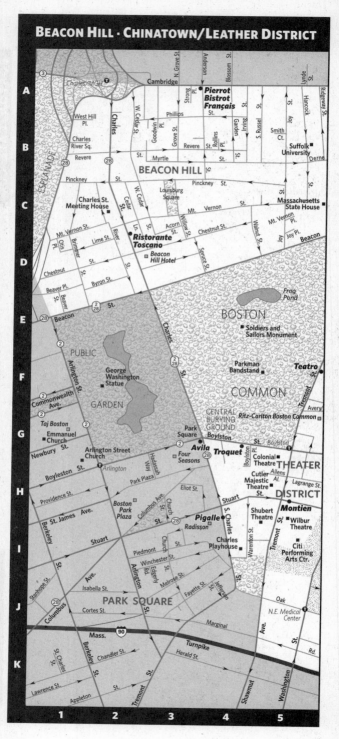

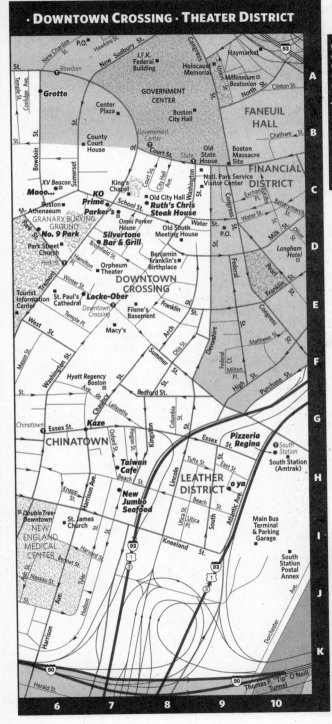

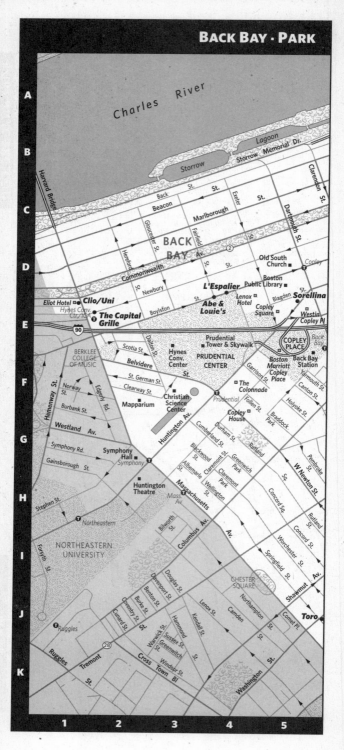

Menus, photos, voting and more – free at ZAGAT.com

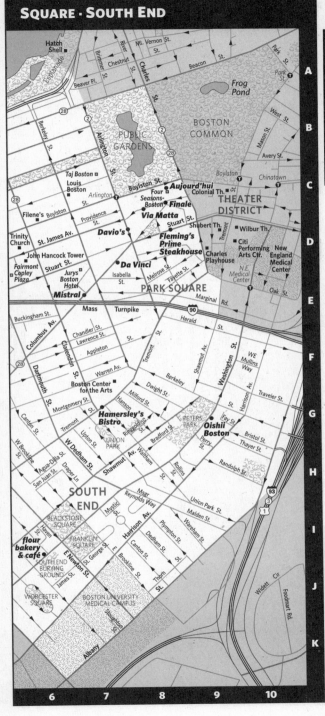

MAPS

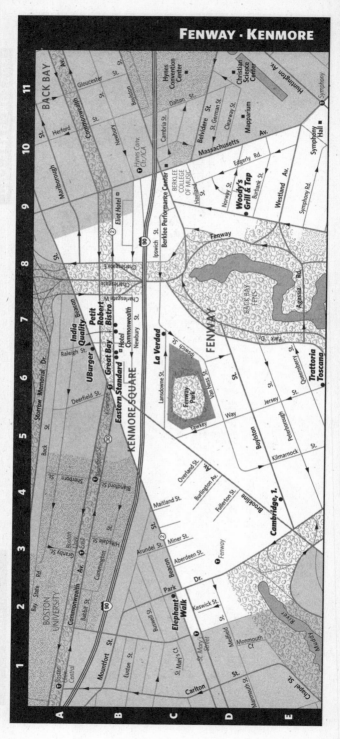

Menus, photos, voting and more – free at ZAGAT.com

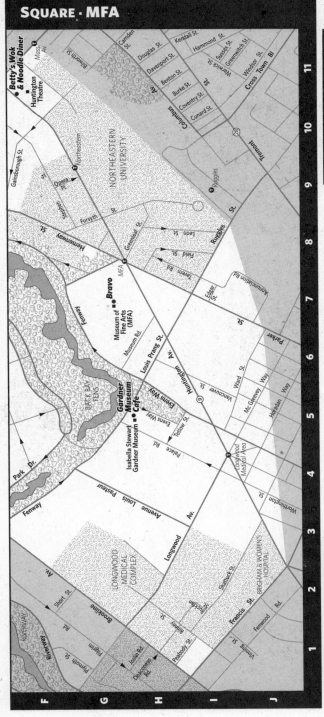

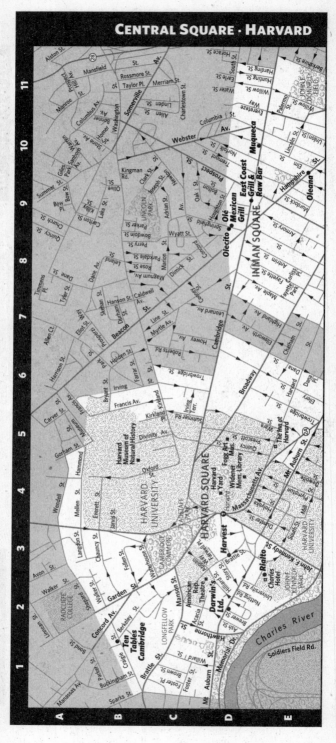

CENTRAL SQUARE · HARVARD

Menus, photos, voting and more – free at ZAGAT.com

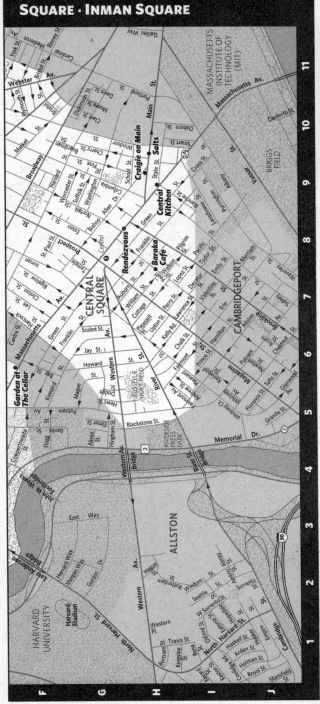

Special Features

Listings cover the best in each category and include names, locations and Food ratings. Multi-location restaurants' features may vary by branch.

BREAKFAST

(See also Hotel Dining)

Arno's | **Nan**	16
Art Cliff Diner | **MV**	24
Baker's Best | **Newton**	22
Bayside Betsy's | **CC**	15
Betsy's Diner | **CC**	18
NEW Bina Osteria | **D'town Cross**	-
☑ Black Dog Tavern | **MV**	19
Black-Eyed Susan's | **Nan**	26
Bon Savor | **Jamaica Plain**	20
Brookline Family | **Brookline**	21
Cafe Edwige/at Night | **CC**	26
Centre St. Bistro | **Nan**	16
Chacarero | **D'town Cross**	-
Charlie's Sandwich | **S End**	23
Deluxe Town | **Watertown**	22
Even Keel | **Nan**	19
Fairway | **CC**	18
flour bakery | **S End**	26
Fog Island | **Nan**	21
Haley House | **Roxbury**	24
Harry's | **Westborough**	20
Hi-Rise | **multi.**	24
Johnny's Lunch. | **Newton**	18
Laureen's | **CC**	23
Mike's | **S End**	20
Neighborhood Rest. | **Somerville**	23
Optimist Café | **CC**	21
Oxford Spa | **Porter Sq**	21
Panificio | **Beacon Hill**	19
Paramount | **Beacon Hill**	23
Rosebud | **Somerville**	16
Rubin's | **Brookline**	19
S&S | **Inman Sq**	18
Sconset Café | **Nan**	21
Sorella's | **Jamaica Plain**	26
Sorelle | **Charlestown**	23
Sound Bites | **Somerville**	22
South End Buttery | **S End**	21
South St. Diner | **Leather Dist**	16
Stars on Hingham | **Hingham**	16

Trident | **Back Bay**	19
Via Lago | **Lexington**	20
Vicki Lee's | **Belmont**	25
Victoria's Diner | **Roxbury**	20
NEW Waterside Mkt. | **MV**	-
Wicked Oyster | **CC**	24

BRUNCH

☑ Abe & Louie's | **Back Bay**	26
Alchemist | **Jamaica Plain**	17
☑ Aquitaine | **S End**	23
Aquitaine Bis | **Chestnut Hill**	23
Ashmont Grill | **Dorchester**	22
☑ Aujourd'hui | **Back Bay**	28
Baker's Best | **Newton**	22
Beacon Hill Bistro | **Beacon Hill**	22
Bleu | **CC**	25
Blue Room | **Kendall Sq**	25
Bombay Club | **Harv Sq**	20
Bon Savor | **Jamaica Plain**	20
Bullfinch's | **Sudbury**	21
Cafe Edwige/at Night | **CC**	26
Café Fleuri | **Financial Dist**	22
Café Polonia | **S Boston**	24
Centre St. Café | **Jamaica Plain**	25
Charley's | **multi.**	18
Columbus Café | **S End**	19
Coonamessett Inn | **CC**	18
dante | **E Cambridge**	24
Delux Cafe | **S End**	21
☑ East Coast | **Inman Sq**	25
Gargoyles | **Somerville**	24
Haley House | **Roxbury**	24
Harvest | **Harv Sq**	25
Henrietta's | **Harv Sq**	23
Johnny D's | **Somerville**	19
☑ J's Nashoba | **Bolton**	26
KingFish Hall | **Faneuil Hall**	22
☑ Legal Sea | **Harv Sq**	22
Lola's | **MV**	22
Lyceum B&G | **Salem**	23
☑ Meritage | **Waterfront**	27

Metropolis Cafe | **S End**	23
Mews | **CC**	27
Middle East | **Central Sq**	17
North St. Grille | **N End**	23
Oceana | **Waterfront**	24
Olecito/Olé | **Inman Sq**	24
Panificio | **Beacon Hill**	19
Park Corner | **MV**	22
Sabur | **Somerville**	22
S&S | **Inman Sq**	18
☒ Sel de Terre | **Waterfront**	23
Sidney's | **Central Sq**	21
Sonsie | **Back Bay**	20
South End Buttery | **S End**	21
Stephanie's | **Back Bay**	20
Stone Soup | **Ipswich**	25
Temple Bar | **Porter Sq**	20
☒ Topper's | **Nan**	27
Tremont 647 | **S End**	21
Tryst | **Arlington**	22
Union B&G | **S End**	24
☒ UpStairs on Sq. | **Harv Sq**	24
West Side Lounge | **Porter Sq**	22
Zaftigs | **Brookline**	21

BUFFET

(Check availability)

Amrheins | **S Boston**	18
☒ Aujourd'hui | **Back Bay**	28
Aura | **Seaport Dist**	22
Bhindi Bazaar | **Back Bay**	22
Blue Room | **Kendall Sq**	25
Bombay Club | **Harv Sq**	20
Brazilian Grill | **CC**	21
☒ Bristol | **Back Bay**	24
Bukhara | **Jamaica Plain**	23
Café Belô | **multi.**	20
Café Fleuri | **Financial Dist**	22
Cafe of India | **Harv Sq**	22
Caliterra | **Financial Dist**	16
Casino Wharf | **CC**	20
Changsho | **Porter Sq**	20
Chatham Bars Inn | **CC**	22
China Pearl | **Woburn**	21
Clink | **Beacon Hill**	19
Coonamessett Inn | **CC**	18
Dan'l Webster | **CC**	20

Diva Indian | **Somerville**	22
Fanizzi's | **CC**	20
Fire & Ice | **multi.**	16
Firefly's | **multi.**	20
NEW Ghazal | **Jamaica Plain**	-
Haveli | **Inman Sq**	-
Henrietta's | **Harv Sq**	23
Himalayan Bistro | **W Roxbury**	24
Hungry i | **Beacon Hill**	24
India Pavilion | **Central Sq**	20
Joshua Tree | **Allston**	15
☒ J's Nashoba | **Bolton**	26
Kashmir | **Back Bay**	23
Kathmandu Spice | **Arlington**	22
Kebab Factory | **Somerville**	24
Laura & Tony's | **CC**	-
Lola's | **MV**	22
Lotus Blossom | **Sudbury**	22
Mantra | **D'town Cross**	18
Martsa's on Elm | **Somerville**	21
Masala Art | **Needham**	23
Mela | **S End**	24
Merchants Row | **Concord**	-
Midwest | **Inman Sq**	20
Namaskar | **Somerville**	23
Neighborhood Rest. | **Somerville**	23
New Mother India | **Waltham**	22
Oceana | **Waterfront**	24
Parker's | **D'town Cross**	22
Passage to India | **Porter Sq**	20
Plaza III | **Faneuil Hall**	21
Rani | **Brookline**	20
NEW Rodizio | **Somerville**	22
Shanti India | **Dorchester**	-
Sidney's | **Central Sq**	21
NEW 606 Congress | **Seaport Dist**	21
Sky | **Norwood**	19
Stanhope Grille | **Back Bay**	23
Sunset Grill/Cantina | **Allston**	20
Tamarind Bay | **Harv Sq**	24
Tanjore | **Harv Sq**	22
Tantric | **Theater Dist**	20
Tavern in Sq. | **multi.**	17
NEW Water St. | **MV**	-
Yangtze River | **Lexington**	17

BUSINESS DINING

Z Aquitaine | **S End**	23
NEW Asana | **Back Bay**	–
Z Aujourd'hui | **Back Bay**	28
Avenue One | **D'town Cross**	18
Azure | **Back Bay**	22
Bambara | **E Cambridge**	20
Beacon Hill Bistro | **Beacon Hill**	22
NEW Bina Osteria | **D'town Cross**	–
blu | **Theater Dist**	21
Z Blue Ginger | **Wellesley**	26
NEW Bokx | **Newton Lower Falls**	23
NEW Bond | **Financial Dist**	–
Z Bristol | **Back Bay**	24
Café Fleuri | **Financial Dist**	22
Caliterra | **Financial Dist**	16
Z Capital Grille | **multi.**	26
Z Clio/Uni | **Back Bay**	27
Cygnet | **Beverly**	21
NEW Daily Grill | **Back Bay**	19
Z Davio's | **Foxboro**	25
Z Eastern Stand. | **Kenmore Sq**	22
Fleming's Prime | **Park Sq**	24
Good Life | **D'town Cross**	17
Great Bay | **Kenmore Sq**	23
Green Papaya | **Waltham**	20
Z Grill 23 | **Back Bay**	25
Z Hamersley's Bistro | **S End**	27
Harvest | **Harv Sq**	25
Henrietta's | **Harv Sq**	23
Z Il Capriccio | **Waltham**	27
Jer-Ne | **Theater Dist**	20
KO Prime | **D'town Cross**	24
Z Legal Sea | **multi.**	22
Z L'Espalier | **Back Bay**	28
Locke-Ober | **D'town Cross**	24
Mantra | **D'town Cross**	18
NEW Market | **Financial Dist**	16
Max Stein's | **Lexington**	18
McCormick/Schmick | **multi.**	21
Z Meritage | **Waterfront**	27
Metropolitan | **Chestnut Hill**	21
Z Mistral | **S End**	27
Mooo... | **Beacon Hill**	24
Z Morton's | **multi.**	25
Z No. 9 Park | **Beacon Hill**	28

Novel | **Back Bay**	–
Z Oak Room | **Back Bay**	25
Oceanaire | **Financial Dist**	24
NEW Olivadi | **Norwood**	–
Z Olives | **Charlestown**	25
Palm | **Back Bay**	23
Papa Razzi | **multi.**	18
Persephone | **Seaport Dist**	25
Plaza III | **Faneuil Hall**	21
Z Radius | **Financial Dist**	26
Z Rialto | **Harv Sq**	26
NEW Rudi's | **Roxbury**	–
Z Ruth's Chris | **D'town Cross**	24
Sandrine's | **Harv Sq**	24
Sasso | **Back Bay**	21
Z Sel de Terre | **multi.**	23
NEW Sensing | **Waterfront**	–
Sidney's | **Central Sq**	21
NEW 606 Congress | **Seaport Dist**	21
Smith/Wollensky | **Back Bay**	23
NEW Sportello | **Seaport Dist**	–
Summer Winter | **Burlington**	24
Turner Fish | **Back Bay**	21
Z UpStairs on Sq. | **Harv Sq**	24
Vinalia | **D'town Cross**	17

BYO

Art Cliff Diner | **MV**	24
Beach Plum | **MV**	25
Z Black Dog Tavern | **MV**	19
Black-Eyed Susan's | **Nan**	26
Café Mangal | **Wellesley**	25
Captain's Table | **Wellesley**	–
Z Clam Box | **Ipswich**	26
Friendly Fisherman | **CC**	24
Home Port | **MV**	20
Lambert's Cove | **MV**	25
Larsen's Fish | **MV**	27
Le Grenier | **MV**	23
Liam's | **CC**	20
Moby Dick's | **CC**	23
NEW Salt Water | **MV**	–
Sushi by Yoshi | **Nan**	25
Sweet Basil | **Needham**	25
Theo's | **MV**	24
Yama | **Wellesley**	22

CELEBRITY CHEFS

Alta Strada | *Michael Schlow* | **Wellesley** — 21

🔁 B&G Oysters | *Barbara Lynch* | **S End** — 26

🔁 Blue Ginger | *Ming Tsai* | **Wellesley** — 26

Bonfire | *Todd English* | **Park Sq** — 21

Butcher Shop | *Barbara Lynch* | **S End** — 25

🔁 Craigie on Main | *Tony Maws* | **Central Sq** — 27

NEW Drink | *Barbara Lynch* | **Seaport Dist** — –

Figs | *Todd English* | **multi.** — 23

Great Bay | *Michael Schlow* | **Kenmore Sq** — 23

🔁 Icarus | *Chris Douglass* | **S End** — 25

Jasper White's | *Jasper White* | **Back Bay** — 21

KingFish Hall | *Todd English* | **Faneuil Hall** — 22

KO Prime | *Ken Oringer* | **D'town Cross** — 24

L'Andana | *Jamie Mammano* | **Burlington** — 25

La Verdad | *Ken Oringer* | **Fenway** — 22

🔁 L'Espalier | *Frank McClelland* | **Back Bay** — 28

Locke-Ober | *Lydia Shire* | **D'town Cross** — 24

🔁 Lumière | *Michael Leviton* | **Newton** — 27

NEW Market | *Rene Michelena* | **Financial Dist** — 16

🔁 Mistral | *Jamie Mammano* | **S End** — 27

Myers + Chang | *Joanne Chang* | **S End** — 23

🔁 No. 9 Park | *Barbara Lynch* | **Beacon Hill** — 28

🔁 Olives | *Todd English* | **Charlestown** — 25

Persephone | *Michael Leviton* | **Seaport Dist** — 25

🔁 Radius | *Michael Schlow* | **Financial Dist** — 26

🔁 Rialto | *Jody Adams* | **Harv Sq** — 26

NEW Scampo | *Lydia Shire* | **Beacon Hill** — 22

NEW Sensing | *Guy Martin* | **Waterfront** — –

Sibling Rivalry | *David/Bob Kinkead* | **S End** — 24

NEW Sofra Bakery | *Ana Sortun* | **Huron Vill** — 26

🔁 Sorellina | *Jamie Mammano* | **Back Bay** — 27

NEW Sportello | *Barbara Lynch* | **Seaport Dist** — –

Summer Winter | *Clark Frasier/ Mark Gaier* | **Burlington** — 24

🔁 Toro | *Ken Oringer* | **S End** — 26

Via Matta | *Michael Schlow* | **Park Sq** — 25

CHILD-FRIENDLY

(Alternatives to the usual fast-food places; * children's menu available)

Adrian's* | **CC** — 16

Amarin Thailand | **multi.** — 22

🔁 Anna's | **multi.** — 22

Ardeo* | **CC** — 20

Arno's* | **Nan** — 16

Art Cliff Diner | **MV** — 24

Artú | **multi.** — 21

Atlantic Fish* | **Back Bay** — 23

Baja Betty's* | **Brookline** — 20

Baker's Best | **Newton** — 22

Bamboo | **Brighton** — 23

Bangkok Bistro | **Brighton** — 22

Barking Crab* | **Seaport Dist** — 16

Bee-Hive Tavern* | **CC** — 19

Bertucci's* | **multi.** — 17

b. good | **multi.** — 19

Bison County BBQ | **Waltham** — 18

🔁 Black Dog Tavern* | **MV** — 19

Blue Fin* | **multi.** — 22

Blue Ribbon BBQ | **multi.** — 25

Boca Grande | **multi.** — 19

Boloco | **multi.** — 18

Border Cafe* | **Saugus** — 19

Bottega | **Brookline** — 24

Brazilian Grill | **CC** — 21

Brown Sugar/Similans | **Boston U** — 25

Cafe Barada | **Porter Sq** — 23

Café Belô | **multi.** — 20

Café Fleuri* | **Financial Dist**	22
Cambridge St.* | **Nan**	-
Canestaro | **Fenway**	19
Cantina la Mexicana | **Somerville**	24
Capt. Frosty's* | **CC**	21
Capt. Kidd* | **CC**	18
Charley's* | **multi.**	18
Chau Chow | **Chinatown**	21
Cheers* | **multi.**	14
Chef Chang's | **Brookline**	20
Chef Chow's | **Brookline**	20
China Pearl | **multi.**	21
☑ Clam Box | **Ipswich**	26
Coolidge Corner* | **Brookline**	17
Cottage* | **Wellesley**	19
Court House* | **E Cambridge**	22
Demos* | **multi.**	21
Dolphin Seafood* | **multi.**	18
Donatello | **Saugus**	24
Durgin-Park* | **Faneuil Hall**	17
Fifty-Six Union | **Nan**	22
Fire & Ice | **multi.**	16
Firefly's* | **multi.**	20
flour bakery | **S End**	26
Fog Island* | **Nan**	21
Frank's Steak* | **Porter Sq**	18
Full Moon* | **Huron Vill**	20
☑ Galleria Umberto | **N End**	26
Golden Temple | **Brookline**	21
Grasshopper | **Allston**	20
Greg's | **Watertown**	19
Halfway Cafe* | **multi.**	17
Hilltop Steak* | **Saugus**	16
Hi-Rise* | **multi.**	24
Home Port* | **MV**	20
Il Panino | **N End**	23
Island Hopper | **Back Bay**	19
Jae's* | **multi.**	20
Jasper White's* | **multi.**	21
Jetties* | **Nan**	14
Joe's American* | **multi.**	16
Johnny's Lunch.* | **Newton**	18
JP Seafood | **Jamaica Plain**	23
Karoo Kafe | **CC**	24
Kowloon* | **Saugus**	17
La Cantina* | **Framingham**	20

La Fam. Giorgio* | **N End**	23
Laura & Tony's* | **CC**	-
☑ Legal Sea* | **multi.**	22
Le's* | **multi.**	21
Lobster Pot* | **CC**	22
Longfellow's* | **Sudbury**	18
Lure* | **MV**	21
Maggiano's* | **Park Sq**	19
Merengue | **Roxbury**	-
Midwest | **Inman Sq**	20
Mike's | **S End**	20
Moby Dick's* | **CC**	23
Morse Fish* | **S End**	21
Mr. Bartley's* | **Harv Sq**	24
Naked Fish* | **multi.**	19
Nantucket Lobster* | **Nan**	19
Neighborhood Rest.* | **Somerville**	23
New Jang Su | **Burlington**	23
No Name* | **Seaport Dist**	19
No. 1 Noodle | **Newton**	18
☑ Not Average Joe's* | **multi.**	18
Offshore Ale* | **MV**	20
Optimist Café* | **CC**	21
Out of the Blue | **Somerville**	22
Paddock* | **CC**	20
Panificio | **Beacon Hill**	19
Papa Razzi* | **multi.**	18
Paris Creperie | **Brookline**	22
Peach Farm | **Chinatown**	25
Peking Cuisine | **Newton**	21
Penang | **Chinatown**	22
P.F. Chang's | **Theater Dist**	19
Phoenicia | **Beacon Hill**	21
Pho Hoa | **multi.**	22
Pho Pasteur | **Chinatown**	23
Picante | **Central Sq**	19
Picco | **S End**	22
Pizzeria Regina | **multi.**	24
Polcari's* | **multi.**	17
Punjab | **Arlington**	25
Purple Cactus* | **Jamaica Plain**	21
Redbones BBQ* | **Somerville**	22
Rubin's* | **Brookline**	19
S&S | **Inman Sq**	18
Scargo Café* | **CC**	20

Sconset Café	**Nan**	21
SeaGrille*	**Nan**	22
Sichuan Garden	**multi.**	22
Siena*	**CC**	21
Skipjack's*	**multi.**	20
Sorella's*	**Jamaica Plain**	26
Sorelle	**Charlestown**	23
Stars on Hingham*	**Hingham**	16
Stir Crazy*	**CC**	23
Sunset Cafe*	**Inman Sq**	19
Tacos El Charro	**Jamaica Plain**	23
Tacos Lupita	**multi.**	25
Taqueria Mexico*	**Waltham**	22
Tom Shea's*	**Essex**	20
Trident	**Back Bay**	19
☑ Union Oyster*	**Faneuil Hall**	20
Veggie Planet	**Harv Sq**	23
Via Lago*	**Lexington**	20
Victoria's Diner*	**Roxbury**	20
Village Smokehse.*	**Brookline**	19
Woodman's*	**Essex**	23
Za	**Arlington**	25
Zaftigs*	**Brookline**	21

DELIVERY

Bamboo	**Brighton**	23
Bangkok Bistro	**Brighton**	22
Bangkok City	**Back Bay**	20
Bertucci's	**multi.**	17
Bluestone Bistro	**Brighton**	17
Brown Sugar/Similans	**Boston U**	25
Cafe Podima	**Beacon Hill**	19
Canestaro	**Fenway**	19
Changsho	**Porter Sq**	20
Chef Chang's	**Brookline**	20
Chef Chow's	**Brookline**	20
Chilli Duck	**Back Bay**	21
Golden Temple	**Brookline**	21
9 Tastes	**Harv Sq**	20
Redbones BBQ	**Somerville**	22
Sichuan Garden	**Woburn**	22
Spice Thai	**Harv Sq**	21
Super Fusion	**Brookline**	27
Trident	**Back Bay**	19
Upper Crust	**multi.**	23
Zen	**Beacon Hill**	24

ENTERTAINMENT

(Call for days and times of performances)

Alchemist	live music	**Jamaica Plain**	17
Amari	live music	**CC**	22
Barley Neck Inn	live music	**CC**	20
Bee-Hive Tavern	live music	**CC**	19
Belfry Inne	jazz/piano	**CC**	25
Bleu	jazz	**CC**	25
Bravo	jazz/piano	**MFA**	21
Bullfinch's	jazz	**Sudbury**	21
Burren	live music	**Somerville**	14
Byblos	belly dancing	**Norwood**	24
Café Brazil	guitar/karaoke	**Allston**	23
Café Fleuri	jazz	**Financial Dist**	22
Café St. Petersburg	piano	**Newton**	19
Casino Wharf	live music	**CC**	20
Chart Room	bass/piano	**CC**	20
Church	live music	**Fenway**	20
Club Car	piano	**Nan**	20
☑ Company/Cauldron	harpist	**Nan**	28
NEW DJ's/Garden	live music	**W End**	–
Dog Bar	live music	**Gloucester**	23
El Sarape	guitarist	**Braintree**	25
Fireplace	jazz/Latin	**Brookline**	21
Glenn's	blues/jazz	**Newburyport**	23
Good Life	DJ	**D'town Cross**	17
Green Briar	bands/DJ	**Brighton**	17
☑ Icarus	jazz	**S End**	25
Jacob Wirth	singalongs	**Theater Dist**	17
Jake's Dixie	blues	**Waltham**	17
Jetties	live music	**Nan**	14
Johnny D's	live music	**Somerville**	19
NEW Jury Room	live music	**Quincy**	19
Karoun	belly dancing	**Newton**	22
Kowloon	varies	**Saugus**	17
La Casa/Pedro	live music	**Watertown**	21
Les Zygomates	varies	**Leather Dist**	22

Lola's | varies | **MV** | 22
Lucky's Lounge | live music | **Seaport Dist** | 18
Matt Murphy's | varies | **Brookline** | 22
Middle East | live music | **Central Sq** | 17
Mount Blue | varies | **Norwell** | 18
Offshore Ale | bands | **MV** | 20
Orleans | varies | **Somerville** | 17
Red Fez | Middle Eastern | **S End** | 18
Redline | live music | **Harv Sq** | 17
Rest. Cesaria | folk | **Dorchester** | -
Roadhouse | jazz/piano | **CC** | 20
Sunset Cafe | Portuguese folk/Brazilian | **Inman Sq** | 19
🔒 Tangierino | belly dancing | **Charlestown** | 24
Tavern in Sq. | DJ | **Central Sq** | 17
🔒 Top of Hub | jazz | **Back Bay** | 20
Tryst | jazz | **Arlington** | 22
28 Degrees | DJ | **S End** | 20
Veggie Planet | folk | **Harv Sq** | 23
Warren Tavern | varies | **Charlestown** | 16
ZuZu! | bands/DJs | **Central Sq** | 20

FIREPLACES

🔒 Abe & Louie's | **Back Bay** | 26
Academy Ocean | **CC** | 22
Aegean | **Watertown** | 21
Alberto's | **CC** | 20
Amari | **CC** | 22
Anthony Cummaquid | **CC** | 18
Aqua Grille | **CC** | 19
NEW Asana | **Back Bay** | -
Atlantica | **Cohasset** | 15
Atria | **MV** | 25
Back Eddy | **Westport** | 22
Barker Tavern | **Scituate** | 23
Barking Crab | **Seaport Dist** | 16
Barley Neck Inn | **CC** | 20
Beacon Hill Bistro | **Beacon Hill** | 22
Beacon St. Tavern | **Brookline** | 20
Bison County BBQ | **Waltham** | 18
Bistro/Crowne Pointe | **CC** | 22
Black Cow | **Newburyport** | 19

🔒 Black Dog Tavern | **MV** | 19
Black Sheep | **Kendall Sq** | 21
Bon Caldo | **Norwood** | 22
Bookstore & Rest. | **CC** | 19
🔒 Bristol | **Back Bay** | 24
Brotherhood/Thieves | **Nan** | 18
Buca's Tuscan | **CC** | 23
Capt. Linnell | **CC** | 22
Chapoquoit Grill | **CC** | 22
Chatham Bars Inn | **CC** | 22
Chiara | **Westwood** | 26
🔒 Chillingsworth | **CC** | 27
Christopher's | **Porter Sq** | 17
Circadia Bistro | **CC** | 23
Ciro & Sal's | **CC** | 20
Coonamessett Inn | **CC** | 18
Cottage | **Wellesley** | 19
Dalya's | **Bedford** | 23
Dan'l Webster | **CC** | 20
DeMarco | **Nan** | 22
Dillon's | **Back Bay** | 16
Dog Bar | **Gloucester** | 23
Dolphin | **CC** | 21
Dolphin Seafood | **Natick** | 18
Donatello | **Saugus** | 24
Dunbar Tea | **CC** | 22
Enzo | **CC** | 24
Euno | **N End** | 24
Finz | **multi.** | 20
Fireplace | **Brookline** | 21
🔒 Gibbet Hill | **Groton** | 24
Gina's | **CC** | 21
Glory | **Andover** | 21
🔒 Grill 23 | **Back Bay** | 25
Harvest | **Harv Sq** | 25
Heather | **CC** | -
🔒 Helmand | **E Cambridge** | 26
Hungry i | **Beacon Hill** | 24
Incontro | **Franklin** | 22
Jae's | **Brookline** | 20
James's Gate | **Jamaica Plain** | 16
Joe's American | **multi.** | 16
Joshua Tree | **Allston** | 15
🔒 J's Nashoba | **Bolton** | 26
🔒 La Campania | **Waltham** | 28
La Fam. Giorgio | **N End** | 23

L'Alouette | **CC**	26
L'Andana | **Burlington**	25
Landing | **Manchester/Sea**	16
Lattanzi's | **MV**	21
Left Bank | **Tyngsboro**	21
Le Lyonnais | **Acton**	23
Longfellow's | **Sudbury**	18
Lyceum B&G | **Salem**	23
Marco Romana | **N End**	26
Marshside | **CC**	15
Merchants Row | **Concord**	-
Metro 9 Steak | **Framingham**	19
Metropolitan | **Chestnut Hill**	21
Mews | **CC**	27
Miel | **Waterfront**	21
ⓩ Mistral | **S End**	27
Mount Blue | **Norwell**	18
Nauset Beach | **CC**	25
Newes/America | **MV**	18
Ocean House | **CC**	25
Offshore Ale | **MV**	20
ⓩ Oleana | **Inman Sq**	28
Olecito/Olé | **Inman Sq**	24
Òran Mór | **Nan**	24
Orleans Inn | **CC**	17
NEW Orta | **Hanover**	-
ⓩ Outermost Inn | **MV**	25
Porcini's | **Watertown**	22
Publick House | **Brookline**	21
Red House | **Harv Sq**	20
Red Inn | **CC**	24
ⓩ Red Pheasant | **CC**	27
Rist. Fiore | **N End**	21
Riva | **Scituate**	26
Roadhouse | **CC**	20
Ross' Grill | **CC**	22
NEW Scampo | **Beacon Hill**	22
Scargo Café | **CC**	20
Scarlet Oak | **Hingham**	20
Sherborn Inn | **Sherborn**	19
Ships Inn | **Nan**	24
Sky | **Norwood**	19
Smith/Wollensky | **Back Bay**	23
South End Buttery | **S End**	21
Stephanie's | **Back Bay**	20
Stockyard | **Brighton**	15

Summer House | **Nan**	20
Taberna de Haro | **Brookline**	23
ⓩ Topper's | **Nan**	27
NEW Townsend's | **Hyde Park**	19
ⓩ 28 Atlantic | **CC**	26
29 Fair St. | **Nan**	22
ⓩ UpStairs on Sq. | **Harv Sq**	24
Vining's Bistro | **CC**	24
NEW Vintage | **W Roxbury**	-
Warren Tavern | **Charlestown**	16
West on Centre | **W Roxbury**	18
Wicked Oyster | **CC**	24
Wild Goose | **CC**	21

HISTORIC PLACES

(Year opened; * building)

1700 | 28 Atlantic* | **CC**	26
1700 | Wicked Oyster* | **CC**	24
1707 | Longfellow's* | **Sudbury**	18
1709 | 29 Fair St.* | **Nan**	22
1716 | Merchants Row* | **Concord**	-
1720 | Chart House* | **Waterfront**	21
1740 | Dunbar Tea* | **CC**	22
1742 | Union Oyster* | **Faneuil Hall**	20
1745 | Newes/America* | **MV**	18
1750 | Landing* | **Manchester/Sea**	16
1750 | Scarlet Oak* | **Hingham**	20
1778 | Chillingsworth* | **CC**	27
1780 | Warren Tavern* | **Charlestown**	16
1781 | Gracie's Table* | **CC**	23
1786 | Red Pheasant* | **CC**	27
1790 | Lambert's Cove* | **MV**	25
1790 | Regatta of Cotuit* | **CC**	25
1796 | Coonamessett Inn* | **CC**	18
1800 | Alchemy* | **MV**	22
1800 | Bistro/Crowne Pointe* | **CC**	22
1800 | DeMarco* | **Nan**	22
1800 | Durgin-Park* | **Faneuil Hall**	17
1800 | Mantra* | **D'town Cross**	18
1802 | Red House* | **Harv Sq**	20
1805 | Red Inn* | **CC**	24
1805 | Terra Luna* | **CC**	24
1825 | Piccolo Nido* | **N End**	24
1827 | Sherborn Inn* | **Sherborn**	19
1830 | Abba* | **CC**	27
1830 | Anthony Cummaquid* | **CC**	18

1830 | Circadia Bistro* | **CC**	23
1831 | Ships Inn* | **Nan**	24
1835 | Capt. Linnell* | **CC**	22
1840 | Brotherhood/Thieves* | **Nan**	18
1840 | Hungry i* | **Beacon Hill**	24
1843 | Lyceum B&G* | **Salem**	23
1847 | 21 Federal* | **Nan**	24
1849 | Optimist Café* | **CC**	21
1850 | Dalya's* | **Bedford**	23
1850 | Dolphin* | **CC**	21
1850 | Le Lyonnais* | **Acton**	23
1850 | Post Office* | **CC**	16
1856 | Parker's* | **D'town Cross**	22
1857 | Living Room* | **Waterfront**	15
1860 | Franklin* | **S End**	26
1860 | Jimmy Seas* | **MV**	23
1860 | Òran Mór* | **Nan**	24
1860 | Pisces* | **CC**	27
1860 | Sweet Life* | **MV**	25
1861 | Bramble Inn* | **CC**	27
1865 | Scargo Café* | **CC**	20
1865 | Wild Goose* | **CC**	21
1868 | Barley Neck Inn* | **CC**	20
1868 | Jacob Wirth | **Theater Dist**	17
1870 | Enzo* | **CC**	24
1875 | Club Car* | **Nan**	20
1875 | Cygnet* | **Beverly**	21
1875 | Locke-Ober | **D'town Cross**	24
1875 | Orleans Inn* | **CC**	17
1876 | Lobster Pot* | **CC**	22
1882 | Doyle's* | **Jamaica Plain**	15
1890 | Amrheins | **S Boston**	18
1890 | Atria* | **MV**	25
1890 | Fireplace* | **Brookline**	21
1890 | Rist. Lucia* | **Winchester**	21
1891 | North St. Grille* | **N End**	23
1891 | Smith/Wollensky* | **Back Bay**	23
1894 | Whitman House* | **CC**	21
1896 | Slip 14* | **Nan**	18
1897 | Cape Sea Grille* | **CC**	26
1898 | Novel* | **Back Bay**	-
1899 | Rani* | **Brookline**	20
1899 | Scollay Sq.* | **Beacon Hill**	19
1900 | Capt. Kidd* | **CC**	18
1900 | Cassis* | **Andover**	26
1900 | Chatham Squire* | **CC**	18
1900 | Chez Henri* | **Harv Sq**	24
1900 | Club Cafe* | **S End**	18
1900 | Elephant Walk* | **Waltham**	23
1900 | Front St.* | **CC**	27
1900 | Mr. Bartley's* | **Harv Sq**	24
1900 | Persephone* | **Seaport Dist**	25
1900 | Prose* | **Arlington**	24
1900 | Santarpio's Pizza* | **E Boston**	25
1900 | Topper's* | **Nan**	27
1901 | Morse Fish | **S End**	21
1902 | Gardner Museum* | **MFA**	20
1903 | Walden Grille* | **Concord**	15
1904 | Coriander Bistro* | **Sharon**	27
1905 | Davide Rist.* | **N End**	24
1906 | UpStairs on Sq.* | **Harv Sq**	24
1907 | Mother Anna's* | **N End**	21
1910 | Tosca* | **Hingham**	25
1912 | Chatham Bars Inn | **CC**	22
1912 | Court House | **E Cambridge**	22
1912 | Oak Room* | **Back Bay**	25
1914 | Mr. Crepe* | **Somerville**	18
1914 | Woodman's | **Essex**	23
1915 | Strega Rest.* | **Salem**	21
1917 | No Name | **Seaport Dist**	19
1919 | S&S | **Inman Sq**	18
1920 | Caliterra* | **Financial Dist**	16
1920 | Nauset Beach* | **CC**	25
1920 | o ya* | **Leather Dist**	28
1920 | Rubin's* | **Brookline**	19
1923 | J's Nashoba* | **Bolton**	26
1926 | Pizzeria Regina | **N End**	24
1926 | Pleasant Cafe* | **Roslindale**	18
1927 | Charlie's Sandwich | **S End**	23
1927 | Rattlesnake* | **Back Bay**	12
1928 | Union B&G* | **S End**	24
1930 | Centre St. Bistro* | **Nan**	16
1930 | Harvard Gardens | **Beacon Hill**	17
1931 | Cantina Italiana | **N End**	22
1931 | Home Port | **MV**	20
1933 | Forest Cafe | **Porter Sq**	20
1933 | Green St.* | **Central Sq**	24
1933 | Greg's | **Watertown**	19

1935	Clam Box*	**Ipswich**	26
1937	Paramount	**Beacon Hill**	23
1938	Frank's Steak	**Porter Sq**	18
1938	Gina's	**CC**	21
1940	Even Keel*	**Nan**	19
1941	Rosebud*	**Somerville**	16
1943	Art Cliff Diner*	**MV**	24
1946	Harry's	**Westborough**	20
1946	Landfall	**CC**	18
1946	Maddie's Sail	**Marblehead**	18
1947	Café at Taj	**Back Bay**	20
1947	Deluxe Town*	**Watertown**	22
1947	South St. Diner*	**Leather Dist**	16
1948	Cobie's Clam	**CC**	19
1948	Joe Tecce's	**N End**	19
1950	Ciro & Sal's	**CC**	20
1950	Fazio's*	**CC**	20
1950	Kowloon	**Saugus**	17
1952	Beach Plum	**MV**	25
1952	Liam's	**CC**	20
1953	La Cantina	**Framingham**	20
1955	Casablanca	**Harv Sq**	22
1955	Charlie's Kitchen	**Harv Sq**	17
1955	Vin & Eddie's	**Abington**	17
1957	Baxter's	**CC**	18

HOTEL DINING

Barley Neck Inn
  Barley Neck Inn | **CC** — 20
Beach Plum Inn
  Beach Plum | **MV** — 25
Beacon Hill Hotel
  Beacon Hill Bistro | **Beacon Hill** — 22
Belfry Inne
  Belfry Inne | **CC** — 25
Blue Dolphin Inn
  Laura & Tony's | **CC** — -
Boston Harbor Hotel
  ☑ Meritage | **Waterfront** — 27
Boston Marriott Burlington
  Summer Winter | **Burlington** — 24
Boston Marriott Long Wharf
  Oceana | **Waterfront** — 24
Bramble Inn
  ☑ Bramble Inn | **CC** — 27

Bulfinch Hotel
  Flat Iron | **W End** — 22
Charles Hotel
  Henrietta's | **Harv Sq** — 23
  ☑ Rialto | **Harv Sq** — 26
Chatham Bars Inn
  Chatham Bars Inn | **CC** — 22
Chatham Wayside Inn
  Wild Goose | **CC** — 21
Colonial Inn
  Merchants Row | **Concord** — -
Colonnade Hotel
  Brasserie Jo | **Back Bay** — 20
Commonwealth, Hotel
  ☑ Eastern Stand. | **Kenmore Sq** — 22
  Great Bay | **Kenmore Sq** — 23
Coonamessett Inn
  Coonamessett Inn | **CC** — 18
Crowne Pointe Historic Inn & Spa
  Bistro/Crowne Pointe | **CC** — 22
Dan'l Webster Inn
  Dan'l Webster | **CC** — 20
Eliot Hotel
  ☑ Clio/Uni | **Back Bay** — 27
Fairmont Battery Wharf
  NEW Sensing | **Waterfront** — -
Fairmont Copley Plaza
  ☑ Oak Room | **Back Bay** — 25
Four Seasons Hotel
  ☑ Aujourd'hui | **Back Bay** — 28
  ☑ Bristol | **Back Bay** — 24
Harbor View Hotel & Resort
  NEW Water St. | **MV** — -
Hilton Boston Financial Dist.
  Caliterra | **Financial Dist** — 16
Hyatt Regency Boston
  Avenue One | **D'town Cross** — 18
Indigo, Hotel
  NEW Bokx | **Newton Lower Falls** — 23
Inn at Blueberry Hill
  Theo's | **MV** — 24
InterContinental Boston
  Miel | **Waterfront** — 21

Jurys Boston Hotel
   Stanhope Grille | **Back Bay** 23

Kelley House
   Newes/America | **MV** 18

Kendall Hotel
   Black Sheep | **Kendall Sq** 21

Lambert's Cove Inn & Restaurant
   Lambert's Cove | **MV** 25

Langham Boston
   NEW Bond | **Financial Dist** -

Langham Hotel
   Café Fleuri | **Financial Dist** 22

Le Languedoc Inn
   Le Languedoc | **Nan** 26

Le Meridien Hotel
   Sidney's | **Central Sq** 21

Lenox Hotel
   Azure | **Back Bay** 22

Liberty Hotel
   Clink | **Beacon Hill** 19
   NEW Scampo | **Beacon Hill** 22

Longfellow's Wayside Inn
   Longfellow's | **Sudbury** 18

Mandarin Oriental
   NEW Asana | **Back Bay** -
   Z Sel de Terre | **Back Bay** 23

Mansion House
   Zephrus | **MV** 20

Marlowe, Hotel
   Bambara | **E Cambridge** 20

Nine Zero Hotel
   KO Prime | **D'town Cross** 24

Omni Parker House
   Parker's | **D'town Cross** 22

Orleans Inn
   Orleans Inn | **CC** 17

Outermost Inn
   Z Outermost Inn | **MV** 25

Outer Reach Resort
   Adrian's | **CC** 16

Park Plaza Hotel
   Bonfire | **Park Sq** 21
   McCormick/Schmick | **Park Sq** 21

Radisson Hotel Boston
   Rustic Kitchen | **Park Sq** 20

Red Inn
   Red Inn | **CC** 24

Renaissance Boston
   Waterfront Hotel
   NEW 606 Congress | 21
   Seaport Dist

Ritz-Carlton Boston Common
   Jer-Ne | **Theater Dist** 20

Royal Sonesta Hotel Boston
   dante | **E Cambridge** 24

Seaport Hotel
   Aura | **Seaport Dist** 22

Sherborn Inn, The
   Sherborn Inn | **Sherborn** 19

Ships Inn
   Ships Inn | **Nan** 24

Stonehedge Inn
   Left Bank | **Tyngsboro** 21

Summer House
   Summer House | **Nan** 20

Taj Boston
   Café at Taj | **Back Bay** 20

Wauwinet Inn
   Z Topper's | **Nan** 27

Wequassett Inn
   Z 28 Atlantic | **CC** 26

Westin Boston Waterfront Hotel
   M.J. O'Connor's | **Seaport Dist** -

Westin Copley Pl.
   Bar 10 | **Back Bay** 17
   Osushi | **Back Bay** 23
   Palm | **Back Bay** 23
   Turner Fish | **Back Bay** 21

White Elephant Hotel
   Brant Point | **Nan** 21

Winnetu Oceanside Resort
   Lure | **MV** 21

XV Beacon Hotel
   Mooo... | **Beacon Hill** 24

LATE DINING

(Weekday closing hour)

Anchovies | 1 AM | **S End** 20
Apollo Grill | 4 AM | **Chinatown** 17
Assaggio | 12 AM | **N End** 24
BarLola | 1 AM | **Back Bay** 18
Bar 10 | 12 AM | **Back Bay** 17

Billy Tse | 12 AM | **Revere**   20

Bluestone Bistro | 12:45 AM | 17
Brighton

Border Cafe | varies | **multi.**   19

Boston/Salem Beer | 12 AM | 18
multi.

Bricco | 2 AM | **N End**   25

NEW Brighton Beer | 1 AM | -
Brighton

Brownstone | 2 AM | **Back Bay**   15

Bukowski Tav. | varies | **multi.**   17

Café Belô | 1 AM | **Somerville**   20

Cafe Escadrille | 12 AM | 19
Burlington

Caffe Paradiso | varies | **N End**   17

Cambridge, 1. | 12 AM | **multi.**   22

Cambridge Common | varies | 17
Harv Sq

Charlie's Kitchen | varies | **Harv Sq**   17

Chau Chow | 3 AM | **Chinatown**   21

Church | 12 AM | **Fenway**   20

Coolidge Corner | 1:15 AM | 17
Brookline

Cornwall's | 12 AM | **Kenmore Sq**   15

Cottonwood | 12 AM | **Back Bay**   18

Deep Ellum | 12 AM | **Allston**   18

Flash's | 12 AM | **Park Sq**   18

Franklin | 1:30 AM | **S End**   26

Z FuGaKyu | 1:30 AM | **Brookline**   25

Gaslight Brasserie | 1:30 AM | 21
S End

Geoffrey's | 1 AM | **Roslindale**   19

Golden Temple | 1 AM | **Brookline**   21

Halfway Cafe | 12:30 AM | 17
Dedham

Harry's | 1 AM | **Westborough**   20

Haru | 12 AM | **Back Bay**   20

Harvard Gardens | 1 AM | 17
Beacon Hill

Imperial Seafood | 3 AM | 24
Chinatown

John Harvard's | 12 AM | **Harv Sq**   16

Jumbo | 1 AM | **Chinatown**   23

Kayuga | 1:30 AM | **Brookline**   24

Kaze | 12 AM | **Chinatown**   23

Kingston Station | 2 AM | 20
D'town Cross

Kowloon | 1 AM | **Saugus**   17

Little Q | 12 AM | **Quincy**   25

Living Room | 12 AM | **Waterfront**   15

Lucca | 12:15 AM | **N End**   25

Middle East | 12 AM | **Central Sq**   17

Miracle of Science | 12 AM | 19
Central Sq

Mission B&G | 12 AM | **MFA**   19

Z Oishii | 12 AM | **S End**   27

Other Side | 12 AM | **Back Bay**   19

Parish Cafe | 1 AM | **Back Bay**   22

Peach Farm | 3 AM | **Chinatown**   25

Pho République | 12:30 AM | **S End**   21

Post Office | 1 AM | **CC**   16

Punjabi Dhaba | 12 AM | **Inman Sq**   24

Rattlesnake | 12 AM | **Back Bay**   12

Red Fez | 12 AM | **S End**   18

Red Sky | 1 AM | **Faneuil Hall**   18

NEW Rist. Damiano | 12 AM | -
N End

Rist. Villa Francesca | 12:30 AM | 19
N End

Salvatore's | 12 AM | **Seaport Dist**   20

Santarpio's Pizza | 12 AM | 25
E Boston

Sasso | 1:30 AM | **Back Bay**   21

Sharky's | 12:30 AM | **MV**   21

South St. Diner | varies | 16
Leather Dist

Stella | 1:30 AM | **S End**   24

Suishaya | 2 AM | **Chinatown**   21

Sunset Grill/Cantina | 1 AM | 20
multi.

Taiwan Cafe | 1 AM | **Chinatown**   23

Z Tangierino | 12 AM | 24
Charlestown

Temple Bar | 12 AM | **Porter Sq**   20

Z Top of Hub | 1 AM | **Back Bay**   20

NEW Townsend's | 12 AM | 19
Hyde Park

NEW Trata Pizza | 1 AM | **Harv Sq**   -

Trident | 11:30 PM | **Back Bay**   19

Via Matta | 1 AM | **Park Sq**   25

Vlora | 1 AM | **Back Bay**   22

MEET FOR A DRINK

Z Abe & Louie's | **Back Bay**   26

Alchemist | **Jamaica Plain**   17

Alchemy | **MV**   22

Aqua Grille | CC	19
NEW Asana | Back Bay	-
NEW Atlantic | MV	-
Audubon Circle | Kenmore Sq	21
Balance | MV	23
Bambara | E Cambridge	20
Z Banq | S End	21
Bar 10 | Back Bay	17
Baxter's | CC	18
Beacon St. Tavern | Brookline	20
Beehive | S End	18
NEW Bina Osteria | D'town Cross	-
Bin 26 | Beacon Hill	21
Black Cow | multi.	19
Blue22 | Quincy	19
Boarding Hse. | Nan	21
NEW Bokx | Newton Lower Falls	23
NEW Bond | Financial Dist	-
Bonfire | Park Sq	21
Bouchée | Back Bay	21
Bricco | N End	25
Z Bristol | Back Bay	24
Burren | Somerville	14
Butcher Shop | S End	25
Cactus Club | Back Bay	16
Cambridge, 1. | multi.	22
Casablanca | Harv Sq	22
Chez Henri | Harv Sq	24
Church | Fenway	20
Clink | Beacon Hill	19
Club Cafe | S End	18
Club Car | Nan	20
NEW Comfort | Watertown	-
Cottage | Wellesley	19
Cottonwood | Back Bay	18
Daedalus | Harv Sq	17
dante | E Cambridge	24
Z Davio's | multi.	25
Delux Cafe | S End	21
Dillon's | Back Bay	16
District | Leather Dist	17
NEW DJ's/Garden | W End	-
Dog Bar | Gloucester	23
Doyle's | Jamaica Plain	15
NEW Drink | Seaport Dist	-
Z Eastern Stand. | Kenmore Sq	22

NEW Ecco | E Boston	-
NEW Erbaluce | Park Sq	-
NEW Estragon | S End	-
Firefly's | Quincy	20
Flash's | Park Sq	18
Franklin | multi.	26
Gaslight Brasserie | S End	21
Glenn's | Newburyport	23
Good Life | D'town Cross	17
Grafton St. Pub | Harv Sq	17
Great Bay | Kenmore Sq	23
Z Grill 23 | Back Bay	25
Harvard Gardens | Beacon Hill	17
Heather | CC	-
Highland Kitchen | Somerville	23
NEW High St. Grill | North Andover	-
Houston's | Faneuil Hall	22
Z NEW Hungry Mother | Kendall Sq	27
Independent | Somerville	18
James's Gate | Jamaica Plain	16
John Harvard's | multi.	16
Johnnie's on Side | W End	17
Joshua Tree | multi.	15
Kingston Station | D'town Cross	20
NEW Lavender Asian | Sudbury	-
La Voile | Back Bay	23
Les Zygomates | Leather Dist	22
NEW Littlest | Financial Dist	-
Living Room | Waterfront	15
NEW Local, The | W Newton	-
Lo La 41° | Nan	21
LTK | Seaport Dist	20
Lucky's Lounge | Seaport Dist	18
Mantra | D'town Cross	18
NEW Market | Financial Dist	16
NEW Marliave | D'town Cross	22
Masa | multi.	23
Matt Murphy's | Brookline	22
NEW Max/Dylan | multi.	-
McCormick/Schmick | multi.	21
Met B&G | Natick	21
Metropolitan | Chestnut Hill	21
Miracle of Science | Central Sq	19
Mission B&G | MFA	19

Z Mistral	**S End**	27
M.J. O'Connor's	**multi.**	–
Z Morton's	**Seaport Dist**	25
Nebo	**N End**	21
Z No. 9 Park	**Beacon Hill**	28
Oceanaire	**Financial Dist**	24
NEW Olivadi	**Norwood**	–
OM Rest.	**Harv Sq**	19
Orleans	**Somerville**	17
NEW Orta	**Hanover**	–
Parish Cafe	**Back Bay**	22
Persephone	**Seaport Dist**	25
Publick House	**Brookline**	21
Rattlesnake	**Back Bay**	12
Red Fez	**S End**	18
Redline	**Harv Sq**	17
Roadhouse Craft Beer & BBQ	**Brookline**	–
Rocca	**S End**	24
RooBar	**CC**	21
Ross' Grill	**CC**	22
NEW Rudi's	**Roxbury**	–
Z Ruth's Chris	**D'town Cross**	24
Sanctuary	**Financial Dist**	19
NEW Scampo	**Beacon Hill**	22
Scollay Sq.	**Beacon Hill**	19
Z Sel de Terre	**multi.**	23
NEW Sensing	**Waterfront**	–
Silvertone B&G	**D'town Cross**	21
NEW 606 Congress	**Seaport Dist**	21
Solea	**Waltham**	23
Sonsie	**Back Bay**	20
Z Sorellina	**Back Bay**	27
Stella	**S End**	24
Stephanie's	**Back Bay**	20
STIX	**Back Bay**	17
Straight Wharf	**Nan**	25
Sunset Grill/Cantina	**Boston U**	20
Tavern in Sq.	**multi.**	17
Tavern on Water	**Charlestown**	13
NEW Tavolo	**Dorchester**	–
Temple Bar	**Porter Sq**	20
33 Rest.	**Back Bay**	20
Z Top of Hub	**Back Bay**	20
NEW Townsend's	**Hyde Park**	19
Z Troquet	**Theater Dist**	27

28 Degrees	**S End**	20
21st Amendment	**Beacon Hill**	17
Z 21 Federal	**Nan**	24
Union B&G	**S End**	24
Via Matta	**Park Sq**	25
Vinalia	**D'town Cross**	17
Vlora	**Back Bay**	22
Vox Populi	**Back Bay**	16
Washington Sq.	**Brookline**	22
NEW Water St.	**MV**	–
West on Centre	**W Roxbury**	18
West Side Lounge	**Porter Sq**	22
Wild Goose	**CC**	21

NOTEWORTHY NEWCOMERS

Asana	**Back Bay**	–
Atlantic	**MV**	–
Bina Osteria	**D'town Cross**	–
Blackfish	**CC**	24
Bokx	**Newton Lower Falls**	23
Bond	**Financial Dist**	–
Brighton Beer	**Brighton**	–
Comfort	**Watertown**	–
Daily Grill	**Back Bay**	19
DJ's/Garden	**W End**	–
Drink	**Seaport Dist**	–
Ecco	**E Boston**	–
Erbaluce	**Park Sq**	–
Estragon	**S End**	–
Franky/Boys	**Brookline**	–
G Bar	**Swampscott**	21
Ghazal	**Jamaica Plain**	–
Grand Chinatown	**N Quincy**	–
Heather	**CC**	–
High St. Grill	**North Andover**	–
Z Hungry Mother	**Kendall Sq**	27
Jerusalem Pita	**Brookline**	–
Jury Room	**Quincy**	19
Lavender Asian	**Sudbury**	–
Littlest	**Financial Dist**	–
Local, The	**W Newton**	–
Market	**Financial Dist**	16
Marliave	**D'town Cross**	22
Max/Dylan	**multi.**	–
Melting Pot	**Park Sq**	20

Olivadi | **Norwood**	-_
Orta | **Hanover**	-_
Pho n' Rice | **Somerville**	-_
Rist. Damiano | **N End**	-_
Rodizio | **Somerville**	22
Rudi's | **Roxbury**	-_
Salt Water | **MV**	-_
Scampo | **Beacon Hill**	22
Sensing | **Waterfront**	-_
Sidecar Café | **MV**	-_
606 Congress | **Seaport Dist**	21
Sofra Bakery | **Huron Vill**	26
Sportello | **Seaport Dist**	-_
Tavolo | **Dorchester**	-_
Thaitation | **Fenway**	-_
Townsend's | **Hyde Park**	19
Trata Pizza | **Harv Sq**	-_
Vintage | **W Roxbury**	-_
Waterside Mkt. | **MV**	-_
Water St. | **MV**	-_
Wheeler's | **Back Bay**	-_

OFFBEAT

Alice's | **Nan**	18
All Star | **Inman Sq**	23
Baraka Cafe | **Central Sq**	26
Barking Crab | **Seaport Dist**	16
Betty's Wok | **MFA**	19
b. good | **Back Bay**	19
Bukowski Tav. | **multi.**	17
Butcher Shop | **S End**	25
Café Polonia | **S Boston**	24
Centre St. Café | **Jamaica Plain**	25
☑ Cuchi Cuchi | **Central Sq**	22
Dalí | **Somerville**	25
☑ Galleria Umberto | **N End**	26
Green St. | **Central Sq**	24
☑ Helmand | **E Cambridge**	26
Karoo Kafe | **CC**	24
LTK | **Seaport Dist**	20
Masala Art | **Needham**	23
Merengue | **Roxbury**	-_
Novel | **Back Bay**	-_
Paramount | **Beacon Hill**	23
Pho République | **S End**	21
Prose | **Arlington**	24
Publick House | **Brookline**	21

Punjabi Dhaba | **Inman Sq**	24
Redbones BBQ | **Somerville**	22
Rest. Cesaria | **Dorchester**	-_
Santarpio's Pizza | **E Boston**	25
Shabu-Zen | **Chinatown**	22
NEW Sidecar Café | **MV**	-_
Stone Soup | **Ipswich**	25
Strip-T's | **Watertown**	22
Trident | **Back Bay**	19
Uncle Pete's Ribs | **Revere**	25
Vinny's at Night | **Somerville**	23
Wine Cellar | **Back Bay**	20

OUTDOOR DINING

(G=garden; P=patio; S=sidewalk; T=terrace)

☑ Abe & Louie's | S | **Back Bay**	26
Academy Ocean | P | **CC**	22
Adrian's | T | **CC**	16
Alberto's | S | **CC**	20
Ashmont Grill | P | **Dorchester**	22
Atasca | P | **Kendall Sq**	23
Atlantica | P | **Cohasset**	15
Atlantic Fish | S | **Back Bay**	23
Atria | P | **MV**	25
Audubon Circle | P | **Kenmore Sq**	21
Back Eddy | P, T | **Westport**	22
☑ B&G Oysters | G | **S End**	26
Bangkok Blue | P | **Back Bay**	21
Barking Crab | T | **Seaport Dist**	16
BarLola | P | **Back Bay**	18
Baxter's | T | **CC**	18
Beacon St. Tavern | P | **Brookline**	20
Birch St. Bistro | P | **Roslindale**	19
Black Cow | T | **Newburyport**	19
Blarney Stone | P | **Dorchester**	16
Bluestone Bistro | P | **Brighton**	17
Boarding Hse. | P | **Nan**	21
Bookstore & Rest. | P, T | **CC**	19
Bottega | P | **Back Bay**	24
Bouchée | P | **Back Bay**	21
Brant Point | T | **Nan**	21
Bravo | T | **MFA**	21
Brotherhood/Thieves | P | **Nan**	18
Bubala's | P | **CC**	16
Bullfinch's | P | **Sudbury**	21
Cactus Club | S | **Back Bay**	16

Cafeteria | P | **Back Bay**	17
Caffe Tosca | P | **Hingham**	24
Canestaro | S | **Fenway**	19
Capt. Frosty's | P | **CC**	21
Capt. Linnell | P | **CC**	22
Casa Romero | P | **Back Bay**	23
Charley's | G | **multi.**	18
Charlie's Kitchen | P | **Harv Sq**	17
Ciao Bella | P, S | **Back Bay**	19
Cinco | P | **Nan**	26
Cioppino's | P | **Nan**	19
Circadia Bistro | P | **CC**	23
☑ Clam Box | T | **Ipswich**	26
Clancy's | T | **CC**	22
Columbus Café | P | **S End**	19
Cooke's | P | **CC**	-
Cottonwood | P | **Back Bay**	18
Daily Catch | P | **Seaport Dist**	24
dante | P | **E Cambridge**	24
☑ Détente | G | **MV**	27
Devlin's | P | **Brighton**	20
Dillon's | P | **Back Bay**	16
Dog Bar | P | **Gloucester**	23
Dunbar Tea | P | **CC**	22
☑ Eastern Stand. | P | **Kenmore Sq**	22
Enzo | P, T | **CC**	24
Even Keel | P | **Nan**	19
Fifty-Six Union | G | **Nan**	22
Finz | T | **Salem**	20
Firefly Woodfire | S | **CC**	20
Fog Island | P | **Nan**	21
☑ Galley Beach | P | **Nan**	24
Gardner Museum | G | **MFA**	20
Grafton St. Pub | P | **Harv Sq**	17
Grapevine | G | **Salem**	25
Green Briar | P | **Brighton**	17
☑ Hamersley's Bistro | P | **S End**	27
Harvest | P | **Harv Sq**	25
Heather | P | **CC**	-
Henrietta's | T | **Harv Sq**	23
Hi-Rise | P | **Harv Sq**	24
Hungry i | G | **Beacon Hill**	24
James's Gate | P | **Jamaica Plain**	16
☑ J's Nashoba | P | **Bolton**	26
Karoo Kafe | T | **CC**	24
KingFish Hall | P | **Faneuil Hall**	22
La Casa/Pedro | P | **Watertown**	21
La Cucina/Mare | P | **CC**	25
Landing | **multi.**	16
Lattanzi's | G, P | **MV**	21
La Voile | P | **Back Bay**	23
Le Languedoc | P | **Nan**	26
L'Étoile | P | **MV**	26
Lo La 41° | P | **Nan**	21
Lure | **MV**	21
Mac's | S | **CC**	24
McCormick/Schmick | P | **Faneuil Hall**	21
Miel | G, P | **Waterfront**	21
Mother Anna's | P | **N End**	21
Neighborhood Rest. | G | **Somerville**	23
☑ Oleana | P | **Inman Sq**	28
Orinoco | S | **S End**	25
Orleans Inn | T | **CC**	17
Other Side | P, S | **Back Bay**	19
Parish Cafe | P | **Back Bay**	22
Piattini | P | **Back Bay**	23
Porcini's | P | **Watertown**	22
Rattlesnake | T | **Back Bay**	12
Red Fez | P | **S End**	18
Red House | P | **Harv Sq**	20
Red Rock Bistro | G, P | **Swampscott**	20
Rist. Fiore | P, T | **N End**	21
Riva | P | **Scituate**	26
RooBar | P | **CC**	21
Ropewalk | P | **Nan**	-
Rustic Kitchen | P | **Hingham**	20
☑ Ruth's Chris | P | **D'town Cross**	24
Salvatore's | P | **Seaport Dist**	20
NEW Scampo | P | **Beacon Hill**	22
Scollay Sq. | P | **Beacon Hill**	19
Scoozi | P | **Back Bay**	18
Sibling Rivalry | P | **S End**	24
NEW Sidecar Café | P, S | **MV**	-
Siena | P | **CC**	21
Siros | T | **N Quincy**	19
Sol Azteca | P | **multi.**	20
Sophia's | P | **Roslindale**	23
South End Buttery | P | **S End**	21
Stanhope Grille | P | **Back Bay**	23

Stella | P | **S End**	24
Stellína | G | **Watertown**	22
Stephanie's | S | **Back Bay**	20
Straight Wharf | P | **Nan**	25
Summer House | **Nan**	20
Sweet Life | G | **MV**	25
Tantric | S | **Theater Dist**	20
Tapéo | S | **Back Bay**	22
Tavern on Water | P | **Charlestown**	13
Temple Bar | P | **Porter Sq**	20
Z Topper's | T | **Nan**	27
Tratt. Il Panino | P | **N End**	23
Tremont 647 | P | **S End**	21
Trevi Café | P | **CC**	-
28 Degrees | P | **S End**	20
29 Newbury | P | **Back Bay**	20
Z 21 Federal | P | **Nan**	24
224 Boston St. | G | **Dorchester**	22
vela | P | **Wellesley**	21
Via Matta | P | **Park Sq**	25
Village Sushi | P | **Roslindale**	23
Vox Populi | S | **Back Bay**	16
Winslow's Tavern | P | **CC**	20
Wonder Spice | P | **Jamaica Plain**	21
Woodman's | G | **Essex**	23
Zen | P | **Beacon Hill**	24

PARKING

(V=valet, *=validated)

Z Abe & Louie's | V* | **Back Bay**	26
Al Dente* | **N End**	22
Amarin Thailand* | **Newton**	22
Antico Forno* | **N End**	23
Z Aquitaine | V | **S End**	23
NEW Asana | V | **Back Bay**	-
Atlantica | V | **Cohasset**	15
Atlantic Fish | V | **Back Bay**	23
Z Aujourd'hui | V* | **Back Bay**	28
Aura* | **Seaport Dist**	22
Avenue One | V | **D'town Cross**	18
Avila* | V* | **Theater Dist**	24
Azure | V | **Back Bay**	22
Bacco* | **N End**	21
Bambara | V | **E Cambridge**	20
Z B&G Oysters | V | **S End**	26
Z Banq | V | **S End**	21
Bar 10 | V | **Back Bay**	17

Beehive | V | **S End**	18
Bertucci's | V* | **multi.**	17
Billy Tse | V | **Revere**	20
Bin 26 | V | **Beacon Hill**	21
blu* | **Theater Dist**	21
Blue Room* | **Kendall Sq**	25
NEW Bokx | V |	23
Newton Lower Falls	
Bombay Club | V | **Harv Sq**	20
NEW Bond | V | **Financial Dist**	-
Bonfire | V | **Park Sq**	21
Bouchée | V* | **Back Bay**	21
Brasserie Jo | V | **Back Bay**	20
Bravo* | **MFA**	21
Bricco | V | **N End**	25
Z Bristol | V* | **Back Bay**	24
Butcher Shop | V | **S End**	25
Café Fleuri | V | **Financial Dist**	22
Cafeteria | V | **Back Bay**	17
Caffe Paradiso* | **N End**	17
Caliterra | V | **Financial Dist**	16
Cantina Italiana* | **N End**	22
Z Capital Grille | V | **multi.**	26
Casablanca* | **Harv Sq**	22
Chart House | V | **Waterfront**	21
Chart Room | V | **CC**	20
Chatham Bars Inn | V | **CC**	22
Chau Chow* | **Chinatown**	21
Cheers* | **Faneuil Hall**	14
Z Cheesecake | V* | **multi.**	18
Ciao Bella | V | **Back Bay**	19
Clink | V | **Beacon Hill**	19
Z Clio/Uni | V* | **Back Bay**	27
Club Cafe | V | **S End**	18
Coonamessett Inn | V | **CC**	18
Cottonwood* | **Back Bay**	18
Z Cuchi Cuchi | V | **Central Sq**	22
dante | V | **E Cambridge**	24
Davide Rist. | V | **N End**	24
Da Vinci | V | **Park Sq**	22
Z Davio's | V* | **Park Sq**	25
District | V | **Leather Dist**	17
Donatello | V | **Saugus**	24
Douzo* | **Back Bay**	24
Durgin-Park* | **Faneuil Hall**	17
Z Eastern Stand. | V | **Kenmore Sq**	22

East Ocean* | **Chinatown**	24
☑ Elephant Walk | V | **Fenway**	23
Exchange St. Bistro* | **Malden**	20
Figs | V | **Charlestown**	23
Fire & Ice* | **Harv Sq**	16
Fishmonger's* | **CC**	18
Fleming's Prime | V* | **Park Sq**	24
☑ FuGaKyu | V | **Brookline**	25
☑ Giacomo's | V | **S End**	25
Golden Temple | V | **Brookline**	21
Grafton St. Pub | V | **Harv Sq**	17
Great Bay | V | **Kenmore Sq**	23
☑ Grill 23 | V | **Back Bay**	25
☑ Hamersley's Bistro | V | **S End**	27
Haru* | **Back Bay**	20
Harvest | V* | **Harv Sq**	25
Henrietta's | V* | **Harv Sq**	23
House of Siam | V | **S End**	24
Houston's* | **Faneuil Hall**	22
Hungry i | V | **Beacon Hill**	24
☑ NEW Hungry Mother* | **Kendall Sq**	27
☑ Icarus | V | **S End**	25
Incontro | V | **Franklin**	22
Ivy Rest. | V | **D'town Cross**	20
Jacob Wirth* | **Theater Dist**	17
Jae's | V | **S End**	20
Jasper White's* | **Back Bay**	21
Jer-Ne | V | **Theater Dist**	20
Joe's American | V | **multi.**	16
Joe Tecce's | V | **N End**	19
John Harvard's* | **Harv Sq**	16
Johnnie's on Side | V | **W End**	17
Joshua Tree | V | **Allston**	15
Jumbo* | **Chinatown**	23
Kashmir | V | **Back Bay**	23
KingFish Hall* | **Faneuil Hall**	22
KO Prime | V | **D'town Cross**	24
La Fam. Giorgio* | **N End**	23
Lala Rokh | V | **Beacon Hill**	23
La Morra | V | **Brookline**	24
L'Andana | V | **Burlington**	25
La Voile | V | **Back Bay**	23
Left Bank | V | **Tyngsboro**	21
☑ Legal Sea | V* | **multi.**	22
Le's | V | **Chestnut Hill**	21

☑ L'Espalier | V | **Back Bay**	28
Les Zygomates | V | **Leather Dist**	22
LiNEaGe* | **Brookline**	23
Living Room | V* | **Waterfront**	15
Locke-Ober | V | **D'town Cross**	24
L'Osteria* | **N End**	23
Lucca | V | **N End**	25
Maggiano's | V | **Park Sq**	19
Mamma Maria | V | **N End**	25
Mantra | V | **D'town Cross**	18
Marco Romana* | **N End**	26
Mare* | **N End**	26
Marshside | V | **CC**	15
Masa | V | **S End**	23
Ma Soba* | **Beacon Hill**	20
Maurizio's | V* | **N End**	25
McCormick/Schmick | V | **Park Sq**	21
NEW Melting Pot | V | **Park Sq**	20
☑ Meritage | V* | **Waterfront**	27
Metropolis Cafe | V | **S End**	23
Metropolitan | V | **Chestnut Hill**	21
Midwest | V | **Inman Sq**	20
Miel | V | **Waterfront**	21
☑ Mistral | V | **S End**	27
Mooo... | V | **Beacon Hill**	24
☑ Morton's | V | **multi.**	25
Mother Anna's* | **N End**	21
9 Tastes* | **Harv Sq**	20
☑ No. 9 Park | V | **Beacon Hill**	28
☑ Oak Room | V | **Back Bay**	25
Oceana | V* | **Waterfront**	24
Oceanaire | V | **Financial Dist**	24
Ocean House | V | **CC**	25
☑ Oishii | V | **S End**	27
☑ Olives | V | **Charlestown**	25
OM Rest. | V | **Harv Sq**	19
Osushi | V | **Back Bay**	23
Paddock | V | **CC**	20
Palm | V* | **Back Bay**	23
Papa Razzi | V | **Back Bay**	18
Parker's | V* | **D'town Cross**	22
Peach Farm* | **Chinatown**	25
Penang* | **Chinatown**	22
Persephone | V | **Seaport Dist**	25
☑ Petit Robert | V | **S End**	24

P.F. Chang's | V | **Theater Dist** 19
Pho République | V | **S End** 21
Pigalle | V* | **Theater Dist** 26
Z Pisces | V | **CC** 27
Plaza III* | **Faneuil Hall** 21
Z Prezza | V | **N End** 27
Z Radius | V | **Financial Dist** 26
Red House* | **Harv Sq** 20
Z Red Pheasant | V | **CC** 27
Rendezvous | V | **Central Sq** 26
Z Rialto | V* | **Harv Sq** 26
Rist. Fiore | V | **N End** 21
Rist. Lucia | V | **N End** 21
Rist. Toscano | V | **Beacon Hill** 24
Rist. Villa Francesca | V | **N End** 19
Roadhouse | V | **CC** 20
Rustic Kitchen | V | **Park Sq** 20
Z Ruth's Chris | V | **D'town Cross** 24
Sage | V | **S End** 24
Salvatore's* | **Seaport Dist** 20
Sandrine's* | **Harv Sq** 24
Saraceno* | **N End** 23
Sasso | V | **Back Bay** 21
NEW Scampo | V | **Beacon Hill** 22
Scarlet Oak | V | **Hingham** 20
Z Sel de Terre | V | **multi.** 23
NEW Sensing | V | **Waterfront** –
75 Chestnut | V | **Beacon Hill** 21
Shabu-Zen* | **Chinatown** 22
Sibling Rivalry | V | **S End** 24
Sidney's | V | **Central Sq** 21
NEW 606 Congress | V | **Seaport Dist** 21
Skipjack's* | **Back Bay** 20
Sky | V | **Norwood** 19
Smith/Wollensky | V | **Back Bay** 23
Sonsie | V | **Back Bay** 20
Z Sorellina | V | **Back Bay** 27
Sorriso | V | **Leather Dist** 20
Stanhope Grille | V | **Back Bay** 23
Stella | V | **S End** 24
Stephanie's | V | **Back Bay** 20
STIX | V | **Back Bay** 17
Strega Rist. | V | **N End** 21
Sunset Grill/Cantina* | **Boston U** 20
Z Tangierino | V | **Charlestown** 24

Tanjore* | **Harv Sq** 22
Z Taranta* | **N End** 27
Tasca | V | **Brighton** 23
Tavern in Sq.* | **Porter Sq** 17
Teatro | V | **Theater Dist** 24
Terramia* | **N End** 26
33 Rest. | V | **Back Bay** 20
Z Top of Hub* | **Back Bay** 20
Z Toro | V | **S End** 26
NEW Townsend's | V | **Hyde Park** 19
Z Tratt. di Monica/Vinoteca | V* | **N End** 26
Tremont 647 | V | **S End** 21
Tresca | V | **N End** 23
Z Troquet | V | **Theater Dist** 27
Turner Fish | V | **Back Bay** 21
28 Degrees | V | **S End** 20
Umbria | V | **Financial Dist** 23
Union B&G | V | **S End** 24
Z Union Oyster | V* | **Faneuil Hall** 20
Z UpStairs on Sq. | V* | **Harv Sq** 24
Via Matta | V | **Park Sq** 25
Vlora | V | **Back Bay** 22
Vox Populi | V | **Back Bay** 16
Wine Cellar | V | **Back Bay** 20
Zócalo Cocina | V | **Brighton** 22

PEOPLE-WATCHING

NEW Asana | **Back Bay** –
NEW Atlantic | **MV** –
Balance | **MV** 23
Z Banq | **S End** 21
Beehive | **S End** 18
NEW Bina Osteria | **D'town Cross** –
blu | **Theater Dist** 21
Boarding Hse. | **Nan** 21
Bouchée | **Back Bay** 21
Bricco | **N End** 25
Butcher Shop | **S End** 25
Cafe Edwige/at Night | **CC** 26
Cafeteria | **Back Bay** 17
Caffe Paradiso | **N End** 17
Charley's | **multi.** 18
Ciao Bella | **Back Bay** 19
Z Clio/Uni | **Back Bay** 27
Club Cafe | **S End** 18

Cobie's Clam | **CC** — 19

Cottonwood | **Back Bay** — 18

Ⓩ Cuchi Cuchi | **Central Sq** — 22

dante | **E Cambridge** — 24

Ⓩ Davio's | **multi.** — 25

🆕 Drink | **Seaport Dist** — –

Ⓩ Eastern Stand. | **Kenmore Sq** — 22

Florentine Cafe | **N End** — 21

Franklin | **S End** — 26

Gaslight Brasserie | **S End** — 21

Great Bay | **Kenmore Sq** — 23

Ⓩ Grill 23 | **Back Bay** — 25

Highland Kitchen | **Somerville** — 23

Jetties | **Nan** — 14

Johnnie's on Side | **W End** — 17

🆕 Jury Room | **Quincy** — 19

KingFish Hall | **Faneuil Hall** — 22

Laureen's | **CC** — 23

Living Room | **Waterfront** — 15

Lo La 41° | **Nan** — 21

LTK | **Seaport Dist** — 20

Mantra | **D'town Cross** — 18

Masa | **Woburn** — 23

🆕 Max/Dylan | **Charlestown** — –

Ⓩ Mistral | **S End** — 27

Ⓩ No. 9 Park | **Beacon Hill** — 28

Parish Cafe | **Back Bay** — 22

Pearl | **Nan** — 24

Persephone | **Seaport Dist** — 25

Piattini | **Back Bay** — 23

Ⓩ Radius | **Financial Dist** — 26

Rattlesnake | **Back Bay** — 12

Roadhouse Craft Beer & BBQ | **Brookline** — –

🆕 Rodizio | **Somerville** — 22

RooBar | **CC** — 21

Ropewalk | **Nan** — –

🆕 Scampo | **Beacon Hill** — 22

Scollay Sq. | **Beacon Hill** — 19

Sibling Rivalry | **S End** — 24

🆕 Sidecar Café | **MV** — –

Sonsie | **Back Bay** — 20

Ⓩ Sorellina | **Back Bay** — 27

🆕 Sportello | **Seaport Dist** — –

Stephanie's | **Back Bay** — 20

Teatro | **Theater Dist** — 24

Temple Bar | **Porter Sq** — 20

Tremont 647 | **S End** — 21

Trident | **Back Bay** — 19

28 Degrees | **S End** — 20

29 Newbury | **Back Bay** — 20

Ⓩ 21 Federal | **Nan** — 24

Via Matta | **Park Sq** — 25

Vox Populi | **Back Bay** — 16

🆕 Water St. | **MV** — –

PRIVATE ROOMS

(Restaurants charge less at off times; call for capacity)

Belfry Inne | **CC** — 25

Bonfire | **Park Sq** — 21

Brotherhood/Thieves | **Nan** — 18

Ⓩ Capital Grille | **multi.** — 26

Capt. Linnell | **CC** — 22

Chanticleer | **Nan** — 25

Chatham Bars Inn | **CC** — 22

Chau Chow | **Chinatown** — 21

China Pearl | **Chinatown** — 21

Coonamessett Inn | **CC** — 18

Dan'l Webster | **CC** — 20

Ⓩ East Coast | **Inman Sq** — 25

Ⓩ Eastern Stand. | **Kenmore Sq** — 22

Ⓩ Elephant Walk | **multi.** — 23

Filippo | **N End** — 21

Fleming's Prime | **Park Sq** — 24

Ⓩ FuGaKyu | **Brookline** — 25

Golden Temple | **Brookline** — 21

Ⓩ Grill 23 | **Back Bay** — 25

Harvest | **Harv Sq** — 25

Heather | **CC** — –

Hungry i | **Beacon Hill** — 24

Ⓩ Icarus | **S End** — 25

Ⓩ Il Capriccio | **Waltham** — 27

Ivy Rest. | **D'town Cross** — 20

Kashmir | **Back Bay** — 23

Kowloon | **Saugus** — 17

Lala Rokh | **Beacon Hill** — 23

Ⓩ Legal Sea | **multi.** — 22

Ⓩ L'Espalier | **Back Bay** — 28

Locke-Ober | **D'town Cross** — 24

Lure | **MV** — 21

Mamma Maria | **N End** — 25

Mantra | **D'town Cross** — 18

McCormick/Schmick | multi.   21

Metropolitan | Chestnut Hill   21

☑ Mistral | S End   27

☑ Morton's | Back Bay   25

Òran Mór | Nan   24

Pearl | Nan   24

☑ Radius | Financial Dist   26

Regatta of Cotuit | CC   25

Saraceno | N End   23

Sibling Rivalry | S End   24

Smith/Wollensky | Back Bay   23

Stella | S End   24

☑ Tangierino | Charlestown   24

☑ Taranta | N End   27

☑ Topper's | Nan   27

Tremont 647 | S End   21

Turner Fish | Back Bay   21

☑ UpStairs on Sq. | Harv Sq   24

Vinalia | D'town Cross   17

Whitman House | CC   21

RAW BARS

Arnold's Lobster | CC   23

NEW Atlantic | MV   -

Back Eddy | Westport   22

☑ B&G Oysters | S End   26

Barley Neck Inn | CC   20

Bookstore & Rest. | CC   19

☑ East Coast | Inman Sq   25

☑ Eastern Stand. | Kenmore Sq   22

Finz | multi.   20

Five Bays Bistro | CC   25

Great Bay | Kenmore Sq   23

Jasper White's | multi.   21

Jetties | Nan   14

KingFish Hall | Faneuil Hall   22

Larsen's Fish | MV   27

☑ Legal Sea | multi.   22

Lobster Pot | CC   22

Locke-Ober | D'town Cross   24

Mac's | CC   24

McCormick/Schmick | multi.   21

Moby Dick's | CC   23

Naked Oyster | CC   25

☑ Neptune Oyster | N End   27

Oceanaire | Financial Dist   24

Orleans Inn | CC   17

Oyster Co. | CC   23

Port | CC   23

Red Inn | CC   24

Ropewalk | Nan   -

Skipjack's | multi.   20

Summer Winter | Burlington   24

28 Degrees | S End   20

☑ Union Oyster | Faneuil Hall   20

Village Fish | Needham   20

Woodman's | Essex   23

ROMANTIC PLACES

Alberto's | CC   20

Amari | CC   22

☑ Aquitaine | S End   23

Ariadne | Newton   21

NEW Asana | Back Bay   -

Assaggio | N End   24

Atasca | Kendall Sq   23

Atria | MV   25

☑ Aujourd'hui | Back Bay   28

☑ Banq | S End   21

Barker Tavern | Scituate   23

Barley Neck Inn | CC   20

BarLola | Back Bay   18

Beach Plum | MV   25

Belfry Inne | CC   25

Bin 26 | Beacon Hill   21

Bistro/Crowne Pointe | CC   22

☑ Bistro 5 | W Medford   27

Boarding Hse. | Nan   21

Bon Savor | Jamaica Plain   20

☑ Bristol | Back Bay   24

Buca's Tuscan | CC   23

Cape Sea Grille | CC   26

Capt. Linnell | CC   22

☑ Carmen | N End   26

Casa Romero | Back Bay   23

Casino Wharf | CC   20

Cassis | Andover   26

☑ Catch | Winchester   27

Chanticleer | Nan   25

Chez Henri | Harv Sq   24

☑ Chillingsworth | CC   27

Cinco | Nan   26

Circadia Bistro | CC   23

Z Clio/Uni | **Back Bay**	27
NEW Comfort | **Watertown**	-
Z Company/Cauldron | **Nan**	28
Z Craigie on Main | **Central Sq**	27
Z Cuchi Cuchi | **Central Sq**	22
Dalia's Bistro | **Brookline**	19
Dalí | **Somerville**	25
Dalya's | **Bedford**	23
Da Vinci | **Park Sq**	22
Z Détente | **MV**	27
NEW Erbaluce | **Park Sq**	-
NEW Estragon | **S End**	-
Euno | **N End**	24
Fava | **Needham**	25
Finale | **multi.**	23
Five North Sq. | **N End**	22
Fleming's Prime | **Park Sq**	24
Z Front St. | **CC**	27
Z Galley Beach | **Nan**	24
NEW G Bar | **Swampscott**	21
NEW Ghazal | **Jamaica Plain**	-
Glory | **Andover**	21
Gracie's Table | **CC**	23
Grain & Salt | **Allston**	-
Grapevine | **Salem**	25
Grezzo | **N End**	23
Grotto | **Beacon Hill**	25
Haveli | **Inman Sq**	-
Heather | **CC**	-
Z Helmand | **E Cambridge**	26
Hungry i | **Beacon Hill**	24
Z Icarus | **S End**	25
Z Il Capriccio | **Waltham**	27
Z J's Nashoba | **Bolton**	26
Z La Campania | **Waltham**	28
Lala Rokh | **Beacon Hill**	23
Lambert's Cove | **MV**	25
L'Andana | **Burlington**	25
La Voile | **Back Bay**	23
Left Bank | **Tyngsboro**	21
Le Languedoc | **Nan**	26
Z L'Espalier | **Back Bay**	28
L'Étoile | **MV**	26
Lucca | **N End**	25
Z Lumière | **Newton**	27
Lure | **MV**	21
Mamma Maria | **N End**	25
NEW Marliave | **D'town Cross**	22
Mews | **CC**	27
Z Oak Room | **Back Bay**	25
Z Oishii | **S End**	27
Z Oleana | **Inman Sq**	28
NEW Olivadi | **Norwood**	-
Òran Mór | **Nan**	24
NEW Orta | **Hanover**	-
Osteria La Civetta | **CC**	-
Z Outermost Inn | **MV**	25
Pagliuca's | **N End**	22
Pierrot Bistrot | **Beacon Hill**	24
Pigalle | **Theater Dist**	26
Z Prezza | **N End**	27
Red House | **Harv Sq**	20
Red Inn | **CC**	24
NEW Rist. Damiano | **N End**	-
Salts | **Central Sq**	26
Z Sel de Terre | **multi.**	23
NEW Sensing | **Waterfront**	-
75 Chestnut | **Beacon Hill**	21
Sol Azteca | **Brookline**	20
Solea | **Waltham**	23
Sorriso | **Leather Dist**	20
Straight Wharf | **Nan**	25
Sweet Life | **MV**	25
Z Tangierino | **Charlestown**	24
Z Taranta | **N End**	27
Tasca | **Brighton**	23
Z Top of Hub | **Back Bay**	20
Z Topper's | **Nan**	27
Tosca | **Hingham**	25
NEW Townsend's | **Hyde Park**	19
Tresca | **N End**	23
Trevi Café | **CC**	-
Z Troquet | **Theater Dist**	27
Tryst | **Arlington**	22
Z 28 Atlantic | **CC**	26
29 Fair St. | **Nan**	22
Z 21 Federal | **Nan**	24
Umbria | **Financial Dist**	23
Z UpStairs on Sq. | **Harv Sq**	24
Via Matta | **Park Sq**	25
Vlora | **Back Bay**	22
NEW Water St. | **MV**	-

West on Centre | **W Roxbury** 18
Wine Cellar | **Back Bay** 20
Zebra's Bistro | **Medfield** 24

SINGLES SCENES

🗲 Abe & Louie's | **Back Bay** 26
NEW Atlantic | **MV** —
Balance | **MV** 23
🗲 Banq | **S End** 21
BarLola | **Back Bay** 18
Blue22 | **Quincy** 19
Boston Sail | **Waterfront** 15
Cactus Club | **Back Bay** 16
Cafe Escadrille | **Burlington** 19
Casino Wharf | **CC** 20
Chatham Squire | **CC** 18
Club Car | **Nan** 20
Cottage | **Wellesley** 19
David Ryan's | **MV** 15
Dillon's | **Back Bay** 16
Fleming's Prime | **Park Sq** 24
Glenn's | **Newburyport** 23
Glory | **Andover** 21
Grafton St. Pub | **Harv Sq** 17
Houston's | **Faneuil Hall** 22
John Harvard's | **Harv Sq** 16
Johnnie's on Side | **W End** 17
Joshua Tree | **Somerville** 15
Living Room | **Waterfront** 15
Lola's | **MV** 22
NEW Max/Dylan | **D'town Cross** —
Middlesex | **Central Sq** 17
M.J. O'Connor's | **Park Sq** —
Orleans | **Somerville** 17
Pho République | **S End** 21
Rattlesnake | **Back Bay** 12
Redline | **Harv Sq** 17
RooBar | **CC** 21
Sanctuary | **Financial Dist** 19
Sunset Grill/Cantina | **multi.** 20
Tavern in Sq. | **Porter Sq** 17
Temple Bar | **Porter Sq** 20
33 Rest. | **Back Bay** 20
28 Degrees | **S End** 20
Village Fish | **Needham** 20
Vox Populi | **Back Bay** 16

SLEEPERS

(Good food, but little known)
Abbondanza | **Everett** 23
Academy Ocean | **CC** 22
Angelo's | **Stoneham** 26
Aura | **Seaport Dist** 22
Balance | **MV** 23
Barker Tavern | **Scituate** 23
Belfry Inne | **CC** 25
Bhindi Bazaar | **Back Bay** 22
bia bistro | **Cohasset** 24
Bistro/Crowne Pointe | **CC** 22
Bistro 712 | **Norwood** 24
Blue Moon Bistro | **CC** 24
Bon Caldo | **Norwood** 22
Brenden Crocker's | **Beverly** 25
Cafe Barada | **Porter Sq** 23
Café Brazil | **Allston** 23
Café Polonia | **S Boston** 24
Cantina Italiana | **N End** 22
Capt. Linnell | **CC** 22
Cassis | **Andover** 26
Catch of the Day | **CC** 25
Chanticleer | **Nan** 25
Cinco | **Nan** 26
Circadia Bistro | **CC** 23
Court House | **E Cambridge** 22
Davide Rist. | **N End** 24
Devon's | **CC** 24
Dog Bar | **Gloucester** 23
Donatello | **Saugus** 24
Dong Khanh | **Chinatown** 22
Don Ricardo's | **S End** 23
🗲 Duckworth's | **Gloucester** 29
Enzo | **CC** 24
Erawan of Siam | **Waltham** 22
Fifty-Six Union | **Nan** 22
Flat Iron | **W End** 22
Friendly Fisherman | **CC** 24
Glenn's | **Newburyport** 23
Gracie's Table | **CC** 23
Grezzo | **N End** 23
Haley House | **Roxbury** 24
HannaH's Fusion | **CC** 24
Himalayan Bistro | **W Roxbury** 24

Menus, photos, voting and more – free at ZAGAT.com

Imperial Seafood | **Chinatown**	24
Incontro | **Franklin**	22
Jasmine | **Brighton**	24
Karoo Kafe | **CC**	24
Karoun | **Newton**	22
Kathmandu Spice | **Arlington**	22
Kayuga | **multi.**	24
Kaze | **Chinatown**	23
La Galleria 33 | **N End**	26
L'Alouette | **CC**	26
Lambert's Cove | **MV**	25
La Summa | **N End**	22
Laureen's | **CC**	23
Le Grenier | **MV**	23
Le Languedoc | **Nan**	26
Le Lyonnais | **Acton**	23
L'Étoile | **MV**	26
Little Q | **Quincy**	25
Mac's | **CC**	24
Masona Grill | **W Roxbury**	25
Mela | **S End**	24
Misaki | **CC**	24
MuLan Taiwanese | **Kendall Sq**	23
Muqueca | **Inman Sq**	24
Namaskar | **Somerville**	23
Navy Yard | **Charlestown**	23
Neighborhood Rest. | **Somerville**	23
NewBridge | **Chelsea**	24
New Jang Su | **Burlington**	23
New Mother India | **Waltham**	22
North St. Grille | **N End**	23
Oceana | **Waterfront**	24
Òran Mór | **Nan**	24
Park Corner | **MV**	22
Pellana | **Peabody**	26
Pho Hoa | **multi.**	22
Piccola Venezia | **N End**	22
Piccolo Nido | **N End**	24
Pi Pizzeria | **Nan**	23
Ponzu | **Waltham**	23
Porcini's | **Watertown**	22
Port | **CC**	23
Prose | **Arlington**	24
Qingdao Gdn. | **Porter Sq**	24
Queequeg's | **Nan**	25

Regatta of Cotuit | **CC**	25
Riva | **Scituate**	26
Ross' Grill | **CC**	22
Sabur | **Somerville**	22
Saporito's | **Hull**	26
Saraceno | **N End**	23
SeaGrille | **Nan**	22
Seiyo | **S End**	25
Seoul Food | **Porter Sq**	22
Sfoglia | **Nan**	24
Shanghai Gate | **Allston**	24
Ships Inn | **Nan**	24
Shogun | **Newton**	23
Sichuan Garden | **multi.**	22
62 on Wharf | **Salem**	24
Soma | **Beverly**	22
Something Savory | **Arlington**	22
Sophia's | **Roslindale**	23
Sorella's | **Jamaica Plain**	26
Sorelle | **Charlestown**	23
St. Alphonzo's | **S Boston**	22
Stanhope Grille | **Back Bay**	23
Stone Soup | **Ipswich**	25
Strip-T's | **Watertown**	22
Super Fusion | **Brookline**	27
Sweet Life | **MV**	25
Tacos El Charro | **Jamaica Plain**	23
Tanjore | **Harv Sq**	22
Taqueria Mexico | **Waltham**	22
Terra Luna | **CC**	24
Theo's | **MV**	24
29 Fair St. | **Nan**	22
Uncle Pete's Ribs | **Revere**	25
Vicki Lee's | **Belmont**	25
Village Sushi | **Roslindale**	23
Vining's Bistro | **CC**	24
Vlora | **Back Bay**	22
Volle Nolle | **N End**	26
Woody's Grill | **Fenway**	22
Wu Chon | **Somerville**	22
Xinh Xinh | **Chinatown**	25
Yama | **multi.**	22
Zabaglione | **Ipswich**	22
Zen | **Beacon Hill**	24
Zon's | **Jamaica Plain**	24

THEME RESTAURANTS

Cheers | **multi.**	14
Durgin-Park | **Faneuil Hall**	17
Fire & Ice | **multi.**	16
Jacob Wirth | **Theater Dist**	17
Kowloon | **Saugus**	17
Lola's | **MV**	22
Optimist Café | **CC**	21
Roadhouse Craft Beer & BBQ | **Brookline**	–
☑ Union Oyster | **Faneuil Hall**	20

TRENDY

Alchemy | **MV**	22
Alta Strada | **Wellesley**	21
Ashmont Grill | **Dorchester**	22
Avila | **Theater Dist**	24
Balance | **MV**	23
☑ B&G Oysters | **S End**	26
☑ Banq | **S End**	21
Beehive | **S End**	18
Bin 26 | **Beacon Hill**	21
Bouchée | **Back Bay**	21
Bricco | **N End**	25
Butcher Shop | **S End**	25
Cafeteria | **Back Bay**	17
Caffe Tosca | **Hingham**	24
Cambridge, 1. | **Harv Sq**	22
Church | **Fenway**	20
Cinco | **Nan**	26
Clink | **Beacon Hill**	19
dante | **E Cambridge**	24
District | **Leather Dist**	17
Douzo | **Back Bay**	24
☑ Eastern Stand. | **Kenmore Sq**	22
Exchange St. Bistro | **Malden**	20
Five Bays Bistro | **CC**	25
Gargoyles | **Somerville**	24
Gaslight Brasserie | **S End**	21
Great Bay | **Kenmore Sq**	23
NEW Jerusalem Pita | **Brookline**	–
KO Prime | **D'town Cross**	24
La Verdad | **Fenway**	22
LiNEaGe | **Brookline**	23
LTK | **Seaport Dist**	20
Mare | **N End**	26

NEW Max/Dylan | **D'town Cross**	–
Mooo... | **Beacon Hill**	24
Myers + Chang | **S End**	23
OM Rest. | **Harv Sq**	19
Osushi | **Back Bay**	23
Pearl | **Nan**	24
Persephone | **Seaport Dist**	25
Pho République | **S End**	21
Pops | **S End**	22
Port | **CC**	23
Rendezvous | **Central Sq**	26
Rocca | **S End**	24
RooBar | **CC**	21
Sibling Rivalry | **S End**	24
Sonsie | **Back Bay**	20
Sophia's | **Roslindale**	23
☑ Sorellina | **Back Bay**	27
Sorriso | **Leather Dist**	20
Stella | **S End**	24
STIX | **Back Bay**	17
NEW Tavolo | **Dorchester**	–
Teatro | **Theater Dist**	24
Temple Bar | **Porter Sq**	20
☑ Toro | **S End**	26
Tremont 647 | **S End**	21
28 Degrees | **S End**	20
29 Newbury | **Back Bay**	20
224 Boston St. | **Dorchester**	22
☑ UpStairs on Sq. | **Harv Sq**	24
Via Matta | **Park Sq**	25
Vox Populi | **Back Bay**	16

VIEWS

Adrian's | **CC**	16
Anthony Cummaquid | **CC**	18
Anthony's | **Seaport Dist**	18
Aqua Grille | **CC**	19
Ardeo | **CC**	20
NEW Asana | **Back Bay**	–
NEW Atlantic | **MV**	–
Atlantica | **Cohasset**	15
Audubon Circle | **Kenmore Sq**	21
Back Eddy | **Westport**	22
Barking Crab | **Seaport Dist**	16
Baxter's | **CC**	18
Bayside Betsy's | **CC**	15
Beach Plum | **MV**	25

Bistro/Crowne Pointe	CC	22
Black Cow	Newburyport	19
☑ Black Dog Tavern	MV	19
blu	Theater Dist	21
Bombay Club	multi.	20
Bookstore & Rest.	CC	19
Boston Sail	Waterfront	15
Brant Point	Nan	21
Bravo	MFA	21
Bricco	N End	25
Bridgeman's	Hull	26
☑ Bristol	Back Bay	24
Bubala's	CC	16
Bukowski Tav.	Inman Sq	17
Café at Taj	Back Bay	20
Cape Sea Grille	CC	26
Capt. Kidd	CC	18
Capt. Parker's	CC	18
Casino Wharf	CC	20
Chart House	Waterfront	21
Chart Room	CC	20
Chatham Bars Inn	CC	22
Circadia Bistro	CC	23
Clancy's	CC	22
Daily Catch	Seaport Dist	24
dante	E Cambridge	24
David Ryan's	MV	15
Devon's	CC	24
Dolphin	CC	21
Enzo	CC	24
Fanizzi's	CC	20
Finz	Salem	20
Fireplace	Brookline	21
Fishmonger's	CC	18
☑ Galley Beach	Nan	24
Gardner Museum	MFA	20
☑ Gibbet Hill	Groton	24
Grafton St. Pub	Harv Sq	17
Hemisphere	CC	17
Home Port	MV	20
☑ J's Nashoba	Bolton	26
Landing	Marblehead	16
Left Bank	Tyngsboro	21
☑ Legal Sea	Waterfront	22
Liam's	CC	20
Lobster Pot	CC	22

Marshside	CC	15
☑ Meritage	Waterfront	27
Mews	CC	27
Miel	Waterfront	21
Net Result	MV	25
No Name	Seaport Dist	19
☑ Not Average Joe's	Newburyport	18
Oceana	Waterfront	24
Ocean House	CC	25
☑ Olives	Charlestown	25
OM Rest.	Harv Sq	19
Orleans Inn	CC	17
☑ Outermost Inn	MV	25
Red Inn	CC	24
☑ Red Pheasant	CC	27
Red Rock Bistro	Swampscott	20
☑ Rialto	Harv Sq	26
Ropewalk	Nan	–
Ross' Grill	CC	22
NEW Salt Water	MV	–
Salvatore's	Seaport Dist	20
Sherborn Inn	Sherborn	19
Sidney's	Central Sq	21
Siros	N Quincy	19
Sonsie	Back Bay	20
Summer House	Nan	20
Tavern on Water	Charlestown	13
Tom Shea's	Essex	20
☑ Top of Hub	Back Bay	20
☑ Topper's	Nan	27
☑ Troquet	Theater Dist	27
Turner Fish	Back Bay	21
☑ 28 Atlantic	CC	26
NEW Water St.	MV	–
Woodman's	Essex	23

WATERSIDE

Adrian's	CC	16
Anthony Cummaquid	CC	18
Anthony's	Seaport Dist	18
Aqua Grille	CC	19
NEW Atlantic	MV	–
Atlantica	Cohasset	15
Back Eddy	Westport	22
Barking Crab	Seaport Dist	16
Baxter's	CC	18

Bayside Betsy's	**CC**	15
Black Cow	**Newburyport**	19
Z Black Dog Tavern	**MV**	19
Bookstore & Rest.	**CC**	19
Brant Point	**Nan**	21
Bridgeman's	**Hull**	26
Bubala's	**CC**	16
Capt. Kidd	**CC**	18
Casino Wharf	**CC**	20
Chart House	**Waterfront**	21
Chart Room	**CC**	20
Chatham Bars Inn	**CC**	22
Clancy's	**CC**	22
Daily Catch	**Seaport Dist**	24
dante	**E Cambridge**	24
Enzo	**CC**	24
Finz	**Salem**	20
Fishmonger's	**CC**	18
Z Galley Beach	**Nan**	24
Hemisphere	**CC**	17
Jetties	**Nan**	14
Landfall	**CC**	18
Landing	**multi.**	16
Left Bank	**Tyngsboro**	21
Z Legal Sea	**Waterfront**	22
Liam's	**CC**	20
Lobster Pot	**CC**	22
Lure	**MV**	21
Mews	**CC**	27
Miel	**Waterfront**	21
No Name	**Seaport Dist**	19
Oceana	**Waterfront**	24
Ocean House	**CC**	25
Orleans Inn	**CC**	17
Z Outermost Inn	**MV**	25
Red Inn	**CC**	24
Red Rock Bistro	**Swampscott**	20
Riva	**Scituate**	26
Ross' Grill	**CC**	22
NEW Sensing	**Waterfront**	-
Siros	**N Quincy**	19
Slip 14	**Nan**	18
Straight Wharf	**Nan**	25
Summer House	**Nan**	20
Tavern on Water	**Charlestown**	13
Tom Shea's	**Essex**	20

Z Topper's	**Nan**	27
Z 28 Atlantic	**CC**	26

WINNING WINE LISTS

American Seasons	**Nan**	25
Angelo's	**Stoneham**	26
Anthony's	**Seaport Dist**	18
Atria	**MV**	25
Z Aujourd'hui	**Back Bay**	28
Bin 26	**Beacon Hill**	21
Blue Room	**Kendall Sq**	25
Z Bramble Inn	**CC**	27
Bravo	**MFA**	21
Butcher Shop	**S End**	25
Z Caffe Bella	**Randolph**	26
Chanticleer	**Nan**	25
dante	**E Cambridge**	24
Great Bay	**Kenmore Sq**	23
Z Grill 23	**Back Bay**	25
Z Hamersley's Bistro	**S End**	27
Heather	**CC**	-
Z Il Capriccio	**Waltham**	27
Z La Campania	**Waltham**	28
Z Legal Sea	**Park Sq**	22
Z L'Espalier	**Back Bay**	28
Les Zygomates	**Leather Dist**	22
Z Lumière	**Newton**	27
Lure	**MV**	21
Mamma Maria	**N End**	25
Mantra	**D'town Cross**	18
Z Meritage	**Waterfront**	27
Z Mistral	**S End**	27
No. 9 Park	**Beacon Hill**	28
Z Prezza	**N End**	27
Z Radius	**Financial Dist**	26
Ross' Grill	**CC**	22
Salts	**Central Sq**	26
Silvertone B&G	**D'town Cross**	21
Smith/Wollensky	**Back Bay**	23
Taberna de Haro	**Brookline**	23
Tomasso	**Southborough**	24
Z Topper's	**Nan**	27
Tresca	**N End**	23
Z Troquet	**Theater Dist**	27
Z 21 Federal	**Nan**	24

BOSTON/CAPE COD

SPECIAL FEATURES

THE BERKSHIRES
RESTAURANT
DIRECTORY

FOOD | DECOR | SERVICE | COST

TOP FOOD

28	Old Inn/Green | Amer.
27	Wheatleigh | Amer./French
	Blantyre | Amer./French
25	Gramercy | Amer./Eclectic
	Elizabeth's | Eclectic

TOP DECOR

28	Wheatleigh | Amer./French
	Blantyre | Amer./French
27	Old Inn/Green | Amer.
25	Jae's Spice | Amer./Pan-Asian
23	Mezze Bistro | American

Aegean Breeze, The Mediterranean   19 | 15 | 18 | $39

Great Barrington | 327 Stockbridge Rd. (State Rd.) | 413-528-4001 |
www.aegean-breeze.com

Great Barrington Grecophiles breeze into this "casual", "fairly priced" Mediterranean for "luscious broiled fish" and other "delicious" "traditional" Hellenic fare proffered by "hospitable" servers; although some find the blue-and-white taverna-style digs "uninteresting", the "attractive" patio is "pleasant" "in warm weather."

allium American   22 | 22 | 19 | $46

Great Barrington | 42-44 Railroad St. (Main St.) | 413-528-2118 |
www.mezzeinc.com

"Food mad" Great Barrington gets a fresh "big-city dining" experience by way of this "sophisticated" New American, a "cool sibling of Williamstown's Mezze" and North Adams' Café Latino; the "limited" but "intriguing" market-based menu served in "chic", "modern" environs impresses most, and though the fussy fume it's "more show than go" with "erratic" service and "pricey" tabs, overall it's a "winner."

NEW Alta Wine Bar Mediterranean   20 | 18 | 21 | $37

Lenox | 34 Church St. (bet. Housatonic & Walker Sts.) | 413-637-0003

"Wonderfully nice owners" set a "friendly" tone at this "fine addition to Lenox", where "terrific" Mediterranean eats are matched by a "great selection" of "reasonably priced" wines; if the "informal" interior is a tad too "young and lively" (read: "noisy"), it's "lovely to eat on the outdoor porch" when weather permits.

Aroma Bar & Grill Indian   21 | 14 | 22 | $30

Great Barrington | 485 Main St. (bet. Maple Ave. & Pope St.) |
413-528-3116 | www.aromabarandgrill.com

A "refreshing alternative" in Great Barrington, this "traditional" Indian offers "generous portions" of "well-priced", "delicious" dishes "spiced to your taste" and served by a "conscientious" staff that "tries hard to please"; as for the decor, some call it "kitschy" and some bill it bland – but "who cares?"

Baba Louie's Sourdough Pizza Pizza   24 | 12 | 18 | $21

Great Barrington | 286 Main St./Rte. 7 (bet. Church & Railroad Sts.) |
413-528-8100 | www.babalouiessourdoughpizzacompany.com

"Waiting crowds are a testament" to the "outstanding" "crunchy", organic thin-crust pizzas purveyed at this "rockin'", "postage-stamp-sized" Great Barrington destination; add "fresh, novel" toppings, "marvelous salads", "first-rate" Italian sandwiches, a "competent staff" and "value" prices, and no wonder it's a "family favorite."

	FOOD	DECOR	SERVICE	COST

Baroods ☒ *French* ▽ 21 | 15 | 19 | $35

Lenox | 18 Franklin St. (Main St.) | 413-637-8222 |
www.baroods.com

Habitués of this French "getaway" say you'll "see the cream of Lenox society" packing into the "tiny" digs for toque team Melissa and Sylvain Noel's moderately priced array of savory and sweet crêpes, plus other "simple" yet "flavorful" bistro classics; if some complain of "variable quality" and service, even they admit dining in the courtyard makes for "a beautiful evening."

Barrington Brewery & Restaurant *American* 15 | 15 | 19 | $24

Great Barrington | 420 Stockbridge Rd./Rte. 7 N.
(Old Stonebridge Rd./Rte. 183) | 413-528-8282 |
www.barringtonbrewery.net

Though it's certainly "not fancy", the "basic" American grub at this "family-friendly" Great Barrington microbrewery "hits the spot" "after a day of leaf peeping" or skiing; "large servings for little cash" come dished up "fast" in a big, "cheerful", "lively" space with working vats on view – oh, and "the beer ain't bad either!"

Bistro Zinc *French* 22 | 22 | 19 | $48

Lenox | 56 Church St. (Housatonic St.) | 413-637-8800 |
www.bistrozinc.com

It's all "trendy" "urban chic" at Lenox's "popular" "replica of a French bistro", where "young and old" gather in "sexy" surroundings that include a "cool bar" for "delightful" fare, which is now created by chef Sylvain Noel of Baroods; if only the prices weren't so "steep", the service were "warmer" and the "tight room" weren't so "zoo-y" in high season (remember, "reservations are a must").

Bizen Restaurant *Japanese* 22 | 17 | 17 | $42

Great Barrington | 17 Railroad St. (Rte. 7) | 413-528-4343

"Yummy", sometimes "edgy" sushi and Japanese grilled dishes make up the "encyclopedic menu" at this "rather pricey" spot in Great Barrington; a "small space" plus "bustling" "crowds" equals often "harried" staffers, so cognoscenti "sit at the bar" and "schmooze" with "knowledgeable" chef-owner Michael Marcus (he also "makes the pottery" on view) or retreat to a tatami room for the prix fixe kaiseki dinner.

☒ Blantyre *American/French* 27 | 28 | 27 | $163

Lenox | Blantyre | 16 Blantyre Rd. (Rte. 20) | 413-637-3556 |
www.blantyre.com

A true "grande dame", this "ritzy" hotel dining room with "a magnificent setting" in Lenox exudes the "luxury" of "a bygone era", from the "fabulous" French–New American à la carte lunches and prix fixe dinners to the "thoroughly professional", "refined staff" to "gorgeous", "romantic" environs filled with "fresh flowers" and soft piano music; yes, the whole "pampering" experience is "over-the-top", just like the "out-of-sight prices" – but this is "one splurge that's really worth the dough"; N.B jacket and tie required, children under 12 not admitted.

Bombay ⓜ *Indian*

23 | 14 | 19 | $30

Lee | Black Swan Inn | 435 Laurel St. (Lake Rd.) | 413-243-6731 | www.fineindiandining.com

"Spicy food"–favorers find "wonderful", "well-prepared" renditions (plus lots of veggie choices) at this "festive" Lee Indian appreciated for "considerate service" and a weekend brunch buffet deemed "one of the best buys anywhere"; if the plain decor seems "peculiar", just "sit at a window" and enjoy the "lovely view of the lake."

Brix Wine Bar ⓜ *French*

22 | 21 | 23 | $40

Pittsfield | 40 West St. (bet. McKay & North Sts.) | 413-236-9463 | www.brixwinebar.com

"Fine" French bistro fare and "a smart wine list" make for "a winning combination" at this "appealing" Pittsfield "hangout" where the "expensive" food tabs are tempered by "good value flights"; an "attentive", "welcoming" staff works the "intimate" gold-and-burgundy room, which the aurally sensitive say gets too "noisy" when everyone else is having too much "fun."

Café Adam *European*

22 | 15 | 19 | $36

Great Barrington | 325 Stockbridge Rd. (bet. Cooper & Crissey Rds.) | 413-528-7786 | www.cafeadam.org

"Imaginative", "well-prepared" contemporary European fare is served "at reasonable prices" alongside an "amazing wine list" at this "casual", "out-of-the-way" Great Barrington cafe where toque-owner Adam Zieminski "settled down" after some swanky cheffing across the pond; diners settle in the minimalist "New York–style interior" with its black accents and matching blackboards (for specials) or nab an umbrella table on the porch when it's nice out.

Café Latino *Nuevo Latino*

22 | 21 | 21 | $32

North Adams | Mass MoCA | 1111 Mass MoCA Way (Marshall St.) | 413-662-2004 | www.cafelatinoatmoca.com

"Jazzy" Nuevo Latino chow offered in "family-sized" portions at "reasonable" rates makes this "upbeat" cafe in North Adams' Mass MoCA complex a "terrific stop before or after a museum visit"; the modern, somewhat "industrial" interior feels "hip" and energetic, while the "inviting patio" is the place for "relaxing" repasts.

Café Lucia ⓜ *Italian*

21 | 17 | 20 | $51

Lenox | 80 Church St. (bet. Franklin & Housatonic Sts.) | 413-637-2640

"If you love osso buco, make a beeline" for this Lenox veteran where the "chef's signature" is the highlight of the "pricey" menu of "reliable" Italian "classics"; even admirers admit the "ordinary" interior of the 1839 house gets too "crowded" and "noisy", but they just ask the "pleasant" staff for a table on the "pleasurable" deck.

Castle Street Cafe *American/French*

19 | 17 | 20 | $44

Great Barrington | 10 Castle St. (Main St.) | 413-528-5244 | www.castlestreetcafe.com

"Popular with transplanted New Yorkers and locals" alike, this "dependable" Great Barrington American-French bistro serves up "old

favorites done well" in lighter preparations at the "lively" bar – which is "enhanced by cool jazz on weekends" (nightly in summer) – and "more pricey" full dinners in the "spacious" dining room; a "courteous" staff is another reason it packs an "invariably full house."

Chez Nous Ⓜ *French* | 24 | 18 | 23 | $50

Lee | 150 Main St. (Academy St.) | 413-243-6397 | www.cheznousbistro.com

"Half the time it's excellent, the other half it's out of sight" pronounce pleased "picky locals" of Gallic chef Franck Tessier's "mouthwatering" French fare and his American wife Rachel Portnoy's "luscious desserts" (she also offers "warm welcomes" as hostess) at this "comfy", costly "country house" in Lee; there's also a "quality wine list", from which the "efficient" staff can suggest "perfect complements."

Church Street Cafe *American* | 21 | 17 | 20 | $43

Lenox | 65 Church St. (bet. Franklin & Housatonic Sts.) | 413-637-2745 | www.churchstreetcafe.biz

A "tried-and-true" "standby for Lenox residents" (as well as tourists heading to Tanglewood), this "relaxed" New American employs an "accommodating staff" to deliver "attractive, delicious food" that's "a bit pricey but worth it"; patrons pick from three "peaceful" rooms, or sit on the "delightful" porch in summertime to "enjoy the scenery" "in the middle of town."

Coyote Flaco Ⓜ *Mexican* | ▽ 21 | 18 | 20 | $30

Williamstown | 505 Cold Spring Rd. (Bee Hill Rd.) | 413-458-4240 | www.mycoyoteflaco.com

"Come hungry" for "real Mexican" "served with flair" advise amigos of this Williamstown branch of the fairly priced, "family-owned" chainlet; even those who declare it "generally mediocre" find places in their hearts for "not-to-be-missed" margaritas and the occasional "mariachi serenade."

Cranwell Resort, Spa & Golf Club *American* | 20 | 23 | 22 | $51

Lenox | 55 Lee Rd./Rte. 20 (Rte. 7) | 413-637-1364 | www.cranwell.com

"What a beautiful place" declare dazzled guests of Lenox's "lovely" Tudor-style mansion resort, where "attentive" staffers serve "wonderful", "expensive" New American fare in the "romantic" Wyndhurst room or Music Room Grill; the less enthused tut it's a tad "hoity-toity" and suggest "sticking to Sloane's Tavern", the home of "good burgers and shareable salads" "at moderate prices", or the spa cafe and its "fresh" light fare.

Dakota *Steak* | 18 | 17 | 19 | $34

Pittsfield | 1035 South St. (Dan Fox Dr.) | 413-499-7900 | www.steakseafood.com

A "family atmosphere" pervades the Pittsfield branch of this "large, popular" steakhouse chain known for its "huge menu" of "predictable", "plentiful" protein in various guises, "amazing salad bar", "magnificent" Sunday brunch and "value prices"; the "pseudo" "big-game-hunter theme" (realized through mounted "elk and

moose heads") is "disconcerting" to some, but the "warm", "caring staff" "never disappoints."

Dish Café Bistro American ▽ 18 | 10 | 16 | $35

Lenox | 37 Church St. (bet. Rte. 183 & Sunset Ave.) | 413-637-1800
"Pleasant" all around pronounce proponents of this "tiny" New American sibling of Stockbridge's Once Upon a Table, whose "varied", "well-prepared" lunch fare gets gussied up for dinner, just as the "narrow" room gets decked out with tablecloths and candles; occasionally "amateurish" service annoys, but the patio is a seasonal "delight."

Egremont Inn Ⓜ American 21 | 20 | 21 | $46

South Egremont | Egremont Inn | 10 Old Sheffield Rd. (Rte. 23) | 413-528-2111 | www.egremontinn.com
South Egremont locals and visitors alike are drawn to this "lovely", "old-fashioned", "typical New England" country inn for "delicious" Traditional American fare served by an "efficient, capable" staff in a freshly painted pale-green dining room or a more "rustic" tavern with beams, fireplace and a lighter, cheaper menu; "live music that can't be beat" on Thursdays and Saturdays remains a plus, so the only concern is whether new owners will maintain the "dedication" to "quality."

Elizabeth's Ⓜ⊅ Eclectic 25 | 13 | 22 | $33

Pittsfield | 1264 East St. (Newell St.) | 413-448-8244
Practically a "cult classic", this "offbeat" Pittsfield Eclectic offers a "limited", "lovingly prepared" menu of "unbelievable pastas" and "bountiful", "spectacular salads", plus one fish and one meat dish (both "amazing") per night; "foodies" "sit in the kitchen" of the "homey" space to watch "scene-stealer" chef Tom Ellis, then marvel at the final "quirk": only checks, cash "or IOU – and they mean it."

Fin Japanese 23 | 13 | 18 | $38

Lenox | 27 Housatonic St. (Church St.) | 413-637-9171
"Tiny but tony", this Lenox "hole-in-the-wall", co-owned by Bistro Zinc's Jason Macioge and his brother, serves "inventive, yummy sushi" and other "complex" "Japanese" dishes "with twists"; while the "roar" and "cramped", "diner"-style digs are negatives, fans find greater comfort at the red-lacquered bar – or when they get it to go.

Firefly American 17 | 17 | 15 | $39

Lenox | 71 Church St. (Housatonic St.) | 413-637-2700 | www.fireflylenox.com
Pros proclaim this "casual" "neighborhood place" in Lenox a "fine choice" for "interesting" New American fare, while cons criticize an "unfocused menu" and "amateur", "disappearing servers"; however, come summer, everyone appreciates the "busy", "pretty bar" and "wonderful porch."

Frankie's Italiano Italian - | - | - | M

Lenox | 80 Main St. (Cliftwood St.) | 413-637-4455 | www.frankiesitaliano.com
Chef-owner Stephane Ferioli set out to create a classic mom-and-pop vibe at this relatively new, casual Lenox Italian in Spigalina's old

	FOOD	DECOR	SERVICE	COST

space where family photos on red felt walls and golden ceilings fashion a cozy backdrop for traditional recipes from his nonna (think lasagna with spinach dough, ragout Bolognese and seafood fra diavolo); spouse Molly meets and greets, and moderate tabs add another friendly note.

Gala ▽ 21 | 24 | 23 | $41
Restaurant & Bar *American/Continental*
Williamstown | Orchards Hotel | 222 Adams Rd. (Main St.) | 413-458-9611 | www.orchardshotel.com
Set in Williamstown's Orchards Hotel, this recently "reinvented" American-Continental's "calm setting" includes "spacious" rooms bedecked with "dark-wood paneling" and "comfortable seats" and a "lovely garden"; an "eager staff" conveys the "beautifully presented" fare, and while it's somewhat pricey, a lighter menu is available in the bar area where "seats by the fireplace are coveted."

☑ Gramercy Bistro *American/Eclectic* 25 | 21 | 23 | $40
North Adams | 24-26 Marshall St. (Rte. 2) | 413-663-5300 | www.gramercybistro.com
"Time your visit to Mass MoCA" so you can eat at this "welcoming" chef-owned American-Eclectic in North Adams, because the "thoughtfully prepared", "updated" bistro classics made with "local, artisanal" ingredients "exceed expectations"; factor in "luscious desserts", "personable service" plus a "warm" vibe, and it's no surprise locals "love it."

Helsinki Cafe *Eclectic/Scandinavian* 19 | 18 | 18 | $34
Great Barrington | 284 Main St. (Railroad St.) | 413-528-3394 | www.clubhelsinkiweb.com
Everything "from gravlax to falafel" can be found on the "eccentric", "ecumenical" Scandinavian-Eclectic menu at this "kooky", moderately priced Great Barrington cafe; maybe "service could be better", but the "souklike", "post-hippie" decor with "mismatched old china and tablecloths" adds a feeling of "terrific fun" – and the adjacent live music venue is "worth checking out" to boot.

Jae's Inn *Pan-Asian* 23 | 21 | 18 | $39
North Adams | 1111 S. State St. (Rte. 8) | 413-664-0100 | www.jaesinn.com
Back in its original North Adams location after a sojourn in Williamstown, this Pan-Asian still dishes up "big portions" of "amazing" Japanese, Korean and Thai fare at "reasonable" rates; fans who are "working their way through the menu" sit at the sushi bar or choose one of the small, "relaxing" dining areas.

🆕 Jae's Spice *American/Pan-Asian* 21 | 25 | 19 | $38
Pittsfield | 297 North St. (bet. Summer & Union Sts.) | 413-443-1234
Already creating a "buzz" in Pittsfield, Jae Chung's "new kid" in the now-defunct Spice's "dramatic" old-department-store space proffers the "Pan-Asian food he's famous for" as well as "mainstream" American dishes, all at "remarkably modest prices"; the decor in the

"gorgeous" space is the same as before albeit with scattered Asian doodads and a sushi bar, so it only remains for "disorganized" service to "smooth out" and all will be "terrific."

John Andrews *American*   25 | 21 | 22 | $55

South Egremont | Rte. 23 (Blunt Rd.) | 413-528-3469 | www.jarestaurant.com

"You want classy in the Berkshires?" – this "charming", "off-the-beaten-track" South Egremont New American is it declare devotees; an "elegant" dining room sets the mood for "masterfully prepared", "sophisticated" cooking "that'll warm your heart", served by a staff that "knows how to keep fussy New Yorkers happy"; wallet-watchers who find it "on the expensive side" opt for the bar where the less expensive, "simpler menu is just as delicious."

Kim's Dragon Ⓜ *Vietnamese*   ▽ 25 | 8 | 18 | $28

Pittsfield | 1231 W. Housatonic St. (bet. Hungerford St. & Lebanon Ave.) | 413-236-0998

"Fresh, well-seasoned", "authentic Vietnamese" vittles are the draw at this "family-run" Pittsfield roadhouse dishing up "plentiful" portions at "reasonable prices"; "waits can be lengthy" and the digs are certainly "not much to look at", nevertheless it remains a "solid", "commendable" choice.

Mezze Bistro + Bar *American*   25 | 23 | 23 | $45

Williamstown | 16 Water St. (Rte. 2) | 413-458-0123 | www.mezzeinc.com

Expect "love at first bite" at this "upscale" New American "surprise" in "the northern Berkshires wilderness" (aka Williamstown), where "refined", "inventive" tastes are matched by a "superb wine list" and "professional service"; the "attractive setting", tricked out in chocolate and cream tones, is "the place to be seen", or come summer, "get an eyeful, if you're into star-watching."

Mill on the Floss, The Ⓜ *French*   23 | 22 | 23 | $49

New Ashford | 342 Rte. 7 (Rte. 43) | 413-458-9123 | www.millonthefloss.com

"An old favorite" in New Ashford, this "time-tested" French spot offers "sophisticated", "pricey" fare in a "lovely, unpretentious" 18th-century farmhouse; sure, it's "a bit dated", but "romantics" "take comfort in the warmth" of its wood-beamed, "cozy", candlelit rooms, while "friendly, helpful service" is another reason it's an "enjoyable" "standby for special occasions."

NEW Mission Bar & Tapas Ⓢ *Spanish*   - | - | - | M

Pittsfield | 438 North St. (Maplewood Ave.) | www.missionbarandtapas.com

Perhaps this Spanish tapas specialist is kind of an "arty place" for Pittsfield, but "young hipsters and older couples" alike pile in for "superb" small plates, charcuterie, "tangy salads" and Iberian wines; works by local artists brighten deep red walls in the long, narrow room where "musicians playing live" add to the "mellow, unrushed atmosphere."

	FOOD	DECOR	SERVICE	COST

Morgan House *New England*

| | 16 | 15 | 17 | $37 |

Lee | Morgan Hse. | 33 Main St. (Mass. Tpke., exit 2) | 413-243-3661 | www.morganhouseinn.com

Lee locals report new owners are "really trying to better" this "quaint" early-19th-century inn, starting with "updating" the decor with fresh paint and a mural of the town; thus far, the New England Regional "comfort food" "remains pretty much the same": "bargain priced" (for the Berkshires) but "pedestrian"; N.B. ratings do not reflect more recent changes.

NEW Napa *Californian*

| | 19 | 18 | 17 | $43 |

Great Barrington | 293 Main St. (Church St.) | 413-528-4311

A "welcome addition" to Great Barrington, this Californian-New Englander (ensconced in the old Union Bar space) "caught on quickly" thanks to "interesting", "well-prepared" dishes ranging from sandwiches and wraps to grilled quail, not to mention "inexpensive wines" (a contrast to the somewhat pricey fare); high ceilings, peach walls and a long bar create a "nice" setting that helps patrons overlook the "noisy sound level" and "needs-improvement" service.

☑ Old Inn on the Green ⑤ *American*

| | 28 | 27 | 25 | $65 |

New Marlborough | Old Inn on the Green | 134 Hartsville-New Marlborough Rd./Rte. 57 (Rte. 272) | 413-229-7924 | www.oldinn.com

"Worth every minute of the drive" to "remote" New Marlborough, this New American "jewel" set in an "exquisite" 1760 inn is "a fabulous find" for chef-owner Peter Pratt's "outstanding" cuisine, matched by "stellar service" and "wonderful wines"; the "impossibly romantic" dining rooms "lit only by candles and fireplaces" might "leave you drowsy with satisfaction", while the tabs will definitely cause your wallet to be considerably lighter – unless you've come on Wednesday or Thursday for the "bargain" $31 prix fixe.

Old Mill *American*

| | 24 | 23 | 25 | $50 |

South Egremont | 53 Main St. (Rte. 41) | 413-528-1421

"Wonderful", "lovingly prepared" American cooking, "gracious" service and a fireside "atmosphere that makes you feel warm and cuddly" explain why this "well-worth-the-cost" "rustic old charmer" in a "beautiful" 1797 South Egremont mill has been "a must" for the past 30 years; the one teeny "turnoff" is the no-rez policy for fewer than five, but even that's made up for by the "lively", "delightful bar to wait in."

Once Upon a Table *American/Continental*

| | 21 | 15 | 23 | $38 |

Stockbridge | The Mews | 36 Main St. (bet. Elm St. & Rte. 7) | 413-298-3870 | www.onceuponatablebistro.com

"Simple, well-cooked" eats are the attraction at this "adorable" Continental–New American "tucked in the mews" next to Stockbridge's Red Lion; a "friendly, efficient" staff works the "pleasant" but "tiny" room, which is "great" for lunch and quickly "full at night" ("reservations are a must").

	FOOD	DECOR	SERVICE	COST

Pearl's *American*

	20	22	17	$49

Great Barrington | 47 Railroad St. (Main St.) | 413-528-7767 |
www.pearlsrestaurant.com

"A little bit of Manhattan" in Great Barrington, this "stylish" bistro attracts a "cool" crowd with its "tasty", "adventurous" New American fare, whether in the "stunning" dining rooms or in the equally "modern" bar where there's a lighter, "lower-priced" menu; too bad the "urban-esque" spirit can include "imperious", "painfully slow" service.

Pho Saigon *Vietnamese*

	∇ 19	10	18	$24

Lee | 5 Railroad St. (Main St.) | 413-243-6288

"Traditional" "homestyle" Vietnamese comes in "good, plentiful" and cheap supply at this "authentic", owner-operated Lee spot; most don't mind that bamboo accents are the only things notable in the no-frills digs, the "cheerful" servers "hardly speak English" or the "kitchen's slow when it gets busy."

Prime Italian
Steakhouse & Bar Ⓜ *Italian/Steak*

	20	20	20	$57

Lenox | 15 Franklin St. (Rte. 7A) | 413-637-2998 | www.primelenox.com
It may "not blow your socks off", but the menu at this "solid" Lenox Southern Italian steakhouse mixes "simple meat and potatoes" with chef-owner Gennaro Gallo's homemade gnocci and the like; manned by a "pleasant" staff, the setting features "smoked glass" dividers on the booths, a lit-from-beneath bar and bright red banquettes.

Red Lion Inn *New England*

	18	22	21	$45

Stockbridge | Red Lion Inn | 30 Main St./Rte. 102 (Rte. 7) | 413-298-5545 |
www.redlioninn.com
This 1773 "quintessential New England inn" – a Stockbridge "icon" – trots out "warhorses like roast turkey" on its "fine", "old-fashioned" menu; a "courteous" staff serves in the "genteel", "high-priced" main dining room, "cozy", "less expensive" Widow Bingham's Tavern or "fun", "reasonable" Lion's Den pub, and even the debonair who decry it's "dowdy" and "stuffed with tourists" declare it's "lovely to eat in the courtyard."

Rouge Ⓜ *French*

	23	18	16	$50

West Stockbridge | 3 Center St. (Hotel St.) | 413-232-4111 |
www.rougerestaurant.com
"A charming couple" runs this "lively" West Stockbridge bistro: chef William Merelle cooks up "exceptional", somewhat pricey French dinners (and "inventive" tapas, served in the bar), while spouse Maggie meets and greets in the "homey" space; *les négatives* are "lapses in service" on "busy" nights, when it's "noisy as a Paris subway", and "cramped" conditions that should be helped by a recent expansion.

Route 7 Grill *American/BBQ*

	23	17	21	$33

Great Barrington | 999 S. Main St. (bet. Brookside & Lime Kiln Rds.) |
413-528-3235 | www.route7grill.com
"Lip-smacking ribs, succulent pulled pork" and other "fantastic" BBQ tops a menu of "delicious" American "comfort-food" at this

"hopping joint" in Great Barrington; "locavores" love its "commitment to regional farmers", while everyone "gives three cheers" for the "festive", "child-friendly" vibe, "cordial" service and "reasonable" tabs; a two-sided fireplace warms up the "spare decor", and there's "a jolly bar too."

Sabor 🅈 🅜 *Pan-Latin* ▽ 21 | 18 | 19 | $33

Pittsfield | 17 Wendell Ave. Ext., downstairs (bet. East & Federal Sts.) | 413-445-5465 | www.sabor-restaurante.com

Not many have discovered this Pittsfield Pan-Latin in the old Allen Hotel, but those who've sampled the "diverse", moderately priced menu, which ranges from tapas to paella to pernil (a traditional Ecuadoran pork dish), say "try it, you'll like it"; dining gives way to dancing after 10:30 PM on weekends when the colorful space fills with live music.

Shiro Sushi & Hibachi *Japanese* ▽ 20 | 19 | 22 | $34

Great Barrington | 105 Stockbridge Rd. (bet. Blue Hill Rd. & Brooke Ln.) | 413-528-1898

"Enthusiastic, goofy chefs" perform a "typical hibachi show" at this "fun" Great Barrington Japanese offering "good robata" and "fresh sushi" in addition to the "theatrical" experience; aficionados advise "don't overlook it" just because of its plain digs "next to a bowling alley."

Siam Square Thai Cuisine *Thai* 18 | 15 | 19 | $27

Great Barrington | 290 Main St. (Railroad St.) | 413-644-9119 | www.siamsquares.com

"Thai food is hard to come by" in the Berkshires, so this "reliable", "welcoming" Great Barrington "landmark" "does the trick" when "noodle cravings" hit, dispensing all "the basics as well as a few unusual options" for "cheap"; the space is "modest and quiet", while the staff is "sweet."

Stagecoach Tavern 🅜 *American* ▽ 20 | 23 | 22 | $41

Sheffield | Race Brook Lodge | Rte. 41 (Salisbury Rd.) | 413-229-8585 | www.stagecoachtavern.net

"A warm hearth beckons" at this "off-the-beaten-path", "rustic" roadside tavern in Sheffield, where seasonal American fare made with local and organic ingredients comes full of "flair and flavor"; the staff is "friendly", while "inviting" decor reflects the inn's 1829 vintage with "beautiful wood" beams and floors, candlelight and "cozy corners for quiet talk."

Sullivan Station Restaurant *New England* ▽ 15 | 15 | 19 | $33

Lee | 109 Railroad St. (Mass. Tpke., exit 2) | 413-243-2082 | www.sullivanstationrestaurant.com

"Weekend crowds, even off-season" confirm that Lee's "delightful" "converted train station" is on the right track with its "variety" of simple, "solid" New England "comfort fare" "at the right price"; it's a "family-friendly" spot that's "literally a hoot" when the Berkshire Scenic Railway tourist ride rolls by.

	FOOD	DECOR	SERVICE	COST

Taylor's *American*

| | - | - | - | M |

North Adams | 34 Holden St. (Center St.) | 413-664-4500 |
www.taylorsfinedining.net

Housed in the storefront once occupied by Gideons, this American newcomer in underserved North Adams draws a mostly mature crowd for "nicely presented" classic steaks and seafood offered at moderate prices; the "helpful" staffers preside over the attractive space with paintings hung on brick walls; N.B. jackets required.

Thai Garden *Japanese/Thai*

| | 20 | 14 | 19 | $28 |

Williamstown | 27 Spring St. (Rte. 2) | 413-458-0004

"A nice surprise in staid Williamstown", this Thai turns out "fresh", "spicy" "standards" – and the "sushi isn't bad either"; the decor is "typical", staff "helpful" and rates "reasonable", so no surprise it's a "favorite of faculty and students", with just a fussy few shrugging it's "nothing special."

Trattoria Rustica *Italian*

| | 23 | 21 | 20 | $45 |

Pittsfield | 26 McKay St. (West St.) | 413-499-1192 |
www.trattoria-rustica.com

"Turn on your GPS" to find this "little corner of Naples" "hidden in the backstreets of Pittsfield", where chef-owner Davide Manzo's "delectable", "pricey but worth-every-penny" Southern Italian meals come via "congenial", "well-paced" service; add a wood oven and "low-lit", "romantic" ambiance in the "pretty" stone-and-brick-walled room and you've got a "winning combination."

Trattoria Il Vesuvio ⊠ *Italian*

| | ▽ 18 | 17 | 20 | $39 |

Lenox | 242 Pittsfield Rd. (bet. Lime Kiln & New Lenox Rds.) |
413-637-4904 | www.trattoria-vesuvio.com

Pros claim "you can't go wrong" with the "red-sauce" classics at this "popular" Lenox Italian presided over by an "accommodating", "down-to-earth" family that "appreciates your company"; cons complain the eats are "simply so-so", but even they appreciate that the "rustic", converted century-old stable is made "cozy" by a wood-fired brick oven.

Truc Orient Express *Vietnamese*

| | 21 | 18 | 19 | $34 |

West Stockbridge | 3 Harris St. (Main St.) | 413-232-4204

"Super" Vietnamese cooking at "fair prices" keeps customers coming "year after year" to this family-run West Stockbridge "standby" that's been "doing something right" for three decades now; an "efficient", "polite" staff plus a "really nice gift shop" are other reasons it's "worth a detour", so though the digs decorated with art from the motherland are "a bit dated", it's "no matter."

NEW Viva Ⓜ *Spanish*

| | ▽ 23 | 19 | 21 | $44 |

Glendale | 14 Glendale Rd. (Rte. 183) | 413-298-4433

"Finally, a real Spanish" spot in "off-the-beaten-path" Glendale cheer those "pleasantly surprised" to find this newcomer near the Norman Rockwell museum; "authentic tastes" can be found in "to-die-for paella", "terrific tapas" and other "fabulous" fare in a "com-

fortable", casual mustard-and-terra-cotta setting jazzed up with a Picasso-esque mural.

☑ Wheatleigh *American/French*

27 | 28 | 26 | $97

Lenox | Wheatleigh | Hawthorne Rd. (Rte. 183) | 413-637-0610 | www.wheatleigh.com

It's "heaven on earth" avow the "wowed" at this "gorgeous" Italianate mansion in Lenox, where "truly lovely" rooms form an "elegant" backdrop for "superb" French–New American cuisine and "extraordinary", "formal service"; it strikes a few as "somewhat stuffy", but most are "left sighing" by the whole "spectacular" experience, and though you may have to "sell your house" to pay the bill, this is one "splurge" that's "worth every penny"; N.B. jackets suggested.

Xicohtencatl *Mexican*

21 | 18 | 21 | $35

Great Barrington | 50 Stockbridge Rd. (Rte. 23) | 413-528-2002

"Upscale", "real Mexican" is the deal at this "colorful" Great Barrington cantina serving "scrumptious" "regional specialties" in "generous" amounts and for relatively "modest costs"; a "staggering selection of tequilas" ensures everyone has "a blast" in the "festive" digs, while "dining on the terrace at sunset is sublime"; P.S. don't sweat the name, just call it "'shico.'"

THE BERKSHIRES
INDEXES

Cuisines

Includes restaurant names, locations and Food ratings.

AMERICAN (NEW)

allium | **Great Barr**	22
Z Blantyre | **Lenox**	27
Castle St. | **Great Barr**	19
Church St. Cafe | **Lenox**	21
Cranwell Resort | **Lenox**	20
Dish Café | **Lenox**	18
Firefly | **Lenox**	17
Gala | **Williamstown**	21
Z Gramercy Bistro | **N Adams**	25
NEW Jae's Spice | **Pittsfield**	21
John Andrews | **S Egremont**	25
Mezze Bistro | **Williamstown**	25
Z Old Inn/Green | **New Marl**	28
Once Upon | **Stockbridge**	21
Pearl's | **Great Barr**	20
Taylor's | **N Adams**	-
Z Wheatleigh | **Lenox**	27

AMERICAN (TRADITIONAL)

Barrington Brew | **Great Barr**	15
Egremont Inn | **S Egremont**	21
Old Mill | **S Egremont**	24
Route 7 Grill | **Great Barr**	23
Stagecoach Tav. | **Sheffield**	20

BARBECUE

Route 7 Grill | **Great Barr**	23

CALIFORNIAN

NEW Napa | **Great Barr**	19

CONTINENTAL

Gala | **Williamstown**	21
Once Upon | **Stockbridge**	21

ECLECTIC

Elizabeth's | **Pittsfield**	25
Z Gramercy Bistro | **N Adams**	25
Helsinki | **Great Barr**	19

EUROPEAN

Café Adam | **Great Barr**	22

FRENCH

Baroods | **Lenox**	21
Z Blantyre | **Lenox**	27
Castle St. | **Great Barr**	19
Mill on the Floss | **New Ashford**	23
Z Wheatleigh | **Lenox**	27

FRENCH (BISTRO)

Bistro Zinc | **Lenox**	22
Brix Wine Bar | **Pittsfield**	22
Chez Nous | **Lee**	24
Rouge | **W Stockbridge**	23

INDIAN

Aroma B&G | **Great Barr**	21
Bombay | **Lee**	23

ITALIAN
(S=Southern)

Café Lucia | **Lenox**	21
Frankie's Italiano | **Lenox**	-
Prime Italian | S | **Lenox**	20
Tratt. Rustica | S | **Pittsfield**	23
Tratt. Il Vesuvio | **Lenox**	18

JAPANESE
(* sushi specialist)

Bizen* | **Great Barr**	22
Fin* | **Lenox**	23
Shiro Sushi* | **Great Barr**	20
Thai Gdn.* | **Williamstown**	20

MEDITERRANEAN

Aegean Breeze | **Great Barr**	19
NEW Alta Wine | **Lenox**	20

MEXICAN

Coyote Flaco | **Williamstown**	21
Xicohtencatl | **Great Barr**	21

NEW ENGLAND

Morgan Hse. | **Lee**	16
NEW Napa | **Great Barr**	19
Red Lion Inn | **Stockbridge**	18
Sullivan Station | **Lee**	15

Menus, photos, voting and more – free at ZAGAT.com

NUEVO LATINO

Café Latino | N Adams 22

PAN-ASIAN

Jae's Inn | N Adams 23
NEW Jae's Spice | Pittsfield 21

PAN-LATIN

Sabor | Pittsfield 21

PIZZA

Baba Louie's | Great Barr 24

SCANDINAVIAN

Helsinki | Great Barr 19

SPANISH

(* tapas specialist)
NEW Mission Bar* | Pittsfield –
NEW Viva | Glendale 23

STEAKHOUSES

Dakota | Pittsfield 18
Prime Italian | Lenox 20

THAI

Siam Sq. Thai | Great Barr 18
Thai Gdn. | Williamstown 20

VIETNAMESE

Kim's Dragon | Pittsfield 25
Pho Saigon | Lee 19
Truc Orient | W Stockbridge 21

Locations

Includes restaurant names, cuisines and Food ratings.

GLENDALE

NEW Viva | *Spanish*   23

GREAT BARRINGTON

Aegean Breeze | *Med.*   19
allium | *Amer.*   22
Aroma B&G | *Indian*   21
Baba Louie's | *Pizza*   24
Barrington Brew | *Amer.*   15
Bizen | *Japanese*   22
Café Adam | *Euro.*   22
Castle St. | *Amer./French*   19
Helsinki | *Eclectic/Scan.*   19
NEW Napa | *Calif.*   19
Pearl's | *Amer.*   20
Route 7 Grill | *Amer./BBQ*   23
Shiro Sushi | *Japanese*   20
Siam Sq. Thai | *Thai*   18
Xicohtencatl | *Mex.*   21

LEE

Bombay | *Indian*   23
Chez Nous | *French*   24
Morgan Hse. | *New Eng.*   16
Pho Saigon | *Viet.*   19
Sullivan Station | *New Eng.*   15

LENOX

NEW Alta Wine | *Med.*   20
Baroods | *French*   21
Bistro Zinc | *French*   22
Z Blantyre | *Amer./French*   27
Café Lucia | *Italian*   21
Church St. Cafe | *Amer.*   21
Cranwell Resort | *Amer.*   20
Dish Café | *Amer.*   18
Fin | *Japanese*   23
Firefly | *Amer.*   17
Frankie's Italiano | *Italian*   -
Prime Italian | *Italian/Steak*   20
Tratt. Il Vesuvio | *Italian*   18
Z Wheatleigh | *Amer./French*   27

NEW ASHFORD

Mill on the Floss | *French*   23

NEW MARLBOROUGH

Z Old Inn/Green | *Amer.*   28

NORTH ADAMS

Café Latino | *Nuevo Latino*   22
Z Gramercy Bistro | 25
   Amer./Eclectic
Jae's Inn | *Pan-Asian*   23
Taylor's | *Amer.*   -

PITTSFIELD

Brix Wine Bar | *French*   22
Dakota | *Steak*   18
Elizabeth's | *Eclectic*   25
NEW Jae's Spice | 21
   Amer./Pan-Asian
Kim's Dragon | *Viet.*   25
NEW Mission Bar | *Spanish*   -
Sabor | *Pan-Latin*   21
Tratt. Rustica | *Italian*   23

SHEFFIELD

Stagecoach Tav. | *Amer.*   20

SOUTH EGREMONT

Egremont Inn | *Amer.*   21
John Andrews | *Amer.*   25
Old Mill | *Amer.*   24

STOCKBRIDGE

Once Upon | *Amer./Continental*   21
Red Lion Inn | *New Eng.*   18

WEST STOCKBRIDGE

Rouge | *French*   23
Truc Orient | *Viet.*   21

WILLIAMSTOWN

Coyote Flaco | *Mex.*   21
Gala | *Amer./Continental*   21
Mezze Bistro | *Amer.*   25
Thai Gdn. | *Japanese/Thai*   20

   Menus, photos, voting and more – free at ZAGAT.com

Special Features

Listings cover the best in each category and include names, locations and Food ratings. Multi-location restaurants' features may vary by branch.

BRUNCH

NEW Alta Wine | **Lenox**	20
Bombay | **Lee**	23
Café Adam | **Great Barr**	22
Café Latino | **N Adams**	22
Dakota | **Pittsfield**	18
Pearl's | **Great Barr**	20
Z Wheatleigh | **Lenox**	27
Xicohtencatl | **Great Barr**	21

BUSINESS DINING

allium | **Great Barr**	22
Cranwell Resort | **Lenox**	20
Gala | **Williamstown**	21
NEW Jae's Spice | **Pittsfield**	21
NEW Napa | **Great Barr**	19
Pearl's | **Great Barr**	20
Taylor's | **N Adams**	-

CATERING

Bizen | **Great Barr**	22
Bombay | **Lee**	23
Castle St. | **Great Barr**	19
John Andrews | **S Egremont**	25
Mezze Bistro | **Williamstown**	25

CHILD-FRIENDLY

(Alternatives to the usual fast-food places; * children's menu available)

Aegean Breeze | **Great Barr**	19
Baba Louie's | **Great Barr**	24
Barrington Brew* | **Great Barr**	15
Bistro Zinc* | **Lenox**	22
Café Lucia | **Lenox**	21
Castle St. | **Great Barr**	19
Church St. Cafe* | **Lenox**	21
Coyote Flaco* | **Williamstown**	21
Dakota* | **Pittsfield**	18
Egremont Inn* | **S Egremont**	21
Elizabeth's | **Pittsfield**	25
Morgan Hse. | **Lee**	16
Old Mill | **S Egremont**	24
Once Upon | **Stockbridge**	21
Red Lion Inn* | **Stockbridge**	18

Rouge | **W Stockbridge**	23
Route 7 Grill* | **Great Barr**	23
Shiro Sushi | **Great Barr**	20
Siam Sq. Thai | **Great Barr**	18
Sullivan Station* | **Lee**	15
Thai Gdn. | **Williamstown**	20
Tratt. Il Vesuvio* | **Lenox**	18
Xicohtencatl* | **Great Barr**	21

DINING ALONE

NEW Alta Wine | **Lenox**	20
Baba Louie's | **Great Barr**	24
Fin | **Lenox**	23
NEW Napa | **Great Barr**	19
Once Upon | **Stockbridge**	21
Pho Saigon | **Lee**	19

ENTERTAINMENT

(Call for days and times of performances)

Z Blantyre | varies | **Lenox**	27
Castle St. | jazz/piano | **Great Barr**	19
Egremont Inn | live music | **S Egremont**	21
NEW Mission Bar | folk/indie rock | **Pittsfield**	-
Red Lion Inn | varies | **Stockbridge**	18
Sabor | DJ/flamenco guitar | **Pittsfield**	21

FIREPLACES

Aegean Breeze | **Great Barr**	19
Barrington Brew | **Great Barr**	15
Z Blantyre | **Lenox**	27
Cranwell Resort | **Lenox**	20
Dakota | **Pittsfield**	18
Egremont Inn | **S Egremont**	21
Gala | **Williamstown**	21
Helsinki | **Great Barr**	19
Jae's Inn | **N Adams**	23
John Andrews | **S Egremont**	25
Mill on the Floss | **New Ashford**	23
Morgan Hse. | **Lee**	16
Z Old Inn/Green | **New Marl**	28

Old Mill	S Egremont	24
Red Lion Inn	Stockbridge	18
Route 7 Grill	Great Barr	23
Stagecoach Tav.	Sheffield	20
Truc Orient	W Stockbridge	21
Z Wheatleigh	Lenox	27

GAME IN SEASON

allium	Great Barr	22
NEW Alta Wine	Lenox	20
Bistro Zinc	Lenox	22
Z Blantyre	Lenox	27
Brix Wine Bar	Pittsfield	22
Café Lucia	Lenox	21
Castle St.	Great Barr	19
Church St. Cafe	Lenox	21
Cranwell Resort	Lenox	20
Egremont Inn	S Egremont	21
Elizabeth's	Pittsfield	25
Firefly	Lenox	17
Z Gramercy Bistro	N Adams	25
John Andrews	S Egremont	25
Mezze Bistro	Williamstown	25
NEW Napa	Great Barr	19
Z Old Inn/Green	New Marl	28
Pearl's	Great Barr	20
Red Lion Inn	Stockbridge	18
Rouge	W Stockbridge	23
Stagecoach Tav.	Sheffield	20
Z Wheatleigh	Lenox	27

HISTORIC PLACES

(Year opened; * building)
1760	Old Inn/Green*	New Marl	28
1773	Red Lion Inn*	Stockbridge	18
1780	Egremont Inn*	S Egremont	21
1797	Old Mill*	S Egremont	24
1817	Morgan Hse.*	Lee	16
1829	Stagecoach Tav.*	Sheffield	20
1839	Café Lucia*	Lenox	21
1840	Jae's Spice*	Pittsfield	21
1841	Chez Nous*	Lee	24
1852	Church St. Cafe*	Lenox	21
1890	Mezze Bistro*	Williamstown	25

1893	Sullivan Station*	Lee	15
1893	Wheatleigh*	Lenox	27
1894	Cranwell Resort*	Lenox	20
1900	Tratt. Il Vesuvio*	Lenox	18
1903	Gramercy Bistro*	N Adams	25
1924	Brix Wine Bar*	Pittsfield	22

HOTEL DINING

Black Swan Inn
| Bombay | Lee | 23 |

Blantyre
| Z Blantyre | Lenox | 27 |

Egremont Inn
| Egremont Inn | S Egremont | 21 |

Morgan Hse.
| Morgan Hse. | Lee | 16 |

Old Inn on the Green
| Z Old Inn/Green | New Marl | 28 |

Orchards Hotel
| Gala | Williamstown | 21 |

Race Brook Lodge
| Stagecoach Tav. | Sheffield | 20 |

Red Lion Inn
| Red Lion Inn | Stockbridge | 18 |

Wheatleigh
| Z Wheatleigh | Lenox | 27 |

JACKET REQUIRED

(* Tie also required)
| Z Blantyre* | Lenox | 27 |
| Taylor's | N Adams | - |

MEET FOR A DRINK

NEW Alta Wine	Lenox	20
Bistro Zinc	Lenox	22
Brix Wine Bar	Pittsfield	22
Castle St.	Great Barr	19
Chez Nous	Lee	24
Gala	Williamstown	21
Z Gramercy Bistro	N Adams	25
Helsinki	Great Barr	19
NEW Jae's Spice	Pittsfield	21
NEW Mission Bar	Pittsfield	-
NEW Napa	Great Barr	19
Old Mill	S Egremont	24
Pearl's	Great Barr	20

Menus, photos, voting and more – free at ZAGAT.com

Prime Italian | **Lenox**	20
Red Lion Inn | **Stockbridge**	18
Sabor | **Pittsfield**	21
Stagecoach Tav. | **Sheffield**	20

MICROBREWERIES

Barrington Brew | **Great Barr**	15

NOTEWORTHY NEWCOMERS

Alta Wine | **Lenox**	20
Jae's Spice | **Pittsfield**	21
Mission Bar | **Pittsfield**	-
Napa | **Great Barr**	19
Viva | **Glendale**	23

OFFBEAT

Barrington Brew | **Great Barr**	15
Elizabeth's | **Pittsfield**	25
Helsinki | **Great Barr**	19
Kim's Dragon | **Pittsfield**	25

OUTDOOR DINING

(G=garden; P=patio; T=terrace; W=waterside)

Aegean Breeze | P | **Great Barr**	19
NEW Alta Wine | P | **Lenox**	20
Baroods | G | **Lenox**	21
Barrington Brew | G | **Great Barr**	15
Café Adam | P | **Great Barr**	22
Café Latino | T | **N Adams**	22
Café Lucia | G, T | **Lenox**	21
Church St. Cafe | P | **Lenox**	21
Dish Café | P | **Lenox**	18
Egremont Inn | T | **S Egremont**	21
Firefly | P | **Lenox**	17
Gala | P, W | **Williamstown**	21
Jae's Inn | T | **N Adams**	23
John Andrews | T | **S Egremont**	25
Z Old Inn/Green | T | **New Marl**	28
Red Lion Inn | P | **Stockbridge**	18
Rouge | T | **W Stockbridge**	23
Shiro Sushi | P | **Great Barr**	20
Sullivan Station | T | **Lee**	15
Tratt. Rustica | P | **Pittsfield**	23
Tratt. Il Vesuvio | T | **Lenox**	18
Xicohtencatl | T | **Great Barr**	21

PEOPLE-WATCHING

allium | **Great Barr**	22
NEW Alta Wine | **Lenox**	20
Bistro Zinc | **Lenox**	22
Mezze Bistro | **Williamstown**	25
Pearl's | **Great Barr**	20

POWER SCENES

Bistro Zinc | **Lenox**	22
Mezze Bistro | **Williamstown**	25
Pearl's | **Great Barr**	20

PRIVATE ROOMS

(Restaurants charge less at off times; call for capacity)

Bizen | **Great Barr**	22
Z Blantyre | **Lenox**	27
Castle St. | **Great Barr**	19
Church St. Cafe | **Lenox**	21
Cranwell Resort | **Lenox**	20
Dakota | **Pittsfield**	18
Gala | **Williamstown**	21
John Andrews | **S Egremont**	25
Mill on the Floss | **New Ashford**	23
Pearl's | **Great Barr**	20
Red Lion Inn | **Stockbridge**	18
Rouge | **W Stockbridge**	23
Stagecoach Tav. | **Sheffield**	20
Z Wheatleigh | **Lenox**	27

PRIX FIXE MENUS

(Call for prices and times)

Bizen | **Great Barr**	22
Z Blantyre | **Lenox**	27
Bombay | **Lee**	23
Z Old Inn/Green | **New Marl**	28
Z Wheatleigh | **Lenox**	27

QUIET CONVERSATION

Z Blantyre | **Lenox**	27
Gala | **Williamstown**	21
Z Gramercy Bistro | **N Adams**	25
John Andrews | **S Egremont**	25
Mill on the Floss | **New Ashford**	23
Stagecoach Tav. | **Sheffield**	20
Taylor's | **N Adams**	-
Z Wheatleigh | **Lenox**	27

RESERVE AHEAD

Bistro Zinc | **Lenox**	22
☑ Blantyre | **Lenox**	27
☑ Old Inn/Green | **New Marl**	28
Once Upon | **Stockbridge**	21
Pearl's | **Great Barr**	20
☑ Wheatleigh | **Lenox**	27

ROMANTIC PLACES

☑ Blantyre | **Lenox**	27
Cranwell Resort | **Lenox**	20
John Andrews | **S Egremont**	25
Mill on the Floss | **New Ashford**	23
☑ Old Inn/Green | **New Marl**	28
Taylor's | **N Adams**	-
Tratt. Rustica | **Pittsfield**	23
☑ Wheatleigh | **Lenox**	27

SENIOR APPEAL

Aegean Breeze | **Great Barr**	19
Cranwell Resort | **Lenox**	20
Gala | **Williamstown**	21
Morgan Hse. | **Lee**	16
Red Lion Inn | **Stockbridge**	18
Taylor's | **N Adams**	-

SINGLES SCENES

NEW Alta Wine | **Lenox**	20
Brix Wine Bar | **Pittsfield**	22
Castle St. | **Great Barr**	19
Helsinki | **Great Barr**	19
NEW Jae's Spice | **Pittsfield**	21
NEW Napa | **Great Barr**	19
Prime Italian | **Lenox**	20
Thai Gdn. | **Williamstown**	20

SLEEPERS

(Good food, but little known)

Bombay | **Lee**	23
Café Adam | **Great Barr**	22
Jae's Inn | **N Adams**	23
Kim's Dragon | **Pittsfield**	25
Tratt. Rustica | **Pittsfield**	23

TAKEOUT

Aegean Breeze | **Great Barr**	19
Baba Louie's | **Great Barr**	24

Barrington Brew | **Great Barr**	15
Bistro Zinc | **Lenox**	22
Bizen | **Great Barr**	22
Café Lucia | **Lenox**	21
Castle St. | **Great Barr**	19
Church St. Cafe | **Lenox**	21
Dakota | **Pittsfield**	18
Gala | **Williamstown**	21
Helsinki | **Great Barr**	19
John Andrews | **S Egremont**	25
Morgan Hse. | **Lee**	16
Once Upon | **Stockbridge**	21
Pearl's | **Great Barr**	20
Rouge | **W Stockbridge**	23
Shiro Sushi | **Great Barr**	20
Siam Sq. Thai | **Great Barr**	18
Stagecoach Tav. | **Sheffield**	20
Thai Gdn. | **Williamstown**	20
Truc Orient | **W Stockbridge**	21

TEEN APPEAL

Baba Louie's | **Great Barr**	24
Barrington Brew | **Great Barr**	15
Coyote Flaco | **Williamstown**	21
Dakota | **Pittsfield**	18

TRENDY

allium | **Great Barr**	22
Bistro Zinc | **Lenox**	22
Bizen | **Great Barr**	22
Brix Wine Bar | **Pittsfield**	22
Café Adam | **Great Barr**	22
Café Latino | **N Adams**	22
Castle St. | **Great Barr**	19
Fin | **Lenox**	23
Helsinki | **Great Barr**	19
NEW Jae's Spice | **Pittsfield**	21
John Andrews | **S Egremont**	25
NEW Mission Bar | **Pittsfield**	-
NEW Napa | **Great Barr**	19
☑ Old Inn/Green | **New Marl**	28
Pearl's | **Great Barr**	20
Prime Italian | **Lenox**	20
Rouge | **W Stockbridge**	23
Xicohtencatl | **Great Barr**	21

Menus, photos, voting and more – free at ZAGAT.com

THE BERKSHIRES

SPECIAL FEATURES

Wine Vintage Chart

This chart, based on our 0 to 30 scale, is designed to help you select wine. The ratings (by **Howard Stravitz,** a law professor at the University of South Carolina) reflect the vintage quality and the wine's readiness to drink. We exclude the 1991–1993 vintages because they are not that good. A dash indicates the wine is either past its peak or too young to rate. Loire ratings are for dry white wines.

Whites	89	90	94	95	96	97	98	99	00	01	02	03	04	05	06	07
French:																
Alsace	24	25	24	23	23	22	25	23	25	26	22	21	24	25	24	-
Burgundy	23	22	-	27	26	23	21	25	25	24	27	23	26	27	25	23
Loire Valley	-	-	-	-	-	-	-	-	24	25	26	22	23	27	24	-
Champagne	26	29	-	26	27	24	23	24	24	22	26	21	-	-	-	-
Sauternes	25	28	-	21	23	25	23	24	24	29	25	24	21	26	23	27
California:																
Chardonnay	-	-	-	-	-	-	-	24	23	26	26	25	26	29	25	-
Sauvignon Blanc	-	-	-	-	-	-	-	-	-	-	-	26	27	26	27	26
Austrian:																
Grüner Velt./Riesling	-	-	-	25	21	26	26	25	22	23	25	26	26	25	24	-
German:	26	27	24	23	26	25	26	23	21	29	27	24	26	28	24	-

Reds	89	90	94	95	96	97	98	99	00	01	02	03	04	05	06	07
French:																
Bordeaux	25	29	21	26	25	23	25	24	29	26	24	26	24	28	25	23
Burgundy	24	26	-	26	27	25	22	27	22	24	27	25	24	27	25	-
Rhône	28	28	23	26	22	24	27	26	27	26	-	26	24	27	25	-
Beaujolais	-	-	-	-	-	-	-	-	-	-	22	24	21	27	25	23
California:																
Cab./Merlot	-	28	29	27	25	28	23	26	-	27	26	25	24	26	23	-
Pinot Noir	-	-	-	-	-	-	-	24	23	25	28	26	27	25	24	-
Zinfandel	-	-	-	-	-	-	-	-	-	25	23	27	22	23	23	-
Oregon:																
Pinot Noir	-	-	-	-	-	-	-	-	-	-	27	25	26	27	26	-
Italian:																
Tuscany	-	25	23	24	20	29	24	27	24	27	-	25	27	25	24	-
Piedmont	27	27	-	-	26	27	26	25	28	27	-	24	23	26	25	24
Spanish:																
Rioja	-	-	26	26	24	25	-	25	24	27	-	24	25	26	24	-
Ribera del Duero/Priorat	-	-	26	26	27	25	24	25	24	27	20	24	27	26	24	-
Australian:																
Shiraz/Cab.	-	-	24	26	23	26	28	24	24	27	27	25	26	26	24	-
Chilean:	-	-	-	-	-	24	-	25	23	26	24	25	24	26	25	24

Menus, photos, voting and more – free at ZAGAT.com

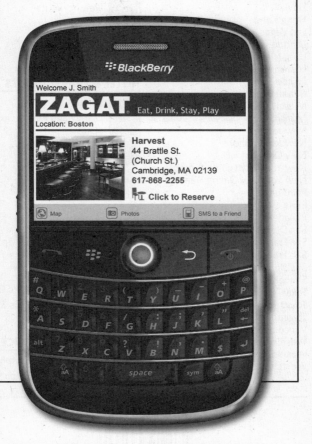

Zagat Products

Available wherever books are sold or at ZAGAT.com. To customize
Zagat guides as gifts or marketing tools, call 800-540-9609.

RESTAURANTS & MAPS

America's Dining Deals
America's Top Restaurants
Atlanta
Beijing
Boston
Brooklyn
California Wine Country
Cape Cod & The Islands
Chicago
Chicago Dining Deals
Connecticut
Europe's Top Restaurants
Hamptons (incl. wineries)
Hawaii
Hong Kong
Las Vegas
London
Long Island (incl. wineries)
Los Angeles I So. California
(guide & map)
Miami Beach
Miami I So. Florida
Montréal
New Jersey
New Jersey Shore
New Orleans
New York City (guide & map)
New York City Dining Deals
Palm Beach
Paris
Philadelphia
San Diego
San Francisco (guide & map)
San Francisco Dining Deals
Seattle
Shanghai
Texas
Tokyo
Toronto
Vancouver
Washington, DC I Baltimore
Washington, DC Dining Deals
Westchester I Hudson Valley
World's Top Restaurants

LIFESTYLE GUIDES

America's Top Golf Courses
Dating/Dumping Guide
(NYC & LA)
Movie Guide
Music Guide
NYC Gourmet Shop./Entertaining
NYC Shopping

NIGHTLIFE GUIDES

Los Angeles
New York City
San Francisco

HOTEL & TRAVEL GUIDES

Beijing
Disneyland Resort Guide
Hawaii
Hong Kong
Las Vegas
London
Montréal
New Orleans
Shanghai
Top U.S. Hotels, Resorts & Spas
Toronto
Vancouver
Walt Disney World Insider's Guide
World's Top Hotels, Resorts & Spas

WEB & WIRELESS SERVICES

ZAGAT TO GO℠ for smartphones
ZAGAT.com℠ • ZAGAT.mobi℠

7 20613 06144 0

ZAGATMAP

Boston Transit Map

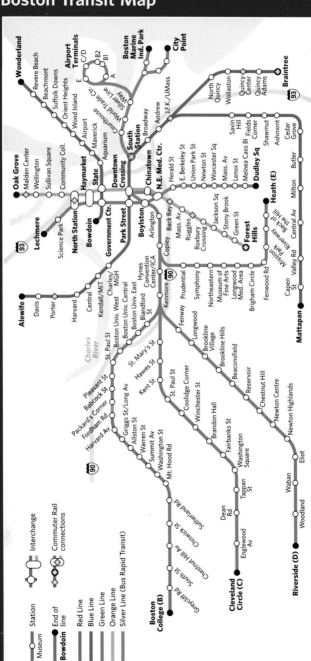

Most Popular Restaurants

Map coordinates follow each name. Those in the Greater Boston area lie in sections A-G (see adjacent map); those in the suburbs, Cape Cod & the Islands lie in sections H-O (see reverse side of map).

BOSTON

1 Legal Sea Foods † (E-5)
2 Blue Ginger (J-2)
3 L'Espalier (E-5)
4 No. 9 Park (D-7)
5 Hamersley's Bistro (F-6)
6 Abe & Louie's (E-5)
7 Oleana (B-3)
8 Aujourd'hui (E-6)
9 Capital Grille † (E-4)
10 B&G Oysters (F-6)
11 Mistral (E-6)
12 Oishii Boston (F-6)
13 Grill 23 & Bar (E-6)
14 EVOO (A-3)
15 Cheesecake Factory † (J-3)
16 Craigie on Main (C-3)
17 Clio/Uni (E-4)
18 Anna's Taqueria † (F-1)
19 Elephant Walk † (F-3)
20 La Campania (J-2)

21 East Coast Grill (B-3)
22 Lumière (J-2)
23 Sel de la Terre † (D-8)
24 Ruth's Chris (D-7)
25 FuGaKyu (F-1, J-2)
26 Rialto (B-1)
27 Petit Robert Bistro (E-4)
28 Union Oyster House* (D-7)
29 Sorellina (E-5)
30 Olives (B-7)
31 Davio's (E-6)
32 Radius (E-7)
33 Helmand (C-5)
34 Il Capriccio (J-2)
35 Giacomo's (C-8, F-5)
36 Morton's (E-5, E-8)
37 UpStairs on the Square (B-1)
38 Aquitaine (F-6)
39 Eastern Standard (E-3)
40 Icarus (F-6)

CAPE COD & THE ISLANDS

1 Abba (L-7)
2 Brewster Fish House (L-7)
3 21 Federal (O-7)
4 Chillingsworth (L-7)
5 American Seasons (O-7)
6 Chatham Bars Inn (M-7)
7 Mews (K-6)
8 Lobster Pot (K-6)
9 Ocean House (M-6)
10 Impudent Oyster (M-7)

11 Cape Sea Grille (M-7)
12 Twenty-Eight Atlantic (M-7)
13 Arnold's Lobster (L-7)
14 Topper's (O-7)
15 Wicked Oyster* (L-7)
16 Chatham Squire (M-7)
17 Nauset Beach Club (L-7)
18 Straight Wharf (O-7)
19 Red Pheasant (M-6)
20 Black Dog Tavern (N-5)

*Indicates tie with above   † Indicates multiple branches

This map is printed using SoyInks on paper containing a minimum 10% post-consumer waste fiber.